Mennonite and Brethren in Christ Churches of New York City

Richard K. MacMaster

Pandora Press
2006

Library and Archives Canada Cataloguing in Publication

MacMaster, Richard K. (Richard Kerwin), 1935-
Mennonite and Brethren in Christ churches of New York City / Richard K. MacMaster.

Includes bibliographical references and index.
ISBN 1-894710-70-3

1. Mennonites--Missions--New York (State)--New York--History. 2. Brethren in Christ Church--Missions--New York (State)--New York--History. 3. Missions--New York (State)--New York--History. 4. Church growth--New York (State)--New York--History. 5. New York (N.Y.)--Church history--20th century. I. Title.

BX8118.N7M32 2006 289.7'7471 C2006-906150-5

MENNONITE AND BRETHREN IN CHRIST CHURCHES OF NEW YORK CITY

Published by Pandora Press
33 Kent Avenue
Kitchener, Ontario N2G 3R2

ISBN 1-894710-70-3

All Pandora Press books are printed on Eco-Logo certified paper.

Design by Cliff Snyder

Cover photographs: (top) Naftali DeLeon and Elias Paulino, pastor, preaching at the Mennonite Evangelistic Tabernacle in Brooklyn; (bottom) visiting after a Sunday morning service at Glad Tidings Church.

13 12 11 10 09 08 07 06 12 11 10 9 8 7 6 5 4 3 2 1

CONTENTS

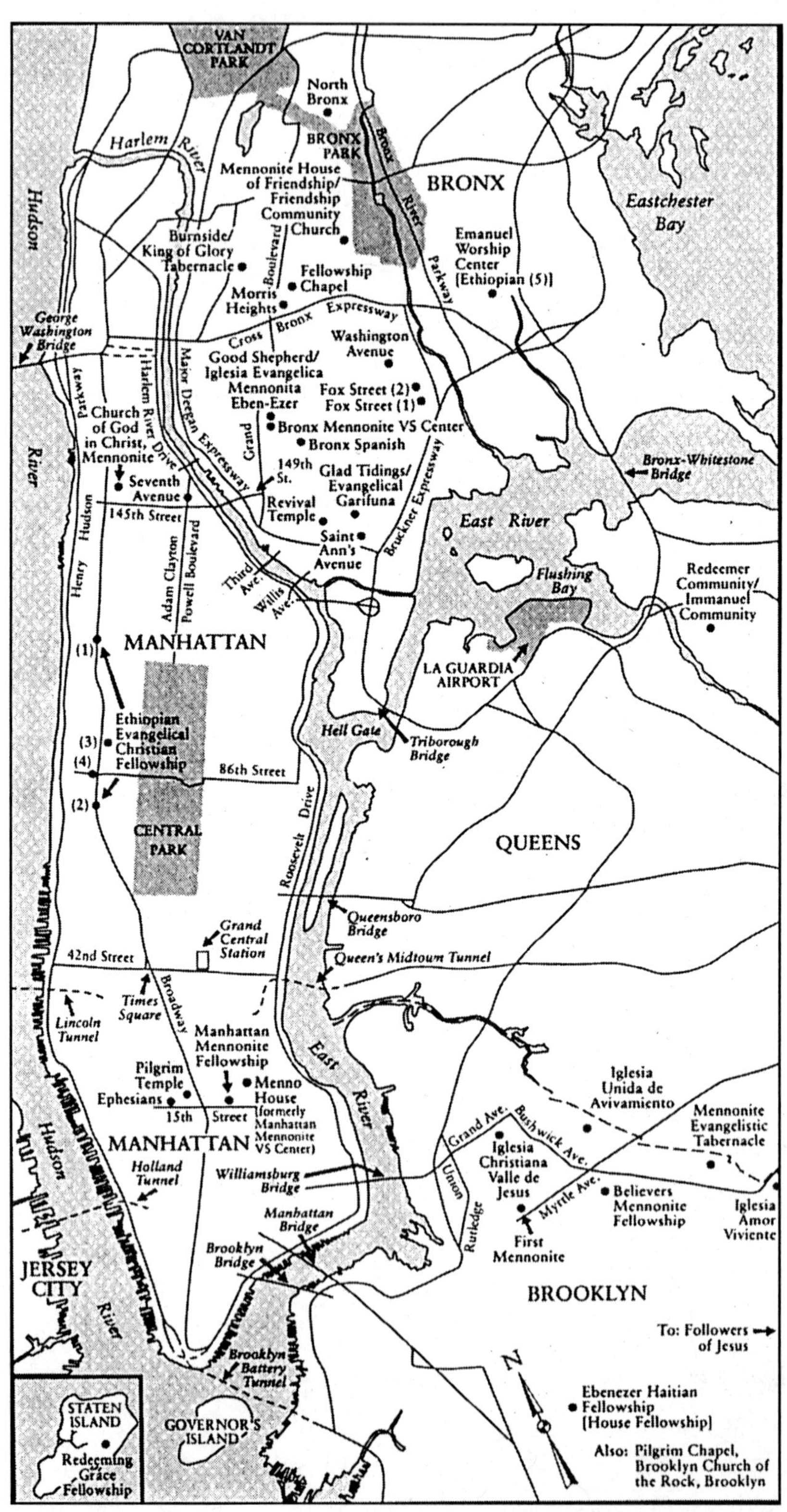
VAN CORTLANDT PARK
North Bronx
Harlem River
BRONX PARK
Bronx River Parkway
Mennonite House of Friendship/ Friendship Community Church
BRONX
Eastchester Bay
Hudson
Burnside/ King of Glory Tabernacle
Boulevard
Emanuel Worship Center [Ethiopian (5)]
Fellowship Chapel
Morris Heights
Cross Bronx Expressway
George Washington Bridge
Washington Avenue
Good Shepherd/ Iglesia Evangelica Mennonita Eben-Ezer
Fox Street (2)
Fox Street (1)
Parkway
Harlem River Drive
Major Deegan Expressway
Church of God in Christ, Mennonite
Grand
Bronx Mennonite VS Center
Bronx Spanish
River
149th St.
Glad Tidings/ Evangelical Garifuna
Bronx-Whitestone Bridge
Seventh Avenue
Revival Temple
Bruckner Expressway
145th Street
East River
Saint Ann's Avenue
Henry Hudson
Adam Clayton Powell Boulevard
Third Ave.
Willis Ave.
Flushing Bay
Redeemer Community/ Immanuel Community
MANHATTAN
(1)
LA GUARDIA AIRPORT
Ethiopian Evangelical Christian Fellowship
(3)
(4)
(2)
Hell Gate
Triborough Bridge
86th Street
CENTRAL PARK
Roosevelt Drive
QUEENS
Queensboro Bridge
Grand Central Station
42nd Street
Queen's Midtown Tunnel
Times Square
Broadway
Lincoln Tunnel
Manhattan Mennonite Fellowship
Pilgrim Temple
Ephesians
Menno House [formerly Manhattan Mennonite VS Center]
15th Street
East River
Iglesia Unida de Avivamiento
Mennonite Evangelistic Tabernacle
Grand Ave.
Bushwick Ave.
MANHATTAN
Hudson
Holland Tunnel
Iglesia Christiana Valle de Jesus
Union
Williamsburg Bridge
Myrtle Ave.
Believers Mennonite Fellowship
Iglesia Amor Viviente
Manhattan Bridge
Rutledge
First Mennonite
Brooklyn Bridge
JERSEY CITY
River
BROOKLYN
To: Followers of Jesus
Brooklyn Battery Tunnel
N
STATEN ISLAND
GOVERNOR'S ISLAND
Ebenezer Haitian Fellowship [House Fellowship]
Redeeming Grace Fellowship
Also: Pilgrim Chapel, Brooklyn Church of the Rock, Brooklyn

FOREWORD

THE MIDDLE OF the 20th century was a time of great change for Mennonites and Brethren in Christ in Lancaster County, Pennsylvania. Because of our culture, in the previous 200 years we had been known as rural people and were rather reluctant to move into the cities and make our living there. This isolation took place as Anabaptists fled persecution in Europe to find a home in the undeveloped America where they could worship God freely and be the quiet in the land. This in spite of the fact that much of the Anabaptist movement centered in the cities of Europe.

However, as we approached the middle of the 20th century this was about to change. Beginning in 1943 young people were graduating from Lancaster Mennonite School with a new appreciation for the Mennonite Church and its mission in the world. During World War II in the early 1940s our young men were drafted as conscientious objectors, and while many of them worked in camps that were somewhat isolated, others who worked in mental hospitals returned home with a new vision for the needs of the world.

During the decade of the 1940s the Mission Boards were encouraging congregations to reach out in evangelism and the slogan was "A mission outpost for every congregation" with the result that many congregations did plant new churches in northern Pennsylvania, throughout the southern states, and other areas. In 1951 the Brunk Tent Revival Meetings began in Lancaster and hundreds of young and older persons made new commitments to Christ, and the course of their lives was radically changed. Then came the Korean War and this time the United States Government required that the conscientious objector go at least 150 miles away from home, and secure a job for two years that would be of national health, safety, and importance in a non profit institution that was on the draft board's approved list.

In 1949 Harold and Dorothy Thomas responded to a request by the Mission Board for them to move to New York City, begin planting a church there, and minister to an extended family living there who had been members of one of our churches in Florida. Having been a body shop mechanic, the only preparation Harold and Dorothy had for this assignment was the new rededication of their lives to Jesus Christ. However, even though he was lacking in formal training, Harold had a heart for people and a remarkable gift from the Lord that few people possess today. He was an evangelist. He was very much at home in meeting new people and could share the gospel message in a very winsome manner. People responded and soon the first Mennonite Church in New York City was born.

Harold's pioneer ministry in these early days was important and effective not only as he reached out to people in New York City, but also in Lancaster County, Pennsylvania, as he came back again and again for speaking appointments in various congregations. What he had to say about his experiences in the big city of New York, and opportunities for service and witness there, were fascinating and captivating for many young people whom God would also call to serve there in the coming years. Many of these young persons came to New York City later on for Voluntary Service, I-W service, jobs, and education, and in their marginal time became a part of the worship, fellowship, and witness of these city congregations.

And so the first Mennonite church in New York City was planted in 1949, the second in 1951, the third in 1954, and on it went until at the turn of the century there were about 20 Mennonite and Brethren in Christ churches scattered over the boroughs of Manhattan, Bronx, Queens, Brooklyn, and Staten Island. At least a dozen of these early pioneer New York City missionaries are no longer living. These churches through the years have not only ministered to the neighborhoods around them but also to hundreds of persons from all over the nation and around the world as youth groups, college students, missionaries, overseas church representatives, and others, hosted by these churches for short periods of time, enlarged their vision and training for service by experiencing the church in the big city.

The first three Mennonite congregations in the city ministered mostly among Hispanic and black people. Later, churches were planted among people from other backgrounds. Even though New York is a city made up of persons from various nations and cultures, there are many neighborhoods in the city where a particular or ethnic group is concentrated, and it is a unique challenge to adapt and share the gospel message in these areas. In some cases it is like being a missionary in a foreign country. Our churches in New York City and Philadelphia and other cities have done a remarkable work as they reached out to these persons.

Richard MacMaster has done a commendable job in bringing together the various parts of this story that was waiting to be told. Richard was uniquely qualified to do this having lived in New York City for a number of years before he had any experience with Mennonites, and then later being a professor at Mennonite and other colleges and universities. He is a historian and has written a number of other books.

A special word of thanks is also due to the anonymous person who gave a sizeable contribution to make this book possible and to the various persons at Eastern Mennonite Missions, formerly Eastern Mennonite Board of Missions, and the Lancaster Mennonite Historical Society who helped to make this book a reality.

John H. Kraybill
September, 2005

PREFACE

"NEW YORK IS like the springtime," a Mennonite farm boy wrote to his family at home in Lancaster County, Pennsylvania. He was thinking of those early spring days back on the farm, when there didn't seem to be enough hours for all the work that had to be done. It was the same for a young man doing two years of voluntary service in the city. "Every time you go outside, you see something else that needs attention."

The first Mennonite and Brethren in Christ mission workers came to New York City as strangers in an unfamiliar place. They saw the city as a field ripe for harvest. They moved into shabby apartment houses and tenements and got to know their neighbors around a kitchen table at suppertime. Neighborhood children came to the storefront churches for youth clubs and vacation Bible schools, so many that classes spilled out onto the sidewalk.

Every year brought new strangers. They came from Pennsylvania and Kansas, Ohio and Ontario, nearly all of them from farms and small towns. They adjusted to congestion and noise, the sounds of traffic in the streets all night and the rattle of the elevated train, to garbage and rats and the rancid smell of poverty. They felt good about themselves when they mastered the intricacies of the rapid transit system and could write: "The city is becoming my home. The subway is becoming my friend."

They came as young couples and single fellows assigned to work in a hospital or with a social welfare agency as alternative service for conscientious objectors to military service. They came as students at one of the church colleges or teenagers in a church youth group to spend a summer in a project that combined adventure with Christian service. They came with a call to preach or teach or listen. Some served their promised term and returned home. Others stayed for years or a lifetime to minister to city people as a pastor in the South Bronx or an elementary school teacher or Head Start director in Harlem.

They found in the city strengths and weaknesses they hadn't recognized in themselves. They discovered handball and coached winning basketball teams. They leaned across sandwich-shop counters and heard things in casual conversation that would not be whispered where they came from. They encouraged some young men of their own age to take a costly stand as non-resistant Christians and others to take the risky step of going to college. They saw a need in themselves for education and made sacrifices to start as older college freshmen with families to support. They drove taxicabs as only a New Yorker can and somehow found time to prepare a sermon and visit church members and prospective members. Whether they stayed in the city or went home, they would never be the same.

They walked boldly, or timidly, down streets that seemed to grow dirtier and more dangerous. The vacant lots, littered with garbage tossed from tenement windows, could be cleaned by eager volunteers from the church. The great swaths cut by highway construction and urban renewal, the burned-out and gutted apartment buildings could not be so easily mended.

The 1950s and the early 1960s were the heyday of fighting gangs battling over the boundaries of their turf. Pastors and youth workers negotiated with gang leaders and tried to show them a better way, or got beaten up for looking like the enemy gang. As drugs settled over the city, some veteran mission workers thought wistfully of the gang era, before the flash of pride in belonging and brotherhood gave way to dulled, vacant eyes.

The power of addiction to alcohol and other drugs came as a shock to inexperienced Christian believers who relied in their own lives on the power of God's Word. This encounter led some voluntary service workers and pastors to explore the psychology of addiction and become better-prepared counselors. The roots of urban poverty, unemployment, racism, housing problems, gang violence, and a host of other realities were equally unfamiliar to young men and women from rural homes. But these problems had to be faced to effectively minister to city people. Mennonite and Brethren in Christ churches became increasingly involved in social justice issues and began to call for more professional training in sociology and social work. At the same time, many church members and mission pastors experienced a new brokenness, a fresh commitment to Jesus Christ, and a new openness to the infilling of the Holy Spirit.

Mennonites and Brethren in Christ with generations of Anabaptist forebears and first-generation Anabaptists who joined Mennonite and Brethren in Christ congregations in New York City made this journey together. No church history is valid that tells only of the comings and goings of evangelists and church planters. The story of the church in New York City is not simply the story of mission workers and voluntary service personnel finding their way in a new setting. It is the story of those from many backgrounds who worked and prayed together "to prepare the members of the people of God to accomplish the task of Christian service and to grow into the Body of Christ." (Ephesians 4:12)

This book would not have been possible without the generous cooperation of many, many people who provided archival material and shared their own memories. Alain Epp-Weaver, then a student at Bethel College, and Dawn Lehman, then a student at Bluffton College, were my research assistants and I would be remiss not to acknowledge their help.

CHAPTER ONE

Mennonites in Early New York City

WHILE RUSH-HOUR traffic snarled on Fifth Avenue on a February evening in 1934, four hundred Lancaster Conference Mennonites met in the Automat restaurant for three hours of prayer and praise. About two hundred New Yorkers who came to the Automat for baked beans or a sandwich and coffee stayed to listen intently to preaching by D. Stoner Krady and John H. Mellinger and to hymns and gospel songs in four-part harmony. This Mennonite worship service in midtown Manhattan was a newsworthy event and all the metropolitan dailies sent reporters to cover it.

To the newspapermen, the visiting Mennonites seemed distanced by more than space from the New Yorkers eating their dinners nearby.

Mennonites from Lancaster County, Pa., singing in an Automat Restaurant in New York City in 1934 as they bid farewell to missionaries leaving for Tanganyika.

"In a roped-off section of the dining-room, the church group, clad in the somber garb of their sect, sang religious songs, thrust coins into the food-vending machines between speeches, and bade Godspeed to three departing missionaries." Mr. and Mrs. John H. Mosemann and Mrs. Elam Stauffer were to sail that night from New York to begin mission work in Tanganyika.[1]

For the Mennonites, who came from Lancaster by special train, New York City must have seemed as strange and foreign as the East African mission field where their friends were going. People rushed by in the cold streets or warmed themselves over a five-cent cup of coffee in the Automat. Who knew what worries troubled them in that Depression winter, what sorrows bore them down? Did they know a Savior who would take their burdens?

The needs of the city had reached the Lancaster Conference Mennonites in earlier years. John H. Mellinger recalled a Sunday school meeting in 1909 when New York City was discussed as a possible mission field. Nothing had come of that impulse, or at least nothing that could be quantified.

Some of the four hundred Mennonite men and women who came to New York City in 1934 must have shared their faith with curious strangers they met on the street. But *Missionary Messenger* carried no stories about witnessing to city folk and no account of the need of the world's largest city for the gospel.

The Lancaster Mennonites sang and prayed and saw the Eastern Board missionaries depart at midnight on the steamer "Deutschland." And they were gone. Next morning a few newspaper readers may have talked about the Mennonites, recalling their own visits to Lancaster County.

Mennonites had been visiting New York City for three hundred years. The old Dutch village at the tip of lower Manhattan had long disappeared under the skyscrapers, with only the name of some twisting downtown street or a historical marker on the wall of a bank building as reminders that it had ever been there. The Mennonite presence left fewer traces. Over the centuries Mennonites had lived and worked, preached and prayed within the limits of Greater New York. There was even one Mennonite missionary hard at work in the Brooklyn slums in 1934. But Mennonite New York City was not a category for even Mennonite visitors in that year.

Mennonite Settlers in New Amsterdam

Mennonites first came to New York City in the seventeenth century among the earliest settlers who began the Dutch colony of New Netherlands.

The little settlement of New Amsterdam at the southern tip of Manhattan Island reflected from the first the religious pluralism of Holland. Toleration of different religious faiths was the glory of the Netherlands at that time. The French Jesuit priest Isaac Jogues, who came to New Amsterdam in 1646, wrote that "there are in the colony Catholics, English Puritans, Lutherans, and Anabaptists, here called Menistes." One of the Dutch Reformed ministers commented in 1655 that "we have here Papists, Mennonites, and Lutherans among the Dutch." Since Mennonites formed a significant minority in the Dutch population at home, it would have been strange if they had not been represented in the Dutch colony.[2]

Was there a Mennonite congregation in New Amsterdam? Probably not. When Lutherans asked permission to open a church in 1653, the Dutch Reformed ministers opposed it since "the Mennonites, as well as the English Independents, who are numerous there, might seek to introduce like public assemblies." The Lutherans renewed their request in 1657 and again the Reformed ministers protested that "if Lutherans should be indulged with exercise of their public worship, the Papists, Mennonites, and others would make similar claims." The Mennonites may have been numerous, but they did not hold public worship services in the 1650s.[3]

If the Dutch Mennonites attempted to organize a congregation then or later, at Manhattan or across the East River in Brooklyn, no record of it has survived. Probably they never did. The Mennonite Church in the Netherlands had a strong sense of the priesthood of all believers at this time, partly reinforced by close ties with the Remonstrants, a group who had rejected the strict Calvinism and authoritarian ways of the Dutch Reformed Church. In 1657 the two Dutch Reformed ministers at New Amsterdam reported that the English and Dutch settlers at Gravesend (now part of the Borough of Brooklyn) were really Mennonites. Why? The two ministers said:

> The majority of them reject the baptism of infants, the observance of the Sabbath, the office of preacher and any teachers of God's Word. They say that thereby all sorts of contentions have come into the world. Whenever they meet [for worship], someone or other reads to them.

The New Amsterdam Mennonites may have met in someone's home for prayer and a reading from a sermon book, as was common in their churches in the Netherlands. An informal fellowship of believers would be as far as they would want to be organized and they may not have wanted even that much structure.[4]

We know the names of a few of these early Mennonites in New York City because there was some other reason for identifying them as Mennonite. Anna Smits, a Mennonite woman, incurred the wrath of the Rev. Johannes Megapolensis of the Dutch Reformed Church by allegedly "using slanderous and calumniating expressions against God's Word and his servants" in 1652. Reformed leaders debated the validity of the baptism of a Mennonite who wished to participate in their communion in 1660. The same year a certain Pieter Pietersen, who lived on Beaver Street, between Broad and William, was called "the Mennonite" in the town records to distinguish him from another Pieter Pietersen, identified as "the carpenter." Other Mennonites lived in the Dutch colony, but the town clerk of New Amsterdam had no reason to identify them as Mennonites in the records he kept. A handful of early settlers at Gravesend had Dutch surnames and could possibly be Mennonites from the Netherlands living in a predominantly English community.[5]

When the English captured New Amsterdam from the Dutch in 1664 and renamed the town New York, migration from the Netherlands naturally slackened, but it did not end altogether. Some Mennonite families came to New York long after the British conquest. Dirck Keyser, a silk merchant from Amsterdam, arrived in New York with his family in 1688. Willem Rittinghuysen [Rittenhouse], a paper manufacturer, settled in New York about the same time.[6]

The growth of Philadelphia as a commercial center, after William Penn established the town in 1682, had more of an impact on New York City. Merchants left New York in significant numbers to set up business in the newer city. By 1690 Dirck Keyser was living in Germantown. A visiting Dutch Reformed minister reported that Reformed, Lutheran, Catholic, and Mennonite people "lovingly meet each Sunday, when a Mennist, Dirck Keyser, from Amsterdam, reads a sermon." William Rittenhouse built his paper mill on the banks of the Wissahickon in 1690, and not on the Hudson. The papermaker became the first ordained Mennonite minister in North America after 1698 and served the Mennonite congregation in Germantown until his death in 1708. He did maintain some ties with New York. In a letter written in the name of the Germantown Mennonite congregation that same year, Jacob Gaetschalk wrote:

> The congregation here is still rather weak to have anything printed. It would cost a great sum to have printing done here, and both here and in New York printing is in English. Hence we, or rather our aged friend and preacher, Willem Rittinghuysen, wrote to New York to have the articles of faith printed in English because there are people

> here who call themselves Mennists who would like to have our articles translated into English.[7]

Philadelphia remained the American metropolis all through the eighteenth century. Philadelphia was not only the most important port, but the financial, industrial, political, and intellectual center of the Colonies and the young republic. Population reflected this dominance. Philadelphia numbered 40,000 in 1786, when New York, the second largest American city, had a population of 23,000.

As the commercial center, Philadelphia became the primary port of entry for immigrants. Mennonites and others who crossed the ocean in the eighteenth century would normally expect to come ashore at Philadelphia. As long as the transatlantic trade of New York remained small, the likelihood that many Mennonites would settle in Manhattan was slight.[8]

Nineteenth Century New York: Immigrant City

New York City began to come into its own after 1815. By that date, the overseas trade of New York outdistanced Philadelphia's and New York edged past Philadelphia in population. As New York City gradually became the commercial and banking hub of the entire nation, it also drew an increasing share of immigrant ships. By mid-century the great majority of European immigrants at least passed through the city on their way to farms in Illinois or Iowa, but many newcomers found work in Manhattan and made New York City their home.[9]

The city grew by leaps and bounds in the nineteenth century. There were more than half a million people on Manhattan Island by 1850, and by 1860 the city (still limited to Manhattan) counted 813,669 inhabitants. The diversity that seventeenth-century visitors found in the Dutch village of New Amsterdam continued to characterize the city, but on a much larger scale. There were 203,740 Irish-born New Yorkers in 1860 and 119,984 people born in Germany. Other immigrant groups were smaller, but every European country had a substantial representation in Manhattan. The soaring population pushed new construction. By 1850 the line of residential blocks and stores had reached 34th Street and by 1860 42nd Street was the frontier, with suburbs and scattered squatter settlements beyond. The bulk of New York City's population was still south of 14th Street in 1860, with many immigrants crowded into the Lower East Side.[10]

The teeming city attracted attention as a mission field. The great revival that began in 1857 with daily prayer meetings in New York's downtown financial district gave impetus to city mission work. The European immigrants, who formed a majority of the urban population, included many Catholics and many others who were distanced from the established Protestantism they had known in their old homelands. The revival had its real beginnings in efforts to visit homes city-wide and establish mission Sunday schools. Early in 1857 over 2,000 volunteers, in teams of two, began regular visits to hold cottage prayer meetings with the unchurched. Crowded conditions, poverty, street crime, and prostitution underscored the need.[11]

Orphans and other poor children wandered the streets, sometimes finding honest work, sometimes falling into crime. The Howard Mission and Home for Little Wanderers was one of several Christian agencies that sprang up in the 1850s to meet this need. Henry B. Brenneman, an Ohio Mennonite, and his brother-in-law Michael Keagy, originally from Virginia, began a long-term association with the Howard Mission before 1857. They contributed financially to its work and helped resettle orphan children in Christian homes. Brenneman, a deacon in the Mennonite Church, continued to be active in this youth work after both men moved to Elkhart, Indiana, in 1867 and worked with John F. Funk on *The Herald of Truth* and *Der Herold der Wahrheit*.[12]

The New York Children's Aid Society undertook a similar ministry in resettling poor children in rural homes. They seem to have advocated sending youngsters anywhere so long as it was outside the city limits. Some of their placements reached Mennonite communities.[13]

A Mennonite Mission in New York City?

If New York City appeared to some as an immigrant city with severe social problems, other rural Americans, including Mennonites, saw it as a land of opportunity. In the years after the Civil War, American cities drew young men and women from the farms and small towns. It was the beginning of urbanization in this country, with the number of city dwellers constantly increasing and the number of farmers declining. Some Mennonites left rural sections in these years to move to cities and larger towns in Pennsylvania and other states.

A meeting of General Conference Mennonites at Bowmansville in Lancaster County, Pennsylvania, in October 1865, recommended mission work as the duty of every congregation. They were thinking primarily of city missions and, the following year, they established First Mennonite Church of Philadelphia as a mission outpost in that city. The focus of this early mission work was on Mennonites who had moved away from established congregations. Andrew B. Shelly asked Eastern Pennsylvania

Conference in 1870: "How are we to regard our scattered members and what is to be done for them?" He believed that a great need existed for "a field preacher to look up such members, visit them, and, when possible, hold public service with them." Shelly himself did this often.[14]

In May 1875 Eastern Pennsylvania Conference appointed A. B. Shelly and two younger preachers, Jacob S. Moyer and Albert E. Funk, as a Home Missions Committee. Under this assignment, Shelly and Moyer visited Mennonite families living in Metuchen, New Jersey, Brooklyn, and Manhattan. This was the first official Mennonite mission activity in New York City.

Moyer and Shelly arrived in New York City on September 20, 1875, and were pleasantly surprised to meet John Fretz Funk of Elkhart, Indiana, editor of *The Herald of Truth*, and David Goerz, who published *Zur Heimat* at Halstead, Kansas. The two Pennsylvanians had arranged to stay with a Mennonite family named Stobbe who lived in Brooklyn. The Stobbe family had moved to Brooklyn from Montgomery County, Pennsylvania, where they were members of West Swamp Mennonite Church.

All four preachers went together to Brooklyn that evening "where we spent very pleasant hours in edifying conversation at the home of the Stobbe brethren." Another family who had moved from Montgomery County joined them. Shelly noted that "The dear Franz brethren were also present here."

Their hosts took them sightseeing the next day. They climbed up a flight of stairs on the Brooklyn Bridge, still under construction, for "a splendid view of New York, Brooklyn, Newark, Jersey City, and out to the ocean." The beautiful panorama spread out before them led Shelly to "wonder about the amount of sin and injustice" in the city. They also visited Greenwood Cemetery, Central Park, and the Central Park Zoo.

That night they held a worship service at the Stobbe home and Jacob Moyer spoke on I John 4:9. "Besides the two Franz brethren and Brother Goerz, Brother Hahn and his wife from New York attended." This may well have been the first Mennonite worship service in New York City.

The next day, September 22, they visited two other Mennonite families who lived in Manhattan, "the brethren Schimmel and Landis and their families," more transplanted Pennsylvania Mennonites.

Moyer and Shelly had made contact with a nucleus of five Mennonite families who already lived in New York City. In his report, Shelly urged "the necessity of having itinerant preachers who are commissioned to visit such places." In this way, the five Mennonite families could be nurtured and, in time, a church planted.[15]

Albert Ehst Funk, the third member of the Home Missions Committee, took responsibility for the work in Brooklyn and Manhattan at this point. He had grown up in the Hereford Mennonite Church, Bally, Pennsylvania, but in his active ministry he was a city preacher, serving the Germantown and First Mennonite of Philadelphia congregations. In May 1876 Funk reported to Conference about a visit with the Stobbe brethren in Brooklyn and worship with them. Occasional visits from Philadelphia nurtured the flickering ember in Brooklyn over the next few years. In 1881 Funk's sister Caroline and her husband, Oliver Schultz, sold their farm in Pennsylvania and moved to New York City to train for urban mission work at Bethany Institute. An unmarried sister, Mary A. Funk, came with them. In May 1882 they all moved to Brooklyn to help the Stobbe and Franz families with a German-language Sunday school as the first step in planting a church.[16]

Eastern Pennsylvania Conference heard this good news at its May 1882 session. The ministers present resolved:

> That the Conference receives with great satisfaction the information that the brethren in Brooklyn desire to establish a missionary congregation, but [the Conference] does not at present see its way clear to provide the necessary funds. Conference however recommends that the brethren should establish a German Mennonite Sunday School and that Brother John B. Baer could be of assistance and that the Home Missions Committee could at stated times preach for them before or after the session of the school, until such time as a regular minister might be placed.[17]

Six months later the situation in Brooklyn seemed less promising. Funk had visited and held devotional services, but he had no expectation that either a mission church or a Sunday school would develop.[18]

It is not clear why circumstances changed so rapidly. Perhaps one or more of the Mennonite families moved away or united with another church. The Schultz family left Brooklyn in October 1882 and went to Oklahoma Territory as General Conference missionaries to the Arapahoe Indians. Albert Funk resigned his Philadelphia pastorate and joined them in Oklahoma at the Arapahoe mission.

Mary A. Funk remained in New York City to complete her nurse's training at Bellevue Hospital. In 1883 Oliver and Caroline Schultz came back to the city, and, in 1885, Albert Funk and his wife followed them. They were all interested in doing Mennonite mission work in New York City, but had no clear leading beyond their commitment to service in an urban setting.

The call came from an unexpected source. Albert B. Simpson, a Canadian Presbyterian minister, was invited to New York City to pastor a church of his own denomination. He resigned to start a non-denominational mission. Simpson invited Albert Funk to join him as co-pastor of the Broadway Tabernacle, with a special emphasis on ministry to German immigrants. Funk was also associated with the Missionary Training Institute from 1886. A year later, in 1887, they organized the Christian and Missionary Alliance. Albert Funk was dean of the Missionary Training Institute when it relocated to Nyack, New York, in 1897, and served there until his death in 1927. Mary A. Funk went to China as a medical missionary in 1888 and spent her life in hospital work there. Oliver and Caroline Schultz established an orphanage at College Point, a German immigrant community, now part of the Borough of Queens. In fact, all but one member of this Mennonite family eventually moved to New York City for urban mission work with the Christian and Missionary Alliance Church.[19]

Urban Ministry and the Social Gospel: Ann Allebach

German and Irish immigrants continued to come to New York City during the years that these city missionaries were trying to be faithful to the Great Commission, but even larger numbers were now coming from Southern and Eastern Europe. Persecution in Russia and economic problems in the Austro-Hungarian Empire encouraged Jews to begin migrating to the United States in the 1880s. Hard times in Sicily and southern Italy brought thousands of Italians every year. The same combination of poverty and government crackdowns on minority groups brought thousands of Armenians, Lebanese, Syrians, Greeks, Macedonians, Poles, Serbs, Croats, Slovenes, Czechs, and Slovaks to Ellis Island each year. Most of the new arrivals settled at first in the old tenement districts of the Lower East Side, but many moved into ethnic villages uptown. By the 1890s New York City had distinct colonies of Chinese in Chinatown, Greeks in Hell's Kitchen, French and Lithuanians in Greenwich Village, Bohemians on the upper East Side, and Syrians just west of City Hall. Italians chose Greenwich Village, East Harlem around East 110th Street, and an area south of Fordham Road in the Bronx.[20]

In 1898 an act of the New York State Legislature united Manhattan, Brooklyn (Kings County), half of Queens County, the southern part of Westchester County (the Bronx), and Staten Island into Greater New York, the largest city in North America with a population of 3.4 million.

With constant pressure from immigration, old neighborhoods became more crowded at the same time that new construction made more and more apartments available in Manhattan. The population of Manhattan Island passed one million in 1880 and had almost reached two million in 1900. Development in the Bronx more than doubled the population there in the ten years between 1890 and 1900, when 200,000 people lived in the borough. New housing in Long Island City, Astoria, Corona, and Flushing nearly doubled the population of the Borough of Queens in the same decade, although large areas remained rural, as did most of Staten Island.[21]

Christian churches of all denominations became more aware of the city and the problems of overcrowded immigrant neighborhoods in the 1890s. Protestant churches often moved to a suburb or a better city neighborhood when non-English-speaking immigrants surrounded them. They sometimes left the community unchurched. The Catholics and Episcopalians were more likely to stay. But new forms of ministry were taking root. Settlement houses brought college-educated Christian workers as permanent residents of the slums. The institutional church provided wholesome recreation for youngsters and their parents with teams and clubs that used the church building all week long. Ministers began to involve themselves in labor disputes, urban planning, transit, housing, police relations, women's issues, and public welfare, as part of their call to preach the Good News. The Fresh Air program began sending children to farms for the summer in the 1890s. Seminary professors and parish ministers began to write about bringing this wider focus to urban ministry as the Social Gospel.[22]

In 1893 a nineteen-year-old Mennonite woman named Ann Allebach accepted a job as a teacher at the East Orange Collegiate School for Women. Ten years later she became its principal. Although she lived in a New Jersey suburb of New York City, she retained her membership in Eden Mennonite Church, Schwenksville, Pennsylvania, and continued to be active in General Conference Mennonite youth programs. In 1907 she began taking courses at Columbia University and at New York University and moved to the Upper West Side of Manhattan. During this time Ann Allebach worked with the Protestant Episcopal Chapel of the Intercession on West 155th Street, where she started "an extensive employment bureau, a stenography class, a clothes bureau, a large kindergarten, mother's society, and church monthly." She also taught a young men's Bible class.

She was ordained as a minister of the General Conference Mennonite Church in 1911. Ann Allebach was the first woman to be ordained in any Mennonite denomination in North America, and it was understood that her ministry would not be with a Mennonite congregation, but with a mission of the Episcopal Church. In describing the ordination service for the readers of *The Mennonite*, the editor commented:

> Everyone felt that it meant a new departure, which, however, would lead to increased usefulness for the church and for consecrated womanhood. Sister Allebach was always an aggressive, earnest and devoted church worker and for four years had been engaged in religious work in New York City where her work was crowned with success.

Ann Allebach's ministry had a decided Social Gospel orientation. Like many Protestant women of the day, she saw her efforts with the Woman Suffrage movement and with the National Purity League, which aimed at suppressing prostitution and rehabilitating young women caught in its snares, as an integral part of the proclamation of the Good News in American cities.

The General Conference *Mennonite Year Book* listed "A. J. Allebach" as one of the Eastern District ministers, located after 1915 in Brooklyn. In 1916 she accepted a call as pastor of the Sunnyside Reformed Church, located on Buckley Street in the Sunnyside section of Long Island City, Borough of Queens. The *New York World* ran a story about the church and its Mennonite pastor.

> Should you chance some Sunday morning to visit Sunnyside Reformed Church, do not be surprised if the service opens thus: "If any of you here present are sick or hungry or need employment or help in your homes, come to me after the service and I will help you." And the Rev. Miss Allebach does help. There are many men and women in New York City who can corroborate this, men and women who know that this woman minister not only preaches but practices the Gospel.

Although serving churches of other denominations, Ann Allebach was always a General Conference Mennonite. She died suddenly on April 27, 1918.[23]

The New York City in which Ann J. Allebach lived and worked had 5.6 million people, most of them crowded into Manhattan and the older urban sections of Brooklyn. New York City surpassed London in 1910 as the most populous city in the world. New apartment houses and row houses were going up in some sections of the West and South Bronx and in Long Island City and Astoria, including the Sunnyside area where she ministered, but much of the Borough of Queens and parts of the Bronx remained essentially rural with farms and country estates. Construction of the subways began to change the landscape. The Interborough Rapid Transit Company completed its lines in Manhattan from the Battery to West 145th Street in 1904 and finished extensions into the Bronx a few years later, so that for five cents a passenger could travel from lower Manhattan to the Bronx Zoo entrance at East 181st Street.

Sunnyside Reformed Church. In 1916 Ann J. Allebach, a member of the General Conference Mennonite Church, accepted a call as pastor of this congregation, which was located in the Sunnyside section of Queens.

In 1913 the city signed a contract with two rapid transit companies for construction of 44 miles of subway and 53 miles of elevated railway. The new lines would bring a large part of the city into the five cent fare zone. New construction offered alternative housing as new sections of the city came into the system. An extension from Grand Central Station through Long Island City to Corona opened in April 1917. At every station band concerts, fireworks, and illuminations marked the day, with real estate developers in the forefront of the celebration. According to the New York Times, several stations were "in the zone which is about to be taken over for the erection of high-class apartments and business blocks" and another station in Elmhurst faced "on all sides the single detached homes of house development of the Queensboro Corporation." The opening of the Lexington Avenue line in July 1917 with its two extensions into the Bronx had the same effect in that "borough of homes." [24]

Developers constructed luxury apartments and detached houses for the upper half of the market, rather than build for the lower half, so they ran a risk of overbuilding high-priced housing. With completion of the Lenox Avenue subway in 1910, property owners in the Harlem section of Manhattan began to feel the pinch. Expensive new apartment buildings stood almost tenantless, but the five cent fare provided a remedy. The

Afro-American Realty Company began recruiting black families from an older neighborhood in the West 50s and 60s. They didn't care how many subdivided an apartment to pay a single rent. black churches followed their members; nearly all of them had relocated to Harlem by 1917. Soon Harlem became the magnet for thousands of blacks migrating from the South in these same years.

By 1920, when over 109,000 blacks lived there, it was clear that the continuing influx of newcomers was overwhelming the resources of Harlem. Repairs were inadequate and the area was already becoming a slum. High rents remained the rule but the low income jobs available to blacks made it impossible for all but a favored few to avoid overcrowding.[25]

Older neighborhoods in Manhattan and Brooklyn changed into slums, too, as Jews, Italians, Irish, Germans, and others with better-paying jobs left old immigrant sections for better housing in the Bronx or Queens. They left their poor relations behind and the latest wave of immigrants took their place. The least desirable housing deteriorated further. Some slum neighborhoods only housed those who could not afford to escape, those with no hope, and the criminals who preyed upon them.

It was these last-ditch slums that attracted a remarkable Mennonite woman missionary who came to New York City in 1923. Elizabeth Foth of Whitewater, Kansas, was a few weeks short of her 32nd birthday when she graduated in 1916 from the Bible Institute of Los Angeles (now Biola University). The Foreign Mission Board of the General Conference Mennonite Church appointed her as a mission worker in India. Her departure was delayed and she returned to North Newton, Kansas, to take nurse's training at Bethel College. Still waiting, she took courses at the Moody Bible Institute in Chicago. Late in 1917, the mission board sent her to San Francisco to sail for India with another missionary, but the shipping company had overbooked and there was no room on the ship for her. Unable to arrange other passage, the mission board sent her to Altoona, Pennsylvania.

Bishop Jacob Snyder of the Mennonite Church began the work in Altoona, before he joined the General Conference Mennonite Church with the four congregations in his district in 1914. Three years later, he appealed to the mission board for help. Elizabeth Foth arrived in Altoona as the first mission worker early in 1918. A year later, Martha Franz of Berne, Indiana, joined her. The two women started a mission Sunday school at Coupon, a small town in the mountains nine miles from Altoona, in addition to their work at the Altoona mission church.

William T. Snyder, Jacob Snyder's nephew, remembered Elizabeth Foth as a kind babysitter who often helped his mother with household chores, "but it was clear she could do anything, nothing would phase her." He believed she would have made an outstanding pastor, "but in those days we expected women to be silent."

Elizabeth Foth, a member of the General Conference Mennonite Church, began her ministry in New York City in 1923.

They demonstrated an independent spirit that caused tension with Jacob Snyder. In 1921 he complained to the mission board about "the lady workers in the field" who "conduct religious services outside of Altoona and select their own speakers and go around for meetings." The board first tried to make Coupon a separate station under Elizabeth Foth, but a large majority of the Altoona church wanted both Foth and Franz to continue working there, too. Finally both women resigned.

The two Mennonite mission workers eventually felt a call to minister in New York City, but neither one had an official appointment from the General Conference Mennonite Church. Martha Franz (later Mrs. J. L. Westrich) worked with the Mariner's Temple, rescue missions on the Bowery and in Chinatown, and then for many years with the New York City Mission Society. She retained her membership in First Mennonite Church, Berne, Indiana, and her home congregation supported her work.

Elizabeth Foth began her ministry in New York City in 1923. Another missionary directed her to the Warren Street Methodist Church, "which had once been in the heart of one of Brooklyn's most fashionable districts and was now in the midst of one of the five major crime centers of New York." The church was dilapidated and the parsonage deserted, as no minister's family would live in it. Miss Foth was called the mission worker and given a room in the empty parsonage. She would have to find her own support.[26]

She began with an apartment-to-apartment canvass of this tough Red Hook neighborhood. Her work soon had its own pattern. She taught Sunday school, an afternoon Bible class, and led prayer meeting after the evening service. Mondays she devoted to visitation. Tuesdays she visited

Kings County Hospital or Raymond Street Jail. She taught a women's Bible study at the church on Thursdays. On Fridays she had a children's meeting in Brooklyn and an evening service at the Mariner's Temple on Chatham Square in Manhattan.

Soon after she came to the city, she met a San Blas Indian from Panama. He and others of his tribe worked as sailors on ships that frequently docked in Brooklyn. This contact led to a life-long work with the San Blas people in New York. In the early days she taught a Sunday afternoon Bible class for them and helped them learn English on Tuesday evenings.

She started a summer Bible camp program in 1925, taking boys and girls, each for a ten-day camp, to Cedar Beach, New Jersey. Facilities were primitive and she was the entire staff. She continued this program through the summer of 1933.

Foth found a vacant store-front in a block of tenements, on Hoyt Street between Baltic and Butler Streets, just two blocks from her Warren Street room, in 1929. She transformed the store-front into a rescue mission and club room for her youngsters. The Hoyt Street Mission in the Boerum Hill section of Brooklyn opened in 1930. The Hoyt Street Mission became the focus for her work for the next seventeen years. In 1946 the city acquired and demolished the building for a housing project and the Hoyt Street Mission closed.[27]

Since she had no financial support from any denomination or mission board, Elizabeth Foth depended on Sunday school classes and individuals in churches that knew of her work. She never asked for donations, but she became a familiar visitor to General Conference and Mennonite Brethren churches in the Midwest and the West. *The Mennonite* published a long account of her work with the Hoyt Street Mission and the San Blas Indians in 1930 and shorter reports at other times. She was always a member of the Gnadenberg (now Grace Hill) Mennonite Church, Whitewater, Kansas, and was considered a Mennonite mission worker.

A new minister at Warren Street Methodist Church asked Foth to leave her parsonage room in 1935. She lived in one furnished room for about a year and then moved to 415 East Third Street, Brooklyn, where she lived for more than twenty years. The little house on Third Street was always full. "Ministers, missionaries, and, during the war, conscientious objectors on leave were our guests." Her nephew Erwin R. Wedel recalled that "Her apartment in Brooklyn was, during the war years, a welcome stop-over place for what she called 'my C.O. boys' who were on their way to or from places of service."[28]

During World War II, Mennonite C.O.s and graduate students formed an All-Mennonite Fellowship that met regularly at the New York Biblical Seminary on East 49th Street in Manhattan. Elizabeth Foth attended the meetings and recruited young Mennonites to help in her mission. Jacob T. Friesen recalled:

> Elizabeth Foth had connections with my home church in Mountain Lake, Minnesota, so she was known to me earlier, but I hadn't met her before she came to the Fellowship meetings. A group of us fellas sang for her at the Mission. She would share incredible stories of her work on the lower east side of Manhattan.[29]

Foth was 62 years old when the Hoyt Street Mission closed in 1946, but her work in New York City had barely begun. She wrote that as one door closed, a larger one opened. She soon had three weekly children's meetings at three Brooklyn public housing projects, and weekly services at Marcy Houses and the Navy Yard Housing Project. She worked with evangelical Episcopalians at St. Paul's House in Hell's Kitchen on the west side of Manhattan. And she began a unique tract ministry on Broadway, at Coney Island, anywhere that large crowds gathered. She carried a large printed sign with a Scripture message and engaged anyone who was willing to listen in earnest conversation.

In her last years in New York City, Elizabeth Foth devoted her major efforts to visiting hospitals, reading the Bible and praying with sick people. She was a volunteer counselor at the Billy Graham pavilion at the New York World's Fair in 1964 and 1965. Her daily round of sharing the Good News of Jesus Christ with the people of New York City continued until 1971, when she was 87 years old. She retired at last to the Mennonite Home in Corn, Oklahoma, after 46 years of active ministry on the sidewalks of New York. She died there on December 12, 1975.[30]

Elizabeth Foth, in New York City, carrying a large printed sign with a Scripture message.

NOTES

[1] *New York Times*, Feb. 22, 1934. *Missionary Messenger*, March and July 1934.

[2] J. Franklin Jameson, ed., *Narratives of New Netherland* (New York, 1909), 260. *Ecclesiastical Records of the State of New York* (Albany, NY, 1901), I, 334.

[3] *Ecclesiastical Records*, I, 317, 320, 386.

[4] *Ecclesiastical Records*, I, 396. Frederick J. Zwierlein, *Religion in New Netherland 1623-1664* (Rochester, NY, 1910), 168-170. Leo Schelbert, "Eighteenth Century Swiss Migration to America," *Mennonite Quarterly Review* [hereafter *MQR*], XLII (July 1968), 164-165.

[5] *Ecclesiastical Records*, I, 485, 504. Berthold Fernow, ed., *Records of New Amsterdam 1653-1674* (New York, 1897), II, 246, III, 70, VI, 124.

[6] Eighteenth-century Baptist historian Morgan Edwards stressed this New York City link to the beginnings of the Germantown Mennonite Church. "Some Mennonite families were in the Province [of Pennsylvania] as early as 1692 who came hither from the New York government. . .They settled in the neighborhood now called Germantown, Frankford, etc." Morgan Edwards, *Materials Towards a History of the American Baptists* (Philadelphia, 1770), I, 94-95. C. S. Keyser, *The Keyser Family* (Philadelphia, 1889), 31. Harold S. Bender, "The Founding of the Mennonite Church in America at Germantown, 1683-1708," *MQR*, VII (October 1933), 233, 236-237.

[7] Harold S. Bender, "Was William Rittenhouse the First Mennonite Bishop in America?" *MQR*, VII (January 1933), 42-47.

[8] Thomas M. Doerflinger, *A Vigorous Spirit of Enterprise* (New York, 1987), 341-342.

[9] Robert G. Albion, *The Rise of the Port of New York* (New York, 1943), 5-13.

[10] Jay P. Dolan, *The Immigrant Church: New York's Irish and German Catholics 1815-1865* (Baltimore, 1977), 12-22.

[11] Timothy L. Smith, *Revivalism and Social Reform* (Baltimore, 1980) 63-65.

[12] W. S. Sedwick to Henry B. Brenneman, March 31, 1862. Henry B. Brenneman Papers, Mennonite Church Archives [hereafter MCA], Goshen, Indiana. I am indebted to Theron F. Schlabach for this reference.

[13] Kenneth D. Miller and Ethel Prince Miller, *The People Are the City* (New York, 1962), 61-64. The informal methods of the Children's Aid Society in shipping teenagers to the Shenandoah Valley of Virginia can be followed in the *Staunton [Virginia] Vindicator*, April 19, 26, May 3, 17, 1878.

[14] Silas M. Grubb, comp., "Eastern Pennsylvania Conference Minutes," typescript in Mennonite Historical Library, Bluffton College, Bluffton, Ohio. [Hereafter MHL-BC.]

[15] *Der Mennonitische Friedensbote*, XX (October 1, 1875), 148-149.

[16] A. J. Fretz, *The Funk Genealogy* (Philadelphia, 1895).

[17] "Eastern Pennsylvania Conference Minutes," MHL-BC.

[18] "Eastern Pennsylvania Conference Minutes," MHL-BC.

[19] Fretz, *Funk Genealogy*.

[20] Oscar Handlin, *The Newcomers* (Cambridge, MA, 1965), 34-35.

[21] George J. Lankevitch and Howard B. Furer, *A Brief History of New York City* (Port Washington, NY, 1984), 97-98.

[22] Ferenc M. Szasz, *The Divided Mind of Protestant America 1880-1930* (University, AL, 1982), 70-75.

[23] Mary Lou Cummings, ed., *Full Circle: Stories of Mennonite Women* (Newton, KS, 1978),

11-15.

[24] *New York Times*, July 9, 1917.

[25] Lankevitch and Furer, *Brief History*, 111-113.

[26] William T. Snyder, Interview, May 30, 1990. Gordon P. Gardiner, *Sowing Beside All Waters: The Story of Elizabeth Foth* (Corn, Oklahoma, 1972), 49-51.

[27] Gardiner, *Sowing Beside All Waters*, 58-67.

[28] Letter to author, July 30, 1990.

[29] Jacob T. Friesen to author, September 10, 1990.

[30] Gardiner. Charles Kraybill supplied other information on Elizabeth Foth.

CHAPTER TWO

Found: A Mission Field

ON ALMOST ANY Saturday morning in the late 1940s, as the first streaks of dawn began to redden the sky, a small group of Mennonite teenagers and young adults could be seen gathering in an empty church parking-lot in Eastern Pennsylvania for the long drive to New York City. Amos K. Mellinger went with the Gospel Beacons, the young people's worker's band of the Chestnut Hill congregation, on one of their regular monthly trips to the city in January 1949. They met at Mellingers meetinghouse

Youth Group from Bosslers Mennonite Church, Elizabethtown, Pennsylvania, about 1950, ready to distribute "The Way" on a Brooklyn street. Left to right: John H. Kraybill, Ralph Longenecker, Norma Garber, Marian (Grove) Wenger, Jean (Kraybill) Shenk, Mel Wenger, Lois Jean (Longenecker) Kreider, Ruth Arlene (Longenecker) Weaver, Jane Roberts, Mary Jean and Simon Kraybill.

before daybreak. Raymond Charles, the Chestnut Hill pastor, led them in prayer and then all ten piled into two cars. They carried a collection of tracts and 1,500 copies of the current issue of *The Way*, an evangelistic monthly published by the Mennonite Church. Mellinger had never been to the city before and acknowledged "I was indeed struck with awe as I beheld the skyscrapers, the tunnels, and the bridges." They drove to Long Island City in Queens and divided into pairs, "each couple going in separate streets distributing *The Way* at the doors of the homes and offering tracts to the folks we met in the street." Most people accepted their literature, but others refused to take a tract.[1]

Groups of Mennonite young people and their elders from both Franconia Conference and Lancaster Conference churches frequently drove to New York City for a day of distributing Christian literature. Sometimes a gospel quartet accompanied them, and they would hold a street meeting.

Mennonites rediscovered New York City in the 1940s as part of a church-wide movement to mission. New horizons opened in these years in unexpected ways. The challenge of itinerant evangelism, with a mission outpost for every established congregation, led many young men and women, in spite of wartime gasoline rationing, to take off for distant places for a season of witnessing and nurturing new Christians. Students at Eastern Mennonite School in Harrisonburg, Virginia, popularized the idea with summer evangelistic teams in Kentucky in 1940 and 1941. During the war years, Lancaster Mennonites began sending itinerant evangelism teams to the southeastern United States. Newlyweds H. Raymond and Anna Lois Charles witnessed in Munson, Florida, in the summer of 1943, Earl and Alta Mosemann worked in Alabama, and Mahlon Hess and C. Z. Martin surveyed possible sites for future evangelism.[2]

World War II disrupted the lives of many young Mennonites who left their home communities for Civilian Public Service camps in distant places. Assignments to mental hospitals and training schools put many CPS men in unfamiliar situations and brought new possibilities for Christian service. CPS men also saw openings for mission work in places where they served, like in Puerto Rico. H. Raymond Charles wrote in 1969 that Mennonite interest in New York City grew out of an experience that one of our young men had in CPS in nearby New Jersey. He urged that the Mennonite Church ought to be doing something in this great city so close to home from which missionaries leave for overseas fields. The youth group at Chestnut Hill responded to this challenge with monthly trips to distribute *The Way* beginning in 1946.[3]

During the war, the number of Mennonite students in graduate school and seminary increased as all branches of the Mennonite family recognized the importance of Christian higher education here and overseas. Some young men studied at Columbia University or New York University to prepare for future teaching careers in one of the church colleges. The New York Biblical Seminary on East 49th Street had the greatest concentration of Mennonites from all groups. Eight Mennonites enrolled at Biblical in 1942 and eleven in 1943. Union Theological Seminary had one or two General Conference Mennonite students in these years.[4]

Paul R. Shelly, an ordained minister in Eastern District of the General Conference Mennonite Church, was a graduate student at Columbia University in 1942-1944. He was one of the Mennonite students who organized the New York Mennonite Fellowship and planned for monthly meetings at New York Biblical Seminary. The Home Missions Board of the General Conference Mennonite Church provided a small stipend for a seminary student who served as coordinator for the Fellowship from 1944 through 1951. Shelly made this contact, although the Home Missions Board began its assistance only after he left New York City.[5]

Stanley C. Shenk, who was a student at Biblical Seminary in 1944-1945, wrote to J. L. Stauffer at Eastern Mennonite: "I have attended only one or two of the meetings of the All Mennonite Fellowship here this winter. I just haven't had time to attend more of them." The Fellowship always met at Biblical Seminary and attracted not only graduate students, but visiting CPS men, missionaries, Mennonite families living in or passing through the city, and resident mission workers like Elizabeth Foth. As Stanley Shenk recalled, "It was simply an inter-Mennonite fellowship and was not in any sense related to church-planting."[6]

In 1945 Paul F. Barkman was executive secretary, although he was "a student at Biblical Seminary and gives only part time to the Fellowship." The General Conference *Year Book* for 1945 described the Fellowship as "an inter-Mennonite work and speakers from various branches are engaged to lead the discussions." Jacob T. Friesen followed Barkman as leader in 1947 and Verney Unruh succeeded him the following year. Orlando Schmidt coordinated the Fellowship in 1949.[7]

The monthly meetings consisted of a worship service with a sermon by a visiting minister or one of the students. Stanley Shenk spoke at the October 1948 meeting. A Mennonite minister who had been a chaplain in the German army during World War II, spoke in November. At the December meeting Marty Friedman, a violinist at Juilliard School of Music, played for the group and John W. Miller gave a Christmas meditation.

John J. Plenert, a General Conference minister from Lansdale, preached on another occasion. The meetings provided an opportunity for isolated city Mennonites to get together. Stanley Shenk's diary mentioned a conversation with Hugh Hostetler, then a student at Union Theological Seminary, about Reinhold Neibuhr's use of Guy Hershberger's *War, Peace, and Nonresistance* in his lectures.[8] Two Russian Mennonite families who lived in New York City and a businessman in Newark came regularly. Jacob Friesen recalled one of the families, the Heibners, had come to New York before the war and were very devoted people. Relief workers and missionaries also dropped in.[9]

Mennonites have a way of finding one another and the fellowship continued after the Home Missions Board ended its subsidy in 1951. The meetings became less frequent and less formal, but John H. Kraybill knew of fellowship meetings of Mennonite students in New York City in 1959 that had been going on "for the past few years."[10]

J. Paul Graybill challenged Lancaster Conference Mennonites to begin missionary work in New York City. At the meeting of Eastern Board of Missions and Charities held at Landis Valley Mennonite Church in March 1946, Graybill "presented to the Board his own deep conviction that a missionary witness be established in New York City—with particular emphasis on Bible teaching centers and points." The Board took no immediate action. But in November 1946, *Missionary Messenger* reprinted an article by a non-Mennonite who was studying in New York City for the overseas mission field. The author had come to realize that New York City was a mission field and the city had needs as great as East Africa or India. By that time, some Mennonites had begun to have the same conviction.[11]

The Franconia Conference Mission Board had established many mission churches and Sunday schools in eastern Pennsylvania since its organization in 1917. Franconia Mennonites, like their brethren in Lancaster Conference, were now looking beyond their immediate borders. In the early months of 1947 Franconia Conference authorized a study of the potential for mission work in Vermont, where they had seen vacant churches and communities without any Christian services, and, at the same time, asked John E. Lapp, Jacob M. Moyer, and Elias W. Kulp to investigate the possibility of mission work in New York City. These three Franconia ministers, each with a long experience in home missions, studied the New York situation and recommended that Franconia Conference send a male quartet and a minister to New York City to conduct street meetings and distribute *The Way* and other tracts during the summer of 1947.

In May 1947 John E. Lapp took the train to New York with Jacob Z. Rittenhouse, minister of the Lansdale Mennonite Church, and Paul H. Martin, a young man who planned to begin his studies at New York Biblical Seminary that fall. They met with William Galvin, who directed a rescue mission in Manhattan, and set out to find a lodging-place for weekend workers and good locations for street meetings. After investigation, they decided to bypass both Manhattan and Brooklyn.

Rittenhouse and Martin returned to the city by car a week later. This time they concentrated on the Borough of Queens. King's Park in the center of the old town of Jamaica seemed ideal for open-air meetings. They found a suitable base for the mission team at the Flushing YMCA on Northern Boulevard. Rittenhouse drove east along Northern Boulevard through the Queens and Nassau suburbs "but was not impressed with mission possibilities." On his return he took a different route, swinging south through Mineola. On his way, Rittenhouse wrote, "I was deeply impressed as I beheld a large section of new homes, some finished and some under construction, with no church building in sight."[12]

New York City, like other metropolitan areas in the United States, was on the verge of vast changes. New housing construction had been almost at a standstill through the Depression and war years. Public housing projects and slum clearance had created new housing units administered by the New York City Housing Authority from 1934. The stimulus of the World's Fair and a modest upturn in the economy brought some new construction of more expensive homes in 1939-1941. None of it could possibly meet the pent-up demand. New York City had a terrible housing shortage in the 1940s. Rents and real estate prices would naturally swing upward as demand overtook supply, but, as a wartime measure, the city imposed rent control. Mayor William O'Dwyer, who took office in 1946, decided to keep rent controls in effect and it is still a city policy. By protecting the tenant against arbitrary rent increases, this policy made investment in existing rental property less attractive.

Emergency housing developments provided one answer to the housing shortage. The city housing authority constructed acres of prefabricated metal barracks and Quonset huts on public land around the city, each with a thousand or more families in residence.[13]

During the summer of 1947, Franconia Conference Gospel teams made house-to-house visits and distributed *The Way* in many of these housing projects, including Northern Boulevard, Linden, Jamaica Bay, and Horace Harding Houses in Queens, and Bruckner Boulevard Houses in the Bronx. They made contact with several families in the Jamaica

Bay Emergency Housing development who allowed them to hold cottage meetings in their homes. The kindness of a police captain permitted them to hold open-air meetings there from early July to late September 1947.[14]

When the weekend missionaries drove from their headquarters at the Flushing YMCA to their preaching stations, they passed through farmland and open fields. Driving east on Northern Boulevard or on Sanford Avenue, they would see large Victorian homes on acre or half-acre lots. To the east and southeast of Flushing a broad belt of farms spread from Bayside through Black Stump and Fresh Meadows. Open country, broken by golf courses or nurseries, separated each of the suburban communities in this part of the Borough of Queens and across the city line in Nassau County. By 1947 real estate developers had targeted almost every acre as construction sites for new developments of single-family homes or garden apartments.

Jacob Rittenhouse and Paul Martin explored some of these new housing developments in June 1947. According to Paul Martin's journal, they found a thousand or more new homes with no churches "in the section" of Queens called Devonshire Village and in adjacent Lakewood Estates just across the city line. These developments lay between Lake Success and the even larger real estate development called Glen Oaks Village in eastern Queens. Rittenhouse prepared and printed a canvassing form and the next weekend he and Martin, joined by Clyde Fulmer, Richard Detweiler, and Lester Moyer, conducted a religious census of the community. They visited 155 families, almost evenly divided between Catholics and Protestants, about twenty families who claimed no religious affiliation and four Jewish families. They found people interested in a summer Bible school and 144 who indicated willingness to attend a Sunday school. Later work in distributing *The Way* raised this number to 280.

Rittenhouse had the experience of nurturing a mission Sunday school begun in Lansdale in 1935 into the Lansdale Mennonite Church. He believed Mennonites could plant a church in an unchurched subdivision. The brethren "investigated the possibility of securing a place for worship" in Devonshire Village. They first thought of renting. "We soon learned that homes in these areas are built to sell. The only possible way to secure a property is to buy it." The difficulty of converting a house into a church made it reasonable "to look for a plot of ground suitable for the erection of a church building." They found a corner lot with an owner eager to sell at a reasonable price. The lot would cost $4,000.

Weekend trips to distribute *The Way* and other tracts in Devonshire Village and in the Northern Boulevard and Jamaica Bay Emergency

Housing complexes continued through the fall and winter months of 1947 and into the summer of 1948. The Franconia Mission Board decided in March 1948 that the cost of erecting a church building in Devonshire Village would be prohibitive. Without a permanent address in Queens, which made it more difficult to secure a permit for outdoor meetings, the board also decided to limit the summer work to literature distribution.[15]

Contemporary church planters would probably endorse the vision for a Mennonite Church in an unchurched Queens subdivision. Rittenhouse and Martin had selected Queens in the first place because it had "the largest percentage of Protestant and Gentile population of the five New York City boroughs." They chose a section of Queens undergoing rapid development, with some 4,000 new single-family homes in the immediate area and others under construction nearby. Every family had moved there within a few months of the beginning of Mennonite work. There were no neighborhood churches, and active church-members had necessarily severed or strained their ties to a former congregation elsewhere in the city. The people in Devonshire Village "are of the middle, working class, kind, and congenial enough to converse." Rittenhouse and Martin both wrote articles for *Mission News* urging Franconia Mennonites to give New York City a fair trial. They knew it would not be easy. Martin wrote:

> Mission work in New York would require a special sort of doing. It would require an understanding of a people radically different from ourselves. It would require a certain specialized type of worker, specialized methods and techniques. The church would need to seek out a leader with years of successful city mission experience and vision in whom could be placed the confidence to engage in experimentation in new ways of doing things.[16]

Jacob Rittenhouse was still hopeful in 1949. He told I. B. Horst that "the Franconia brethren are praying for the direction of the Holy Spirit in the finding of a more permanent witnessing point" in New York City. In 1949, a dozen Franconia Mennonites went once a month to distribute *The Way* in different sections of Queens. But the moment for church planting in Queens had passed. It would be 1983 before Mennonites again attempted to start a congregation in a stable, middle-class section of the city and saw it as an integral part of city mission strategy.[17]

The families who moved to new developments like Devonshire Village and Glen Oaks came, for the most part, from older neighborhoods in the Bronx, Brooklyn, or Manhattan. New construction of single-family homes and garden apartments within the city and the surrounding suburban counties gave them alternatives to the inner-city. Better-off Jewish families had aspired to an apartment on or near the Grand Concourse in the Bronx in the early 1940s, but most of them now looked for a home in a suburban tract. Younger and more prosperous Italian, Irish, and German families made similar choices. The old neighborhood, as earlier in New York City history, became greyer and poorer, with old parents and less prosperous neighbors left behind. A continuing housing shortage masked the fact that demand had begun to slacken for rental property in unfashionable sections of Manhattan, Brooklyn, and the Bronx. Rent control and the temporary housing shortage, moreover, removed any incentive for landlords to upgrade rental property.

As in earlier years the latest wave of immigrants moved into the least desirable rental units. Wartime job opportunities brought a steady stream of black families from the rural South to Harlem and by 1950 about a million blacks lived in the city. Regular air flights at low cost from Puerto Rico encouraged over half a million people to leave that impoverished island for work in New York City in the fifteen-year period beginning in 1941. The high cost of new housing and other factors perpetuated segregation. Black newcomers moved into Harlem and the Bedford-Stuyvesant district of Brooklyn and into apartments in the Morrisania section of the South Bronx made available by whites migrating to the newer developments. Puerto Ricans also clustered in a traditional Puerto Rican neighborhood in East Harlem, spreading out as Italian and other neighbors moved elsewhere. They also developed strong enclaves on the Lower East Side and Upper West Side and in the East Bronx. The rent control laws encouraged landlords to subdivide apartments or to let them as furnished rooms at greatly increased cost, with the tenants taking in lodgers to help pay the rent. "The poor housing in the Bronx thus became worse and the apartments on the West Side which had often been good were downgraded." These changes, if less visible than new houses going up in rural Queens, were also in full swing when Mennonites began mission work in New York City.[18]

The young people's worker's band of the Chestnut Hill congregation, known as the Gospel Beacons, had continued distribution of *The Way* around the city since 1946. Through mission workers at Tampa, Florida, they made contact with a family who had attended Mennonite services there before they moved to New York. By 1948, the Gospel Beacons were regularly visiting the Emmanuel Cruz family and holding prayer meetings in their apartment. As Amos K. Mellinger wrote of their trip in January 1949:

> We had the privilege of visiting in a certain home in a large apartment building located in the Bronx. The members of this home, which was also contacted on a previous trip, consisted of father, mother, two daughters, one son-in-law and three grandchildren of school age. The father and mother and one daughter are Mennonites and are in fellowship with the Ybor City Mission in Tampa, Florida. They were converted last winter when Brother John S. Hess was the evangelist, but sometime after having been received, they moved to New York.

The Cruz family naturally hoped that the Mennonite Church would begin work towards a permanent congregation in New York City and offered their own apartment as a starting place until a more suitable location could be found. Mennonites had now found "a more permanent witnessing point" and focused their attention on the Mott Haven section of the South Bronx.[19]

Emmanuel Cruz family who moved from Florida to New York City about 1948. Left to right: Mrs. Cruz, daughter Catherine (Cruz) DeLaFe, granddaughters Josie and Ruthie DeLaFe.

H. Raymond Charles and his Chestnut Hill congregation continued to send carloads of willing workers to the city. Other Lancaster churches had joined in the work. The Christian Workers group of the Weaverland congregation distributed *The Way* in the Jackson Heights section of Queens beginning in October 1948. Eastern Mennonite College students investigated the city in the summer of 1948 and recruited others for mission work, gradually involving their home churches in the project.[20]

By the early spring of 1949 a Mennonite congregation was beginning in the Bronx, nurtured by regular visits from Lancaster County. Earl W. Witmer coordinated the weekend evangelism teams from different Lancaster churches and reported to his own Mellinger congregation that:

> Each Sunday a group of Christians from around Lancaster goes to New York City to have a time of fellowship with the Cruz family in their home. Our service consists of prayer, singing, a discussion of the Sunday school lesson and a short evangelistic message. Every two

> weeks either Bro. Martin Hershey or John S. Hess go along to give instructions on the Christian life to four applicants.[21]

The emphasis on evangelistic outreach through distribution of tracts and street meetings continued. Witmer recruited four Eastern Mennonite College students who formed the Crusaders Quartet to come to New York as part of a summer evangelism team. Roy Kreider and Eugene Souder recalled that Earl Witmer was the speaker. He had fitted a loudspeaker on top of his Studebaker car. They would park anywhere where there was a crowd and Kreider, Souder, Aaron King, and Paul Swarr would sing.[22]

In April 1949, Witmer led a group of twelve men from Mellingers including Bishop Elmer Martin, Martin Hershey, Aquilla Riehl, and Harold Thomas. They distributed copies of *The Way* and witnessed to people on the street. With "three baptized members and two persons under instruction," the group were also "investigating a building which could be bought to further the work." The four-story building would be appropriate for "holding services and Sunday school" as well as "for summer Bible school, living quarters for the workers, and lodging for in-coming and out-going missionaries."[23]

Crusaders For Christ Quartet and speaker, in 1949, with their car that had loudspeakers installed on the roof, ready to leave for another trip to "sing and speak the message of salvation" on New York City streets. Left to right: Roy Kreider, Eugene Souder, Paul Swarr, and Aaron King, the quartet, and Earl Witmer, speaker.

This trip to New York was apparently the first for both Harold Thomas and Aquilla Riehl. Harold Thomas had an auto body business in Lancaster. In October 1948 Harold and his wife Dorothy attended a weekend meeting where George Brunk preached. Thomas was 28 years old and had been a Christian since he was twelve, but that day he made a real commitment to the Lord. Dorothy Thomas was sitting on the women's side near the coat rack in the rear. She had a similar experience. Harold went to see Raymond Charles. "I said there is something gnawing at me. He said it is a burden for souls." In April 1949 the Thomas family went with the Clair Shenks to Alabama to work in itinerant evangelism. They were prepared to return to the rural South, but when Thomas visited Henry Garber, the head of the Mission Board, he had other ideas. "He was sitting back in his rocking chair and he said, "You're a city boy. We don't have many of them. You should think about New York City."

B. Harold Thomas family, pastor of St. Ann's Mennonite church. Front row: Peggy, Barbara. Second row: Dorothy, Harold Jr, Harold. They are standing in front of the St. Ann's Mennonite Church building.

After that first visit, Harold and Dorothy Thomas went every week to the Bronx with the Earl Witmers. Aquilla Riehl joined them later that summer and taught the intermediate Sunday school class. He wrote that "My interest in New York City mission work began when invited to travel there weekends from Lancaster County with the Harold Thomas family to help in the Sunday school and worship services. Earl Witmers also traveled back and forth to help."[24]

The Cruz family apartment was already too small for the growing congregation. Caspar Delgado made his real estate office on East 167th Street available and the first public service was held there on May 1, 1949, with about 25 New Yorkers in attendance. After six or eight weeks, Delgado abruptly withdrew his offer. They found a new location several blocks away on Vyse Avenue, but on the second Sunday, the building's owner told them they could not return. By this time they had made arrangements for the property at 1127 Fox Street, just two blocks from the Delgado real estate office. The first service there was on July 31, 1949.[25]

Aquila Riehl, right, pastor of Fox Street Mennonite Church, with his wife, Ella Mae, center, and a friend Hans Weiler, left, in front of the St. Ann's Mennonite Church building.

Meanwhile, the Executive Committee of Eastern Mennonite Board of Missions and Charities had taken action. At its meeting on May 10, 1949, the committee heard reports on New York from Harry Frank and from H. Raymond Charles about his congregation's "experience in tract distribution and surveys over the past year and a half." After lengthy discussion, the Executive Committee agreed:

> that the time is ripe for this Board's fuller entry into New York City, and that a *location be found* (preferably for renting) where two couples could live, and from which they could serve in Jewish and non-Jewish interests, and as a center from which our church's witness in New York could be managed and developed.

Ira Buckwalter, Mission Board treasurer, had responsibility for identifying a suitable property.[26]

As a result of this decision, Orie O. Miller asked Irvin B. Horst to work with Ira Buckwalter in a survey of New York City as a mission field. In his letter to them, Miller outlined the Executive Committee's expectations. They were to develop "an overall grasp of the area in terms of racial sub-areas, Protestant and evangelical church and mission occupancy" and the contacts already made by different groups of Mennonites. On this basis they were to determine at "what point would be best for us to establish the proposed center" so that "the expanding program could be best directed and co-ordinated." Miller envisioned a center with living quarters for the two couples, guest rooms, meeting room and library, and he thought the mission would have other sub-stations for Sunday school and other purposes elsewhere. As for the two couples, one would be "responsible for the center and for the total co-ordinated program" and the other would represent "the Jewish Evangelism Committee for particular contact with Jews."[27]

The Mission Board had in mind something quite different from the work begun by Lancaster Conference Mennonites in the Bronx. The center, as I. B. Horst understood it, was to be in Manhattan, "located conveniently in terms of transport, and in a respectable neighborhood." There would also be "the mission point in the Bronx." The primary focus of Mennonite mission in New York City would be ministry to Jews. So far Mennonites had sought to evangelize New Yorkers of every background and concentrated on a Puerto Rican community in the Bronx.

On his first day in New York City, Horst visited the Fox Street church.

> Without too much difficulty I located the store front where our folks have been having services. Together we had a nice service of about 30 persons, chiefly Puerto Rican children and the Cruz family. I have the impression that a good work has been started. It is a pretty big task for the folks to travel from Lancaster County, get the building in order, and haul some children, all on a Sunday morning before ten o'clock.

The first Fox Street Mennonite Church building at 1127 Fox Street, Bronx, a rented store front building.

The Bronx Mennonite workers hoped that Horst "would solve their problem of finding a more permanent witnessing point," but he understood that "my assignment has nothing to do with the problem of a property there."[28]

Ira Buckwalter did not agree. He felt that if "the work that is being done in the Bronx is in a good general area to witness to" both Jews and Puerto Ricans, then Horst ought to look for properties in that area. Indeed, board members would expect "good reasons why another area would be better than this one." He did not know whether the proposed center needed to be in a central location in Manhattan, as Horst suggested.[29]

At the close of his first week, Horst recognized "that our folks will likely want to have a witness among Puerto Ricans and the Jews, and that the Bronx or upper Manhattan and Brooklyn will likely be the places respectively for this witness." He still favored a Mennonite center somewhere in Manhattan to serve these needs. When he wrote his final report in August 1949, he acknowledged that "one might begin mission work almost at any spot in New York City," but he gave first priority to Jewish work, "one of the most difficult fields." Horst and Buckwalter also identified "new housing projects, Italians, refugees arriving from Europe, students in Brooklyn College and New York University, and emigrants from Puerto Rico" as likely targets for mission work.

The Franconia Mennonite Conference, based primarily in the Bucks-Montgomery Counties of Eastern Pennsylvania, efforts at church planting in new housing developments in Queens still seemed viable in 1949 and the Lancaster churches should leave that field to them. The Bronx mission should be developed as a ministry to Puerto Ricans. The proposed mission center in Manhattan, which was to be located near New York University, could combine both Jewish witness and ministry to college students. At some future date, the Mission Board might consider starting work among Jews in the Bronx or Brooklyn, Italians in Brooklyn, or Puerto Ricans in East Harlem.

The Mott Haven-Morrisania section of the Bronx, where Mennonites were at work, was in transition in 1949. "This particular area of the Bronx is strongly Jewish," Horst noted, but in recent years Negroes and Puerto Ricans were "shifting northward from the Harlems into the Bronx." He concluded that "if we are interested in serving these folks, we are no doubt located at a desirable place."[29]

The Executive Committee discussed the Horst-Buckwalter report at a meeting on August 30. They took action on only one point:

> that Harold Thomas continue to superintend the Sunday school for Puerto Ricans at 1127 Fox Street, but that a more suitably located and adapted facility be found and rented for the continuing program.

The committee members also agreed to invite the Lester Brubakers to serve as part-time workers in New York City. A general meeting in September again discussed the survey report and approved the Executive Committee decision.[30]

Harold and Dorothy Thomas had only made two Sunday morning trips to the Bronx, when Earl Witmer asked Harold to take responsibility for the next week's program. Harold Thomas reported that the Witmers felt a call to itinerant evangelism in Alabama. Earl reported that bishop Martin had told him he could no longer serve in New York City because he had discontinued wearing a plain coat. The Thomas family kept the work in New York City going. Harold Thomas had a warmth and friendliness that made it possible for him to talk to anyone. He and his wife shared a vital personal faith that soon became evident in any casual conversation. Those who worked with Harold and Dorothy Thomas recalled how well he related to people, his friendliness and zeal to bring lost wanderers to a personal knowledge of Jesus Christ. He was quick to invite neighborhood children to Sunday school and to follow up with a visit with their parents. Under the severe handicap of spending only one day a week in the Bronx, Harold and Dorothy Thomas nevertheless gathered a growing family of inquirers. At the first service at the Fox Street store front in July, 41 children and adults attended and a week later there were 71 present. Dorothy Thomas and her mother had come from Lancaster during the week to clean and scrub the former grocery store. On Sunday morning everything was ready.

> As it was a new location, the children had to be invited in and the neighborhood made acquainted with the work being started. While Harold made several trips in his car to the former meeting places to pick up children, the Cruz children and we went along the street distributing literature and telling those we met of the service at 10:30.

In those early months at Fox Street, Harold Thomas made the acquaintance of the Pierantoni and Trespalacios families. Louis Pierantoni and Roland Trespalacios were in the first group baptized by Bishop Elmer Martin, and both boys began attending Lancaster Mennonite School in the autumn of 1949. Their fathers helped with driving children to the Sunday school.[31]

In December 1949 the Thomas family moved to New York City. In spite of the severe housing shortage, Harold Thomas located an apartment on East 28th Street in Manhattan. They lived there with their two small daughters for more than a year. Since they were self-supporting missionaries, Harold Thomas had a full-time job in addition to his responsibilities at Fox Street.

Earl and Marguerite Witmer, Aquilla Riehl, and John H. Landis came from Mellingers on a regular basis, teaching one of the four Sunday school classes at Fox Street. Aquilla Riehl began classes at Eastern Mennonite College in January 1950. Anna Buckwalter moved to New York about the same time. The store front had a seating capacity of 75 which was put to the test each week by an average attendance of 75-80 children and adults.[32]

Four Sunday school classes at Mellinger Mennonite Church covered the expenses of the Fox Street mission, including travel to and from the Bronx. Youth groups and older members from Mellingers, Weaverland, and Chestnut Hill visited regularly to distribute tracts in the neighborhood. Bishop Elmer Martin and preachers Martin Hershey and John S. Hess took turns preaching for the congregation. J. Paul Sauder came several times to preach in Spanish. Some of the older Puerto Rican people knew little or no English. Catherine DeLaFe, a daughter of the Emmanuel Cruz family, worked with the children's crafts program one night a week. There was another week night service and a Bible study on another evening.[33]

Elmer G. Martin, Mennonite bishop

Summer Bible school gave a fresh impetus to the work at Fox Street. Roy Kreider, Paul Swarr, Robert Stetter, Jr., from the East Petersburg congregation in Lancaster County, and Eugene J. Souder from the Souderton Mennonite Church in Montgomery County moved to the Bronx in June 1950 for five weeks as a city Mission Evangelism Unit. The four young men had sung together at Eastern Mennonite College as the Crusaders Quartet. Earl Witmer had recruited them for this ministry, which was supported by the Mission Board. He wrote soon after they arrived in New York that "Paul, Roy, Robert, and Eugene sing very harmoniously. These fellows can testify as to how the Lord saved them, too." They planned "to sing and speak the message of salvation to New Yorkers," mostly "on the sidewalks." And they would do visitation.

Roy Kreider and Eugene Souder both recalled that Earl had installed a loudspeaker on top of his car. They would park anywhere that there seemed to be a crowd. They sang and preached in Central Park and on Wall Street and on Saturday night in Times Square. They would sing in the car or take the mike out on the street. Fox Street was their base and they were to relate to ministries already there. They worked in the summer Bible school in July and did follow-up visits on responses to *The Way*, going two by two. "It was pretty tough going. People were hard to find, often not at home, and unresponsive if they were home." The people who had checked and mailed a card often had many physical needs beyond the ability of their visitors. The experience introduced these young men to the realities of urban mission.

Contact with Dick Hightower and Bill Kinnamon introduced the Crusaders to the possibilities of radio ministry. When they returned to Harrisonburg for college classes in September 1950, they approached WSVA and obtained free time for a religious program. In March 1951 this became the Mennonite Hour.[34]

Summer Bible school operated for two weeks in July with volunteer teachers from Lancaster County churches. The attendance was about 50 each day. Bishop Elmer Martin and D. Stoner Krady held evangelistic meetings at Fox Street the following week.

The Fox Street congregation was growing. In October 1950 Bishop Elmer Martin baptized nine converts, reinstated one lapsed member, and the following day had communion for 28 members.

In October 1950 Henry Garber, Ira Buckwalter, Elmer Martin, and Harold Thomas inspected a four-story building at 200 St. Ann's Avenue in

St. Ann's Mennonite Church building at
200 St. Ann's Avenue, Bronx, a store front building.

the Bronx and decided to enter into a contract to purchase it for $13,000. This building, located in a Spanish-Puerto Rican section near the homes of several recently-baptized members at Fox Street, had a vacant store on the first floor and three six-room apartments on the floors above. The Mission Board decided to provide living quarters for the Thomas family and for another mature couple "at this center to be in charge of the Board's overall interests and strategy in New York, and to develop the facilities from this center." In other words, the ministry begun at Fox Street would be relocated. The new center on St. Ann's Avenue near East 136th Street would be in the same section of the Bronx in a neighborhood more predominantly Puerto Rican than Fox Street, which was mixed Jewish and Puerto Rican. The advantages of the St. Ann's Avenue site would be in the improved facilities for mission workers. In other respects it simply duplicated the outreach already begun at Fox Street.[35]

In January 1951 Harold Burkholder, Ralph Weaver, and Donald Kautz, three sixteen-year-old boys from Mellinger's, went to New York City with a retired carpenter named Henry Stauffer and his wife to remodel the building on St. Ann's Avenue. They spent three weeks repairing the building. It was a cold winter in New York and the vacant building had no heat. Ralph Weaver recalled how difficult it was to sleep because of the cold and the unfamiliar street noises. They took down the old partitions on the first floor, removed tons of plaster from walls and ceiling, built a new partition at the front of the building, made two new doorways through a solid brick wall, did carpentry, laid bricks, plastered, painted, and anything else that needed doing. Two carloads of men from Hershey's and Strasburg churches came to help paint.[36]

The Harold Thomas family moved into one of the apartments in June 1951. Their apartment was open to church members and inquirers and to visiting groups from the Lancaster churches. For example, H. Raymond Charles and his family took a busload of young people to the Bronx in the summer of 1951, to witness to people on a moonlight cruise on one of the Hudson River Dayliners. They returned to St. Ann's Avenue to help with Sunday school and worship services at St. Ann's and Fox Street. "Breakfast was served to all by the Thomases." "Dinner was served cafeteria style (as were all of the meals on Sunday) at the Thomas residence." "We had supper again with the Thomases."[37]

Summer Bible school brought more short-term voluntary service workers to New York City. The Mission Board again sponsored a New York City Mission Evangelism Unit for three weeks in the summer of 1951. Roy Kreider, Harold Shearer, Eugene Souder, and Paul Swarr helped with Summer Bible school, worked with street meetings and other evangelistic programs and did personal witnessing. During the three weeks the Crusaders Quartet was in the City, Walter Keener, Jr., Noah Hershey, Jr., and David Thomas held evangelistic meetings every night at both the St. Ann's Mennonite Mission and Fox Street Mennonite Mission. "Some of the fellows who attend the mission regularly helped us to distribute invitation and announcement cards of the services to the apartments in the blocks surrounding the chapels." One evening they had a prayer meeting with the Hernandez family and the father said he would accept Christ and join his wife and children in the Mennonite Church.[38]

The New York mission needed long-term volunteers, too. Aquilla Riehl had completed his course work at Eastern Mennonite College and came to the city with his wife Ella Mae in the summer of 1951. "We moved to the heart of the Puerto Rican immigrant section in the Bronx as self-supporting workers." He recalled that "All the early missionaries earned their livelihood by working as cab operators, hospital workers, in vehicle maintenance, appliance repair, etc." The New York workers, Harold and Dorothy Thomas, Aquilla and Ella Mae Riehl, and Anna Buckwalter asked the Mission Board for "additional organization and worker help." The Executive Committee agreed in September 1951 "to favor an ordination from the present worker group" and to ask Chairman Henry Garber to work with the Bishop Board "for a second ordained helper." They also asked H. Raymond Charles as director of Voluntary Service to send more workers to the city. The November 1951 issue of *Missionary Messenger* carried an announcement that

> A Voluntary Service Unit of up to four persons has been approved for this mission. This unit is to assist our mission workers in teaching, in visitation, in household cares, and in operating a program of crafts which we hope to develop. This unit will need one married couple and can include several single sisters. We hope to operate this unit this winter.[39]

On December 16, 1951 Aquilla Riehl was ordained to the ministry by lot. He was the first to be ordained for pastoral work in New York City. Everyone had anticipated that Harold Thomas, who had been given responsibility for the work in New York City almost from the beginning, would be the ordained leader. Early in 1952 the Bishop Board approved the ordination of B. Harold Thomas without the use of the lot. This was unusual in Lancaster Conference at that time. He became mission superintendent at St. Ann's Avenue and Aquilla Riehl became superintendent of the Fox Street mission. These decisions made it difficult for Harold Thomas to continue as the superintendent of the mission he'd begun. Until December 1951, the intention was evidently to move the mission to the better facilities at St. Ann's Avenue and close the Fox Street outpost. A mission worker reported that St Ann's was described as a new outreach (and it was that too) but basically it was a church split. The two locations together had a membership of 28 in January 1952, seventeen baptized members at Fox Street and eleven at St. Ann's Avenue. Both congregations were predominantly Hispanic.

The neighborhoods were changing, with Irish and Jews moving away and Puerto Ricans and blacks moving in, and a few other people of different backgrounds attending on Sundays. Aquilla Riehl had studied some Spanish earlier. He remembered:

> In light of our labors being primarily with Puerto Ricans, and the benefit of giving at least some teaching in Spanish, I at various times attended night school and summer school in the city, plus I concentrated several months in Puerto Rico to get me "over the hump" and unafraid to initiate Sunday school classes in Spanish.

Both congregations took an interest in outreach to Jews by 1952.[40]

The Jewish Evangelism Committee of Lancaster Conference had long been urging a mission to Jewish people in New York City. In May 1948 D. Stoner Krady, Martin Z. Miller, Abner Stoltzfus, and D. Frank Hertzler met with Mission Board Chairman Henry Garber "for the purpose of considering work in New York City." Abner Stoltzfus, minister of the Maple Grove Mennonite Church near Atglen, had already begun occasional visits to the city for friendship evangelism among Jews. He was also exploring "the possibilities of a summer farm to provide summer vacation privileges for Jewish persons." In August 1949 the Mission Committee of the Maple Grove congregation made a proposal to D. Stoner Krady for Stoltzfus to work half-time at Jewish evangelism in New York "and be supported proportionately by our Board and the Maple Grove congregation." When Krady took this suggestion to Garber and the Lancaster Bishop Board, the difficulty of working across conference lines proved a fatal objection. Maple Grove belonged to the Ohio and Eastern Conference.

Abner Stoltzfus continued his somewhat independent ministry to Jewish people. In 1950 he approached Mennonite Board of Missions, Elkhart, Indiana, with a request that they initiate a mission to Jews in New York City. In March 1950 J. D. Graber of Mennonite Board of Missions met with Stoltzfus and Earl W. Witmer in Lancaster County. Witmer

Abner Stoltzfus, right, and his brothers: Reuben, left, and Jake, center, spend a relaxing day at Camp Deerpark.

had recruited the Crusaders Quartet as a summer evangelism team for New York City and was open to work with the Elkhart board rather than Lancaster Conference. Both Graber and Levi C. Hartzler were reluctant to enter into competition with Eastern Board, but they wanted to keep lines of communication open with Stoltzfus. The Mennonite Board of Missions let the matter rest there until 1955.

Lancaster Conference sent its first Jewish mission worker to New York in 1952. Mrs. Olive Lucas, "an experienced worker among Israel," and member of the Norris Square Mennonite Mission in Philadelphia, Pennsylvania felt led to go to New York, and in May 1952 the Jewish Evangelism Committee agreed to provide a monthly allowance for her. Aquilla Riehl recalled that:

> One unforgettable character associated with our mission churches in New York City was Sister Olive Lucas, an aged sister who wholeheartedly adopted our Mennonite faith and practices. She was well acquainted with the Scriptures, and fearless and able in using them as a witness to, and for, the Jewish people who, next to her Savior, were her first love. Sister Lucas, who had a ready arsenal of Scripture verses, and could level them at any whom she felt needed them, spent the last years of her life at the Welsh Mountain Mission in Pennsylvania.

Her own letters indicate that she was a staunch supporter of the fledgling State of Israel and this was a point of contact with Jewish friends.[40]

Sister Lucas made her headquarters at St. Ann's Avenue, where Harold and Dorothy Thomas "cleaned and completely furnished the small store building adjoining the main mission hall, turning it into a most comfortable apartment." A window display invited Jewish passersby to come in and receive a Testament in Yiddish or English. Ralph and Catherine (Cruz) DeLaFe helped Sister Lucas greatly. He worked "in an office with many Jewish people" and she was "faithful in witnessing to Jews."

Frances and Jacob Thomas with two of their sons: Dwight, left, and Arthur, right, in their home on Hampden Place, Bronx.

Jacob and Frances Thomas had also come to the Bronx in the interests of Jewish evangelism. In September 1952 D. Stoner Krady invited them to consider a ministry to Jews in New York City. They were already living in the Bronx at that time and "have opened their hearts and home to God's covenant people." The Jewish Evangelism Committee "agreed to compensate

Left to right: Ruth Burkholder, Grace Kautz and Frances Thomas, at the Thomas home on Hampden Place.

Anna Buckwalter at the microphone with a group of singers at Burnside.

them for literature and car mileage expense incurred in Jewish evangelism." The Jacob Thomas family, like the other missionaries, were self-supporting mission workers with full-time jobs. They did not live at either mission, but had their own home on Hampden Place, just off Fordham Road, which eventually became the center for ministry to Jews.

Anna Buckwalter, who had been in the city since 1950, and Lillian Bruckhart, who came to New York to do Jewish evangelism in 1953, both helped in this witness. Lillian Bruckhart later married Bernard Spanier, a Jewish convert who attended the Fox Street mission.[41]

Mabel Herr, left and Lillian Bruckhart Spanier, right.

Another important ministry began in 1952. Work with children and youth was the cornerstone on which both Fox Street and St. Ann's Avenue missions had built their outreach to the community. The summer Bible school was one of the most important ways of contacting neighborhood families. In August 1952 the first group of youngsters selected by the Mennonite mission workers in the city went to Lancaster County for two weeks with financial support from the New York Herald-Tribune Fresh Air Fund. This work centered at St. Ann's Avenue and its successor Glad Tidings Mennonite Church in the Bronx. Over the years thousands of children took part in this program.

Abner Stoltzfus had the vision for a summer away from the city as an opportunity for evangelism. In 1950 the Conestoga and Maple Grove churches developed Camp Tel Hai at Honey Brook, Pennsylvania, as part of an outreach to Jews. Harold D. Lehman was the director of Tel Hai Camp in the summers of 1951 through 1955. In the camp's first season a small group of Jewish girls came for the first part of July, a very large group of girls recommended by the Lutheran Inner City Mission later in July, a smaller group from the East Harlem Protestant Parish in August, and a group from the Fresh Air Fund later the same month. In August 1952 Harold Thomas and his co-workers at St. Ann's Avenue sent 30 girls to Tel Hai. They were the first group sent to camp by the Mennonite mission in New York City.[42]

Dorothy Martin came to New York City from Erbs Mennonite Church in 1952 as a full-time voluntary service worker. Lois Thomas, a cousin of Harold Thomas, came from Mt. Vernon Mennonite Church a few months later. They were assigned to the St. Ann's Avenue mission. In her first summer at St. Ann's, Dorothy Martin wrote that:

> Bible school started July 7 with nearly 200 children attending. Since this group was too large for our chapel we had the assembly right on the street. Eight sisters from Lancaster assisted in teaching the seventeen classes we had on all four floors of the apartment. Ten children accepted Christ during the two weeks. The attendance at Sunday school has increased since Bible school closed.[43]

Left to right: Elsie Anza, Velma Landis, Fannie Landis, Rhoda Buckwalter

Teachers for summer Bible school were not always easy to recruit. In 1952 "Velma Landis and Bessie Good answered a last minute call for teachers for summer Bible school in New York from Raymond Charles." They stayed at St. Ann's Avenue for the two weeks of the program there. Harold Thomas asked Velma Landis to come back for the following summer. In addition to work in the house and with the summer Bible school, she took responsibility for the Fresh Air program. Velma Landis stayed at St. Ann's and continued to work with this program for eighteen years. In the summer of 1953, she wrote:

> I helped teach four weeks of Bible school, two weeks at St. Ann's Avenue and two at Fox Street. There were about ninety children sent to the country this summer. As we went into the homes of these children to register them, we had an opportunity to meet their parents and to witness. The children were sent at different times and we took them to the station when they left and met them when they returned.

In time the program grew to involve more than 500 children every summer. It was not just for Sunday school children, Velma Landis recalled, but Sunday school children were guaranteed they would go. Most of them stayed in Mennonite homes in Pennsylvania. The Herald-Tribune took care of medical examinations, insurance, and transportation costs. The children gathered at St. Ann's, later at Glad Tidings. "We had children running around all day long. Some were coming back and others were leaving. Each child had to wear a tag around the neck with name, host's name and destination. We had to carry the luggage and get them on the train. The smallest child would always have the biggest suitcase. We would take them to the train or bus station and meet them when they returned with tomatoes and corn. It was fun, but a lot of work." The Fresh Air children usually had a two-week stay, so groups were coming and going continuously in July and August. Some children got to stay all summer. Many deep and lasting relationships were formed as they returned year after year to the same host family.[44]

Charles and Lucille Isaacs, a Baptist preacher who provided good fellowship and encouragement to the NYC Mennonite Churches for a number of years. While serving with Civilian Public Service in World War II as a conscientious objector he had learned to know Mennonites.

The camping program helped develop local leadership. In July

1953, 33 girls from the St. Ann's Avenue mission went to Camp Tel Hai for two weeks. Lancaster Conference provided the counselors. Three young men from the Bronx accompanied the 29 boys who went to Tel Hai in August. Camp director Harold Lehman especially commended Paul Espinosa and Tony Audinot for their work with the boys. There were some difficult adjustments. Camp routine and camp discipline seemed strange to some of the city boys. "Camp property and anything moveable took a beating from these boys" and some "expressed their feelings by a constant throwing of stones at each other." All in all, it was a good experience and the program continued at Tel Hai through the summer of 1955 and later at Camp Men-O-Lan and Camp Hebron.[45]

With the leadership of Harold and Dorothy Thomas, the New York mission developed a youth center in 1952. Dorothy Martin wrote:

> Half way between St. Ann's and Fox Street, the basement of an apartment house has been cleaned up and painted for our new youth center which was opened this week by our young people starting a Bible school. The attendance the first night was fifty-eight. Sixteen of these were teenagers. We plan to make this a place for teen-agers to get together for crafts and recreation; also a place where our people can go any time of the day to spend time by themselves. One room will be furnished with a good library for this purpose.

The youth center had a sewing room, which doubled as a prayer room, a crafts room, and a shop equipped with a band saw, jig saws, lathe, and other tools.

Ralph DeLaFe, Sunday school superintendent at St. Ann's, was in charge of the shop project. He also worked with youth and children, hauling youngsters to Sunday school and summer Bible school classes in his car. Ralph DeLaFe died suddenly on August 18, 1953. The Sunday night before he died, "Ralph called his wife and family to the front of the church where they sang 'On Christ the Solid Rock I Stand.'" At his funeral Catherine DeLaFe said, "If Ralph were here now, he would say to you folks in this service who are not Christians, 'Give your life to Jesus.'"[46]

From the beginning of mission work in the Bronx, there was a vision for an outpost in Harlem. Mrs. Olive Lucas put a few dollars aside to help, but nothing happened until the summer of 1953. A group from St. Ann's Avenue began an open air summer Bible school in a vacant lot on West 147th Street between Seventh and Eighth Avenues. During those two weeks,

> A Bible class was held for boys and girls in a vacant lot where blankets were laid on the ground for them to sit on. We sang with the children,

> told a Bible Story, and taught them a memory verse. When the boys and girls were dismissed, each one received a church paper, *Words of Cheer* for the older ones and *Beams of Light* for the small children. The first night we went there the children were called in off the street to come and listen to the Bible story. It didn't take long to gather thirty-two boys and girls. The highest attendance was fifty. After the class for children, we had a street meeting which consisted of testimonies, singing and preaching. Some people would listen from the street and others would lean out of their apartment windows as high as the fourth and fifth floors. Tracts were given out.

This was the beginning of the Seventh Avenue Mennonite Church.

John H. Kraybill had been in New York City with the youth group from Bosslers Mennonite Church and knew the workers at Fox Street and St. Ann's Avenue. He had attended the Ontario Mennonite Bible Institute in 1951-1952 and 1952-1953, but was drafted before he could begin the third year of the program. He asked his draft board if he could do 1-W service in New York City. Bellevue Hospital was on the approved list and Kraybill worked there for two years beginning in 1953. He was the first 1-W man to serve in New York City.

He was somewhat involved in the St. Ann's Avenue mission and shared the vision there for work in Harlem. As a result of the summer Bible school, they had contacts with a number of families. It was difficult

John & Thelma Kraybill family, pastor of Seventh Avenue Mennonite Church. Left to right: Fred, Rose, Thelma, Janet, John, and Charles.

Minese Hamilton, center, Olive Lucas, right, with a friend in front of Seventh Avenue Mennonite Church store front, 2526 Seventh Avenue, Manhattan.

to find a good location to begin work in the same neighborhood. Just around the corner from the original vacant lot, Kraybill discovered a little novelty store on Seventh Avenue between West 146th and West 147th Streets had gone out of business. He bought the store's contents and an auctioneer in Manheim sold the contents for $800. The mission workers rented the store from the owner of the building, which contained two stores and thirteen apartments. They fixed up the store as a church. By January 1954 the Harlem Mennonite Church, later known as Seventh Avenue Mennonite Church, was ready. John H. Kraybill and his new bride

A Sunday Morning Worship group in front of Seventh Avenue Mennonite Church, 2526 Seventh Avenue, after the store front was removed and a brick front installed.

Glad Tidings Mennonite Church building at 344 Brook Avenue, Bronx, before the store front was removed.

Glad Tidings Mennonite Church building at 344 Brook Avenue, after the store front was removed and a brick front installed.

Thelma (Snyder) Kraybill had responsibility for the new mission and he was licensed as a minister the same month. The first Sunday services were held on January 17, 1954. Sunday school, midweek service, summer Bible school, and home visitation helped the new congregation grow. Willis Johnson and Minese Hamilton were among the most faithful helpers in getting the church started. Glenn and Florence Zeager moved to New York City for his 1-W service in the spring of that year. When the building was advertised for sale, the Kraybills and Zeagers bought it for $26,000. John and Thelma Kraybill moved from the St. Ann's Avenue youth center building to an apartment above the store-front church in June 1954.[47]

Other changes were on the way in 1953. The New York City Housing Authority announced that the mission center at St. Ann's Avenue would be demolished as part of a slum clearance program and public housing built on the site. The Mission Board bought a new property at 344 Brook Avenue, four blocks from the St. Ann's Avenue location, a four-story building with six apartments above a store. Volunteers remodeled the Brook Avenue building. On the first Sunday in July, 1954 Bishop Elmer Martin, Henry Garber, and Harold Thomas led a parade from the old church on St. Ann's to the new church on Brook Avenue, followed by the congregation carrying banners and placards.[48]

The springtime of Mennonite work in New York City was a season of planting. In the five years from the first cottage prayer meetings at the Cruz family apartment, self-supporting mission workers from Lancaster Conference had begun three congregations at Fox Street, St. Ann's Avenue-Brook Avenue, and Seventh Avenue in Harlem. They had begun ministering in communities that were predominantly Puerto Rican and black and had also undertaken outreach to Jews. New persons had committed their lives to Jesus Christ and been baptized. The number of believers was steadily increasing. The mission workers themselves were young, twenty or twenty-one when they moved to the city. Harold Thomas, who was twenty-eight when he began coming to New York City in 1949, was the old man of the group. In those first years there was work to be done on every side and young committed workers ready to do it.

NOTES

[1] Amos K. Mellinger, "A Lay Member's Impression of the Field—New York City," *Missionary Messenger*, March 1949, 4.

[2] Mahlon Hess, "Opportunities and Possibilities in Itinerant Evangelism," *Missionary Messenger*, June 13, 1943, 5-7; H. Raymond Charles, "Witnessing in Munson," *Missionary Messenger*, September 12, 1943, 2-3; Russell J. Baer, "Evangelism in Kentucky," *Missionary*

Messenger, June 1946; Hubert R. Pellman, *Eastern Mennonite College 1917-1967 A History* (Harrisonburg, Va., 1967), 161-162.

3 H. Raymond Charles to Gerald Meck, October 3, 1969, as quoted in Gerald Meck, "History of the Mennonite Church in New York City," Term Paper, Eastern Mennonite College, 1969. Melvin Gingerich, *Service for Peace: A History of Mennonite Civilian Public Service* (Akron, Pa., 1949), 268.

4 Irvin B. Horst, "Report on New York City Survey Study and Investigation," 1949, 9. Archives, Eastern Mennonite Missions, Salunga, Pennsylvania. [Hereafter EMM].

5 *Year Book of the General Conference of the Mennonite Church of North America* (Newton, Kansas, 1944-1952. Lois Barrett, *The Vision and the Reality* (Newton, Kansas, 1983), 155.

6 J. L. Stauffer to Stanley Shenk, March 19, 1945, Stanley Shenk to J. L. Stauffer, March 27, 1945. J. L. Stauffer Papers, Eastern Mennonite College, Harrisonburg, Va. Stanley Shenk to Richard MacMaster, September 12, 1990.

7 *Year Book of the General Conference* (Newton, 1945), 23; *Year Book* (Newton, 1946), 24; *Year Book* (Newton, 1947), 13; *Year Book* (Newton, 1948), 17.

8 Stanley C. Shenk, Diary, as quoted in Stanley Shenk to Richard MacMaster, September 12, 1990. LMHS.

9 Jacob T. Friesen to Richard MacMaster, October 24, 1990. LMHS.

10 John H. Kraybill to Paul G. Landis, February 12, 1959. Kraybill Papers.

11 Missionary Messenger, 23(April 1946), 4. "Found: A Mission Field," *Missionary Messenger*, November 1946, 4.

12 Jacob Z. Rittenhouse, "Mission Activities of Our Conference in New York City," *Mission News*, 12 (July 1948), 5-6. J. C. Wenger, *History of the Mennonites of the Franconia Conference* (Telford, Pa., 1937), 332-338. "Pioneer Workers Recall Early Days, First Mennonite "Churches in Vermont," *Franconia Conference News*, 54 (November 1990), 4-5.

13 George J. Lankevitch and Howard B. Furer, *A Brief History of New York City* (Port Washington, N.Y., 1984), 229-250, 252.

14 Rittenhouse, "Mission Activities," *Mission News*, 12 (July 1948), 6.

15 Paul H. Martin, June 8-July 6, 1947. Typescript copy. EMM. "Devonshire Village," *Mission News*, 12 (September 1948), 4. Wenger, *History*, 337.

16 Paul H. Martin, "What Confronts the Church in New York City?" *Mission News*, 12 (July 1948), 4-5. Rittenhouse, *loc. cit.*

17 I. B. Horst, "Report on New York City Survey," 1949, EMM. John I. Smucker, "Reflections and Implications of Urban Mennonite Mission in the South Bronx," Ph.D., Union for Experimental Colleges and Universities, 1985, 176-177.

18 Oscar Handlin, *The Newcomers* (New York, 1956), 48-51, 93-94. George Sternlieb and James Hughes, *Housing a People in New York City* (New York, 1973), 42-44.

19 *Missionary Messenger*, (March 1949), 4.

20 Horst, "Report," EMM. Paul G. Burkholder, "A History of the New York Mennonite Churches," *250 Years Mellinger District 1717-1967* (Lancaster, Pa., 1967), 3.

21 *Mellinger's Notes*, May 29, 1949.

22 Interviews with Roy Kreider and Eugene K. Souder, June 19, 1990.

23 *Mellinger's Notes*, May 1, 1949.

24 Interview with Harold and Dorothy Thomas, August 16, 1990. Harold Thomas testimony, *Mellinger's Notes*, March 1949. Trip to Alabama, *Mellinger's Notes*, April 17, 1949. Aquilla Riehl, *Mellinger's Notes*, September 18, 1949. Aquilla Riehl to Richard MacMaster, September 23, 1990.

25 Harold and Dorothy Thomas Interview. I. B. Horst, "Report." First service at Fox Street, *Mellinger's Notes*, August 21, 1949.

26 EMBMC Executive Committee, May 10, 1949. *Mellinger's Notes*, May 1, 1949 reported (prematurely) that the Mission Board "took an option on the building mentioned."

[27] Orie O. Miller to Irvin B. Horst and Ira Buckwalter, July 1, 1949, EMM.

[28] Irvin B. Horst to Ira Buckwalter, August 3, 1949, EMM.

[29] Irvin B. Horst to Orie O. Miller, August 5, 1949. Horst, "Report," EMM.

[30] EMBMC Executive Committee, August 30, 1949, September 12, 1949, EMM.

[31] Interviews with Harold and Dorothy Thomas, August 16, 1990, Louis Pierantoni, August 18, 1990, Eugene Souder, Roy Kreider, June 19, 1990. *Mellinger's Notes*, May 15, 1949, June 12, 1949, August 21, 1949, December 11, 1949.

[32] Interviews with Harold and Dorothy Thomas, August 16, 1990. *Mellinger's Notes*, December 11, 1949. *Gospel Herald*, XLIII (February 21, 1950), 185. *Mellinger's Notes*, January 8, 1950. Aquilla Riehl to Richard MacMaster, September 23, 1990.

[33] *Mellinger's Notes*, February 19, 1950, March 19, 1950.

[34] *Mellinger's Notes*, July 9, 1950. "Report of Activities of the Voluntary Service Committee From January 1, 1950 to January 1, 1959." EMBMC. Interview with Roy Kreider and Eugene Souder, June 19, 1990.

[35] Ira J. Buckwalter to Eastern Board and Bishop Board Members, October 31, 1950. Executive Committee EMBMC, October 26, 1950, November 6, 1950.

[36] *Mellinger's Notes*, February 4, 1951. Donald Kautz, "Voluntary Service in Action—in a Temporary Builders Unit," *Missionary Messenger*, (December 1951), 9. Interview with Ralph Weaver, August 18, 1990.

[37] *Mellinger's Notes*, June 24, 1951, August 19, 1951.

[38] "Report of Activities of the Voluntary Service Committee From January 1 to December 31, 1951." EMBMC. Paul Swarr, "Voluntary Service in Action—In New York City Evangelism," *Missionary Messenger*, 28 (December 1951), 8.

[39] Aquilla Riehl to Richard MacMaster, September 23, 1990. Quarterly Meeting EMBMC and Lancaster Conference Board of Bishops, September 18, 1951. *Missionary Messenger*, 28 (November 1951), 2, (December 1951), 5, (February 1952), 5.

[40] Jewish Evangelism Committee Minutes, May 20, 1948, July 5, 1948, August 11, 1949, October 3, 1949, August 1, 1951, May 5, 1952. EMBMC. J. D. Graber to Abner G. Stoltzfus, March 14, 1950. Levi C. Hartzler to Abner G. Stoltzfus, March 31, 1950. Archives of the Mennonite Church, Goshen, Indiana. (Hereafter AMC) Esther Eby Glass, "Town and Country Preacher," *Christian Living*, (December 1959), 3-5, 32. Aquilla Riehl to Richard MacMaster, September 23, 1990.

[41] Olive Lucas, "Echoes from the Field," *Gospel Herald*, XLV (December 16, 1952), 1232. Jewish Evangelism Committee Minutes, September 2, 1952, November 4, 1952, January 7, 1953, March 9, 1953, March 30, 1953. EMBMC.

[42] Interview with Harold D. Lehman, June 20, 1990. Tel Hai records in Lehman Papers.

[43] Dorothy Martin, "St. Ann's, New York," *Missionary Messenger*, 29 (October 1952), 12. Interview with Dorothy Martin Freed, August 18, 1990.

[44] *Mellinger's Notes*, July 20, 1952. Velma Landis, "V. S. in New York City," *Mellinger's Notes*, September 27, 1953. Interview with Velma Landis, August 17, 1990.

[45] Harold D. Lehman to B. Harold Thomas, August 28, 1953. Lehman Papers. Interview with Harold D. Lehman, June 20, 1990.

[46] Dorothy Martin, "St. Ann's, New York," *Missionary Messenger*, 29 (October 1952), 12. *Mellinger's Notes*, September 27, 1953.

[47] Velma Landis, "V. S. in New York City," *Mellinger's Notes*, September 27, 1953. Interview with John H. Kraybill, August 17, 1990. Ira J. Buckwalter to Orie O. Miller, May 5, 1959. EMBMC. "Seventh Avenue Mennonite Church. Self-Analysis of Congregation, August 1965." EMBMC.

[48] *Missionary Messenger*, 30 (December 1953), 14. Evelyn Hertzler, "Report of Glad Tidings and Community, 1965." EMBMC.

CHAPTER THREE

The Church Was Not There

EASTER 1951 WAS as early as it ever can be. On a brisk and chilly Sunday morning in March a procession of children, youth, and adults, a choir, and a young minister walked from the store-front Church of Our Redeemer on East 102nd Street in Spanish Harlem to a vacant lot between tenements on East 101st Street. As they walked, they sang "Christ the Lord is Risen Today" in English and Spanish. At the vacant lot they met another procession from another store-front church on East 100th Street.

A dozen members of the Young Lords gang had cleaned garbage and trash from the lot and raised a large home-made cross. The Young Lords turned up for service, standing together self-consciously. Hugh Hostetler, the Church of Our Redeemer pastor, had befriended the Young Lords and led some of them to faith in Jesus Christ.

About three hundred people attended the Easter service in the vacant lot, which had been notorious for narcotics and prostitution. Archie Hargreaves, the black pastor at East 100th Street, preached in English. Hostetler preached the Spanish sermon. They took Communion together, singing "Let Us Break Bread Together On Our Knees," after they baptized five new Christians.

The East Harlem Protestant Parish had deliberately chosen a section of Manhattan where the poorest Puerto Rican immigrants crowded into over-age tenements in a decaying Italian neighborhood, where rival gangs fought over turf, and drugs and prostitution were already a way of life. They came with a message of resurrection and a new life in Christ.[1]

Hugh Hostetler had worked with the East Harlem Protestant Parish from its inception. The General Conference Mennonite Church ordained him as missionary with the East Harlem Protestant Parish in January 1950 and sent voluntary service workers each summer to help him.

Hostetler was drafted soon after graduation from Bethel College. His Civilian Public Service experience began that summer in a Relief and Reconstruction Unit at Goshen College, followed by four months in Grottoes, Virginia, and six months in Mulberry, Florida. He spent the next two years in Puerto Rico. After discharge in 1946, he taught math, algebra, physics, Spanish, and physical education at Ransom [Kansas] High School for a year. In September 1947 he entered Union Theological Seminary in New York City. With his experience in Puerto Rico and his knowledge of Spanish, Hostetler was giving serious thought to work as a missionary in Latin America. His field work assignment from the seminary sent him to a Puerto Rican congregation in the Bronx.

Two of Hostetler's fellow students, Don Benedict and George W. (Bill) Webber, both in their senior year in 1947-1948, had a vision for a ministry in the city. Only a few blocks from the Union Seminary campus was one of the worst slums in America. East Harlem, extending from East 96th Street to East 125th Street between Central Park and the East River, was the most crowded section of the city with more than 200,000 people jammed into a square mile. In October 1947 Benedict and Webber surveyed the neighborhood. They brought their conclusions to the Division of Home Missions of the National Council of Churches in January 1948, proposing a three-man team to work in East Harlem, each man with responsibility for a store-front church. They would begin their work by visitation, recreational leadership, and cooperation with community agencies. These activities would be followed up with worship services, Sunday schools, and participation in local politics. As Don Benedict put it: "The churches' primary emphasis would be on religious life, and at the same time the church would be a focal point around which life's problems could be attacked."

Bill Webber and Don Benedict approached Hugh Hostetler and asked him to be part of the work in East Harlem. "They were impressed by my ability to hit a softball as much as anything." Since he was a second-year student at Union Theological Seminary, he could work only part-time as a youth leader with the East Harlem Protestant Parish. He moved into an apartment on East 100th Street, between First and Second Avenues, a neighborhood with 4,000 people packed into one street of tenements.[2]

The East Harlem Protestant Parish began there in the summer of 1948 with vacation Bible school attended by sixty children recruited from that one block. When the parish opened its first store-front church in October 1948, Hostetler's youth work increased, too. The Sunday school soon had an enrollment of 55 children, and the same children attended weekday programs. "The weekday program for the children consists of church clubs for both girls and boys; a choir; hikes and other recreational trips; and in general providing a 'home' for them, giving them advice, counsel, and (the most important) just plain friendship at all hours possible. The group leaders have to originate new techniques constantly for, by and large, these children have never had any group experience; know no family life that is meaningful spiritually; and have no religious background outside of very casual contacts." The workers contacted all the families in one apartment house and invited them to an agape meal or love feast on Friday evening. Six of eight families came to the apartment Hostetler shared with Norman Eddy, another seminarian, and they kept returning every Friday.

> These agape meals have all the elements of a genuine worship service—prayer; Scripture with exegesis; fellowship around a simple lunch; and then laying plans for a common community action project. This first group has undertaken the cleaning of vacant lots in the neighborhood, the work being done on Saturdays.

Like the weekly meals, a work project cleaning up the garbage and litter tossed out of apartment windows, built up an identity with each other among isolated tenement dwellers, who could not yet be called a church.[3]

The East 100th Street Block Church, as it was first known, opened its doors in January 1949 as the second of the store-front churches. In building the church in East Harlem, the leaders believed it was first necessary to gain the confidence of the neighborhood people. "The first attention was given to the overwhelming mass of children who flocked into the church" on East 100th Street. Outreach into the adult community began in earnest only in the summer of 1949 with a program of adult evangelism. Norm Eddy and Hugh Hostetler resided on the block so as to "grow into the life of the people." By the end of the summer, the East 100th Street congregation had a "core of dedicated Christians, committed to Christ, and a body of worshipers." The congregation was giving greater attention to worship. They had a devotional service each evening. The agape groups had increased in number and a membership class was meeting.[4]

The growth of the East Harlem Protestant Parish in the summer of 1949 reflected the dedicated work of seven voluntary service workers, all but one of them Mennonite, who came to the city for the entire summer. Peter Bartel of the Mennonite Central Committee and the General

Conference Voluntary Service Committee worked together to develop a unit of five young women and one young man. "Daily vacation Bible school would be the chief assignment," Hostetler wrote, along with "an intensive program of follow-up work, making it an all-day affair with planned recreation, crafts, plus an active program of visitation, touching the youngsters on the home and family level."[5]

The East Harlem Protestant Parish team ministry was still feeling its way in the summer of 1949. Mary Moyer and Mary Wiens, two Bethel College students assigned to work with Hugh Hostetler and the East 100th Street Church, conducted a vacation Bible school for 56 children, worked with five different boys' and girls' clubs, a nursery school and a day camp, and took youngsters on all-day outings to Bear Mountain and other country places. When the summer was over and the Mennonite VSers had gone back to college, the team ministry concluded that the summer volunteers "need more carefully defined responsibilities" and, in the absence of clear direction, time was lost in "milling around."[6]

The first summer VS workers in the East Harlem Protestant Parish were all Mennonite college students. Joanna Bowen was between her sophomore and junior year at Bluffton College. Mary Moyer, Mary Wiens, Katharine Enns, and Leo Miller all came from Bethel. It was not easy for young people from strong Mennonite communities and sheltered Mennonite campuses to be suddenly thrust into the realities of Spanish Harlem. Joanna Bowen recalled "total culture shock" in her first summer. "I'd visited Chicago, but I'd never lived in a ghetto. I was totally bewildered." Living in a rat-infested tenement, with poverty, drugs, crime and degradation on the doorstep, made her question the easy assumptions of home and college. Her pastor urged her to return to East Harlem the next summer to regain the faith she thought she had lost there. She did.[7]

The East Harlem Protestant Parish group ministry reported to their administrative board in March 1950 that:

> In June Hugh Hostetler becomes available and will undertake a third experiment in ministry in our area. He will begin in a crowded block as a missionary living in one of the tenements and starting out without any other headquarters. Working with the people, learning to know them, perhaps starting several agape groups, Hugh will not bring any framework to his ministry, but seek to work freely as a friend and servant of his people. He will be supported in large part by the Mennonite Church which has ordained him as a missionary for the Parish.[8]

The Parish gave Hugh Hostetler a tough assignment. They assigned him to the block of East 101st Street between First and Second Avenues, "one of the most challenging blocks in our whole Parish area." This was a predominantly black neighborhood. "This particular block is very politically-conscious, and it is oriented very much and very deeply towards the extreme left." Congressman Vito Marcantonio and his American Labor Party considered it one of their strongholds. "It is one of the numbers racket centers on the East Side, well protected by the police." Drugs had invaded the block, with "several known dope centers which specialize in the heroin trade." The block had "many more broken homes" and "more unmarried mothers" than other East Harlem blocks, and "open prostitution is carried on here to a far greater degree" than was evident elsewhere.

Hostetler made his first contacts on the street, in candy stores, on door stoops, in vacant lots, wherever people congregated. Esther Berky, a young Mennonite VSer, worked with him in the summer of 1950 to set up a day care nursery. A women's group met on Tuesdays. Hostetler himself had some success with a Puerto Rican junior gang called "The Golden Wings."

Three Mennonite college students volunteered for summer service in 1950 with the East Harlem Protestant Parish. Joanna Bowen and her Bluffton College classmate Esther Berky were the first on the list. Esther Berky went to Washington, D.C., the previous summer as part of a Congress of Racial Equality interracial workshop for college students. The purpose of this summer program was to help "eliminate segregation and discrimination against Negroes in the national capital" and "to learn methods to be used in challenging prejudice in our own communities." She took part in sit-ins and other non-violent efforts to successfully integrate the Greyhound bus terminal, movie theaters, and swimming pools and picketed the White House on behalf of jailed conscientious objectors. With this background of commitment to interracial justice and the city, she wrote to Hugh Hostetler about full-time service with the East Harlem Protestant Parish after graduation. He suggested that she come for the summer and see how the Parish worked.[9]

The third Mennonite volunteer was Ernest Goertzen, a student at Bethel College. He had served in CPS, taught school, and worked a summer under MCC with migrant workers and "has deep Christian convictions which carry him to volunteer for work like this." By the time he was accepted in April 1950, the whole summer program had changed. Ray Horst, MCC assistant director of voluntary service, wrote him:

> I understand that East Harlem is taking on a quite different form and is becoming an international, interagency, interracial, interdenominational work camp. For this reason the different groups will be supplying only a limited number of persons.[10]

The World Council of Churches chose East Harlem Protestant Parish as the site for their first American work camp, "following the pattern and standards of the European and Asiatic World Council work camps." The eighteen volunteers included students from India, the Netherlands, and Switzerland. Four of the American vsers were Presbyterian, three Mennonite, two Methodist, two Disciples, a Baptist, a Congregationalist, and a Lutheran.[11]

Ernest Goertzen "felt somewhat like a shy Kansas farm boy in a big city among sophisticated fellow work campers from Yale, Harvard, and other big schools." They worked well together. The men had rooms on the lower level of an apartment building a few blocks from one of the store-front churches.

> To start with, we hung out on the street. I got out a sketch pad and started drawing. It didn't take long for a small group of curious boys to gather. When we mentioned the word "club" there was immediate interest. But the Italian boys didn't want any of the Puerto Rican boys to belong and the Puerto Rican boys wanted to keep the Italians out. No, we said, this would be for everybody and they'd have to learn to get along. There was a little grumbling occasionally, but they got along fine. We played ball in Central Park, tried to have some Bible school in one of the store-fronts, took them on the subway to the beach, went swimming in a big pool within walking distance (on the way back, the boys stopped for pizza slices, my first introduction to pizza), took the ferry to Staten Island, played marbles on the sidewalk, and visited families of the boys. I recall Don Benedict making the comment at the end of the summer that the most tangible result of the summer's work camp was that a family of one of our boys had decided to join the parish.[12]

By the end of the first summer, Hostetler had begun the search for a store-front on East 101st Street. The General Conference Home Missions Board pledged the money needed to rent one, but finding a suitable place proved more difficult. That same summer Mary Foreman and Ed Knopf were taking "an avowed and direct religious approach" to the next block on East 102nd Street, seeking "out those who would form a church for specifically religious reasons," rather than the Parish's usual effort to simultaneously evangelize and deal with social problems. They also located a suitable store-front on their block. Hugh Hostetler opened the third church in the parish in a store-front located at 324 East 102nd Street. They called it the Church of Our Redeemer. It was not a Mennonite congregation, although it had a Mennonite pastor. As Hostetler explained in an article written for *The Mennonite,* "the situation calls for a united ministry" of all Protestants "for the common job of bringing the Gospel into the blighted sections of our cities." The Church of Our Redeemer held its first services on November 19, 1950 with forty children and twelve adults, mostly women, in attendance. Young people organized a choir. Mothers volunteered to work with children's groups. The hall they rented had been used by a gambling syndicate and "for a number of months after we took it over, men and women of all descriptions used to stop in to lay their bets!"[13]

For both regular staff and summer work campers the East Harlem Protestant Parish was an unending challenge. Esther Berky wrote in 1950 that "For me at least, it took almost a whole summer to come to a clear understanding of my responsibilities, which I now feel more than ever boil down to being friendly and understanding." She worked with Anne Benedict, Don Benedict's wife. Her duties involved organizing a cooperative nursery on the 104th Street block, and the first step "meant doing my share of systematic calling or a survey of the block." She enjoyed this work. "Adult calling was the most interesting part of my work. I like dealing with people as individuals, one at a time." Anne Austin, who worked as an industrial chaplain with the Parish team in 1949, noted that:

> The emphasis of the Parish is upon adaptability, elasticity of the program, upon feeling its way along. Another dilemma lies in the fact that the Parish leaders constantly take on more than they can handle, yet to hit the community from all sides they must.

For the summer volunteers this sometimes translated into a lack of organization. Both the nursery and vacation Bible school were left to Esther Berky's ingenuity for curriculum, materials, equipment and crafts supplies. Summer volunteers did not always like the burden of having to come up with their own ideas, but that was the continuing pressure on everyone working in the Parish. The Bluffton College senior raised more fundamental questions than planning or leadership style. She wrote:

> The East Harlem Protestant Parish has done wonders for the people of East Harlem from a psychological and material standpoint, but I don't believe the religious message has gotten across. The four

> disciplines of the group ministry help carry the Gospel into the lives of those who accept them. I wish they could someday become the disciplines of the entire church fellowships in the Parish and that the lines between staff members and church members could gradually be dissolved. . . .It seems to me that there must be more really frank discussions with parishioners of all Parish problems in which they are treated as equals and not handed down half the story. Many attempts to organize the adults around various projects have failed simply because they were imposed from above and the motivation was not there. If it is not possible to develop leadership from East Harlem itself, then the Parish becomes a failure as far as I can see.[14]

Bill Webber asked the General Conference Mennonites to "again consider placing a unit in East Harlem" for the summer of 1951. Edith Claassen, the director of voluntary service, began recruiting at once. As it turned out, only one Mennonite worked with the East Harlem Protestant Parish that summer—Velma Jean Krehbiel, a Bethel graduate from Deer Creek, Oklahoma. Perhaps in response to Esther Berky's concern about developing local leadership, the five college students lived and worked with eleven of the most promising boys and girls from the Youth Division of the Parish "who showed leadership potential."[15]

The following summer Rebecca Sprunger from Goshen College and George Eicher from Bluffton College spent two months in East Harlem. They worked under Hugh Hostetler's supervision. George Eicher recalled:

> As a unit we had several projects that ranged from cleaning and painting a church, providing leadership in worship services, and conducting a community survey. Usually this work was done in the mornings. In the afternoons each member of the unit had specific work assigned. I helped a doctor give free medical exams to young people. I can remember one young man was preparing for the Golden Gloves boxing tournament and the doctor tried to talk him out of participating. Some of the other youth were going to camp and needed pre-camp medicals. I took boys on camping trips in the mountains and supervised recreation programs for boys. We needed a place to play softball, so we worked for several days clearing a vacant lot of garbage. The first day we were really able to play on the lot we got there and people had thrown garbage back on the lot. We were never able to play softball on it. The boys invited me into their homes so I was able to see the living conditions of the families. I felt accepted by the families to a degree. My inability to speak Spanish was a barrier. The youth were so appreciative of the things I did and their enthusiasm helped to rise above their first reactions. I learned, after

> working there for a month, that people thought I was a dope pusher because I spent so much time with the kids.[16]

Mennonite college students in summer VS programs helped the East Harlem Protestant Parish accomplish some of its goals in reaching into the neighborhood. But questions about the vision and ministry of the Parish had reached the Home Missions Board of the General Conference Mennonite Church, and they decided to drop summer projects in East Harlem pending further discussion.

The East Harlem Protestant Parish leaders broke new ground in defining what it meant to be the church in the city. They consciously challenged the idea that the ministry of a typical suburban or small town congregation could adequately meet the needs of people in an urban slum. They saw their work as including a wide variety of social services and as mediating between the power structures and the poor people of East Harlem. But, as Hugh Hostetler forthrightly put it in a 1951 article:

> The Parish is not a settlement house, it is not a social center. It is a church, and our efforts are directed towards bringing people the good news of redemption through Christ. In doing so we are called to stray from normal middle-class church patterns of the ministry.[17]

Some General Conference Mennonites thought that the Parish had strayed too far. The Rev. John Thiessen, General Secretary of the Mission Board, visited East Harlem in July 1951. He wrote Hugh Hostetler that:

> What I saw of your work, I honestly felt you are doing a great work, a real mission work. But some people in this area feel that it is chiefly a social service venture and nothing more. So I suggest that you emphasize as strongly as possible that the total aim is Christ-centered, and the sum total aim is to bring people together with our Savior.

Hostetler agreed that this was the fundamental point; the East Harlem Protestant Parish is "a group of churches where the Gospel is heard, and interpreted in action, as fully as we are able to do so."[18]

The young pastor of the Church of Our Redeemer worked well with teenage gangs. By the summer of 1951 his store-front church had a Sunday evening youth worship service and a weekly recreation night. The emphasis in the first year was on the younger children who flocked to the newly-opened church. Gradually mothers and fathers began to take an interest. A men's club developed spontaneously in 1951, and the women's clubs had an average attendance of twenty five by the end of the first year.[19]

This was no ordinary congregation, slowly growing as the worship services and outreach program took hold. The people who attended services, two-thirds of them on welfare, faced every day a confusing and often hostile world. Police officers, nervous about their own safety, treated neighborhood people with contempt. Landlords ignored requests for repairs, elimination of rats, and even neglected heat, water, and sewage. Housing inspectors, welfare officials, school teachers could not spend time with the people who could not articulate their problems. Hostetler had to learn how the system worked and negotiate every day for his church members in the police station, the welfare office, the housing department and other city agencies.[20]

The East Harlem Protestant Parish protested police brutality in the shooting of Sergio Rodriguez. They worked together to produce "Dope", a play about the evil of narcotics, in vacant lots. Hugh Hostetler was chair of the Parish narcotics committee and served on Mayor Wagner's first citywide narcotics committee for a year. Jackie Robinson, the Brooklyn Dodgers star, came to Hostetler's church to urge youngsters to avoid drugs. The Parish ministers worked together on a housing survey, secured additional building inspectors, ran a rat control drive, and petitioned for improved ambulance service. It was all in a day's ministry.[21]

In 1952 Hugh Hostetler and Harriet Smith were married. She had come to New York during the summer of 1950 as a Denison College student to work with the East Harlem Protestant Parish. The newlyweds moved to an apartment in the same building as the store-front church. Harriet Hostetler recalled "I felt safer there than anywhere else in New York City. People lived on the streets, hung out the windows, and knew who belonged there. We could be part of the community and share their problems."

The Church of Our Redeemer began to put more emphasis on agape meal groups in apartment house buildings. Hostetler wrote:

> We've had one such group going all winter. Somehow at those meetings some of the true essence of propagation of the Christian faith is present, people are gathered because of common concern to meet for prayer, fellowship, and concrete action... These meetings remind me of the early Christian cells which also met in homes because they too faced crises in their lives. I feel the church as a whole would profit greatly if this method of *evangelization* were tried in even some of our more supposedly Christian communities.[22]

By March 1953 the Church of Our Redeemer had twenty-six members who felt ready to reach out to the whole community on their block through five agape groups, four youth groups with an average attendance of 70 youth and young adults. Two women from the congregation staffed a play school for day-care youngsters, and 85 children were enrolled in Released Time classes and children's programs. The congregation brought together blacks, Italians, and Puerto Ricans and services were in both English and Spanish.

Hugh Hostetler believed his own inexperience "has hindered in his ability to 'convict' people of their need for God." He also felt that a multipurpose hall did not contribute to a setting for worship. "A number of people have commented that they simply cannot worship in a place on Sunday when they know it has been used for a party Friday night."[23]

Late in 1953 the congregation of the Church of Our Redeemer finally secured a large storefront on East 102nd Street that provided, for the first time, adequate facilities for worship. They acquired a building at 340 East 102nd Street formerly used as a furniture refinishing factory. The congregation took full responsibility for making needed repairs and renovations and for meeting the cost of renting the building.[24]

It took several months to renovate it with the congregation and pastor working side by side without any outside help. This gave them a large sanctuary and another large room for recreational purposes. They dedicated the new church on October 22, 1953. "Our church with twenty active members, two-thirds of whom are on welfare, have raised and contributed over $600 to help make this possible." Another fifteen members had moved away or dropped out. Ten new members joined the Church on Christmas Day, 1953. The members had all attended an eight-week membership class and committed themselves to the disciplines of the Congregational Christian Church. There were Junior High and Senior High classes in the Bible and Christian faith. Hostetler added:

> Our case load in employment and welfare problems is unusually heavy these days—we feel very keenly every business recession. The battle for better housing continues daily: one church member counted five rat bite cases in her family in a period of one week. A number of our young people have run afoul of the law, demanding our attention in court. And so it goes.[25]

Angel Camacho, a gang leader from the neighborhood, became a Christian and the influential youth leader at the Church of Our Redeemer. "Angel Camacho who worked at the Church of Our Redeemer decided on the basis of his summer work to enter full-time service." He became part of the Parish staff in 1954. "Angel came up through our youth program, originally from a gang; he has felt a real call to work with the youth here."[26] He took over as youth director under Hostetler's supervision.

The Home Missions Board of the General Conference Mennonite Church contributed $2,700 a year to the East Harlem Protestant Parish, a larger contribution than came from any other single source except for the Congregational Christian Conference and the Reformed Church in America. John J. Plenert, pastor of Grace Mennonite Church in Lansdale, Pennsylvania, had served on the East Harlem Protestant Parish board since 1950 and made frequent visits to Hostetler and the Parish.

In his official capacity Plenert also became aware of the widespread erosion of Mennonite support for the East Harlem Protestant Parish. "Some of our pastors in the East are questioning our work and support of this kind" and had doubts about the approach to evangelism and church work taken in East Harlem. Other board members were more direct. Daniel J. Unruh of Newton, Kansas, expressed his conviction that the Mission Board should take steps to withdraw from the East Harlem Parish Mission and

> that we direct our mission energies to a program that is fundamentally sound and evangelistically geared to the program of winning souls for the Lord Jesus Christ. I am told by Mennonite Christian workers in New York that the work among the Negroes in the Harlem Parish follows the social program of the Federal, now National, Council of Churches, under whose supervision the work is conducted, and that in this social program there is little of the Gospel but much emphasis upon social gatherings and sponsoring such activities as square dancing.[27]

The Home Missions Board struggled with East Harlem over many months. Thiessen summed up the issues in a letter to Plenert in December 1952.

> Please read Hugh's letter which I enclose. Notice the passion to help those people in the name of Christ. I for the life of myself cannot condemn that effort, and I feel our Board, as a whole, does not either. What we object to is some of the methods....Could those keen minds of the parish find a substitute for the dance? I am sure they could.

Thiessen asked Plenert to share their concerns, telling Hostetler "how we all admire him for his sacrifice" and of "our appreciation of the desperate need," but asking for "a standard that our best people can approve of."[28]

The Board passed a resolution of disapproval at its annual meeting in December 1952, but decided to hold it in abeyance while they continued to work with Hostetler and the Parish ministry. Thiessen polled the board members in March 1953. S. F. Pannabecker's response was typical.

> I feel our concerns at the Board meeting were justified, although the work has many good points. Perhaps it would be all right to continue some support but not to send young people there for summer service. On the other hand, why support with money, if not with personnel?[29]

Most board members spoke enthusiastically of the work done by the Parish. The only specific objections raised by board members were to the approval given by the East Harlem Protestant Parish to dancing and their failure to condemn the use of tobacco. The Parish leaders saw smoking and moderate use of alcohol as lesser problems in an area rife with hard drugs, Mafia activities, numbers, prostitution, and political corruption at every level.

Plenert made it clear that he never "came to the place where he thought that the General Conference should withdraw its support" even though "he was rather uneasy about the whole thing."[30]

Wilmer Shelly of Bally, Pennsylvania, took John Plenert's place on the East Harlem board in December 1953. The annual meeting of the Board of Missions directed Shelly and Sam Goering to visit Hostetler in New York. John Thiessen, who had supported the East Harlem Protestant Parish all along, reported to Hostetler their "intention of finding a way to interpret the East Harlem program to our churches," since "a considerable group in our churches question anything that seems too much like 'social service.'"[31]

The Mission Board had misgivings about East Harlem, but they recognized the good work going on there. The General Conference Mennonite Church continued to support East Harlem Protestant Parish.[32]

"Housing is still the plague of East Harlem," the editor of the *Parish Newsletter* complained in April 1954. Much work went into dealing with eight different city agencies to restore heat to a single tenement. In comparison with the problem, "Such successes are scanty." East Harlem was being torn apart by wrecking balls and bulldozers in 1954. Relocation of tenants from sites being cleared for low-income housing projects was a major problem. "Families often get moved two or three times in a year, keeping one jump ahead of the wrecking crews." Many of them did not qualify for public housing. The George Washington Houses cut a swath south from East 104th Street. The Thomas Jefferson Houses cleared the blocks between East 112th and East 115th Streets and First to Third Avenues.

The East Harlem Protestant Parish experienced serious growing pains in 1954-55. The Group Ministry had mushroomed from three to eighteen members in the six years since they began work. As it grew, the group itself absorbed a great deal of time and thought, leaving less time for ministry. As Esther Berky had observed in her summer in East Harlem, the Group Ministry made all the decisions and left little real power in the hands of the church members. This was especially true in financial matters. Bruce Kenrick commented on these changes that resulted in "a courageous and thoughtless activism, a dehumanizing realm which served men more than it loved them, the giving of the life of the staff in necessary, costly, and superficial service, galvanizing the church into action instead of helping its members came alive with the life of Jesus Christ." One of the Group acknowledged in 1955 "We were less concerned with worship than with activism." The religious discipline of the original Group Ministry was by this time "a discipline in name only."[33]

Harriet Hostetler taught in the vacation Bible school in the summer of 1954 and filled in as director of Christian education. She had completed a degree in social work that year. With their first child expected, the Hostetlers began to think seriously about moving from East 102nd Street. The Parish turned out for farewells to Hugh, Harriet, and baby Sara Vaughan Hostetler on September 1, 1955. They remained in New York. Hugh became a full-time student at the American Foundation of Religion and Psychology in 1955 and went into private practice as a psychologist in 1957.[34]

The Mennonite connection with East Harlem Protestant Parish continued after Hugh Hostetler left. The Mission Board increased their contribution for 1956.[35] Ward Shelly became the Mennonite representative to the Parish board in August 1956. He reported favorably to the Board at its November meeting, but budget constraints led to a decision to "not continue a definite commitment to East Harlem in 1957."[36] John Thiessen sent personal contributions and collections taken in the Newton office. "I personally regard your work very highly and believe it is fully in accord with Matthew 25:35-36," he wrote in 1958.[37] The same year Leo Driedger made inquiries about renewed involvement of Mennonite Voluntary Service with the parish.[38]

In 1960 Leo Driedger visited East Harlem and determined to revive the General Conference Mennonite link. He wrote Bill Webber in March 1961 proposing a summer VS unit with three to five Mennonite volunteers, but by that time East Harlem Protestant Parish was so well known that they had many more applications for summer service than they could possibly accept.[39]

East Harlem Protestant Parish invited Mennonite Voluntary Service in 1963 to again supply a summer intern. Adolf Ens of the Newton VS office sent the proposal to Leland Harder at the Mennonite Biblical Seminary in Elkhart. Donald and Elvira Schierling, students at the seminary, agreed to spend the summer of 1964 in East Harlem. Don was a member of Bethesda Mennonite Church in Henderson, Nebraska, and had served overseas for three years with the Pax program in Greece and Germany in 1954-1957. They were assigned to the Church of the Resurrection on East 102nd Street. They found their summer work a stretching experience, "adjusting my middle-class values to the situation" and "struggling with the nature of the church."[40]

The Schierlings worked with the summer camping program and vacation church school and co-sponsored a young adult group and coached a junior high softball team. Elvira worked primarily with a tutoring program. They also "participated in the Family Freedom Week" which "involved a study of Negro history."[41]

The summer in East Harlem raised questions for the Schierlings as for others who had worked there earlier. "Why does the Church shy away from areas of conflict such as East Harlem? How does the Church speak out against these gross injustices? What is our responsibility to people who are depressed by environment, filled with apathy, yet looking for hope?"[42]

East Harlem Protestant Parish workers were enthusiastic about the Schierlings and requested another seminary student for the summer of 1965. Darrell Fast visited the Schierlings in East Harlem in 1964 and asked Leland Harder about working there.[43] Fast, a student at the seminary in Elkhart, was also from Henderson, Nebraska. Bethesda Mennonite Church provided financial support for his internship as the Mennonite Men had done for Don and Elvira Schierling.[44]

Darrell Fast spent the months of June, July, and August 1965 with the East Harlem Protestant Parish.[45] He reported to his home congregation early in his stay: "It is exciting to be a part of this congregation in its worship and fellowship. My responsibility will involve primarily teaching and assisting in the summer program of vacation church school. But already I have discovered that I will be doing more learning than teaching."[46]

He worked with the Church of the Ascension on East 106th Street, and took part in weekly Bible study meetings with groups of adults in their apartments that ran for three or more hours. "Many people have a keen understanding of the Bible, for they know what Moses meant when he told Pharaoh, 'Let my people go;' they understand the fact of Israel living in a foreign land; and some have experienced the reality of being one in Christ where there is neither Jew nor Greek, bond nor free."[47]

After he returned to Elkhart for his final year of seminary, Fast took responsibility for short-term voluntary service under the Board of Christian Service of the General Conference Mennonite Church. He was anxious to see the relationship with East Harlem Protestant Parish continue and hoped to recruit both a seminary intern and a volunteer for the summer remedial reading program.[48]

A young couple from Indiana seemed ideal, but their commitments to a local church kept them busy that summer. No one from the General Conference volunteered for East Harlem in 1966, but Fast began working at once to find a seminary intern and one or two college seniors for the reading program. Several Bethel College students volunteered and Faye Edwards, director of the remedial reading program, narrowed her choice to two of them. As summer drew nearer, both withdrew their names. Fast made a final effort to locate a qualified Bethel student, but this student also made other plans. The East Harlem Protestant Parish was "in very bad financial straits" in 1967 and forced to trim budgets in "an austerity program." Summer volunteers would need to be heavily subsidized by the denomination or their home church.

Restructuring began in late 1965 in response to the growing involvement of lay members, the emergence of new secular structures connected with the Poverty Program, and a perceived need for a more open-ended approach to urban ministry.[49] "The Parish is greatly changed and is in a period of transition now, as is the whole community. Bill Webber's books are no longer as relevant to us." In this time of change, the Mennonite connection with the East Harlem Protestant Parish came to an end.[50]

East Harlem Protestant Parish pioneered in methods and approaches that had become commonplace in urban ministry by the 1960s, but they attracted international attention in the 1950s. Young ministers from many different denominational backgrounds came to East Harlem to share in the group ministry and study the Parish firsthand, so they could begin similar work in inner-city neighborhoods of Chicago or Glasgow. Books by Ross Sanderson, Bill Webber, Bruce Kenrick, Geoffrey Shaw, and others made the East Harlem experiment familiar to divinity students and other interested Christians around the world.[51] *Time*, *Newsweek*, *The Reporter*, *The Saturday Evening Post*, and *The New Yorker* and denominational magazines profiled the Parish and brought it momentarily to the attention of thousands more across the country.

A new generation had come of age in Harlem by the late 1960s, and taken control of their own lives. Angel Camacho, one-time gang leader and youth worker with Hugh Hostetler's church, was administering poverty programs in the Bronx. Another youngster from the Church of Our Redeemer was an administrator with the Department of Rehabilitation. They were typical of many in the black and Hispanic communities who were ready to take charge.

"The demise of the Parish was due to a change in perception about who should be there," Hugh Hostetler observed. "We had too many white people, with some blacks, but overwhelmingly white middle-class. We were acutely aware we were white, educated, and had all kinds of avenues out. We couldn't be truly one with the people who lived there, but we made every effort that we knew how to be part of their community."

"It's hard to explain to people who have never been there. We experienced their tragedies. We shared with them. We saw lives changed. We all had a Christian religious impetus to try to live what we've been taught. I love the moment in the Gospel where Jesus opens the scroll and reads from it...'to bring good news to the poor, to let the oppressed go free.'"

"And it was really a political issue. We were asking where does power lie? What are *they* doing about this? The rich were getting richer, the poor poorer. That's consumerism. To focus on that meant rattling some cages."[52]

The East Harlem Protestant Parish workers had rattled cages about everything from public housing to contraceptives. They had been unabashedly political, campaigning against Congressman Marcantonio and for Liberal Party candidates. They had organized the neighborhood and made people aware of their rights and of grievance procedures. By the late 1960s ministers all over the city, including Mennonites, were going regularly to City Hall to plead for housing, health care, schools, and anti-poverty programs. They saw advocacy as integral to their ministry, "to bring good news to the poor."

NOTES

[1] *New York Times*, Mar. 26, 1951. East Harlem Protestant Parish, Report to the Administrative Board, Apr. 11, 1951.

[2] Interview with Hugh Hostetler, 24 September 1990. Bruce Kenrick, *Come Out the Wilderness*, (New York, 1962), 29-31, 53.

[3] Hugh Hostetler, "They Found the Church NOT There," *The Mennonite*, (February 1949), 4-6.

[4] The East Harlem Protestant Parish also worked with the First Spanish Methodist congregation which met in the Methodist Church of the Savior at East 111th Street and Lexington Avenue. "Report to the Administrative Board, East Harlem Protestant Parish," 26 January 1949, 23 September 1949, 26 October 1949. Hostetler Papers.

[5] Peter S. Bartel to Hugh Hostetler, 26 February 1949. Hugh Hostetler to Peter S. Bartel, 3 March 1949. MHLA.

[6] "Report to the Administrative Board, East Harlem Protestant Parish," 8 June 1949, 23 September 1949. Hostetler Papers.

[7] Interview with Joanna Bowen Gillespie, 5 October 1990.

[8] EHPP Report to Administrative Board, Mar. 1, 1950.

[9] Interview with Esther Berky Reed, 26 September 1990. Esther Berky to Bertha Fast, 22 March 1950. Bertha Fast to Esther Berky, 4 April 1950. Bertha Fast to George W. Webber, 15 April 1950. MHLA. *Summer Interracial Workshop Bulletin*, 15 July 1949, 30 July 1949. BCA.

[10] Ernest Goertzen to Richard MacMaster, 12 October 1990. Ray E. Horst to Ernest Goertzen, 11 April 1950. Bertha Fast to George W. Webber, 15 April 1950. MHLA.

[11] Bill Webber to Bertha Fast, 27 March 1950. "East Harlem Protestant Parish Work Camp. Final Report, 3 October 1950." MHLA.

[12] Ernest Goertzen to Richard MacMaster, 12 October 1990.

[13] East Harlem Protestant Parish, Report to the Administrative Board, Nov. 21, 1950. MHLA.

[14] Esther Berky, "Parish Report, 31 August 1950." MHLA. Anne Austin, "The Crisis Parish of East Harlem," *Social Action*, 16(January 1950), 23-33.

[15] Edith Claassen to Louisa Shotwell, 13 January 1951. "Voluntary Service for 1951,"n.d. Edith Claassen to Velma Jean Krehbiel, 19 February 1951, 19 April 1951. East Harlem Protestant Parish, Report to the Administrative Board, 25 September 1951. MHLA. "Concrete Vineyard," *Time*, Aug. 29, 1955, 65.

[16] George Eicher to Richard MacMaster, 19 November 1990, 24 January 1991.

[17] Hugh Hostetler, "The Church and the City," *The Mennonite*, 16(1951), 700-701.

[18] John Thiessen to Hugh Hostetler, 20 October 1951. Hugh Hostetler to John Thiessen, 22 October 1951. MHLA.

[19] East Harlem Protestant Parish, Report to the Administrative Board, Sept. 25, 1951. MHLA.

[20] Hugh Hostetler, Interview, Sept. 24, 1990.

[21] Henry L. Cossit, "God Sent Them to the Slums," *Saturday Evening Post*, July 5, 1952. East Harlem Protestant Parish, Report to the Administrative Board, April 1953. Hugh Hostetler, Interview, Sept. 24, 1990. Helen Kromer, "Ministering in East Harlem," *Advance*, Sept. 3, 1951, 16-17.

[22] Hugh Hostetler to John Thiessen, May 9, 1952. MHLA.

[23] EHPP, Report to the Administrative Board, March 1953, Oct. 1953.

[24] Hugh Hostetler, "Visit East Harlem," *Missionary News and Notes*, Dec. 1953, 14.

[25] Hugh Hostetler to John Thiessen, Dec. 1, 1953.

[26] Harriet and Hugh Hostetler to Dear Friends, Christmas 1954. MHLA. William Harlan Hole, "Going Down This Street, Lord," *The Reporter*, Jan. 13, 1955, 15-18.

[27] John J. Plenert to John Thiessen, June 7, 1952. Daniel J. Unruh to John Thiessen, July 9, 1952. MHLA.

[28] John Thiessen to John J. Plenert, Dec. 20, 1952. MHLA.

[29] S. F. Pannabecker to John Thiessen, Apr. 8, 1953. MHLA.

[30] Arthur S. Rosenberger to John Thiessen, Nov. 24, 1953. MHLA.

[31] John Thiessen to Hugh Hostetler, Dec. 19, 1953. MHLA.

[32] Arthur S. Rosenberger to John Thiessen, Nov. 24, 1953. Hugh Hostetler to John Thiessen, Jan. 9, 1954. John Thiessen to Hugh Hostetler, Jan. 14, 1954. Donald W. Strickler to Wilmer S. Shelly, Mar. 24, 1954. MHLA.

[33] Bruce Kenrick, *Come Out the Wilderness*, 134-142.

[34] Hostetler, Interview.

[35] John Thiessen to Donald W. Strickler, Dec. 20, 1955. Bill Webber to John Thiessen, Jan. 3, 1956. Donald W. Strickler to John Thiessen, Jan. 10, 1956. MHLA.

[36] John Thiessen to East Harlem Protestant Parish, Dec. 6, 1956. MHLA.

[37] John Thiessen to "Christian Friends at Eastern Harlem Protestant Parish," Jan. 2, 1958, June 16, 1958, Oct. 15, 1968. MHLA.

[38] G. W. Webber to Leo Driedger May 12, 1958. MHLA.

[39] Leo Driedger to G. W. Webber, March 10, 1961. G. W. Webber to Leo Driedger, March 23, 1961. MHLA.

[40] Adolf Ens to Leland Harder, Dec. 10, 1963. Adolf Ens to Donald and Elvira Schierling, Jan. 16, 1964. Adolf Ens to Robert Nichol, Feb. 12, 1964. MHLA. Adolf Ens to Richard F. Graber, July 10, 1964.

[41] Donald Schierling Report, East Harlem Protestant Parish, Church of the Resurrection, n.d. 1964. MHLA.

[42] Don and Elvira Schierling to Richard F. Graber, Sept. 21, 1964 with enclosure: Don and Elvira Schierling, "God's People in East Harlem," n.d. MHLA.

[43] Walter Paetkau to Leland Harder, Oct. 9, 1964. Leland Harder to Walter Paetkau, Oct. 24, 1964. Walter Paetkau to Robert Nichol, Oct. 28, 1964. Robert Nichol to Walter Paetkau, Nov. 10, 1964. MHLA.

[44] Walter Paetkau to John Gaeddert, Dec. 7, 1964. John Gaeddert to Walter Paetkau, Dec. 17, 1964. Alfred Epp to Walter Paetkau, Jan. 8, 1965. Walter Paetkau to Alfred Epp, Jan. 13, 1965. MHLA.

[45] Robert Nichol to Darrell W. Fast, Mar. 10, 1965. Walter Paetkau to Darrell Fast, Mar. 17, 1965. Bob Nichol to Darrell Fast, May 14, 1965. MHLA.

[46] Darrell Fast to "Dear Members of Bethesda," June 26, 1965. MHLA.

[47] Darrell Fast to "Dear Members of Bethesda," July 31, 1965. MHLA.

[48] Darrell Fast to Robert Nichol, Sept. 28, 1965. Darrell Fast to Faye Edwards, Sept. 28, 1965. Bob Nichol to Darrell Fast, Oct. 13, 1965. Darrell Fast to Faye Edwards, Dec. 7, 1965. Faye Edwards to Darrell Fast, Dec. 13, 1965. MHLA.

[49] Letty M. Russell, "Changing Structures in the East Harlem Protestant Parish," *Union Seminary Quarterly Review*, 21 (Mar. 1966), 333-338.

[50] Laverne Basenitz to Darrell Fast, May 2, 1966. Darrell Fast to Margarita Miranda, May 17, 1966. G. W. Webber to Darrell Fast, June 7, 1966. Darrell Fast to Letty Russell, Sept. 7, 1966. Darrell Fast to Margarita Miranda, Oct. 8, 1966. Letty Russell to Darrell Fast, Oct. 21, 1966. Darrell Fast to Leland Harder, Oct. 22, 1966. Linda Hiebert to Faye Edwards, Nov. 27, 1966. Faye Edwards to Darrell Fast, Feb. 19, 1967. Faye Edwards to Darrell Fast,

Mar. 27, 1967. Darrell Fast to Faye Edwards, Mar. 29, 1967. Darrell Fast to Letty Russell, Apr. 13, 1967.

[51] Ross Sanderson, *The Church Serves the Changing City,* (New York, 1955), 190-231. G. W. Webber, *God's Colony in Man's World,* (New York, 1960). G. W. Webber, *The Congregation in Mission,* (New York, 1964). Bruce Kenrick, *Come Out the Wilderness,* (New York, 1962).

[52] Hugh Hostetler, Interview, Sept. 24, 1990.

CHAPTER FOUR

"We Can Work Together"

1954–1964

A Decade of Change

THE YOUNG CHRISTIANS who worked with the East Harlem Protestant Parish deliberately chose inner-city social problems as the context for their ministry. The social problems of the inner-city increasingly crowded in on the young Mennonite mission workers in the Bronx and provided the setting for their ministry.

Change was a constant factor in the Bronx neighborhoods where Mennonites had begun churches. Even the most stable New York City communities experienced major changes in the 1950s and 1960s, but in the southwestern Bronx communities of Morrisania, Melrose, Mott Haven, and Hunt's Point change was a fact of life. The population grew from 407,000 in 1950 to an estimated 426,000 in 1953 and increased at about the same rate through the decade. In addition to the steady increase in population, the ethnic composition of the South Bronx shifted dramatically. When the Mennonite congregation moved from St. Ann's Avenue to Brook Avenue in 1954, the immediate Glad Tidings neighborhood was largely Puerto Rican with a few Irish and German remaining. The *New York Times* described the Brook Avenue section in 1950 as "a squalid Puerto Rican quarter" with blocks of "solid, grimy five-story tenements." By 1965 "only a small minority of Irish are found, but many Spanish and Negroes have moved in." The Fox Street community to the northeast had been predominantly Jewish. "Only a few older Jewish people" still lived there in 1965 and the Fox Street church stood on the boundary between two ethnic groups. "To the west is a large Negro community and to the east and south is a Spanish Puerto Rican community." The Fox Street Church was "experiencing a change from Spanish folks to Negro folks. Those who have been attending the church for a number of years are largely Spanish while those who have begun attending more recently are largely Negro."[1]

The South Bronx was always working-class with mixed neighborhoods where many different ethnic groups lived. Some groups were more numerous in certain sections: the Irish in Mott Haven, Italians west of Third Avenue, Jews east of Brook Avenue. As people progressed economically, they tended to move to slightly more prosperous Bronx neighborhoods. Population shifts in the 1950s merely accelerated the pace.[2] It was never the sort of neighborhood where families lived in the same house for two or three generations. In 1953 half the people in the South Bronx had lived fewer than five years at their present address and nearly one in five had lived there less than a year.[3]

Slum clearance and construction of new public housing projects forced many families to relocate, often to double-up with relatives or friends. The new expressways eliminated whole neighborhoods in their path and scattered the residents. The South Bronx offered a refuge for families evicted from buildings in Manhattan scheduled for demolition, and the South Bronx had more than its own share of low-income housing projects, partly to keep them out of more affluent neighborhoods. Patterson Houses opened in 1950, Melrose in 1952, Forest in 1954. The St. Ann's Avenue church was razed in site clearance for Mill Brook Houses which was still under construction, along with St. Mary's Park Houses, in 1956. Six more projects were in various stages by the end of 1956. The South Bronx communities had 5,418 new low-income housing units and another 6,960 under construction or in planning stages by December 1956. What had that meant in terms of demolition of old walk-up apartments and of dislocation of old tenants? Mill Brook, James Mitchel, and Mott Haven were all in walking distance of Glad Tidings. One neighborhood resident recalled Mill Brook as "huge, ugly, unsafe," tall towers massed in the center of razed blocks. "Few of the old tenants became new tenants. People in the projects were afraid."[4]

The pattern of disruption and deterioration continued through the 1950s and early 1960s. Esther Petersheim remembered other changes in this South Bronx neighborhood in those years. "There were still some very lovely buildings with large apartments, then some agent came in and divided them into small apartments and filled them with welfare clients." Glad Tidings and Fox Street churches "constantly faced the problem of knowing the best way to relate to the human need surrounding them." What Carl Good wrote of the Fox Street neighborhood in 1965 was true of the whole South Bronx: "This community is very much a transitional community and suffers from serious problems of poverty and disorganization. These problems make it a distasteful place for people to choose to live."

Building a stable congregation in the midst of instability and change proved nearly impossible. Slum clearance in the St. Ann's Avenue neighborhood scattered many families at the time the church moved to Brook Avenue. "People who came to Glad Tidings had to move because of their houses being torn down in the St. Ann's area and these people didn't continue to come to Glad Tidings." Others moved away to better their circumstances. At Fox Street "some of the younger member families moved to better communities." Some of the other members "are living in other needy communities" at a distance, "but come to Fox Street for worship."[5]

Change was less apparent in Harlem, but Seventh Avenue Mennonite Church had some of the same inner-city problems. Lucy Vance noted in 1965 that half the members lived near the church, with the other half scattered throughout the city. "Those who live in other areas probably do so for a variety of reasons, some of which are proximity to jobs, better housing, and better schools." The Seventh Avenue Mennonites were all employed, with only one church member on welfare. One respondent commented on the excessive rent charged for housing in Harlem. Sociologist Kenneth B. Clark published a study of Harlem in 1965 in which he observed that 44 percent of the buildings in Harlem were officially classified as dilapidated or deteriorating in 1960 and that rent "is often higher in Harlem than for better-equipped buildings downtown." Clark documented the high level of unemployment and under-employment with 64 percent of employed men and 74 percent of employed women relegated to low-paid unskilled and service jobs. Although still overcrowded—more than 1,000 people lived in the same block as the church—the population of Harlem was steadily declining in the 1950s and 1960s as young couples moved to other parts of the city and suburbs, "shifting to other ghettos."[6]

The accelerated pace of change in these three urban neighborhoods reflected larger changes in the city. Construction of new expressways and both public and private housing developments required demolition of existing buildings and tenant relocation on a massive scale. The Major Deegan-Bruckner Expressway, completed in 1955, and the Cross-Bronx Expressway, completed in 1960, cut a wide swath of destruction through crowded, stable neighborhoods. The United States Supreme Court upheld a lower court decision allowing Stuyvesant Town, a Manhattan development, to refuse to rent to people of color in 1950, and New York City did not have a fair housing law outlawing racial discrimination until 1958, so black and Puerto Rican tenants had few choices for new housing. Existing black and Puerto Rican neighborhoods became more crowded, and housing deteriorated further.

Although the mission workers had no reason to study the already alarming statistics, New York City was losing jobs as the garment industry, printing and other kinds of manufacturing plants moved out of the metropolitan area. The type of employment that enabled previous waves of newcomers to work up the ladder had thus become scarcer. The garment industry alone lost 87,000 jobs between 1950 and 1960. Unions became nervous and worried more about protecting their present members than opening opportunities to other workers.[7]

Dissent and Renewal

Fox Street remained the most conservative among the New York City churches through the 1950s. Looking back at the early days at Fox Street, John Freed wrote in 1965 that "The first few years were prosperous ones. A fine group of young people responded and became members of the church. They were enthused, interested, and looked forward to being part of the church." At the same time, "Deep internal struggles developed within the core of workers. The pastor and several of the team felt a deep commitment to develop a Christianity with all the external expressions of their background and culture. Several of the other members of the team felt as deeply committed to a Christianity that gave new Christians the freedom to develop their own culture and make the adaptations that seemed wise to make."[8]

Esther Petersheim was the first young woman from the Weavertown Amish Mennonite Church to go into voluntary service. It seemed natural for her to go to Fox Street since Aquilla Riehl, the pastor, came from her home congregation. She arrived in New York on June 1, 1953. The Riehls left for a visit to family in Iowa and Esther's first duty in the unfamiliar city was to rent a store-front for vacation Bible school. "We rented the store-front, and cleaned it up." When the first day of class came, "I never saw more children in my life. We had to have classes on the sidewalk. It was so hot. I can feel that city heat now."

Aquilla Riehl had a sincere conviction and expressed his concern to "hold the standards of the conference." Despite their shared background, Esther Petersheim had difficulties with plain dress. "I dressed Weavertown fashion for at least two years until I changed my membership in 1956. I chose to dress as I did, but I couldn't see imposing that on new believers to the degree he did. I didn't quite do what he thought I should do. He was very unhappy with my relations with the youth group. Fellows and girls weren't supposed to sit beside each other. We had very strict regulations in dress and behavior."

Esther had responsibility for the young women, and Lloyd Wenger, who was doing his 1-w service at Presbyterian Medical Center, worked with the young men. Both of them disagreed with Lancaster Conference standards as applied to the youth group. By 1956 this had reached a crisis. "Esther resents any correction that is given to any of the young people with whom she has to do," Anna Buckwalter wrote. "For me, I feel if we do not correct them we do not love them." Lloyd Wenger was asked to leave Fox Street in July 1956 because of his "willingness to mix Christian and non-Christian youth for fellowship" and his "attitude about television and radio in the Christian home." He went to Seventh Avenue and worked with the youth group there. "I am still praying for the workers at Fox Street that there may be more unity among them," he wrote H. Raymond Charles. Esther Petersheim also left Fox Street. She would have returned home, but in October 1956 Harold Thomas invited her to Glad Tidings. One person recalled that whenever there were tensions or disagreements at Fox St, the person involved was invited to come to Glad Tidings.[9]

The Fox Street team were all committed to spreading the gospel and reaching new neighborhoods. In 1956 Earl and Maggie Denlinger began a new outpost on Washington Avenue, teaching Sunday school and children's Bible clubs in a rented storefront. Bill Overholt, a Beachy Amishman from Norfolk, Virginia, and Daniel and Anna Ruth Lapp from the Weavertown Amish Mennonite Church staffed this work in 1958. They were all working full-time in 1-w service at Frances Delafield Hospital. Victor and Ruth Weaver had also come to the city for his 1-w service. They lived on Fox Street and worked with the Washington Avenue outpost. They recalled the difficulty of keeping contact with youngsters and their parents in a distant neighborhood. City people were generally wary of strangers and unfriendly to their neighbors, but they responded warmly when Ruth Weaver greeted them as she pushed her baby-carriage, and she made many friends in their own neighborhood.[10]

In the summer of 1957, the Riehl family left the Bronx to settle on a farm near Wallkill, New York. Aquilla continued as pastor at Fox Street, but Victor Weaver took over as mission superintendent.[11]

In February 1958 Aquilla Riehl asked to be relieved of his pastoral duties at Fox Street. In August he and Victor Weaver met with Raymond Charles to chart the future course for the mission. They agreed that John Freed should be invited to take over the work whenever the Weavers left the city. Victor Weaver had completed his two years of alternate service, but drove a city cab for another year. The Weaver family moved back

Victor and Ruth Weaver family.
Left to right: Ruth, Janice, Julia, and Victor holding Linford.

John and Dorothy Freed, pastor of Fox Street Mennonite Church, with their children, Lamar and Dottie Jean, in front of the first Fox Street church building.

to Chester County, Pennsylvania in 1959. John and Dottie Freed moved to Fox Street from Glad Tidings when he received an appointment as mission superintendent in February 1959.[12]

Mabel Herr came from Lancaster County in 1958 and lived with the Weavers, helping with the children. She found a new apartment on Grant Avenue, sharing with Norma Brenner, a registered nurse. Eighteen months later their apartment would be the center of a new outreach.

The Denlingers closed out the Washington Avenue store-front mission, but remained in the Bronx until 1960, working with the Fox Street congregation. Daniel and Anna Ruth Lapp also moved to Fox Street in February 1959.[13]

Aquilla Riehl continued to be active in the Fox Street mission after he resigned as pastor. He sometimes preached in Spanish on Sundays and taught in Spanish at a Bible conference held at Fox Street in February 1961.[14]

Fox Street was not unique in experiencing "deep internal struggles" among the inner core of mission workers. The younger workers at Glad Tidings often disagreed with the pastor on issues of discipline and discipleship, which he interpreted as meaning that they were unwilling to work with the Church. Jacob and Frances Thomas, Merritt and Esther Robinson, Paul and Miriam Burkholder, John and Dorothy Freed, John and Thelma Kraybill and others had this experience.

George R. Brunk had pitched a tent in a field alongside Manheim Pike near Lancaster in 1951 and announced a week of evangelistic services. He was already well-known as a preacher and speaker in churches, but he was venturing into a new way of preaching the gospel. The response of Lancaster Mennonites and others who jammed the tent week after week convinced him that this was the Lord's leading, and Brunk Brothers Revival began.

In the early days of the Brunk Crusades, Merritt Robinson took care of the tent and handled some of the logistics. Merritt and Esther (Zimmerman) Robinson felt called to mission work in New York City and became self-supporting mission workers at St. Ann's Avenue in 1953.[15] They helped begin Harlem Mennonite Church, later Seventh Avenue, but remained part of the Glad Tidings team after the move from St. Ann's.[16]

Esther Robinson edited the newsletter and the church bulletins, and did secretarial work. Merritt Robinson was the youth leader, coaching winning softball teams for Glad Tidings. The Mennonite teams played in Central Park and attracted some attention from passersby. He also taught Sunday school and served as Sunday school superintendent.

With his experience in the Brunk revivals, Merritt Robinson was the natural choice to head the "Christ for You" evangelistic campaigns in the city. B. Harold Thomas was the evangelist. Robinson rented a vacant lot on Jackson Avenue and set up a tent for the first campaign in July and August 1954. Five people responded in the first meetings that summer and asked to join the Mennonite Church. After instruction, four of them were baptized together at Glad Tidings on May 15, 1955. The fifth was baptized later. Others expressed a renewed faith. The following summer they held another series of evangelistic meetings at the Jackson Avenue site. In 1956 the "Christ for You" tent meetings moved to a vacant lot on East 146th Street, four blocks from Glad Tidings. The final campaign ran from August 3 to August 25, 1957 at the same site with B. Harold Thomas

Bronx Gospel Tent Campaign, sponsored by the New York City Mennonite Churches.

A womens trio sings during a service in the tent. Left to right: Esther Robinson, Lois Thomas, and Dorothy (Martin) Freed.

as evangelist. Jesus Constantin, who lived across the street, came to the tent meetings out of curiosity. He accepted Jesus Christ as his Savior and led his family into the Mennonite Church. Related "Christ for You" crusades were held across the Hudson in North Bergen, New Jersey, with Noah Hershey as the revival preacher, and at Moonochie, New Jersey.[17]

Paul and Miriam Burkholder moved to New York in April 1954 with two small children and a third on the way. They had been attending the Vine Street Mission in Lancaster because Paul had cast off his plain coat and could not continue worshiping at his home church. Paul put on the plain coat again to go to New York. "It felt somewhat noble to be involved in the mission of the church, but we had come to the end of ourselves spiritually." The Burkholders originally planned to work with Jacob and Frances Thomas in Jewish evangelism, but Harold Thomas, Miriam's cousin, persuaded them to come to Glad Tidings, where her sister Lois was in V.S.

"I held no significant position in the church, only teaching Sunday school and helping with the tent campaign," Paul Burkholder recalled. Harold Thomas was in great demand as a speaker. "He was being called back to Lancaster all the time to preach so he asked Bishop Elmer Martin for an assistant pastor. Elmer said no to the request for an assistant pastor, but he told Harold, 'I need a deacon to help me serve communion when I come to New York.' Harold decided he'd make [whoever is chosen] a preaching deacon." Merritt Robinson, Richard Valentine, and Paul Burkholder were in the lot. "The bishops had no problem with the first two, but I gave them fits. I had told them I could not require other people to put on plain clothes." The lot fell to Burkholder and he was ordained at Glad Tidings on January 2, 1955. In his ministerial questionnaire, he wrote "I think perhaps in our City Missions where this practice is unknown we should be patient with new Christians."Both Paul and Miriam Burkholder encountered Jesus Christ in a new way early in their first year in the city. Glenn and Florence Zeager and Herbert and Erma Maust encouraged them in their renewed faith. They had been refreshed by fellowship with Mennonite missionaries, back in Pennsylvania on furlough, who had come to a new understanding of discipleship through the East African Revival.

Paul and Miriam Burkholder family, pastor of Glad Tidings Mennonite Church. Rear: Miriam, and Paul holding Jim, front: Judy, Renee, Marilyn, and Glenn.

The Glad Tidings congregation counted 25 New York City converts among its members in 1956. Richard Valentine was one of the native members and with his wife Emma Mohler Valentine, a former VSer, a self-supporting worker at Glad Tidings. The average attendance on a Sunday morning was 85, most of them children and teenagers. Mennonites assigned to 1-W alternative service jobs in the city also attended Glad Tidings and many of them helped the mission workers as Sunday school teachers and song leaders.

About twenty young Mennonites did their 1-W alternative service at Northport Veterans Hospital on eastern Long Island in 1953-1955. Curtis Godshall, Eugene Souder and others had a vision for a Mennonite church in nearby Centereach and began holding services in the Fire House. Others

Visiting on the sidewalk after a Sunday morning service at Glad Tidings. Left to right: Wilbert Lind, Esther Petersheim, Anna Maestre, Nellie (Villanueva) Beiler, Don Sensenig, pastoral intern, and Paul G. Burkholder, pastor.

came occasionally to the Bronx to help with the churches there. John L. Freed, one of the 1-w men at Northport already knew Merritt and Esther Robinson from the Brunk meetings in Perkiomenville, his home community in Montgomery County, Pennsylvania. He came to Glad Tidings the first time with three others from Northport to sing in a quartet. After the service and a fellowship meal, Harold Thomas sent him to the kitchen to help Dorothy Martin with the dishes. Freed became a frequent helper at Glad Tidings and spent many evenings washing and drying dishes with Dottie Martin after his 1-w service ended in 1955. They were married on March 24, 1956. John Freed joined the Glad Tidings team, serving as Sunday school superintendent. He was the only one from Franconia Conference working in the city.[18]

Paul Burkholder had followed John H. Kraybill's example and supported his family driving a New York City cab. John Freed also became a taxi driver.

Harold Thomas had full-time employment repairing and selling automobiles, specializing in cabs. His work with taxi cabs had suggested cab driving to Kraybill and the others. Although he was good at repairing cars, Harold Thomas had too kind a heart to take advantage of anyone when it came to selling them. He sold cars at low prices to poorer people and often took a loss on the deal. In order to support his family, he needed to give more time to his business, located just across the George Washington Bridge in New Jersey. In July 1957 John Freed took over the duties of mission superintendent at Glad Tidings. Harold Thomas remained the pastor.[19]

Merritt Robinson may have felt that he was passed over in choosing someone with less experience in the work of the mission, but Merritt and Esther continued to carry other responsibilities at Glad Tidings.[20] He succeeded John Freed as Sunday school superintendent, at Harold Thomas' request. Freed reported that "Brother Harold is having a harder time 'letting go'" than he had at first anticipated."[21]

The Fall Communion at Glad Tidings in 1957 brought problems there to a crisis. The preparatory service prior to Communion was the traditional time for the bishop and ministers to determine whether each member of the congregation was at peace and in order. "We became aware that several of the girls were not wearing their coverings all the time," Freed wrote. When it came time for council meeting, preparatory for Communion, two members did not hand in favorable reports on the state of the congregation. Only Harold Thomas knew the contents of their

John Kraybill standing by the taxi he drove for the Yale Service Corp., a fleet of 65 taxis whose garage was located one block from the Seventh Avenue Church building. Paul Burkholder also drove for the same company.

written reports and he instructed John Freed to inform Conference that all was well. Bishop Elmer Martin accordingly set a date for Communion and traveled to New York. Nothing had been said "to any of those who answered negatively till Sunday morning after our regular services, and then they were talked to fifteen minutes before our communion service," Paul Burkholder explained. Elsie Anza, one of "the two girls who said they did not believe in wearing the veiling," had talked about her problem months earlier with Paul and Miriam Burkholder and they found themselves in agreement with her. The Burkholders "constantly encouraged them to wear it for the sake of obedience to the church," but the young women stopped wearing the covering except at services. On the morning of communion service Elsie attempted to explain her actions. Harold Thomas indicated that Paul Burkholder was responsible for the lack of unity in the congregation. "After this brother Elmer decided we should not have communion."[22]

Harold Thomas moved more and more "in the direction of coming back to full responsibility" for the Glad Tidings congregation. In March 1958 the Mission Board again appointed him as mission superintendent. In a reorganization at that time, Merritt Robinson and Esther Petersheim were responsible for youth work, John Freed and Esther Robinson for the Release Time program for elementary school pupils, and John Freed and Aubin Huertas for vacation Bible school. Velma Landis continued in charge of child visitation and the summer camp program. Carol De La Fe, Velma Landis, and Rosita Morales served on the young people's program committee and Elsie Dickens, Elsie Anza, and Esther Petersheim on the shut-in committee.[23]

Instead of a tent evangelism campaign in the summer of 1958 the Glad Tidings workers conducted a community survey of their neighborhood between East 132nd and 149th Streets and Cypress and Willis Avenues, including the Mill Brook public housing development. They joined with Fox Street to hold weekly street meetings on Saturday evenings and youth rallies once a month. They had as yet no plans for Spanish services, but Glad Tidings began a Spanish Sunday school. Over 200 children participated in the summer Fresh Air and camping programs. Average attendance on Sundays was 120.[24]

In September 1958 the Robinsons announced that they had talked with Bishop Henry Ginder of the Brethren in Christ Church and planned to work with their new mission in New York.[25] A few months later Raymond Charles asked Harold Thomas to release John and Dottie Freed to Fox Street.[26]

The Harlem Mennonite Church on upper Seventh Avenue was also going through a period of change. In 1955 John H. Kraybill completed his two years of 1-w service, and stayed in New York as a self-supporting pastor. Glenn Zeager still had his 1-w job, which interfered with his mission work to some extent. The Harlem workers appealed for help.[27] Help came from unexpected places. Mennonite Central Committee had established a new service unit in 1951 at Wiltwyck School at Esopus, New York. This was a home for troubled youth and most boys were sent there by New York City juvenile courts. Because of this, Wiltwyck maintained an office in Manhattan and, in January 1955, Lucy Vance, an MCC volunteer, arrived in New York to staff it. She was a Mennonite from Pendleton County, West Virginia, and had attended Eastern Mennonite College before moving to Washington, D.C. to work in a government office. She finished college at George Washington University in 1953. Her first contacts with city Mennonites were at Fox Street. Lucy Vance attended her first worship service at Seventh Avenue Mennonite Church on Easter Sunday, 1955, and promptly became part of the congregation. Lloyd Wenger, assigned to 1-w work at Presbyterian Medical Center, came in 1956 from Fox Street. Jacob and Grace Good, in 1-w service at Presbyterian Medical Center, first lived at Fox Street, but moved to Seventh Avenue. In February 1956 Jacob Good was Sunday school superintendent and Florence Zeager, Lloyd Wenger, Lucy Vance, Jacob Good, Glenn Zeager, Thelma Kraybill, and Earl Herr, also doing 1-w work at Presbyterian, taught the classes. The church sent seven boys to Camp Men-O-Lan in 1955. The Harlem Church had one baptized member who was a native New Yorker and seven others were under instruction. The average Sunday attendance of 48 included four adults in addition to those considered mission workers.[28]

Glenn and Florence Zeager in their home on University Avenue, Bronx.

The Seventh Avenue Church, like all the Mennonite city missions depended heavily on 1-w men and their wives to help with a variety of ministries. Since Kraybill and Zeager were themselves veterans of the 1-w program, young men and women who came to New York for alternative service felt a kinship there. In March 1957 a group of these young men presented a program at Seventh Avenue on "the Value of Nonresistant Love." Charles Marrero, Lloyd Wenger, and William Overholt discussed non-resistance on the job. Jacob Good spoke on non-resistant love in leisure time. Earl Herr talked about non-resistance in the Church and Victor Weaver gave the Scriptural basis.[29]

The VS Center

More than a dozen young men had come to the city for 1-w service since 1953 and taken an active part in the Lancaster Conference missions. In 1954 H. Raymond Charles first proposed setting up a VS Center where they could live in Christian community. The Executive Committee of Eastern Board authorized implementation of the idea in April 1957. The plan called for locating a rooming house or other suitable building on the east side of Manhattan in the neighborhood of 14th Street for the 1-w workers and spouses and a resident full-time director. The director should already have city mission experience. The Executive Committee specified that the center would operate as a VS center, not as a church.[30]

Paul Landis and Paul Kraybill made several trips to New York in the Spring of 1957, working with John H. Kraybill in locating the building they needed. In June the Mission Board appointed John H. Kraybill as unit leader for the VS Center. They decided that he continue as pastor of the Harlem Mennonite Church for some indefinite time.[31]

A year later the Mission Board approved an agreement for the purchase of the building at 314 East 19th Street that John H. Kraybill had located. John and Thelma Kraybill moved there in September 1958 with their infant son Charles.[32]

Paul G. Landis, Eastern Mennonite Board of Missions VS Director.

The first residents moved in soon after the Kraybills did. James and Rosetta Kreider and John and Miriam Buckwalter were followed by Harold and Connie Stauffer and Marvin and Lois Weaver. These four young couples were employed in the NYU-Bellevue Hospital complex. Daniel and Anna Ruth Lapp soon joined them. He worked at Frances Delafield Hospital and she became the first unit cook at the VS house. The unit was completely staffed with the arrival of Dale and Doris Stoltzfus early in 1959.[33]

The VS unit looked uptown. The Lapps continued to take responsibility for the Washington Avenue mission Sunday school, just as the Kraybills kept their pastoral duties in Harlem. The Harold Stauffers and James Kreiders taught in the Glad Tidings Sunday school and Dale and Doris Stoltzfus and John and Miriam Buckwalter taught at Seventh Avenue. Marvin and Lois Weaver taught at Fox Street. The VS unit began a community survey in February 1959. They discovered that their immediate neighborhood was 45 percent Catholic, 25 percent Protestant, 15 percent Jewish and 15 percent claimed no religious affiliation.

The seven couples who made up the original unit found time to do other things together. They attended the New York Flower Show and an Intercollegiate Peace Seminar at the UN and went to an evangelistic film "Heart of a Rebel" at the DeWitt Church on Rivington Street. They heard Guy Hershberger talk on "The Way of the Cross in Human Relations" and entertained him at the VS Center. They went witnessing in Union Square and Anna Ruth Lapp and Doris Stoltzfus packed a picnic lunch for the unit to take to Van Cortlandt Park.[34]

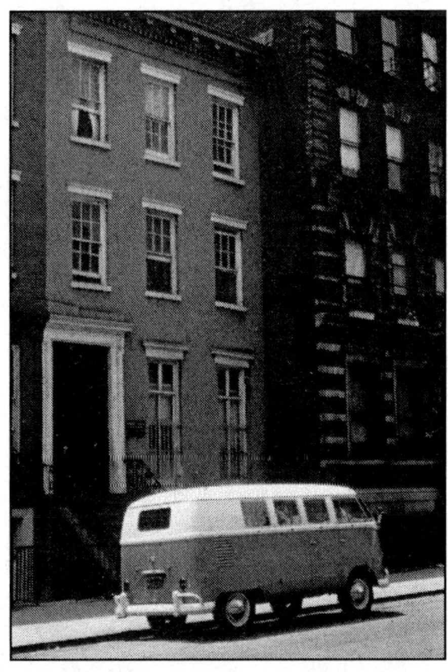

Mennonite Voluntary Service Center, 314 East 19th Street, Manhattan, with the Center's Volkswagen van parked in front of the building. Later, this building became Menno House when the VS Center moved uptown to the Bronx.

The VS Center developed outreach in its own neighborhood as time went on. By the time David W. Shenk took over as unit leader in October 1959, the unit staffed a club program for neighborhood children involving 30 children from 24 families. "Some of the unit members continue to meet with interested community people in the center on Sunday mornings for Bible study." Shenk told Paul Landis that the unit members were "perplexed as to which direction we should move in regards to community outreach." Some of the 1-W workers wanted to concentrate on their own East Side neighbors for evangelism, while others put all of their energy into helping in the uptown missions.[35]

The VS Center was itself a force for change as young Mennonites shared their own experiences in adapting to an unfamiliar city. They saw no harm in setting up a Christmas tree for the youngsters in the club program, but it scandalized some of the older Conference leaders.[36] Carl Frey, working with the Police Athletic League in his 1-W placement, had significant contacts with tough youth in Hell's Kitchen, but his job seemed in jeopardy because of his unashamed sharing of his Christian faith with them.[37] He kept his job and found himself in the middle of a gang war between the Crowns and the Sinners. His patient work bore fruit when gang members turned over their zip guns to him and accepted Carl's invitation to spend a few days with his family in Lancaster County.[38] The clubs that met at the center had their effect, too. Paul Landis joined in "thanking the Lord with you for those teenagers who gave their hearts to the Lord last Saturday night."[39]

In 1960 Evelyn Hertzler began investigating the potential for a nursery or day care program at the VS Center. She found facilities at the East 19th Street house inadequate and language was a barrier for a nursery with Spanish-speaking neighborhood children. She and Lucy Vance considered a day-care program in Harlem a better idea.[40]

The first group of seven couples who lived in the 19th Street VS Center. Front row, left to right: James and Rosetta Kreider, Thelma Kraybill holding Charles, John Kraybill, director, holding Fred. Back rows, left to right: Doris and Dale Stoltzfus, Miriam and John Buckwalter, Connie and Harold Stauffer, Anna Ruth and Dan Lapp, Lois and Marvin Weaver.

Paul Landis commented in 1960 that "the clubs for children on Saturdays continue to open the door for contacts with the community." Don Hertzler reported the clubs met on Saturday afternoon from 1 to 2:30 for boys 6 to 9 and from 2:30 to 4:00 for boys 10 to 14. The boys made lamps and book shelves and put models together. The last 15 minutes were devoted to Bible study. In addition to the club work, the fellows at the center began hauling children to Camp Hebron every Saturday that summer. Paul Hill from Fellowship Chapel in the Bronx began a series on Revelation at the VS Center, attended by several adults from the neighborhood.[41]

Praying and Working Together

The Billy Graham Crusade that began on April 14, 1957 had major impact on the city missions. The taxi-driving pastors had many contacts with Graham staff people, although none of them managed to pick up Billy Graham himself. Mission workers from Fox Street, Glad Tidings, and Seventh Avenue and from the new Mennonite House of Friendship sang in the massed choir and volunteered for training as counselors to work with those who made a decision for Christ at Madison Square Garden. This was the beginning of closer cooperation between the Eastern Board and Mennonite Board of Missions workers. As John I. Smucker recalled, the Graham Crusade "gave us much courage and inspiration."[42] They saw that they were not alone in a hostile environment. And working together in the Crusade brought pastors closer together. John Smucker wrote:

> I went with Raymond Charles and John H. Kraybill to Yankee Stadium to the Billy Graham Meeting. After the Meeting, Raymond Charles specifically told me that he hopes that John H. and the other Lancaster Conference pastors and us would be able to work together. I appreciated his attitude very much. So in the near future there is a Mennonite Pastors' Fellowship that is going to be held, perhaps at John H. Kraybill's home, to discuss problems of evangelism that Mennonites face here in New York area. This is what we have been praying for and hoping that we would at least be able to discuss problems together and work together to that extent.[43]

The reconciling message of the East African Revival also gave new life to the city missions and brought them into closer fellowship. Herbert and Erma Maust spent part of several summers helping with the vacation Bible school at Seventh Avenue Mennonite Church and drove to the city at other times in the year to meet with mission workers for prayer and fellowship. They brought encouragement and spiritual renewal in a time of trial for many of the city missionaries. John I. Smucker recalled: "A Mennonite

Spirit-filled saint, Erma Maust, came many times to visit." Don Jacobs, Elam Stauffer, John Leatherman and others from the East African mission field carried the message of renewal to the city churches. Roy Hession, an English evangelist who brought the central ideas of the East African Revival to millions in his book *The Calvary Road*, visited the New York City Mennonites in May 1958 and returned in January 1959 with Dr. Joe Church to preach at the House of Friendship. John Leatherman preached at Seventh Avenue and the House of Friendship in April 1959. Smucker's diary recorded five visits by Erma Maust in August 1959 when she was helping at Seventh Avenue. Don Jacobs addressed all the Mennonite workers on mission strategy at the House of Friendship in October 1959.[44]

Glenn Zeager experienced a deeper commitment to Christ before he came to New York through missionaries who told about the East African Revival at Goods Mennonite Church. Herbert and Erma Maust from Goods began helping each summer with the Bible school at Seventh Avenue Mennonite Church and visiting the Zeagers during the year with words of encouragement. The Paul Burkholders, who had had a similar renewal experience soon after they came to New York in 1954, joined the Mausts and Zeagers in a fellowship group. The John Freeds became part of the group a little later, as did John and Irene Smucker from the Mennonite House of Friendship. In 1958 Paul Burkholder invited Merritt and Esther Robinson, Esther Petersheim, and Velma Landis, but, like John H. Kraybill, they were sympathetic without being deeply involved in the fellowship. David W. Shenk knew the East African Revival at first hand and it had shaped his spirituality, too. As unit leaders at the VS Center on East 19th Street in 1959-1961 David and Grace Shenk promoted a fellowship group there.

Glenn and Florence Zeager had lived in one of the apartments above the Seventh Avenue Mennonite Church. In 1959 they purchased a large house at 2190 University Avenue in the Bronx, primarily to have room for meetings of the Fellowship and for visiting missionaries to stay. They dedicated their new home with a fellowship meeting on October 29, 1959. Like the "Balokole" in East Africa, those who had been influenced by the Revival formed a close supportive community, "walking in the light," confessing their faults, and sharing their joys with one another. By centering on Jesus Christ, and being themselves broken at the foot of His cross, they found it possible to work together across conference lines and across denominational lines.[45]

Others in the New York mission felt excluded or saw the influence of the East African Revival as a divisive threat to traditional boundaries.

In February 1960 Harold Thomas resigned as pastor of Glad Tidings. He cited the ideas brought to New York by Erma Maust as a divisive element that undercut loyalty to Lancaster Conference and its standards. Bishop Elmer Martin and Harold Thomas had tried to uphold the Conference rules and found the Mission Board no longer stood behind them. His own failing business and impending bankruptcy made it necessary for him to resign as a minister. The Mission Board attempted to help resolve his financial problem but larger issues were sweeping the Church with waves of change.[46]

The Lancaster Mennonite Conference New York churches felt the need for new approaches to urban ministry. In March 1960 John H. Kraybill wrote in their name, "We have kept silent long enough and the time is come for us to speak our convictions." The theme in the preparatory service before Communion at the Harlem church "was examining ourselves and the main emphasis which took up the greater part of the message was plain clothes." On Sunday morning it was neckties and on Sunday afternoon cape dresses and television. "Paul [Burkholder], John [Freed] and I are feeling that the time is here to make an appeal to conference on this matter, in an official way." Raymond Charles arranged for the New York pastors to meet with David Thomas and later with the full Bishop Board.[47]

After their meeting, the Conference leaders decided to invite D. Stoner Krady to provide "more mature guidance" for the city churches on regularly scheduled visits, but stopped short of appointing him as overseer of an autonomous bishop district. Paul Burkholder stressed the need for greater autonomy and suggested Krady be made bishop.[48]

Soon afterward the Eastern Board appointed John H. Kraybill property manager and mission coordinator for the Lancaster Conference work in the city. The mission board provided partial support "for giving overall leadership" to the New York mission workers and suggested monthly meetings of all the city pastors. Kraybill continued driving his cab on a part-time basis and serving as pastor at Seventh Avenue.[49]The early outposts in the Bronx resembled children's churches. Harold Thomas and the other pioneers had concentrated on inviting neighborhood kids and hauling youngsters by car to Sunday school from other neighborhoods. They hoped to draw the parents through the children. In 1962 Glad Tidings and Fox Street stopped hauling children. "I suppose to many stopping our hauling program here looked like a relatively simple thing. But for some of us here it was far from that...One of the big things in the minds of some is the club programs which they have with their

Sunday school classes. Many parents don't want their children going out on the streets after dark by themselves and rightly so."[50] Both churches put more emphasis on person-to-person evangelism and less on the street meetings and tent meetings that Harold Thomas had relied on to pave the way for personal contacts. The two churches cooperated in joint Sunday evening services and began to hold more Spanish-language services. Paul Landis preached in Spanish for a series of special meetings at Fox Street in October 1960. Jesus Constantin, Serafin Rivera, Paul Burkholder and John Freed planned for other Spanish speaking preachers to visit.

In February 1961 Glad Tidings and Fox Street had a Bible conference with Aquilla Riehl as the Spanish language Bible teacher. Glad Tidings counted ten native New Yorkers as members in 1961 and had an average attendance of 55 on Sundays. Members included the families of Jesus Constantin on East 146th Street, William Dickens on East 137th, Miss Micah Gianetti on Jackson Avenue, Paul Espinosa and William Anza who lived in the church-owned apartments on Brook Avenue. The Espinosas, the first baptized members, moved out in November 1960 and Paul Hill of the Brethren in Christ mission helped them find a new apartment. Mrs. Margaret Huertas and her son Aubin moved from Fox Street, when the Housing Authority demolished their building for a new project. With more attention to Spanish language services, attendance rose.[51] Spanish preaching became a regular part of the service by 1962.[52] Both churches had Spanish Sunday school classes for adults. Jesus Constantin taught the adult class at Glad Tidings. "Our attendance Sunday mornings would average about 90," Paul Burkholder reported, which was "about as high as it has ever been here." The Spanish Sunday school class was a big factor. "Our Adult English class has not shown much growth but Brother Constantin's Spanish class continues with very good interest." Some of the 1-w men from the VS center were helping start woodworking and crafts classes.[53]

The future of Fox Street became an issue in this period of close cooperation. In September 1960 the New York City workers discussed closing Fox Street and consolidating the work at Glad Tidings. The decision was made to sell the property at 1129 Fox Street owned by Eastern Board, an apartment building where mission workers lived,and it was sold in June 1961 for $17,000. The Fox Street church met next door at 1127 Fox Street in very inadequate quarters. John and Dorothy Freed, Bernard and Lillian Spanier, James and Shirley Hershey, Wesley and Marian Newswanger, Daniel Ness, Mabel Herr, Norma Brenner, and Anna Buckwalter met at

Fox Street in November 1961 to plan for better facilties for the church and to support Norma and Mabel's Bible club. After slow, careful planning, the building committee composed of John H. Kraybill, John Freed, Serafin Rivera, Carl Metzler, and Ralph Villanueva met for the first time in July 1963.[54]

Paul Burkholder and John Freed began studying Spanish two nights a week. Don Sensenig took over some of the Glad Tidings routine to give Paul time for his classes. In August 1962 Don and Evelyn Hertzler moved from the VS Center, where they had lived for two years of 1-w service, to an apartment next door to Glad Tidings. Don Hertzler became the treasurer of the congregation and Evelyn Hertzler, a full-time public school teacher, worked with classes for young people and children. With her experience in VS, Glad Tidings and Fox Street began to explore the possibilities of a day care center. Paul Burkholder wrote:

> I wonder if we ought to be thinking of an uptown VS Center? Brother John Freed at Fox Street certainly needs a new building, and I think this might be an opportunity to incorporate a number of new ideas. I would like to see along with a new Fox Street church such things as a self-supporting day care center, perhaps operated by and in a VS center nearby or connected with the church, the day care center turned into a youth center at night, also operated by VSers.[55]

The Grant Avenue Bible Clubs

Mabel Herr and Norma Brenner, two Fox Street members, began a new mission outreach in another Bronx neighborhood in September 1960. They shared an apartment at 1117 Grant Avenue and spent part of their time at the nearby home of Norma's Jewish parents. They decided to invite neighborhood children to come to the apartment once a week for a Bible Club, where they would have crafts and games and study Old Testament stories. Nine children came to the first meeting. By June 1961 seventy attended regularly, although "some of our members moved away during the year, and others dropped out because of opposition from their priest or rabbi." The neighborhood was a mixed Jewish and Catholic area, but most of the original club members came from Jewish homes.[56]

Classes met each day after school in five different age groups from five to twelve years old. A group of 25 slightly older girls was forming. "Most of the parents have been here to see us" and Mabel and Norma contacted the mothers of the other children. An adult Bible class developed. In

Mabel Herr teaching a Craft Class at the Grant Avenue Bible Club.

November 1961 three Jewish women and one Jewish man met with Mabel and Norma weekly for a study of Genesis and the children's clubs counted 145 members. H. Raymond Charles noted on a visit that, apart from attending the Sunday service at Fox Street, "their work has little, if any, relationship to Fox Street work." The two women met all the expenses of the clubs for rent and crafts supplies themselves; supplies alone cost $100 a month.

Norma Brenner was hospitalized in the autumn of 1961 and Lillian Spanier took her place while she was convalescing. She informed Eastern Board of the need to support this burgeoning mission with a building of its own. In December 1961 the mission board asked John H. Kraybill to look for a suitable location. He reported that the Grant Avenue section was "until recently a strong Jewish neighborhood but the Negroes are moving in."[57]

Norma Brenner teaching a Club Class at the Grant Avenue Bible Club.

Paul Landis questioned this move. "I would be very hesitant to see us place in New York City a 'Jewish worker' who does not have any special training or experience and whose program would eventually evolve into just another point among a Puerto Rican or Negro population." Instead of beginning new work, shouldn't the existing mission churches be strengthened?[58]

Mabel Herr and Norma Brenner reported on the activities of the Grant Avenue Bible Club in the 1961-1962 school year. They taught eleven children's classes each week with an average attendance of 115 and a high point of 130 one week. Fifteen mothers were meeting in one group and a dozen other adults were studying Genesis and Exodus. Nineteen children from the Bible club spent two weeks in Lancaster County homes and seven others went to Camp Hebron. Dorothy Freed brought teenagers from Fox Street to weekly club meetings and five club members went to Fox Street for Sunday school.[59] "I believe that they have contact with almost as large a group of people as any of our missions in New York City," John H. Kraybill concluded. The club work could be made part of the outreach of an existing church or continue to be independent of the other missions. If it continued on an independent basis, Kraybill suggested, "a hospitality center" rather than a church setting and "avoiding a nationality label" so as to make it a neighborhood outreach rather than a mission to Jews. Eastern Board decided to recognize the Bible Club "as the fifth witness point in New York City and that the present approach be continued and strengthened." Although the two women had worked virtually alone, aided only by Dorothy Freed and Lillian Spanier, in carrying the club work to this point, the executive committee determined that a male superintendent was needed and a larger apartment to accommodate the many children enrolled. John and Miriam Buckwalter were appointed mission superintendent. The Buckwalters had come to the city in 1958 and remained seventeen years after he completed his VS and 1-W service in October 1960. John Buckwalter worked for Glenn Zeager as the dispatcher in his private car company. John found a double store front, a block northwest of Mabel and Norma's apartment, and rented 1156-1158 Sherman Avenue for what now became the Sherman Avenue Bible Club.[60]

Norma, Mabel, and Lillian continued to do all the teaching and crafts work in the winter of 1962-1963 in addition to their regular employment. Norma Brenner was a nurse at Fordham Hospital, working two days a week, and Mabel worked in an office every morning. When classes began in September there were 355 children enrolled, a number which dropped to 215 by December 1962. Only seventeen Jewish children attended at the close of the session. This reflected changes in the neighborhood as black families moved in and Jewish families moved out, but the progress in Bible stories from Old Testament to New Testament was probably a more significant factor. Norma Brenner and Mabel Herr had some hope that the return to Old Testament stories and beginner's Hebrew classes the next year would "bring back the Jewish children who dropped out." More than half the children in the clubs were Protestant and 39 percent Catholic.[61]

The phenomenal growth of the Bible Club from 1960 on was mirrored by a slower consolidation at the older missions. With the leadership of John H. Kraybill as mission superintendent, a New York City committee made long-range plans and the three taxi-driving pastors helped the original mission stations emerge as autonomous local congregations. "We here in New York feel that we have just come through a time when program has practically collapsed," John Freed wrote, "But we too are praising God that He needed to collapse the program for us workers to get to Him."

The selection of Paul Landis as bishop with oversight of the New York churches in 1962 was a welcome surprise, since his responsibility for Voluntary Service projects gave him personal experience of the city and his knowledge of Spanish was a decided asset. The ordination of Paul Burkholder as pastor of Glad Tidings in 1963 and John L. Freed in 1964 as pastor at Fox Street began another phase of church life. John Kraybill believed that "a measure of self-government" with a church council in each congregation and an acceptance that "patterns of church life find different expression in different areas" would move the churches in the direction of partnership and indigenous leadership. The New York pastors agreed "that we should build up the present program in the three churches we now have before thinking about beginning anything new." If new work were to be started, it should be "in the area of the VS Center where very significant groundwork is now being laid through the club and home visitation program." This would be a new field, since "the three churches are in Negro and Puerto Rican neighborhoods." As it happened, the door seemed to be opening for a new church planting in another South Bronx neighborhood.[62]

Mennonite Bishop Paul and Ann Landis.

As Lancaster Conference churches worked at indigenizing the city mission outposts, they also built structure for inter-Mennonite cooperation. A Ministers' Fellowship provided a meeting place for Mennonite pastors from the Lancaster Conference with John I. Smucker of the House of Friendship and Paul Hill of the Brethren in Christ Fellowship Chapel by 1960. All of the Mennonite and Brethren in Christ churches joined together for an Easter sunrise service at Crotona Park in 1960. A city-wide Mennonite Youth Fellowship began in May 1960, and a renewed Mennonite Graduate Students Fellowship met periodically at the VS Center. The idea of a Mennonite camp first came under discussion at a meeting of pastors at the House of Friendship on November 5, 1961. As the decade progressed, Mennonite believers found new ways of working together.[63]

Paul Landis recalled that:

> Up until 1962, the New York City churches were part of the Mellingers District of Lancaster Conference and the pastors met with that group of pastors in the Lancaster area, with Elmer Martin as bishop. There were more rigid dress requirements for the city members than for the Pennsylvania members because those churches were less conservative historically. This relationship was nearly at a breaking point when I was ordained as bishop in the Mellingers District in 1962. I had previously spent a good bit of time in the city in developing and administering the Voluntary Service Unit, so I had some awareness of the situation before having the bishop responsibilities. We immediately formed a new district of Lancaster Mennonite Conference called the New York City District. We had our own meetings, agenda, and priorities. I was the link with the Conference and Bishop Board. This had its own set of problems for me as the departures from conference rules were now more focused, but we tried to stick together as a unit.[64]

There were two lines of administration for the New York City churches that related to Lancaster Conference. The Conference, through the bishop, dealt with ecclesiastical matters, such as membership requirements, baptism, communion, ordination of ministers and deacons, and issues touching on the nature of the congregation. Eastern Board of Missions worked directly with the churches in matters of strategy, finances, purchasing and maintaining buildings, and appointing mission workers. Paul Landis served a dual role, after 1962, as bishop and as area mission superintendent for the mission board. As a result of this integration of functions, the city churches had greater autonomy and more responsibility for priorities and decisions.

Paul Landis added that:

> This transition was costly in terms of pressure and stress, but helped us move forward together and prepared the stage for more cooperation with the other churches that developed under other conferences and mission boards. This led to the New York City Council of Mennonite Churches. This development became a pattern that other mission areas in Lancaster Conference soon developed which resulted in a life change in the Bishop Board as the mission areas soon had their own mission area superintendents who became local bishops and brought a new focus for the Bishop Board as its numbers increased with bishops who had vision for church planting and a relevant pattern of church life.

The mission churches, in East Africa and in Harlem and the South Bronx, brought new vitality to the sending churches in Lancaster Conference. Renewal and new strength of purpose changed the Mennonite Church in its historic congregations and in the most recent church plantings in response to the promptings of God's grace that flowed from the newest to the oldest members of His family.

Discipline and Discipleship

"New York City was the cutting edge for the conference," Paul Landis recalled. Issues that became important in Lancaster Conference and in the wider Mennonite Church seemed to surface there first. New Yorkers challenged rules on plain dress and radio and television. "We had our first divorce and remarriage case there." Cooperation across conference and denominational lines and a new emphasis in Mennonite piety created a fresh basis for community in the city.[65] A comparative study by Robert Weaver of Mennonite attitudes in Lancaster County and in New York City showed how far the city had caused a rethinking of traditional ideas by 1963. More than half the Pennsylvania respondents thought plain dress important, only three percent of the New York Mennonites agreed. Two thirds of the Pennsylvania respondents considered a high school education adequate for their children, more than half the New York Mennonites considered four years of college essential for their children. The New York City Mennonites were nearly unanimous in agreeing that Christians have a responsibility to speak out on political issues; their counterparts in Lancaster County were much more diffident. Two thirds of the city Mennonites intended to vote in the presidential election; two thirds of the county group said they would not vote in any election. New York City Mennonites were almost unanimous that preaching the Gospel was not enough to meet the needs of the people in their community, the Church had to respond to social problems as well.[66]

Of all the changes in the New York City Mennonite churches, the shift from plain dress was the most symbolic—and the most traumatic. Ethnic folkways from rural Pennsylvania could be excess cultural baggage in an American metropolis or an East African village. But, as Paul Landis wrote to a city pastor in 1964, "changing your suit and using a piano in the worship service" raised deeper issues. At stake was the Mennonite understanding of the church as more than a collection of individuals who had encountered Jesus Christ. The Mennonite congregations were under "pressure to become another Protestant Church with little emphasis on a disciplined life, a committed brotherhood, and the Anabaptist concepts of church and conversion."[67] Would the city churches and the Mennonite Church as a whole be able to keep these values alive in a decade of rapid change?

The question of dress had never been included in the *Lancaster Conference Discipline* before 1943. It was one of those areas of life that needed no legislation because the Mennonite community had absorbed a taste for modest and unadorned clothing. As historian Steven Nolt observed, the 1954 *Discipline* was twice as long as the 1943 edition and even more weighted toward discipline of personal lifestyle, because "the need to define previously assumed lifestyle patterns and choices...required extended description and comment."[68]

The older leaders of the New York City mission saw no distinction between accepting the Gospel as a rule of life and working with the Conference Discipline. Both demanded obedience and humble submission to a disciplined brotherhood. To many of the young Mennonite mission workers in New York City, on the other hand, the requirements of the Conference Discipline seemed to place an additional burden on their converts.

Jacob and Frances Thomas moved to New York in 1952 to witness to Jews about the Messiah. As self-supporting mission workers they had many opportunities in their office jobs and in street meetings. Since they did not have strong convictions on plain dress, Fox Street and Glad Tidings excluded them and they attended the more tolerant Seventh Avenue Mennonite Church. In 1955 Jacob Thomas contacted the Mennonite Board of Missions in Elkhart, Indiana, to explore the possibilities of more extensive Jewish evangelism. From these conversations the Mennonite House of Friendship emerged in 1956 as a new mission station with John and Irene Smucker as full-time workers and Abner Stoltzfus continuing his part-time friendship evangelism in New York and in his Lancaster County summer cabin. B. Harold Thomas and other workers from the existing missions attended the dedication of the House of Friendship on January 22, 1957, but there was some tension between the Lancaster Conference and Ohio and Eastern Conference mission workers. It went back to the founding of the Neffsville Mennonite Church in Lancaster County where Mennonites who chafed under Lancaster Conference dress restrictions were welcomed as members of Ohio and Eastern Conference. The same thing seemed to be happening in New York when the Jacob Thomas family and others moved their membership to the House of Friendship. John H. Kraybill wrote with regret of "the barriers that now exist" to prevent close association with the House of Friendship. "I trust that the Lord shall soon show us as Mennonite believers we must stand united in our witness if it is to be effective in this city."[69]

Long before they began their work in the city streets, Mennonites had begun to separate the plan of salvation from the evidences of a renewed life that followed from it. When a young man or woman from the city had clearly been saved by the grace of God, it seemed to them pharasaic to withhold baptism.

In 1961 John H. Kraybill wrote in behalf of all the New York pastors:

> The principles back of these points are very good but wouldn't it be much better if we approached these applications as aims rather than demands whereby we refuse baptism until the person complies in every point? When there is genuine evidence that a person is born again and is growing spiritually how can we refuse to receive him into the fellowship because he does not yet have conviction on a minor application or two? We believe that time should be given after the person is received for their understanding of other matters pertaining to the Christian walk.[70]

NOTES

[1] The term "South Bronx" was used only of the four neighborhoods mentioned in the text in the southwestern corner of the Borough. Later the term became almost a euphemism for urban blight and was extended to all the deteriorating neighborhoods of what would have been called "West Bronx" or "East Bronx" in the 1950s. Meryl Ruoss, comp., "Area Master Plans Protestant Churches New York City. Area 1 South Bronx," mimeographed for New York City Protestant Council Day of Planning, December 27, 1956. Evelyn Hertzler, "Report of Glad Tidings and Community," 1965. John L. Freed and Carl Good, "Fox Street Mennonite," July 1965. EMBMC. Jill Jonnes, *We're Still Here: The Rise, Fall, and Resurrection of the South Bronx* (Boston, 1986), 100.

[2] The South Bronx was half Jewish in 1920, but the Jewish population declined to a third by 1930, a fifth by 1940, a tenth by 1950, and virtually disappeared over the next few years.

[3] Ronald H. Bayor, *Neighbors in Conflict: The Irish, Germans, Jews, and Italians of New York City 1929-1941* (Urbana, IL, 1988), 152-155. Ruoss, "Area Master Plans, 1."

[4] Ruoss, *loc. cit.* Jonnes, *We're Still Here*, 117, 125.

[5] Esther Petersheim, Interview, August 17, 1990. Freed and Good, "Fox Street Mennonite," July 1965. Hertzler, "Report of Glad Tidings," 1965, EMM. Glad Tidings Questionnaires, 1965. Paul Burkholder Papers.

[6] Lucy Vance, "Seventh Avenue Mennonite Church," July 1965, EMM. Kenneth B. Clark, *Dark Ghetto: Dilemmas of Social Change* (Middletown, Conn., 1989), 30-35, 59.

[7] Jonnes, *We're Still Here*, 93-94, 123-124.

[8] John Freed and Carl Good, "Fox Street Mennonite," July 1965, EMM.

[9] Aquilla Riehl to Lloyd Wenger, July 15, 1956. Anna Buckwalter to Raymond Charles, September 15, 1956. Interview with Esther Petersheim, August 16, 1990. Lloyd Wenger to Raymond Charles, July 25, 1956, Sept. 15, 1956. H. Raymond Charles to Aquilla Riehl, Oct. 17, 1956. EMM.

[10] John H. Kraybill to Paul Landis, October 4, 1958, EMM.

[11] Aquilla Riehl to Raymond Charles, Aug 26, 1957. Raymond Charles to Victor Weaver, Sept. 9, 1957, Sept. 30, 1957, EMM.

[12] Aquilla Riehl to Raymond Charles, February 2, 1958. Victor R. Weaver to Raymond Charles, Oct. 15, 1958. John L. Freed to Raymond Charles, Feb. 13, 1959. Raymond Charles to John Freed, Feb. 23, 1959. H. Raymond Charles to Aquilla Riehl, Feb. 23, 1959. Raymond Charles to Daniel Lapp, Feb. 16, 1959, EMM.

[13] H. Raymond Charles to Aquilla Riehl, Feb. 23, 1959, EMM.

[14] Ira J. Buckwalter to Mary E. Landis, May 19, 1959, EMM.

[15] George R. Brunk to Richard MacMaster, Apr. 15, 1991.

[16] Seventh Avenue Mennonite Church, Self-Analysis of Congregation, Aug. 1965, f. 1, EMM.

[17] *Missionary Messenger*, Feb. 1954, 10, March 1954, 4. Esther Robinson, "God's Continuous Miracle," *Missionary Messenger*, November 1954, 5, August 1955, 10, August 1956, 5.

[18] John L. Freed, Interview, August 18, 1990.

[19] H. Raymond Charles to Paul Burkholder, July 22, 1957, EMM.

[20] H. Raymond Charles to Merritt Robinson, June 26, 1957, EMM.

[21] John L. Freed to H. Raymond Charles, October 24, 1957, EMM.

[22] Paul G. Burkholder to H. Raymond Charles, October 18, 1957. John L. Freed to H. Raymond Charles, October 24, 1957, EMM.

[23] John Freed to H. Raymond Charles, February 24, 1958, Minutes, Glad Tidings Business Meeting, March 26, 1958, EMM.

[24] Glad Tidings Report, September 8, 1958. LMHS.

[25] H. Raymond Charles to Merritt Robinson, October 1, 1958. Elmer Martin to Merritt Robinson, October [September?] 6, 1958, EMM.

[26] H. Raymond Charles to B. Harold Thomas, February 5, 1959, EMM.

[27] *Missionary Messenger*, August 1955, 12.

[28] Seventh Avenue Mennonite Church, Report, February 1956. LMHS. Lucy Vance, Interview, August 18, 1990, April 16, 1991.

[29] Seventh Avenue Mennonite Church, Program, March 31, 1957. LMHS.

[30] "Report of Study Reference Possible 1-w VS Center in New York City," July 1, 1957, EMM. John H. Kraybill, "Voluntary Service in New York City," *Missionary Messenger*, December 1958, 2.

[31] John H. Kraybill, to H. Raymond Charles, June 12, 1957. H. Raymond Charles to John H. Kraybill, June 27, 1957. John H. Kraybill to H. Raymond Charles, June 27, 1957. H. Raymond Charles to John H. Kraybill, July 1, 1957. Paul Landis to VS Committee, July 19, 1957. H. Raymond Charles to Members of Harlem Mennonite Church, July 25, 1957, EMM.

[32] Ira Buckwalter to John H. Kraybill, June 18, 1958. Paul Landis to Peace Section, MCC, September 8, 1958, EMM.

[33] J. Harold Sherk to Paul Landis, September 13, 1958. J. Harold Sherk to Director, N.Y.C. Selective Service System, September 13, 1958. John H. Kraybill to Paul Landis, October 4, 1958, EMM. *Missionary Messenger*, December 1958.

[34] New Notes from Mennonite VS Center, March 1, 1959, April 29, 1959, May 5, 1959, May 13, 1959. 1-w Mirror, May 4, 1959. N.Y.C. Committee Meeting Minutes, April 6, 1959, EMM..

[35] Paul Landis to John H. Kraybill, October 27, 1959. David W. Shenk to Paul Landis, November 4, 1959. Paul Landis, "Report of Visit to N.Y.C. V.S. Unit, November 23-25, 1959, EMM.

[36] David W. Shenk to Paul Landis, Dec. 22, 1960, EMM.

[37] David W. Shenk to Paul Landis, Mar. 14, 1960, EMM.

[38] "News Notes," Oct. 17-24, 1960, Mar. 14-21, 1960, EMM.

[39] Paul Landis to David W. Shenk, Jan. 26, 1960, EMM.

[40] David W. Shenk to H. Raymond Charles, Aug. 2, 1960, EMM.

[41] Paul Landis, "Report of Visit to NYC VS Unit," October 28-30, 1960. "News Notes," July 25-Aug. 7, 1960. Don Hertzler, Report, n.d. (1961?), EMM

[42] Fern Lehman, "Yankee Stadium," *Gospel Herald*, August 13, 1957, 716. John I. Smucker, "Joy of Counseling," *Gospel Herald*, September 17, 1957, 806.

[43] John I. Smucker to Nelson E. Kauffman, September 10, 1957. AMC.

[44] John I. Smucker, *Urban Mennonite Mission in the South Bronx*, 106-107, 310, 315-319.

[45] Paul and Miriam Burkholder, Interview.

[46] B. Harold Thomas to H. Raymond Charles, February 7, 1960. H. Raymond Charles to Ira Buckwalter, September 28, 1959, EMM.

[47] John H. Kraybill to H. Raymond Charles, March 22, 1960. H. Raymond Charles to John H. Kraybill, April 1, 1960. H. Raymond Charles to John H. Kraybill, April 20, 1960, EMM.

[48] Ira Buckwalter to H. Raymond Charles, August 18, 1960. H. Raymond Charles to John H. Kraybill, August 18, 1960. H. Raymond Charles to Paul Burkholder, June 13, 1960. Paul Burkholder to Ira Buckwalter, July 13, 1960, EMM.

[49] Ira Buckwalter to H. Raymond Charles, August 18, 1960. H. Raymond Charles to John H. Kraybill, August 18, 1960, EMM.

[50] Paul Burkholder to H. Raymond Charles, January 30, 1963, EMM.

[51] Paul Burkholder to Ira Buckwalter, July 28, 1960, November 7, 1960. Paul Burkholder to Ira Buckwalter, November 29, 1961, EMM.

[52] Paul Burkholder to Ira Buckwalter, November 29, 1961, July 2, 1962, EMM.

53 NYC Committee Meeting Minutes, September 24, 1960, November 20, 1960. Paul Burkholder to Ira Buckwalter, February 21, 1961, November 29, 1961, EMM.

54 NYC Committee Meeting Minutes, September 24, 1960. Ira Buckwalter to H. Raymond Charles, March 30, 1961, May 4, 1961, EMM.

55 Paul Burkholder to Ira Buckwalter, July 2, 1962, EMM.

56 Mabel Herr, "Challenge of Bible Club Work," July 1961, EMM.

57 H. Raymond Charles Report of Visit to NYC, July 5, 1961. Lillian Spanier to Ira Buckwalter, Oct. 24, 1961, D. Stoner Krady to H. Raymond Charles, Nov. 2, 1961. Ira Buckwalter to Jewish Evangelism Committee, Dec. 22, 1961. Ira Buckwalter to John H. Kraybill, Dec. 26, 1961. Ira Buckwalter to H. Raymond Charles, May 11, 1962, EMM.

58 Paul Landis to H. Raymond Charles, April 12, 1962, EMM.

59 Norma Brenner and Mabel Herr, "Report of Grant Avenue Bible Club, September 1961 to June 1962." EMBMC-A.

60 H. Raymond Charles to Executive Committee, June 6, 1962. H. Raymond Charles to Executive Committee, August 10, 1962. John Buckwalter to H. Raymond Charles, November 3, 1962. EMBMC-A.

61 John Buckwalter to H. Raymond Charles, January 29, 1963.

62 Paul Burkholder, Interview. John L. Freed to H. Raymond Charles, Mar. 22, 1961. John H. Kraybill, "Aims and Goals for the Future of the Witness in New York City."

63 Smucker, "Reflections," 323. House of Friendship Prayer Newsletter, May 18, 1960. MBM-MCA.

64 Paul G. Landis to Allen Brubaker, Sept. 19, 1995.

65 Paul Landis, Interview, August 15, 1990.

66 Robert Weaver, "The Effect of Social Change Upon the Mennonite Community in New York City," Term Paper, EMC, January 1964.

67 Paul Landis to Paul Burkholder, May 7, 1964.

68 Steven M. Nolt, "Church Discipline in the Lancaster Mennonite Conference: The Printed *Rules and Discipline*, 1881-1968," *Pennsylvania Mennonite Heritage*, XV (Oct. 1992), 6-7.

69 John H. Kraybill to Raymond Charles, June 12, 1957, EMBMC

70 John H. Kraybill, "Aims and Goals for the Future of the Witness in New York City," March 15, 1961.

CHAPTER FIVE

Brethren in Christ Beginnings in the City

1953–1964

A STIRRING SERMON challenged delegates at the 1953 annual conference of the Brethren in Christ church to new visions of mission. They responded with a recommendation that the Home Mission Board begin work in New York City and Los Angeles, "the two great metropolitan cities," as soon as possible. The chairman of the Home Mission Board, Bishop Henry A. Ginder, and the secretary, Albert H. Engle, made preliminary investigations in New York City through the Protestant Council's Planning Office and took responsibility for getting the project off the ground.[1]

Ginder and Engle returned to the city in March 1954 for a more extended survey. They again paid a visit to Dr. Meryl Ruoss, director of planning for the Protestant Council, and with his help targeted four areas. They did not respond to his suggestion that "some new housing developments of 7,000 people have no church within four miles." They looked first at "a needy area in Central Brooklyn," near the Long Island Railroad Station. The next day they visited the East Harlem Protestant Parish and met with Hugh Hostetler. Bishop Ginder wrote:

Brethren in Christ Bishop Henry Ginder.

> His church is a small "store front" type of church, with thirty members, and an average of eighty in Sunday school. This is a very needy area—of course largely Negro. The most thickly populated street in the world is East 100th Street. Between First and Second Avenues, that one street has 4,000 people in one block. They tell us that on warm spring days the children come out into the street like honey bees.

After visiting East Harlem, they concentrated on the Upper West Side from West 60th Street to Morningside Heights, exploring the long blocks between Broadway and Amsterdam Avenue all the way to West 160th Street. They gave the rest of their time in the city to this area of Manhattan and had clearly made their choice of a mission field for the Brethren in Christ. Bishop Ginder wrote to the Mission Board members sharing his own enthusiasm for the project: "We both felt we would just love to move in with a staff of workers and bring the story of our wonderful Saviour to a portion of New York's needy millions."[2]

The Home Mission Board moved quickly to implement this vision. By the time the Conference met at Messiah College in June 1954 to approve "taking the necessary steps to open a work in the city of New York," the preliminary investigations were completed, a course of procedure outlined, and William and Willa Lewis appointed as the first Brethren in Christ mission workers in New York City.[3]

On July 5, 1954 William and Willa Lewis arrived in New York and began looking for an apartment "from which they could conduct a careful on-the-field study of the situation." The board expected this might take three or four months, but, at any rate, they would have recommendations ready for action by the board members at their December meeting.

Through a real estate agent, Lewis soon found a building at 323 West 108th Street used by the Methodist Church for mission work among Japanese students.

> This five-story building which is already adapted to begin, in a small way, a gospel work is located in a very desirable section of Manhattan. Being on West 108th Street it is near the boundary of an area which Columbia University has been able to maintain as a sort of restricted zone. The eight blocks between it and the university constitute a part of the section where Columbia's 20,000 students are housed.

Lewis telephoned Engle on July 6 with the news and the next day Bishop Ginder and Engle went through the building, which they found to be "neglected on the inside," but nevertheless serviceable. Bishop H. N. Hostetter and Howard Landis, a building contractor from Souderton, Pennsylvania, joined them for a closer look some days later. After a careful study of the building from the basement to the roof, all agreed it was a good building, basically sound, well-located, and easily adapted to their program. The five men negotiated with the Methodist church representatives and agreed with them on a price of $27,100 and possession no later than February 1, 1955. The Brethren in Christ Church now had a New York City outreach.[4]

The Methodists had difficulty getting a clear title to the building where they had planned to move. They were eager to give possession of the West 108th Street property as soon as they could locate something else. The Brethren in Christ Home Mission Board could find no other property as well suited to their purpose and remained convinced that "the Lord has led us to the location and building where He would have us carry on gospel work in New York City." Negotiations continued through 1955 and into 1956 without breaking the deadlock.[5]

The Home Mission Board did not lose heart. When the Annual Conference met at West Milton, Ohio, in June 1957, Albert H. Engle reported "new prospects that we may be able to secure possession within the current year of the property at 323 108th Street for which we have been negotiating since the summer of 1955." But once again the bright prospects quickly dimmed and the board abandoned all hope of securing the Morningside Heights property.[6]

William and Willa Lewis stayed in Manhattan only long enough to locate the West 108th Street building and begin negotiations for its purchase, but they did make a few contacts in that short time. As long as there was hope of a New York City mission, the Lewises were ready to return. Eventually they took another assignment.[7]

Miss Mary Wenger became the second Brethren in Christ missionary in New York City. With her appointment early in 1957, the Home Mission Board began a new approach to urban mission. She had worked for three years as a missionary in Israel, but serious illness prevented her returning there after a furlough in 1954. For a time her health precluded any mission assignment. With the Upper West Side mission center in jeopardy and no workers in the city, "After prayerful study, it was decided to assign Sister Mary Wenger to New York City to explore the possibility of a testimony among the Jews."[8]

Mary Wenger.

In launching this new ministry the Brethren in Christ Home Mission Board worked closely with Mennonites. Bishop and Mrs. Henry Ginder drove Mary Wenger to New York City on March 25, 1957 where she had already found an apartment at 2255 Hampden Place in the Bronx, across the street from Jacob and Frances Thomas. She wrote Ginder two days later:

> The Thomases invited me to go along with them to the House of Friendship last night. They are very willing to help me in any thing I may wish them to do. I enjoyed the fellowship session last night. Mr. Thomas showed slides from N.Y. and Pa. Afterwards we visited. Bro. Stoltzfus was not there until at the end. They invited me to go along again this evening to their prayer meeting at the same place.[9]

She found support not only from Jacob and Frances Thomas and Abner Stoltzfus, but also from the Glad Tidings congregation.

> Sunday I was invited to spend the day with the Robinsons who work with the Harold Thomases in a Spanish work here in the city. Also met the Zeagers who have a work among the (Mennonite) colored people in Harlem. I did not realize there were so many works here of the Mennonites, however, the House of Friendship is the only Jewish work.

She went with the Thomases to the Seventh Avenue Mennonite Church, where they invited her to teach Sunday school and help with the summer Bible school. She also spoke at the House of Friendship.[10]

Mary Wenger helped as a counselor at the Billy Graham Crusade, but the board expected her help in locating a definite site for Brethren in Christ work in the city. If the West 108th Street location could not be purchased, it was time to look for another.[11]

In October 1957 she moved to the Mennonite House of Friendship, sharing a room with Verna Beiler, until she could find a more permanent headquarters. She led a Jewish woman to Christ and followed other contacts made through the Graham meetings. And she continued to look for a new site for a Brethren in Christ mission.[12]

When the Home Mission Board met at Messiah College, they decided: "Due to restriction in personnel and finances, the Board is reluctant to be aggressive in planning for beginning a more permanent unit in the city." They did not want to "discontinue our interest in New York City" and made Henry Ginder and Albert Engle "fully responsible for continuing study of the work in New York City." The board suggested shifting attention to "new housing developments near the city, probably over in Long Island."[13]

Bishop Ginder and Mary Wenger "endeavored to explore the thinking of the Home Mission Board" about church-planting in the suburbs. They toured Long Island communities and visited the Mennonites at Centereach, but remained unconvinced. Consultations with the Protestant Council raised other questions about the West 108th Street area.

They heard about the Brownsville section of Brooklyn, a very needy area with widespread juvenile delinquency and a third of the residents on welfare. The northeastern Bronx still had large predominantly Jewish sections and offered other possibilities for mission. After the passage of so much time, the Brethren in Christ work was still at the first step, but with an important difference. They knew that the choice of a location would determine the nature of the work done there.

Abner Stoltzfus took them with a realtor to see a property on Sedgwick Avenue in a residential section of the northwest Bronx known as Kingsbridge Heights. The 12-room house would be available for $27,000. Ginder had some hesitation "whether this is the proper community in which to work," but, if the Board determined to purchase this property, "we would need to find the very best young man available to lead and develop our work in New York City."

Ginder saw the need for a thorough canvass of the neighborhood to assess community needs. Jane Burkholder, Ruth Kreider, and Ethel Engle came to New York City to help Mary Wenger with house-to-house visitation. The 1950 census showed about 12,000 people in the neighborhood, with one in four foreign-born, mostly Irish, Germans, and Polish Americans. The March 1958 survey confirmed a significant Jewish population and some strong Catholic areas. "Shall we think in terms of a Jewish work? This seems a good place for such."[14]

The Sedgwick Avenue property purchase needed Board approval. "While we delayed signing the contract until our Board met in full session, the property was sold." After this disappointment, the Home Mission Board left New York City on the back burner, with no "aggressive planning" for the immediate future. Mary Wenger worked with the Seventh Avenue Mennonite summer program.[15]

Esther Robinson.

In August 1958 Bishop Ginder invited Merritt and Esther Robinson to his home for a visit. He was especially impressed by Esther Robinson's definite gifts for missionary work. They agreed the Robinsons would transfer their membership after the Brethren in Christ Mission Board acquired a building. The Robinsons were then Mennonite mission workers at Glad Tidings. "We will not ask for rigid dress requirements as they practice." But plain dress was not the main issue. Merritt Robinson had apparently felt his gifts were not recognized. Six months after they moved their membership, Ginder would request ministerial credentials for Merritt Robinson. He looked to the Lord's direction whether Robinson should assist another pastor or be the sole pastor. Ginder had some hesitation because he saw Robinson as an impulsive type of personality.

By September 1958 Mary Wenger had located a suitable building of fourteen rooms for $22,000. Ginder talked with Bishop Elmer Martin about releasing the Robinsons. He was most cooperative and gave them the option of continuing in Mennonite mission work after changing their membership. The Robinsons united with the Mount Pleasant Brethren in Christ Church in Pennsylvania on November 30, 1958.[16]

Fellowship Chapel

Ginder hoped to get board approval for an energetic beginning in New York. On October 13, 1958 Bishop Ginder, Isaac Kanode, and Albert Engle, representing the mission board, and Souderton contractor Raymond Hess investigated the four-story building at 246 East Tremont Avenue, located "not far from where Sister Wenger now resides." They found it in good condition with an almost new heating plant and a good roof. The realtor had it listed at $35,000 but he was sure a lower figure could be

Second location of Fellowship Chapel, 240 East Tremont Avenue, Bronx. 2005 photo.

negotiated. "It would require very little remodeling as it has been used for recitals in connection with its use as a music and dance school." The committee agreed that "it is now time to renew aggressive effort to secure a building which provides a place to begin service, [and] living quarters for workers."[17]

Mary Wenger and the Robinsons were understandably "eager for a place of worship, Christian fellowship and service" in New York City and Tremont Avenue seemed to be the right location. Early in January Mary Wenger met with David Carlson, a Brethren in Christ member living in the city, and set off a flurry of activity. This culminated in a meeting in New York on January 14, 1959 of representatives of the Home Mission Board with Mary Wenger, Esther Robinson, and David Carlson. Albert Engle reported: "It was a most rewarding conference and we apparently emerged with a united front to work together with our efforts centering in the Tremont property if the Lord would open it up." Before the day was over, they met with their attorney and "gave the green light for him to draw up a contract for sale."[18] It did not prove as simple as that. There were delays and a promised drop in price failed to materialize. The owners finally signed early in March. "This means that if the city authorities approve our proposed plans for alteration and use of the building we will get possession by October 30, 1959."[19]

The stress and strain of those weeks contributed to Mary Wenger's collapse. She wrote Albert Engle in February "expressing good hopes of recovery of strength," but telephoned him on the first of March "and regretfully relayed her doctor's orders that she should have someone with her." The Engles drove to New York City the next day and brought her back to Grantham, Pennsylvania. She did not return to the city, but her pioneering laid the groundwork for the Brethren in Christ Church in the metropolis.[20]

The Home Mission Board agreed that Paul D. Hill was their choice as pastor of the church that would develop in the Bronx. The Hills were from the rural Midwest, but they had urban mission experience. Paul Hill came from Wheeler, Michigan, and had attended Messiah College. His wife Evelyn was from Englewood, Ohio. They had served a small church in northern Michigan and in 1955 moved to Detroit to direct the mission program there. The board decided that the Hills should make an exploratory trip to New York and meet with those closer to the situation. They visited the city with Albert Engle and Bishop Ginder on April 10, 1959.

Negotiations over the property had hit a snag. While the Hills, Engle, and Ginder were eating lunch at a Howard Johnson, Engle telephoned the attorney and learned that the board's check had been returned and the contract voided. After a frustrating afternoon of phone calls and meetings, they all went to the Robinson apartment for dinner with the Robinsons and Carlsons where "we reported our disappointing experiences and had united prayer about the situation." Then Ginder and Engle met with the couple who owned the building and "were able to talk over 'on a human level' both sides of the problems." Before they left, both parties agreed to the original contract. The sale would go through. The Hills accepted the new assignment. Fellowship Chapel was born.[21]

Paul and Evelyn Hill and their two small daughters moved to the Bronx in August and rented a temporary furnished basement apartment. They moved into the building at 246 East Tremont Avenue September 10, 1959.[22]

The final closing on the property happened on October 16, but the New York City Building Permit did not finally come until December 11. "The next morning a carload of six men arrived from Pennsylvania," led by Earl Martin. "They began at once to demolish the walls, pull down the ceilings and begin construction of the chapel." Over the next few weeks different men from Mount Pleasant, Hummelstown, Chambersburg, Hanover, Cross Roads, Manheim, and Grantham Brethren in Christ churches traveled to the Bronx to help with remodeling. Raymond Hess put in the steel and supervised major construction. C. R. Heisey supervised the painting crew.[23]

Fellowship Chapel pastor Paul Hill, standing second from right. His wife Evelyn, seated with their two daughters.

Paul Hill noted in his diary on January 3, 1960 that "Our first service was held in the 2nd floor living room with 17 present. The text was Ephesians 1:9 'The Mystery of His Will.'" A month later, with the main part of the renovation work completed in the chapel area and only a second coat of paint needed to finish it, they held the first service in the chapel on February 7 with eight present. "It was a real warm service and we were truly blessed because of all that the Lord has wrought up to this time."[24]

On February 16 Hill "met and worked with Paul Espinosa in remodeling." This was a significant meeting. Paul and Irma Espinosa began attending worship at Fellowship Chapel in September and became key members of the congregation. They had been among the first baptized members of the Glad Tidings Mennonite congregation.[25]

Fellowship Chapel was ready for a dedication service on March 20, 1960. There were 74 for the fellowship dinner and 77 for the dedication service. Nearly all of them were, of course, visitors from Pennsylvania. Growth was slow. Rose, Angel, Ramon and Benito Martinez came for the first time in July. In August Hill noted "twelve community people" at the Sunday morning service.[26]

Brooklyn Brethren in Christ Church

Meanwhile, another outreach had begun across the East River in the Bedford-Stuyvesant section of Brooklyn. Carl Glinton and his wife, an African-American couple, were members of the Hanover Brethren in Christ Church who moved to the city. Mary Wenger began holding prayer meetings at their home on Greene Avenue. The Robinsons joined later on after she became ill. The door had opened for a mission in the black community.[27]

Bishop Ginder visited the Glintons in May 1959 along with the Robinsons and gave a mission message in their apartment. On his return he recommended "that the work in Brooklyn be considered our project for the present time" and "that the Board give consideration to the assigning of Merritt and Esther Robinson to that phase of the movement in New York." The Glintons were already looking for a public meeting place to rent. They found a vacant room, which earlier served as a storefront church, about four blocks from where they lived. The church could seat 45 people and had rest-room facilities. Its location at a busy intersection with two banks and a subway station made it visible to the community. The rent would be $80 a month.[28]

Ginder returned to the city with Isaac Kanode on May 29 and rented the building. On his return home he drafted a formal resolution recommending "that the Board give consideration to opening of work among the colored folk at 948 Bedford Avenue" and "the assigning of Bro. and Sr. Merritt Robinson as workers under the superintendency of Bro. Paul Hill." He proposed that "the program shall consist of Sunday school and worship in the morning of each Lord's Day, a mid-week service, a youth program and a Bible Club, or any other as deemed necessary."[29]

Albert Engle sent the Robinsons official confirmation of their appointment in June. "Of course our goal is that the Lord may prepare some Negro Christian to take over this responsibility." Although the new church would have a white pastor, Carl Glinton was appointed treasurer and Sunday school superintendent. Volunteers came from Lancaster County to help distribute announcements of services. On July 12, 1959 the new Brooklyn Brethren in Christ Church at 948 Bedford Avenue opened for the first Sunday school and worship service with seventeen in attendance. That afternoon there was a dedication service with Bishop Ginder, Samuel Lady, B. Harold Thomas, and Eugene Witter participating. Ginder very much appreciated the presence of "Bro. and Sr. Harold Thomas, the Robinsons' former pastor" in the service. Bishop Ginder preached the dedication sermon based on Matthew 16:18, "And the gates of Hell shall not prevail against it." That evening Esther Robinson led a children's meeting with fourteen neighborhood children and Samuel Lady preached an evangelistic appeal to the unsaved.[30]

Merritt and Esther Robinson, pastor of Brooklyn Brethren in Christ Church, 948 Bedford Avenue, Brooklyn. Merritt had previously served as tent manager for the Brunk Brothers Evangelistic Crusades.

The Brooklyn Brethren in Christ Church was located in an historic black community that was rapidly becoming a totally black neighborhood. The Bedford-Stuyvesant section centered along the two avenues of those names in what was generally called Central Brooklyn in the 1930s and 1940s. The opening of the Fulton Street subway line in 1936 led local boomers to talk enthusiastically of modernization and rising real estate values, but the stagnant Depression economy and the fact that the section was largely built-up already meant little change was possible. The area was a very mixed one with large numbers of foreign-born residents, some sections heavily Jewish, others predominantly Italian, and others mainly African-American. The black population made up 25 percent of the total in 1940. The number of blacks in Brooklyn nearly doubled in the 1940s. "It was during this decade that Bedford-Stuyvesant as a large, impacted, overwhelmingly black ghetto was forged... The classic urban demographic pattern of black growth and white decline accelerated during the 1950s."[31]

By September 1959, when Bishop Ginder visited next, things were moving along. Thursday and Saturday evening services drew "several adults and several children in from the community" and attendance at Sunday worship was 39. The Robinsons hoped to move to Bedford-Stuyvesant. "They should, and want to live in the area." They planned to develop a youth center and expand the Sunday school. Bishop Ginder observed: "Merritt may need help to render a more dignified and stable type of leadership. I counselled a bit in this direction."[32] Although the Home Missions Board paid a small allowance and the church schedule was heavy, Robinson was expected to be self-supporting. "We surely are sorry that Merritt does not have work at the present time," Ginder wrote in December 1959. This was a problematic start for the Bedford-Stuyvesant mission.

The 1959 report for the Handbook of Missions included a summary of the Brooklyn mission:

> The Brethren in Christ Church also has an active work among the Negroes in New York City. The services are conducted in a rented hall at 948 Bedford Avenue in Brooklyn, New York. This work was opened in July with Rev. and Mrs. Merritt Robinson in charge. The Sunday school has experienced a steady growth and there have been definite conversions for which we thank God. This church is also offering a released-time program of Christian Education in which a fine group of community children are receiving Bible instruction.[33]

The Home Missions Board moved ahead in 1960 with plans to buy the building adjoining the rented store-front on Bedford Avenue for $10,719. The building, which was in good repair, had a main floor similar to the chapel, suitable for a youth center, a second floor with four rooms and bath, where the pastor could live, and a similar third floor apartment. The Brooklyn Brethren in Christ Church grew steadily through 1960:

> At the Brooklyn church attendance has grown beyond present facilities. For the Christmas program 119 crowded into the chapel that 60 would fill. It seems an answer to prayer that the property next door was offered for sale at a very reasonable price. The three-story

> building would provide space for Sunday school classes, youth center, and residence for the pastor in the local area.[34]

The situation changed early in 1961. Paul Hill reported that Merritt and Esther Robinson were having a domestic crisis. Bishop Ginder held a series of meetings with them in April 1961 that brought their problems into the open, if they did not resolve them. Their marriage had been in trouble for at least four years. Merritt was prepared to resign his pastorate and intended to leave his wife for a young Jewish woman. Bishop Ginder accepted his resignation, lifted his ministerial credentials and suspended his church membership. Esther Robinson would continue in the mission. By early May Merritt had moved out. Carl Glinton was leading the services and the Sunday school with 36 attending.[35]

In this crisis for the fledgling church, the Home Mission Board invited Harold Bowers, a young minister and recent Messiah graduate, to take over:

> Rev. and Mrs. Harold Bowers assumed this pastorate in July 1961. They had assisted in a Mennonite Mission in Steelton, Pennsylvania, among Negroes, and Mrs. Bowers taught in Harrisburg with mostly Negro pupils. This was excellent background for their work in our Brooklyn Mission, which is predominantly Negro.

The Sunday school grew rapidly and it was necessary to rent a room in the next building to the Mission Hall for a youth center and Sunday school Department. On Friday and Saturday evening there were activities planned for the young people. On Thursday afternoon there was a release time from school for the purpose of Religious Education Classes. Approximately forty-seven pupils were enrolled.[36]

Cathy and Harold Bowers, pastor of Brooklyn Brethren in Christ Church, with their children Deanne and Carlton.

Isaac Kanode reported in October 1961: "The Bowerses are doing a good job. There were 54 in Sunday school last Sunday and 58 for worship. They have 37 release-time pupils in their religious instruction classes." The Brooklyn church seemed to "need more room desperately" and the store next door was for rent. Should they expand now?[37]

Bishop Ginder noted on his visit a few weeks later that attendance had dropped again. "It appeared that the lack of visitation contact was reflected in this lower attendance." He believed it "important that the Bowerses would soon live in Brooklyn." They were still living at Fellowship Chapel in the Bronx.[38]

A year later the situation was much the same. Home Missions Board chairman Charles Rife and Isaac Kanode "heartily agreed we *must* move the Bowerses to Brooklyn soon." Their inability to visit in the neighborhood every day and the failure to acquire a suitable building seemed to doom the Brooklyn mission.[39] The Home Missions Board finally arranged to move the Bowers family to Brooklyn, near the church in the fall of 1962.

Program did well enough. "The Bible school in July was outstanding in attendance with an average of 70, and in conversions with 11 colored children finding the Lord." In the weekly Release Time classes "an average of 20 colored children meet in the chapel for Bible instruction." Sunday morning showed a growing attendance. "To make room for this growth the chapel has been enlarged."[40]

The VS Center

"On one of our times to New York," Henry Ginder later recalled, "Isaac Kanode and I visited the Mennonite Voluntary Service Unit. As we traveled home on the New Jersey Turnpike, I asked Isaac to get out a piece of paper and a pen and start writing down some notes. So as we headed home we put down many ideas and figures on what it would cost to have a Voluntary Service unit in the Bronx and how we might operate it."[41]

In June 1960 the Home Missions Board approved the idea of developing the fourth floor at Fellowship Chapel into a 1-w VS Center, assuming clearance from Selective Service, and working in cooperation with the Peace, Relief and Service Committee of the Brethren in Christ Church. The two bodies met and appointed a sub-committee to study how best to implement the decision. Isaac Kanode, Henry Ginder, and Clair Hoffman formed the sub-committee. On July 19 they met with H. Raymond Charles at the Eastern Mennonite Board of Missions office in Salunga and found him helpful and encouraging. The following week they went to New York City for extended meetings with Paul Hill and with John H. Kraybill. Based on his own experience in starting the Mennonite VS Center, Kraybill suggested a unit of six, preferably married couples. He advised them to seek the approval of Selective Service for 1-w work at Fellowship Chapel, enabling the unit leader to assist the mission with club programs and maintenance work. 1-w job openings were plentiful in New York and Kraybill made a list of openings available to the committee. With this encouragement, the sub-committee recommended action.[42]

On May 7, 1961 Mary Lou Ruegg of Ridgeway, Ontario, came to Fellowship Chapel as the first VS worker assigned to the new unit. She was to stay more than thirty years. Kathy Kreider, a short-term VSer, and Dallas Robinson of Williamsburg, Pennsylvania, who was to do his 1-w service at St. Barnabas Hospital, arrived in June.[43]

When Bishop Ginder visited in July, the fourth floor tenants had still not vacated the apartment and the four VSers were staying with the Hills. They were in good spirits and busy with their new jobs. Kathy Kreider was caring for a handicapped Spanish child and Mary Lou Ruegg had "a very fine job in the Interchurch Center on Riverside Drive." Harold and Catherine Bowers were living temporarily in the youth center in the basement. Ginder decided against making them unit leaders in addition to their Brooklyn assignment. Once the fourth floor opened, they would move to the Robinson apartment. Esther Robinson would move to the VS Unit as hostess and would also take responsibility for the layette distribution and home visitation program for new mothers in the community. She was to be officially released from the Brooklyn mission as soon as vacation Bible school ended. "A farewell service will be planned for Sunday evening July 23" and the Brooklyn congregation would be informed the previous Sunday.[44]

On December 10, 1961 the Bronx congregation received its first four members into fellowship. Paul and Irma Espinosa moved their membership from Glad Tidings. Richard Tange and the pastor's sixteen-year-old daughter Gloria Hill were baptized.

Pastor Paul Hill with four young men at Fellowship Chapel.

The VS Unit was also growing. Edna Hill, a friend of Mary Lou Ruegg's from Ridgeway, Ontario, came after Christmas and Eber Wingert, Darrel Gibble, and Paul Kennedy arrived together on New Year's Day 1962. Wingert and Gibble were both from Chambersburg, Pennsylvania, and both did their 1-w service at New York University Hospital. Kennedy, from Greencastle, Pennsylvania, joined Dallas Robinson at St. Barnabas Hospital for his alternative service. As the year progressed, the VS unit gained more married couples. Don and Dorothy Alvis of Thomas, Oklahoma, and Leon and Frances Kanagy came to the city for 1-w service. Paul Kennedy married Mary Martin of Greencastle in April and Eber Wingert brought his new bride Dolores to join the VS center in October.[45]

Fellowship Chapel grew slowly. Isaac Kanode noted in the 1961 report that "The layette distribution is proving to be a great ministry, opening many doors in the community." The church had six members and an average attendance of 27 on Sundays.[46]

The Han Chin family joined the church in 1962. "One of the interesting experiences coming out of the chapel is the interest and witness of a lovely Chinese family who operate a laundry business. These people are devoted Christians and in each package of laundry they place a tract, New Testament, or some announcement concerning the chapel."[47]

Attendance at morning worship and Sunday school increased steadily in 1963 averaging 50 and in 1964 averaging 61. Fellowship Chapel counted thirteen members in 1963 and sixteen members in 1964. Eliezer and Maria

Pastor Paul Hill preaching at Fellowship Chapel.

Molina were received as members early in 1964. Paul Hill reported "The youth program, with a full time director, has shown marked advancement during 1963. The purchase of Camp Brookhaven has added much to the total program of the New York City work."[48]

Mark and Faye Peachey brought youth club work to a new level when they came to Fellowship Chapel in 1963 for 1-W service. After Isaac Kanode visited the Bronx in February 1964, he reported: "Mark and Faye are doing an excellent job with the young people. This phase of the program is carried entirely by themselves. Mark has approximately 50 boys which he is working with presently, and Faye has probably one-half this number of girls."[49]

The Brooklyn Brethren in Christ Church was also growing. On Thursday in Holy Week 1963 Bishop Ginder came to the Brooklyn church for their first communion service. "Pastor Bowers and Pastor Hill directed it nicely. The feet washing service was included. Carl and Martha Glinton assisted. There were 20 present."

Ginder found problems, too. Could a white pastor effectively minister to a black congregation in Bedford-Stuyvesant in a time of increased racial awareness and Black Pride? "The Bowerses have experienced an awareness of some anti-white feelings in the congregation. I believe it was helpful for them to discuss this. Cathy is learning to live with those who do not fully share her views."[50]

During 1963 Harold and Cathy Bowers made an increased effort "to reach the young people of the community through the development of a choir and through times of fellowship in the pastor's home. The teenagers have also been given added responsibilities in the church." But the Brooklyn church had no members, apart from the pastor and his wife. Community interest seemed to be dropping. Attendance at Sunday worship fell from 48 in 1963 to 37 in 1964 and Sunday school slipped from 42 to 31. The vacation Bible school in the summer of 1963 attracted 55 children, a drop from 70 the year before. Kanode found the service somewhat lifeless and "not geared to the people present," who only numbered 24, when he visited early in 1964.[51]

The major event of the year was the location of a building to "adequately house both the church facilities and the parsonage." Despite some misgivings, the Home Missions Board had determined unanimously in September 1963 to purchase a four story building at 958 Bedford Avenue as a more permanent place of worship and mission outreach. On March 6, 1964 Bishop Ginder, Isaac Kanode, Paul Hill, Harold Bowers, and Roy Mann made final settlement of $10,317.77 for the property. Remodeling progressed well under Roy Mann's supervision and the first service in the newly remodeled chapel was held on Sunday, May 24, 1964.[52] With two functioning missions, the Brethren in Christ Church had come to New York City to stay.

NOTES

[1] *Minutes of the 83rd Annual General Conference of the Brethren in Christ Church* (Nappanee, Indiana, 1953), 93-4. E. Morris Sider, *Leaders Among Brethren* (Nappanee, Indiana, 1988), 106.

[2] Henry A. Ginder, "Report of Second Trip to New York City to Study Possibilities for Opening Mission Work," n.d. (April 1954), Ginder Papers in the archives of the Brethren in Christ Church at Messiah College, Grantham, Pennsylvania. [Hereafter BCA-MC.]

[3] *Minutes of the 84th Annual General Conference of the Brethren in Christ Church* (Nappanee, Ind., 1954), 97 and 101.

[4] *Evangelical Visitor,* 67 (August 16, 1954), 9.

[5] *Minutes of the 85th Annual General Conference of the Brethren in Christ Church* (Nappanee, Ind., 1955), 106. *Brethren in Christ Handbook, 1955,* (Nappanee, Ind., 1955), 95-6. *Minutes of the 86th Annual General Conference of the Brethren in Christ Church* (Nappanee, Ind., 1956), 83.

[6] *Minutes of the 87th Annual General Conference of the Brethren in Christ Church* (Nappanee, Ind., 1957), 84.

[7] *Brethren in Christ Handbook of Missions, 1955* (Nappanee, Ind., 1955), 96.

[8] Mary Wenger, "Glimpses from Life in Israel," *Evangelical Visitor,* 67 (December 6, 1954), 8 and 16. *Evangelical Visitor,* 67 (November 22, 1954), 14. *Minutes of the 87th Annual General Conference of the Brethren in Christ Church* (Nappanee, Ind., 1957), 84.

[9] Henry A. Ginder to Esther Ebersole, March 19, 1957; Mary Wenger to Henry A. Ginder, March 27, 1957. Ginder Papers. BCA-MC.

[10] Mary E. Wenger to Henry A. Ginder, April 2, 1957. Ginder Papers, BCA-MC. Mary E. Wenger to Henry A. Ginder and Albert H. Engle, Apr. 15, 1957. BCA-MC.

[11] Mary E. Wenger to Henry A. Ginder, May 17, 1957, Ginder Papers, BCA-MC.

[12] Mary E. Wenger to Henry A. Ginder, Oct. 17, 1957, Ginder Papers, BCA-MC.

[13] Henry A. Ginder to Mary E. Wenger, Jan. 6, 1958, Ginder Papers, BCA-MC.

[14] Henry A. Ginder, "Report re New York," Feb. 1958. Albert H. Engle to Home Mission Board, Feb. 24, 1958, Apr. 4, 1958. Mary E. Wenger to Henry A. Ginder, Mar. 25, 1958, Ginder Papers, BCA-MC.

[15] Mary E. Wenger to Henry A. Ginder, June 30, 1958. Henry A. Ginder to John I. Smucker, July 3, 1958, Ginder Papers, BCA-MC.

[16] H. A. Ginder to Albert H. Engle, Sept. 26, 1958, Oct. 28, 1958. Ginder Papers. BCA-MC. H. Raymond Charles to Merritt Robinson, Oct. 1, 1958. Earl G. Martin to Merritt Robinson, Oct. 6, 1958, EMM. .

[17] Albert H. Engle to Board of Home Missions, Oct. 17, 1958. Home Missions File, BCA-MC.

[18] Albert H. Engle to Home Mission Board, Jan. 15, 1959, Home Mission, BCA-MC.

[19] Albert H. Engle to Home Mission Board, Jan. 20, 1959, Feb. 5, 1959, Mar. 6, 1959, Home Mission, BCA-MC.

[20] Albert H. Engle to Home Mission Board, Mar. 6, 1959, Home Mission, BCA-MC.

[21] Albert H. Engle to Home Missions Board, Apr. 13, 1959. "The Hills of San Francisco," (c.1983). Home Missions, BCA-MC.

[22] Albert H. Engle to Home Mission Board, Sep. 10, 1959. "Diary Jottings of Reverend Paul D. Hill 1959-1966." Home Mission, BCA-MC.

[23] Reverend Paul D. Hill, "Diary Jottings." Albert H. Engle to Home Mission Board, Sep. 10, 1959, Sep. 15, 1959. Henry A. Ginder, "Report of Visit to Bronx, September 23 to 25, 1959." Isaac S. Kanode to Paul Hill, Nov. 6, 1959. Home Mission, BCA-MC. *Evangelical Visitor*, 73 (January 25, 1960), 15.

[24] Paul Hill, "Diary Jottings." Paul Hill to Henry A. Ginder, Feb. 11, 1960. Ginder Papers, BCA-MC.

[25] Paul Hill, "Diary Jottings," BCA-MC. Paul Burkholder to Ira Buckwalter, July 28, 1960, Nov. 7, 1969, EMM.

[26] Hill, "Diary Jottings," BCA-MC.

[27] Henry A. Ginder to Carl Clinton, Nov. 11, 1958. Henry A. Ginder to C. W. Boyer, Nov. 11, 1958. Ginder Papers, BCA-MC.

[28] Henry A. Ginder to Albert Engle, May 15, 1959, May 19, 1959. Ginder Papers, BCA-MC.

[29] Draft, "Re: Colored Work New York City," n.d. Ginder Papers, BCA-MC.

[30] Henry A. Ginder to Graybill Wolgemuth, Jun. 27, 1959. Draft, "Brooklyn Brethren in Christ Church," (July 1959), Program "Official Opening and Dedication of Brethren in Christ Church 984 Bedford Avenue, Brooklyn, N.Y. July 12, 1959." Henry A. Ginder to Albert H. Engle, Jul. 14, 1959. Esther Robinson to "Dear Interested Friends," July 1959. Ginder Papers, BCA-MC.

[31] Harold X. Connolly, *A Ghetto Grows in Brooklyn*, (New York, 1977), 71, 76, 130.

[32] Henry A. Ginder, "Report of Visit to Brooklyn, September 22 and 24, 1959." Ginder Papers, BCA-MC.

[33] *Handbook of Missions Brethren in Christ Church*, 1960, 20.

[34] *Handbook of Missions Brethren in Christ Church*, 1961, 57.

[35] Memoranda, Apr. 10, 1961, Apr. 14, 1961, Apr. 24, 1961. Merritt Robinson to Henry A. Ginder, Apr. 20, 1961. "Notes on Visit to New York Churches May 5, 6, and 7, 1961." Ginder Papers, BCA-MC.

[36] *Handbook of Missions Brethren in Christ Church*, 1962, 20.

[37] Isaac Kanode, "Report of Trip to New York City, October 2-3, 1961," BCA-MC.

[38] Henry A. Ginder, "Report on Visit to New York City," Oct. 21-27, 1961.

[39] Isaac S. Kanode, "Report of Visit to New York City," October 18, 1962, BCA-MC.

[40] *Handbook of Missions Brethren in Christ Church*, 1963.

[41] E. Morris Sider, *Leaders Among Brothers* (Nappanee, Indiana, 1988), 107.

[42] Albert H. Engle to Paul Hill, June 25, 1960. "Report of the New York City 1-w VS Study Committee," 1960, BCA-MC.

[43] Paul Hill, "Diary Jottings." New York City Voluntary Service Committee Minutes, Apr. 10, 1962, BCA-MC.

[44] Henry A. Ginder, "Notes of My Visit to New York City, July 5 and 6, 1961." Ginder Papers, BCA-MC.

[45] Hill, "Diary Jottings." N.Y.C. Volunteer Service Committee Minutes, Apr. 10, 1962, BCA-MC.

[46] *Brethren in Christ Church Handbook of Missions*, 1962, 19-20, 37.

[47] Hill, "Diary Jottings." *Brethren in Christ Church Handbook of Missions*, 1963, 61.

[48] Hill, "Diary Jottings." *Brethren in Christ Church Handbook of Missions*, 1964, 23, 43.

[49] Isaac Kanode to Henry Ginder, Feb. 27, 1964. Ginder Papers, BCA-MC.

[50] Henry A. Ginder to Isaac Kanode and Charles Rife, Apr. 13, 1963, Ginder Papers. BCA-MC.

[51] Isaac S. Kanode to Henry A. Ginder, Feb. 27, 1964. Ginder Papers, BCA-MC. *Brethren in Christ Church Handbook of Missions*, 1964 23, 41.

[52] Isaac Kanode, press release, Oct. 12, 1963; May 16, 1964. Board of Home Missions and Extension, Minutes June 8, 1964, BCA-MC.

CHAPTER SIX

The House of Friendship

1952–1963

THE JEWISH EVANGELISM Committee of Lancaster Conference invited Jacob and Frances Thomas, already living and working in New York, to undertake a ministry to Jews in 1952 as self-supporting missionaries. In January 1953 the committee encouraged them "to give more time or full time as the Lord leads and the work may warrant." Ira Buckwalter went to New York to share this wider vision with the Thomas family. They decided to continue as part-time workers under the committee and bought a house at 2266 Hampden Place in the Bronx as the center for evangelism among Jewish people. The Thomases made personal contacts with Jewish neighbors and co-workers, held meetings and did friendship evangelism at their home and, except in the winter months, held public meetings in the city parks. In July 1954, for instance, Jacob Thomas reported that "They go to the park two or three nights a week, give a Gospel message, distribute literature, and answer questions that come from the audience."

The Jewish Evangelism Committee saw its work as independent of other church-planting efforts. When Harold Thomas met with the committee in 1954, he suggested "Jewish Evangelism should be tied in with our regular church program" and the committee "decided that Bro. Stoner [Krady] and Bro. Elmer Martin should visit the work in New York." Early in 1955 they approved "Bro. Thomas's request for a Sunday afternoon service" at Hampden Place, giving him a certain autonomy.[1]

Jacob Thomas was not in full agreement with the leaders at Fox Street and Glad Tidings on the question of plain dress. This had caused difficulty, as Thomas explained in 1955 "that we had not been used at two of the missions here for some time" because of "the dress question."[2] This estrangement from the other Mennonite centers created some problems for the witness to Jewish people. Aquilla Riehl, superintendent at Fox Street, complained of "Jacob Thomas' inability to work with the church." Lillian

Bruckhart, sister Olive Lucas and Verna Beiler, all interested in Jewish evangelism, were self-supporting workers at the Fox Street mission.[3]

Thomas made the initial contact with the Elkhart board and with Abner Stoltzfus, inviting them to "help in the work" in New York. In May 1955 Nelson E. Kauffman, secretary of Home Missions for Mennonite Board of Missions, arranged a meeting at the Thomas home on Hampden Place to study "the best procedure, location and method to open among the Jewish people" in New York City a mission under the administration of the Elkhart board. He invited Lloyd Weaver, who had been effective in a ministry to the Jewish community in Newport News, Virginia, Abner Stoltzfus, and Jacob Thomas to share their insights.

The four agreed that the mission board should "lease for a year with option to buy, a two or three family house, in a nice neighborhood, adjacent to a predominantly Jewish neighborhood, preferably in the Bronx or Queens" and invite Lloyd and Sara Weaver to give full-time to the work. Abner Stoltzfus believed that Maple Grove congregation would release him for part-time work. Thomas stressed the importance of self-supporting workers and "since he is not supported by Lancaster and has had some differences with them, he would like to cooperate with our program."

The proposed program followed lines already developed by Stoltzfus and Thomas "of personal contacts, home visitation, entertaining folks in homes, some street and park work, with literature distribution," but it would be "a program of Christian witness that would not single the Jew out, because he resents this." On this visit, Nelson Kauffman met some of the 36 ninth graders and five teachers at a Jewish school who had accepted Abner Stoltzfus' invitation earlier that month to spend a week at Camp Tel Hai and to visit Lancaster County Amish and Mennonite homes. With that successful experience as an example it was appropriate that "The program would include camp work, inviting of Jews into homes in the country and the acceptance of the invitation to have selected young people visit in Jewish homes." There would also be "youth activities in recreation, crafts, and Bible classes" at the proposed center.[4]

When Kauffman presented the plan to the Mennonite Board of Missions executive committee, he was given "approval to move ahead." He informed Lancaster Conference and let the Jewish Evangelism Committee know about the conversations with their man in the Bronx. On June 8 Kauffman met with D. Stoner Krady at Lancaster. Krady "felt there was room in New York City for a number of folks to open work." Kauffman assured him that he would not "attempt to lure" Thomas "away from your

Board or your work" and any decision "with regard to cooperation with our work" would be his own.[5]

Thomas hoped that the two mission boards could sponsor a joint Jewish witness in New York. His conversations with Stoner Krady indicated that this was not likely, but he continued to press the point with both Elkhart and Salunga offices. In April 1956 Thomas wrote "Frances and I have decided to work with the General Mission Board. Since we have been working together as two conference bodies the past six months, and plans for furthering this work have developed as they have, we feel this is the Lord's definite leading at this time."[6]

Maple Grove congregation voted to release Abner Stoltzfus for three days a week in New York City. Abner and Lena Stoltzfus began officially as MBM workers on October 1, 1955 receiving half support.[7]

Stoltzfus and Thomas continued their ministry as before for just over a year. Nelson Kauffman met with them in the Bronx in June 1956, to inspect a house located on Southern Boulevard, opposite the main entrance to the Bronx Zoo, and to discuss with an architect what changes would be needed to remodel it as the Mennonite House of Friendship. Jacob Thomas had noticed the house for sale and saw its possibilities. A spacious two-story frame house shaded by maple trees, it had been the home of a Bronx County judge. The house was in a predominantly Jewish neighborhood with synagogues nearby. It would serve as a center for

Mennonite House of Friendship original building at 2283 Southern Boulevard, Bronx. The assembly room was in the basement. 2005 photo.

Jewish evangelism, but the decision had already been made "that our work include a witness to the total community so that it is not distinguished as Jewish witness." The mission board had learned from the experience of Lloyd Weaver and others.

Recruiting personnel took time. Kauffman talked with Martin Bender, a student at Eastern Mennonite College. Bender, originally from Grantsville, Maryland, had spent the previous summer at Camp Tel Hai and planned to return for the summer of 1956. Kauffman found him "definitely interested in the New York program." Abner Stoltzfus knew him and was ready to work with him.

But Stoltzfus had another young man to suggest. John I. Smucker, from Bird in Hand, Lancaster County, a member of his own Maple Grove congregation, was also a student at EMC. Kauffman had explored the possibility of home mission work in different places with John and Irene Smucker. He had known John Smucker since 1952, when he had worked in voluntary service in the Hannibal, Missouri, mission, and at that time he encouraged the younger man to go to college and pray about a call to the ordained ministry. In August Smucker wrote that his summer school classes would be over in a week. "If neither New York or St. Louis open up, we plan to continue in school work either at EMC or Goshen." Kauffman had not yet had a reply from Bender. He wrote immediately to Smucker that the St. Louis mission was still in the planning stage, "However, in New York we do have the house and the program is going, and we would be ready to have you move in."[8]

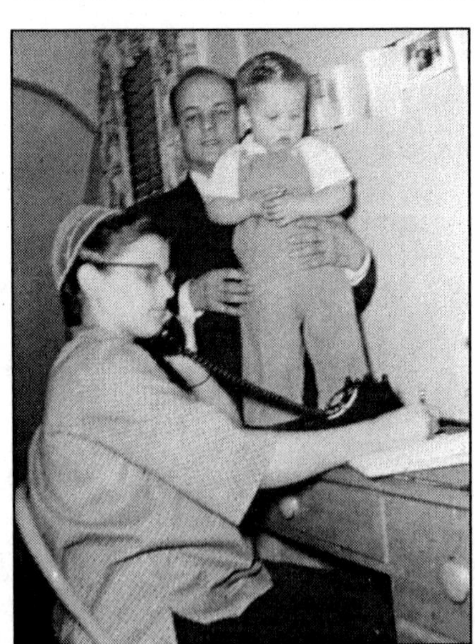

Irene and John Smucker and son Dennis. John was pastor of Mennonite House Of Friendship.

The Smuckers arrived in the Bronx with their six-month-old son on January 2, 1957. "I wore the Mennonite plain coat," Smucker recalled, and "my wife wore the little white Mennonite prayer veiling for several years." Like the other Mennonite urban missionaries of that era, John and Irene Smucker were both in their twenties. They were in an unfamiliar environment, but they wanted to save New York City people and bring them to Christ. Verna Beiler moved from Fox Street to the House of Friendship at the same time. She continued as a self-supporting mission worker and lived in the two-room apartment on the first floor.

Nelson Kauffman returned to the Bronx for a formal service of dedication on January 22, 1957. Harold Thomas, pastor at Glad Tidings, read the Scripture. Jacob Thomas offered the prayer. Abner Stoltzfus explained the purpose of the House of Friendship. Nelson Kauffman emphasized in his talk that:

> This House is to be a haven of quietness and worship where people in need may find friends whose love and knowledge of the truth of God will enable them to lead people into a relationship to God through Christ that is completely satisfying and will give them security and peace in this world of tension.[9]

The Mennonite Board of Missions and its workers in the Bronx saw the House of Friendship as a means of reaching individuals and leading them to the Lord. John and Irene Smucker, Verna Beiler, Jacob and Frances Thomas, Abner Stoltzfus, and soon Mary Wenger understood their ministry as primarily a witness to individuals and primarily to Jewish people. In March Smucker wrote:

> We are slowly getting oriented to New York City. In the month of February there were from 40 to 50 contacts made by Abner, Verna, Irene and I. Abner showed his pictures [of Palestine] at the B'nai B'rith in Brooklyn and in a Jewish synagogue in Manhattan. Abner, Paul Erb and I attended the American Christian Palestine committee Conference downtown last week.[10]

After many years in urban ministry Smucker recalled the difficulty of those first months of making initial contacts, when they had to go into the streets and knock on doors to reach people. He recalled their "strange dress and Pennsylvania accent" as barriers.

> With all these many personal contacts and witnessing to people about Christ, so few made a commitment to Christ and joined the church. We entertained people, gave them free meals, spent hours with them. Jews loved to debate the Bible and the Gospel, but few ever attended even one Sunday worship service. We said we were using the method of fellowship evangelism. Over a cup of tea or a meal in a restaurant or in our apartment we fellowshipped with persons. But the method seemed to be hard work with little result.[11]

Monthly reports to Elkhart indicated "a few more people come to our door" and kept a tally of personal contacts on street, train, subways, barber shop. "The Jacob Thomas family also makes a number of contacts especially while at work." Mary Wenger, "who is witnessing here as a full-time worker with the Brethren in Christ Church has a deep concern for the Jewish people of this city." Bernard Spanier, a converted Jew, whom Thomas had led to Christ, and Lillian Bruckhart were also helping. "This month he and his girl friend passed out about 1,000 tracts."[12]

The Billy Graham Crusade in New York City in April 1957 provided a wider opportunity for the workers at the House of Friendship. Smucker reported that "The Billy Graham meetings open the way to much discussion to anyone on religious subjects." He said "Each night hundreds of people come forward to be counseled by a trained counselor. My wife and Verna both sing in the choir." Jacob Thomas and his son Donald sang in the choir, too. Mary Wenger and Jacob Thomas both served as counselors for the Billy Graham Crusade.

A group of women leave a meeting at Mennonite House of Friendship.

At the same time, a fresh point of tension arose. The Jacob Thomas family wanted to transfer their membership to the House of Friendship. Smucker knew that the Elkhart board had been slow to act on this, because it was "a very tender situation" and they wanted to avoid even the appearance of "dragging him away from Lancaster Conference", but "he has already transferred his work here." Jacob Thomas was superintendent of the Sunday School, teacher of the adult class, and a member of the House of Friendship council. Nelson Kauffman wrote Thomas expressing appreciation for his role in "our total Mennonite witness to the Jews in New York." He added: "I am writing to Johnny Smucker suggesting that from now on we consider the House of Friendship workers a congregation and at a later time take up the matter of conference affiliation." This was a significant development. The House of Friendship had had Sunday morning worship services, Sunday school, and prayer meetings, but its major purpose was as a base for outreach and evangelism. Mennonite Board of Missions would now see it as more of a church-planting effort.[13]

Problems at her Hampden Place apartment led Mary Wenger to move to the House of Friendship, sharing the apartment with Verna Beiler. Early in 1958 she moved into her own apartment on Southern Boulevard next door to the House of Friendship and continued there through the year.

The pattern of fellowship evangelism continued through 1957 and 1958. One or another from the House of Friendship made contact with interested Jews and the Smuckers invited them to the house for meals. All of the workers made door-to-door calls and in the summer of 1958 they held open-air meetings in lower Manhattan. Abner Stoltzfus invited Jewish friends to his Lancaster County cabin. Many welcomed this opportunity and the cabin was filled even in winter. He also reached students from many different countries and some of these international students stayed at the cabin.[14]

Melvin and Naomi Huyard came to the House of Friendship while he was doing his alternative assignment. John Smucker reported "We appreciate very much the 1-w couple we have... They have many witnessing opportunities in the hospital and fit in with the local congregation very well."[15]

The House of Friendship moved towards "a parish approach to Jewish evangelism" emphasizing a welcoming congregation open to people of all races and national backgrounds. Roy Kreider's visit in March 1958 pointed Smucker in this direction. "We were impressed with his use of the parish approach to the Jewish people." John Smucker advocated this method at a Jewish Evangelism Conference held at the House of Friendship in September.[16]

A survey of the immediate neighborhood in 1958, including 368 homes, revealed that two thirds were Catholic, a quarter Jewish, 4 percent Protestant and 5 percent other or no religion. Children made up only 13 percent and teenagers 11 percent of the population. The East Tremont area was an older community with a decreasing population. Young families were moving away and the ethnic composition of the neighborhood was changing, although not as rapidly as it would later. The Catholic and Jewish proportion of the community dropped to 60 percent and 20 percent respectively by 1961.[17]

The House of Friendship had completed its transition from a center for Jewish evangelism to a local congregation by 1959. John I. Smucker was ordained in March as pastor. The small chapel room had already become the worship center for the congregation. They installed an organ in February 1959.[18]

In 1959 Elaine Ackerman Clemmer was the first convert baptized at the House of Friendship, but others who had shown interest were slipping away and attendance was low. Smucker reported an average attendance of 25 in 1959, and five converts and eight transfers of membership from other Mennonite churches brought the attendance to only 32 in 1960.[19]

Five persons joined the congregation in March 1961 and a teenage girl was baptized Easter Sunday. Geraldine Sherman, a Jewish convert, was baptized in October 1961. By 1962 the House of Friendship Church counted 42 members and by 1963 there were 52 on the membership roll. Part of this steady growth came from Mennonites who moved to the New York area from Pennsylvania and from Mennonites who moved away from the South Bronx churches to better neighborhoods in the Bronx or Queens. An analysis of the congregation in 1963 showed that 33 of 52 members came from Mennonite backgrounds. While many nationalities were represented, the members included six of Jewish ancestry, nine Puerto Ricans, one Italian and one black. Only 23 percent lived in the East Tremont nighborhood and these included the pastor and his family and the VS personnel. The rest were about evenly divided between the Bronx and other city and suburban areas.[20]

The neighborhood was changing around them. The old Italian Catholic neighborhood to the north and especially the old Jewish neighborhood to the south were both disintegrating by 1960. Black and Hispanic families took their place. The House of Friendship stood on one boundary line and gangs began to battle over turf.[21]

The problem of relating to the changing neighborhood was one that faced all of the city churches. The House of Friendship still followed traditional patterns of outreach. A Released Time program for public elementary school children began in 1960 with five children. Besides the high school Sunday school class led by Marcus Smucker and Donald Thomas, there was one for older youth taught by Hans Hubert and Cecil Grove, who was also youth leader. Carmen Colon was the MYF leader and Robert Weaver directed the boys' club.

Milagros (Millie) Hernandez led the first Spanish-language service on October 16, 1960. Ed and Milagros (Hernandez) Mullen and Angel Torres served together on the evangelism committee. In 1962 Milagros Mullen was in charge of "Evangelism and Spanish Work," while Ed Mullen had responsibility for visiting and witnessing at Welfare Island on Sunday afternoons. As key personnel moved away, the work of the evangelism and Spanish committee became less vigorous by the end of 1963, John Smucker recalled.[22]

A new approach to the neighborhood emerged in 1962 from meetings of The Bronx Clergy Fellowship. The first meetings of the Bronx Park West Community Renewal Study were held at the House of Friendship and at St. Martin of Tours Catholic Church in July 1962. The City Planning Commission had targeted a 30-block area bounded by Southern Boulevard, East 185th Street, Belmont Avenue, and East 179th Street for rehabilitation. The Bronx Park West Steering Committee brought together community leaders from the predominantly Italian Catholic Belmont Civic Association and the primarily Jewish East Tremont Neighborhood Association and local clergy and elected officials.[23]

The House of Friendship became a congregation of the Ohio and Eastern Conference in April 1962. The congregation worked through a policy on receiving divorced persons at the same time. Plans for building expansion began in 1960 with the creation of a building fund. The basement chapel had a seating capacity of 70 and membership had grown to nearly that number. On June 29, 1963 the congregation approved a $60,000 building project to provide an adequate place for worship and Christian education. But they evidently had second thoughts. Most members lived at a distance. Neighborhood contacts were relatively few. The building committee proposed moving to an entirely new site in the Pelham section of the East Bronx, but ultimately decided to stay. The major problems facing the House of Friendship at the end of 1963 involved "accepting Spanish people, building funds, and the increasing mobility of the congregation."[24]

NOTES

[1] Jewish Evangelism Committee Minutes, January 7, 1953, March 9, 1953, July 5, 1954, September 6, 1954, EMM.

[2] Jacob Thomas and family to Nelson Kauffman, December 3, 1955, Mennonite Board of Missions, Archives of the Mennonite Church, Goshen, Indiana. (Hereafter MBM-AMC.) Thomas sent copies of this letter to D. Stoner Krady, H. Raymond Charles, Ira J. Buckwalter and Abner Stoltzfus.

[3] Aquilla Riehl to H. Raymond Charles, February 23, 1956, EMM..

[4] Nelson E. Kauffman, "Report of Investigation on Jewish Mission Work in New York, May 11-12-13, 1955." Jacob Thomas and family to Nelson Kauffman, December 3, 1955, MBM-AMC.

[5] Nelson E. Kauffman to D. Stoner Krady, June 13, 1955, MBM-AMC.

[6] Jacob Thomas and family to Nelson Kauffman, December 3, 1955, MBM-AMC. Jacob and Frances Thomas to Paul N. Kraybill, April 14, 1956, EMM.

[7] Nelson E. Kauffman to Abner Stoltzfus, October 4, 1955. Aaron F. Stoltzfus to Nelson Kauffman, October 7, 1955. Gladys K. Mumaw to Abner Stoltzfus, November 23, 1955. H. Ernest Bennett to Abner Stoltzfus, December 20, 1955, MBM-AMC.

[8] Nelson E. Kauffman, "Report on New York," June 11, 1956. Abner Stoltzfus to Nelson Kauffman, July 23, 1956. John I. Smucker to Nelson Kauffman, August 13, 1956. Nelson Kauffman to John I. Smucker, August 16, 1956, MBM-AMC. John I. Smucker, "Reflections and Implications of Urban Mennonite Mission in the South Bronx," Ph.D. dissertation, Union Graduate School, 1985, 62. John I. Smucker, "Light in the Concrete Jungle," Youth's Christian Companion (November 8, 1959), 710.

[9] Nelson E. Kauffman, "Mennonite House of Friendship," n.d. MBM-AMC. Smucker, "Reflections," 55, 67.

[10] John I. Smucker to Nelson Kauffman, March 7, 1957, MBM-AMC.

[11] Smucker, "Reflections," 69.

[12] Mennonite Board of Missions and Charities Activities Report, Mennonite House of Friendship, January-April 1957. John I. Smucker to "Dear Friends in the Lord," May 1, 1957, MBM-AMC.

[13] Nelson Kauffman to Jacob Thomas, Sept. 16, 1957, MBM-AMC.

[14] Esther Eby Glass, "Town and Country Preacher," *Christian Living*, Dec. 1959.

[15] John I. Smucker to Nelson Kauffman, Aug. 18, 1958. Nelson Kauffman to Ernest Bennett, Jan. 21, 1959, MBM-MCA. John I. Smucker, "Light in the Concrete Jungle," *Youth's Christian Companion*, Nov. 8, 1959, 709-711.

[16] Smucker, "Reflections," 310. John I. Smucker, "The Parish Approach to the Jewish People," *Missionary Messenger*, Aug. 1960, 3-4.

[17] Nelson Kauffman to Ernest Bennett, Jan. 21, 1959, MBM-MCA. Smucker, "Reflections," 307, 322.

[18] Smucker, "Reflections," 317.

[19] Smucker, "Reflection," 319-321.

[20] John I. Smucker, "A Sketch of the House of Friendship Mennonite Church," Oct. 1, 1963, MBM-MCA. House of Friendship Prayer Newsletter, June 7, 1961.

[21] House of Friendship Prayer Newsletter, June 7, 1961.

[22] House of Friendship Annual Business Meeting, Feb. 27, 1962. Church Council Minutes, Oct. 8, 1962, MBM-MCA. Smucker, "Reflections," 325.

[23] Smucker, "Sketch," Oct. 1, 1963, MBM-AMC. Smucker, "Reflections," 331-332.

[24] Ibid., 333-334; 341.

CHAPTER SEVEN

Island in the City

1957–1966

A NEW MENNONITE congregation began in Brooklyn in 1957 through the faith and witness of a young mother and her children who had recently come to the city from Puerto Rico. Aquilina Torres and her daughter Ana Hilda shared what they had found in a personal knowledge of Jesus Christ with friends and neighbors. Gladys Widmer, a mission worker home on furlough, and Samuel Miller, who taught Spanish at Eastern Mennonite College, helped them from the start. La Primera Iglesia Evangelica Menonita de Brooklyn took root in the Hispanic community and bore fruit. The fledgling congregation soon reached out to establish a second Spanish-speaking Mennonite church in the South Bronx.

In the later 1990s a reception was held to honor Gladys Widmer [center] at the First Mennonite Church of Brooklyn which she helped to plant.

The Mennonite Church came to Puerto Rico in 1943 with the first three men assigned to a Civilian Public Service unit in the La Plata Valley. The C.P.S. men began a mission Sunday School and soon a congregation was emerging. Lester T. Hershey came to Puerto Rico in 1947 as pastor of the first congregation to be established, Calvary Mennonite Church in La Plata. A hospital, rural clinics, schools, and new churches followed in the next few years. The Puerto Rican Mennonite Church was in its first generation, composed entirely of recent converts and, like the first generation of Anabaptists in Europe, they were ready to share their faith with whoever would listen.[1]

An increasing population and a colonial economy forced many Puerto Ricans to leave their homes in search of work on the island or far away in Brooklyn or the Bronx. The large-scale production of sugar made profits for some, while reducing small farmers to agricultural laborers. Ironically, the sugar industry only existed because of U.S. tariff laws favoring domestic sugar producers. A contemporary study noted, "Land ownership is concentrated in huge estates; cane workers are seasonally unemployed; since so much of the available land is devoted to sugar, the island must import about half its foodstuffs at high costs... As a sugar-producing area, Puerto Rico shares the economic fate of plantation economies: her people are poor, undernourished, and landless."[2]

Sugar cane cultivation initially expanded at the expense of coffee and tobacco. High taxes and tight credit forced "many former coffee *hacendados*, small independent farmers, and peasants to give up their land holdings or see them repossessed or sold on the auction block." This also meant a "rapid decline in the acreage dedicated to subsistence farming." As a result many people had to seek work in Puerto Rico's towns and cities, where there were five unemployed laborers for every unskilled job. "Many of the displaced *campesinos* that flocked to the urban areas did so as an intermediate step towards migration to the mainland."[3]

Wages in the cities, as in the countryside, remained low. In March 1945 agricultural workers earned an average of $5 a week, and in manufacturing jobs the average wage was $12. Weekly earnings in manufacturing in the mainland United States averaged $47.50 in the same month and Puerto Ricans paid approximately the same prices for food and consumer goods as were charged in New York City.[4] Mennonite mission workers observed in the 1940s and early 1950s that many Puerto Ricans had an annual income of less than $100. Many people had to spend 90-95% of their income on food. The poverty of Puerto Ricans was "intensified by the exploitation of American owners."[5]

The first years of Mennonite mission work in Puerto Rico coincided with the greatly accelerated migration from Puerto Rico to New York City. Puerto Ricans began moving to New York in response to the employment opportunities created by the First World War and kept coming in substantial numbers through the 1920s. The Depression slowed the flow of migrants from the island and the Second World War halted it almost completely. After 1945 Puerto Rican Americans again began coming to New York in very large numbers. Nearly all of them remained in the city. In 1950 fully 82 percent of all the Puerto Ricans living on the United States mainland made their homes in New York City.[6]

With so many Puerto Ricans coming to the city in the later 1940s and 1950s, at least a few among them would have known the Mennonite Church in their former home. Newcomers from Puerto Rico had settled originally around the Brooklyn Navy Yard and in Harlem. These old community centers were expanding in the 1950s from East Harlem to the South Bronx and from the Navy Yard northeast into the Williamsburg section of Brooklyn. New Yorkers from Puerto Rico chose to live in these crowded sections of the city because these Hispanic neighborhoods supported Spanish-speaking churches, stores, and social clubs, restaurants and stores that sold familiar foods, and an environment where language, customs, interests and attitudes maintained a sense of Puerto Rican identity in an unfamiliar, sometimes hostile, English-speaking city. Immigrant groups had always created such neighborhoods. In addition, "many migrants were likely to return to the island and migrate to the mainland again within a five-year period" and relatively low air fares allowed others to visit family and friends. "This phenomenon was the root of the close links which existed between the island and the mainland [Puerto Rican] communities."[7]

A Mennonite Congregation in Brooklyn

Julio and Silita Colon attended the Coamo Mennonite Church before they moved to Brooklyn in the early 1950s. At the request of Mennonite Board of Missions, Aquilla Riehl contacted them and visited them on a regular schedule for several years. The Colons found a Spanish-speaking Baptist Church near their home and became very active in it, although Doña Silita remained a member of the Coamo Mennonite Church. She had been interested in finding a Mennonite congregation when the family arrived in the city, but the family's involvement with a neighborhood church and the difficulty of traveling to Fox Street raised obstacles to any serious effort.[8]

The request for pastoral visits to the Colon family came from Gladys Widmer, a mission worker in Puerto Rico under Mennonite Board of Missions. She had arrived in Puerto Rico in July 1951 assigned to teach in the school at Pulguillas. She was almost immediately sent to Rabanal to work in a clinic attached to the Good Shepherd Mennonite Church. She served in other places before coming to Coamo in 1954 where she remained until 1957. Gladys Widmer kept in touch with church members who moved to New York City, visiting them herself on furlough, and arranging for the New York pastors, like Aquilla Riehl, to visit.[9]

Angel and Aquilina Torres lived in the Coamo area before they left Puerto Rico to make a new beginning in the city. Angel was a sugar cane worker, and his family lived in a small house owned by the sugar plantation. In addition to his other work, he had to rise early every morning to care for the dairy cattle. He and his wife decided to go to New York City and find work. They left their four children with the grandparents until they had a place to live and could send for them.

Angel and Aquilina Torres like most people in Puerto Rico, were Catholics. Her mother, Librada, had begun worshiping with the Coamo Mennonites and little Ana Hilda Torres went to church and Sunday school with her grandmother. When the children joined their parents in Brooklyn, Ana Hilda carried her Bible in her suitcase and the hymns she had sung in Sunday School in her heart. Her mother disapproved and sent Ana and the other children to a Catholic school. Grandmother came from Coamo to visit the family in the city and shared her faith with them. Aquilina Torres went back to Puerto Rico in the summer of 1956 to visit her mother and other family members. After she came back to Brooklyn, she often took Ana Hilda's Bible to her bedroom and read it. Aquilina had attended her mother's church and felt drawn to its teachings, but she was also resistant. When Gladys Widmer came to visit Ana Hilda and Aquilina, in January 1957, Aquilina Torres opened her heart and accepted Jesus Christ as her Savior while they prayed together at the kitchen table.

Gladys Widmer contacted Nelson Kauffman who was visiting the Mennonite House of Friendship in the Bronx. The following week John Driver, a missionary in Puerto Rico on furlough, came to the Torres apartment. On January 28, 1957 he baptized Aquilina Torres in the presence of family members and neighbors.[10]

Aquilina Torres immediately began inviting friends and neighbors to come together for prayer and Bible study. A short time later, Nelson Kauffman and John Smucker held a Communion service at the home of Doña Silita Colon who was helping the new Christians. John I. Smucker reported in March that "Aquilla Riehl is going over every couple of weeks on a Saturday to teach them. They have meetings about twice a week among themselves." Nelson Kauffman had spoken to Aquilla about the new group in Brooklyn and invited him to include them in his visits.[11]

Gladys Widmer returned to Brooklyn in April, after spending time with her family in Iowa, and arranged for John Smucker to hold meetings in the Torres apartment with Gladys interpreting for him. John Driver also came to help. Julio Camacho committed his life to Jesus Christ at this time.[12]

Samuel E. Miller, a veteran missionary and professor of Spanish at Eastern Mennonite College, had planned to spend the summer of 1957 taking courses at New York University and had arranged for a room at the House of Friendship. Early in June J. D. Graber wrote him:

> I want to say how happy we are that you are there this summer. No one would be better qualified than you to give spiritual direction and teaching to that new church that is coming into being. I hope that this will not interfere at all seriously with your school work, but even if it should interfere somewhat I am certain you would consider it a good investment. I hope you feel free to move right on ahead as the Holy Spirit leads and as your best judgment dictates in making arrangements for the church, baptizing and disciplining members, nurturing the group into a definite church self-consciousness, and planning the whole church program as you deem will best serve for their development... With regard to finding a place to worship, no doubt it would be desirable to have a place apart from somebody's living room, although I think that we can do more by having meetings in a living room than we sometimes think.[13]

While he helped build the church in Brooklyn, Miller completed his Master's degree. He returned to Harrisonburg at the end of the summer. It was arranged for him to come back to Brooklyn once a month and for John Litwiller, a missionary in Argentina studying at Hartford Seminary, to also visit once a month. Gladys Widmer also arranged to be in New York that Fall.[14]

In September Aquilina Torres and the others looked for a hall to rent. They finally found a place they could afford; they rented a former Chinese laundry at 8 Suydam Street for $40 a month. "The people decided to rent the cheaper hall, in fact they could afford no other but we didn't wish the decision on them," Samuel Miller wrote. The laundry building was a dirty place, but they were not discouraged. "They are enthusiastic about cleaning it up and getting ready." Aquilina Torres, and the others set to work with mops and scrubbing brushes. They cleaned and painted the place and were ready to hold services there on September 29, 1957.[15]

The new congregation decided to begin with a week of evangelistic services. Victor Ovando, a Mennonite pastor from Defiance, Ohio, came in October for the special meetings. Ovando had a reputation as an anti-Catholic speaker. Samuel Miller hoped to tone him down, since the Brooklyn group "have not been antagonistic toward the Catholics as so many of their relatives whom they are trying to win are still Catholic." This suggestion was misunderstood and Ovando "came to New York deeply wounded." The week went well enough, although attendance was small. "For some unknown reason [Ovando] refused to give any invitations to make definite decisions to accept Christ, but one person did so in visitation in spite of this." Lucia Lopez, a good friend of Aquilina Torres, had disapproved of her friend's witnessing for Christ but on October 18, 1957 Lucia opened her heart to the Lord in her own home. A week later Aurelio Rodriguez made the same decision in prayer at home. He was baptized in December, but Lucia postponed baptism until her husband could be baptized with her.[16]

Serafin Rivera and his wife, members of the Fox Street Mennonite Church, came from the Bronx to worship with the new Christians in Brooklyn. Serafin preached for them on the first anniversary of Aquilina Torres' baptism. Both Glad Tidings and Fox Street were still English-speaking churches. Angel and Celia Torres, who also lived in the South Bronx, began attending worship in the former laundry. They were both baptized in April 1958.[17]

The new church was making "slow but steady progress" with four baptized members in March 1958. They "are very enthusiastic, witnessing to their neighbors and friends. Bro. Aurelio Rodriguez led those of the group who were able to go in the Sunday afternoon visitation program. He took us into the homes of two of his old friends where we read Scripture, sang, and he gave his testimony. One of these young men came out in the evening. Aurelio has changed his job so as to be able to have Saturday and Sunday free to help. He is very enthusiastic."[18]

Samuel Miller sometimes stayed for the Sunday evening meeting, "riding the bus during the night to get back for my Monday morning classes" at Eastern Mennonite College. Both he and John Litwiller normally left at noon on Sundays after morning worship, leaving the Brooklyn congregation without a Spanish-speaking minister for the Sunday evening service, "the best attended meeting of the week." Gladys Widmer again came to the rescue. She told Rev. Isaias who was working at the Editorial Caribe bookstore about their problem. He suggested a graduate of the Latin American Seminary in Costa Rica who had been preaching in an Independent Baptist church in Brooklyn. His name was Guillermo Torres.

He came to the Brooklyn Mennonite Church the next Sunday and favorably impressed Samuel Miller as "a mild-mannered, early middle-aged man of nice appearance and good diction," with a wife and four young children. He had served an Alliance Church in Puerto Rico and met Lester Hershey, Paul Lauver, John Driver and others there. He refused to take any money for preaching in the evening, even though he was without a job. Miller concluded: "Now, our people have been praying for a resident minister and this truly looks like an answer to prayer—a seemingly sensible, well-prepared, sympathetic man of God at our very doorstep!"[19]

Paul Lauver visited the Brooklyn church in April for the baptism of Celia and Angel Torres. "As to Bro. Guillermo Torres, I do not know how to express in words what his presence has meant to all of us during these meetings. I know that it was a sacrifice for him to attend these meetings... Bro. Torres' presence seemed to add a certain joyfulness to the whole service, and his humbleness and expectancy seemed to draw the message of God from me."[20]

Samuel Miller conducted a service at the home of the Angel Torres family in the Bronx on his next visit as well as the Sunday morning service in Brooklyn. Sunday evening he stayed to hear Guillermo Torres preach. "I was again much impressed with his simple, convincing Gospel message." He had found another member of the Coamo Menonite church and brought him along to the Brooklyn service. They were moving slowly, but they had found a pastor at least.

Summer plans were developing, too. "A girl from the Bronx by the name of Milagros Hernandez plans to come every two weeks to carry on work with the children." She attended the House of Friendship. There was a possibility of Angel Luis Miranda "coming to New York for the summer and helping with the visitation and teaching program." Miller encouraged this. "He could be a great help to Aurelio Rodriguez."[21]

J. D. Graber of Mennonite Board of Missions counseled caution about calling a pastor. "I hope that step by step he can grow together with them and if it is the Lord's will I hope he can become their leader in due course. We must, however, resist the temptation of getting in a hurry and doing something we might need to regret later."[22]

On June 7, 1958 the Brooklyn fellowship organized as La Primera Iglesia Menonita de Brooklyn and had an official business meeting. They chose Lucia Lopez as secretary and Aurelio Rodriguez as treasurer. The next day they had a communion service.

When promised teachers from the House of Friendship failed to materialize, Fernando Cains and Angel Luis Miranda, teachers at the

Mennonite school in Pulguillas, Puerto Rico, taught the vacation Bible school. Samuel Miller wondered whether this traditional Mennonite mission vehicle was imposed on the Brooklyn group. Shouldn't an indigenous church he allowed to make its own decisions at its own pace?[23]

As to calling a pastor, "the people of Brooklyn who very much want a Mennonite witness are very favorable to Bro. Torres... But there is a limit to what one can ask of a man who lives in New York City with a family of four whom we have not been helping financially." How much could the Brooklyn church help? With Gladys Widmer absent and Doña Silita and Don Julio on the periphery of the congregation, support had to come from two women whose husbands were not enthusiastic about Mennonites and a young single man. Could the Mission Board help?[24]

First Mennonite Church of Brooklyn building at 23 Marcus Garvey Boulevard, Brooklyn. 2005 photo. Formerly Sumner Avenue.

J. D. Graber and Samuel Miller met in September with Guillermo Torres. He continued working at his job as a janitor at Brooklyn College and accepted a call from the congregation to serve as a part-time pastor. On November 30, 1958 Guillermo and Maria Torres formally united with the Mennonite Church and that evening he was installed as pastor. John Litwiller, Aurelio Rodriguez, Samuel Miller, and Paul Lauver took part in the installation service. Jose Luis Jimenez led a Gospel quartet.[25]

In March 1959 La Primera Iglesia Menonita de Brooklyn became part of the Puerto Rican Conference of the Mennonite Church.

The church moved in August 1959 to a new location on DeKalb Avenue, a few doors from the Lopez apartment. They had to move again in 1961 because the city planned to demolish buildings along DeKalb Avenue for a new housing project. They found a new location on the third floor of a building at 1050 Broadway. The elevated subway trains passed outside the windows shaking the building and making a loud roar. A club on the lower floor was almost as noisy, especially on Saturday nights, but, with limited funds, they had no other choice.[26]

The Mt. Clinton Mennonite Church in Rockingham County, Virginia, invited Fresh Air children from the Brooklyn congregation. Eleven children between nine and thirteen years old formed the first group in June 1960.

Pastor Torres continued to be employed full-time at Brooklyn College. There was no possibility of moving to half-time. Samuel Miller urged the Mission Board to make it possible for him to work full-time with the church. "I feel Bro. Torres has proved his sincerity and that our Mission would be wise in using him full-time."[27] Gladys Widmer was in Brooklyn in July helping with summer Bible school and added her recommendation.[28]

In September Nelson Kauffman, John Smucker, Samuel Miller, and Gladys Widmer met with the members of First Mennonite of Brooklyn and agreed that Guillermo Torres be full-time pastor with a subsidy from the Mennonite Board of Missions of $400 a month.[29]

Sarah Ann Classen, a student at New York Biblical Seminary, began going to Brooklyn to teach a Sunday school class. She moved into the neighborhood and "helped with young people's activities, music, and summer Bible school."[30]

Blanquita Adorno was baptized in 1960 and the next year Mercedes Gonzalez, Consuelo Inesta and Jeremias Soto became members of the church. Nelson Kauffman reported:

> The present program now has twelve members in the church, and attendance of 40 to 46. The adults attending are increasing. Brother Torres has a list of 100 families in the area of the church, and gives literature personally. He is also beginning to have Bible studies in the homes of interested people. Just recently he baptized a class of two persons, and received one into the church by confession.[31]

By October 1961 the church had fifteen members. "Brother Torres is visiting regularly and their attendance is increasing."[32]

On the last Sunday in December 1962 six persons were baptized "and Mrs. Julio Camacho surprised us all by joining the group. She had taken the lessons years ago." Those baptized in 1962 were Miriam Arroyo, Miguel Alvarado, Jennie Mendez, Frank Mendez, Elba Torres, Ana Hilda Torres, Julio Camacho, and Maria Ester Rodriguez.

The congregation had to move again in 1963. A Fire Department inspector came to the third story loft at 1050 Broadway and warned them to hunt for a new meeting room "as the place is too high up for so many children to get to safety in case of fire." The preacher of a Pentecostal congregation offered the building he was renting, "just a half block from the Myrtle Avenue elevated station." The new location at 12 Jefferson Street served the congregation until 1965.[33]

A women's fellowship was organized in 1961 with meetings every Tuesday evening. "Their first meetings were for prayer: that God might work in the hearts of the husbands, for wisdom and understanding in what to do, and for more members."

Helen Rufenacht from the VS Center on East 19th Street began teaching Sunday school at the Brooklyn church in 1961. "This represents quite a sacrifice on her part for the service is all in Spanish and she needs to travel alone. Also, there is real need to have her help during the week and so she will be facing conflicts in her interests with the program here also." Rhoda Ebersole joined the VS Unit in September 1961 and began helping in the Brooklyn church soon after she arrived. Their work with the Sunday school and youth group was greatly appreciated. They worked primarily with the teenagers in the youth group who all spoke English in school and with their friends. They also assisted in Sunday afternoon services in the Angel Irizarry home on Saratoga Street. In February 1962 "Helen Roofnot and Roada Ebersoul (according to a valentine from Brooklyn) had five of the young people from their Spanish church come to the center from Saturday afternoon until Sunday morning. They worked on a crafts project, went to a Calvary Baptist service Saturday night, and slept here overnight." Both Helen and Rhoda left the city before the end of 1962.[34]

The youth group met on Saturday evenings and studied the Gospel of John in their first year. The group formally organized in January 1963 with Ana Hilda Torres as president, Jerry Soto as vice-president, and Miriam Arroyo as secretary-treasurer.[35]

The church continued to make progress. Elena Adorno, Obed Maldonado and Ray Pacheco joined the church early in 1964. On a five week visit in May 1964, Gladys Widmer reported:

> There is spiritual advance in individual believers, there are new Christians, there are members from our Puerto Rican churches continually arriving. The high point of inspiration comes from the active youth group, many of whom are new believers. Obed Maldonado from Honduras Mennonite Church of Puerto Rico is their Sunday school teacher and also president of the youth group.[36]

They felt a need for help of the kind VSers Helen Rufenacht and Rhoda Ebersole supplied. Gladys Widmer appealed to the Mennonite Board of Missions and they asked Eastern Board whether the VS Center could supply personnel. John H. Kraybill believed two VSers could be found. If the church wanted them to live in Brooklyn, it would have to be a 1-W couple. Paul Burkholder wondered, "Is this truly a request from the local group or from Gladys Widmer?" He suggested direct communication with Pastor Torres. "All of us here have the highest regard for him, and his love for us seems to abound yet more and more—a very dear brother."[37]

Bronx Spanish Mennonite Church

As early as 1963 the idea of a separate Bronx Spanish Mennonite Church came up for discussion. Integrating a Spanish-speaking group into the House of Friendship congregation seemed an unlikely solution. Samuel Miller after one meeting commented, "I feel that an integrated program is more than taking a few culturally assimilated Puerto Rican families into a totally English-oriented church situation."[38]

Angel and Celia Torres, who had been baptized at the Brooklyn church in 1959, were the natural leaders of this emerging group in the Bronx. They expressed a concern for a Mennonite witness lest Pentecostal influences overwhelm the scattered Puerto Rican Mennonites. In October 1964 Guillermo Torres and Gladys Widmer held the first service for the Bronx group in the home of Miguel and Rosa Santiago with ten people present. These Friday evening services in homes continued for about a

Bronx Spanish Mennonite Church met in the Melrose Reformed Church, Elton Avenue and 156th Street, Bronx. 2005 photo.

month. Angel Torres rented the Melrose Reformed Church at the corner of Elton Avenue and East 156th Street for $50 a month. The first service there was held on Friday evening, December 4, 1964.[39]

John H. Kraybill, John Freed, and Paul Burkholder met with Gladys Widmer and John Smucker in October to discuss "a concern to reach a group of Spanish-speaking people, who live in the East Bronx," many of whom "have come from Puerto Rico and were members of the Mennonite Church there." They learned that "some steps are being taken to organize this group into a separate congregation." They had some reservations about the direction this was taking, since "most of the people in this group are within walking distance of the Glad Tidings and Fox Street churches."[40]

The Sunday afternoon meetings at the Reformed Church continued as an outreach of First Mennonite of Brooklyn. Lay members of the Brooklyn church traveled to the Bronx each week to bring the message and lead the worship service. Obed Maldonado, Ray Pacheco, and Aurelio Rodriguez were faithful in this ministry. Samuel Miller and Ross Goldfus also preached for the group on occasion.[41]

Meanwhile in Elkhart, Nelson Kauffman was looking for a pastor for the Bronx Spanish congregation. Samuel Miller proposed Ronald Collins, who was then teaching at Christopher Dock School in Lansdale, Pennsylvania. Collins had gone to Puerto Rico for a voluntary service assignment and stayed on to attend the university there. His wife had worked in a hospital in Puerto Rico. Both were fluent in Spanish. Kauffman suggested an invitation to Ron Collins and his wife to visit the Bronx Spanish congregation and come regularly for a while so as to become acquainted with the people.[42]

Ronald Collins began driving to the Bronx every other Sunday afternoon to preach for the group. The Bronx church had problems with no place of their own for worship and had to fit the schedule of the Reformed Church. They had to postpone a baptismal service because of schedule conflicts.[43]

The same problem of no permanent location for the church came to a happy solution for the Brooklyn congregation. In March 1965 Guillermo Torres invited John Smucker and Gladys Widmer to inspect a synagogue on Sumner Avenue that the congregation was considering buying. The Mennonite Board of Missions approved the purchase of the synagogue and granted them $12,000 for this purpose. In July the Jewish congregation accepted their offer of $21,500 for the former synagogue. The church understood bank financing would be available at a favorable rate. But there were still hurdles to be overcome. The bank turned down their loan application and they had to begin again with another bank. The attorney had already concluded it would take at least four weeks before the Brooklyn church could expect to get the key to the synagogue building. They were only beginning to determine what repairs and remodeling would be necessary.[44]

Negotiations with the bank delayed the transfer of title through much of the year. After Christmas 1965 Samuel Miller brought youth from Mt. Clinton Mennonite Church to help clean up the building. "We built a platform, washed windows, cleaned and varnished benches." People from the Brooklyn congregation plastered the cracks and painted the ceiling. "I think that their money is dwindling and there is still a lot to be done. They probably expected better response on voluntary help."[45] Despite the initial problems and discouragements, the congregation of La Primera Iglesia Evangelica Menonita de Brooklyn had found a more than adequate building for worship and other activities. The church still meets at this location at the time of this writing.

The congregation in the Bronx formally organized as a church on September 21, 1965. Gladys Widmer had played a major role in nurturing this church as she had the First Mennonite Church of Brooklyn. "It seems that Gladys has done a wonderful job in the Bronx, gathering people together, and we have now a nucleus of believers organized into a fellowship church of ten members. Three more are soon ready to be baptized and brought into the fellowship." The original members of the congregation were Angel and Celia Torres, Serafin and Zenaida Rivera from the Fox Street Church, Luis and Sonya Santiago, Blanca Marrero, Paula Rivera, Tomasita Castillo, and Felicita Hernandez.[46]

Addona Nissley, pastor of the Coamo Mennonite Church, was invited to spend a week in New York with the two Puerto Rican Conference churches. He believed that "Gladys works too hard and too fast and finds herself obligated to take a rest. Her heart and soul is in the work and she finds it difficult to work at a pace that allows her to maintain good physical health." The new congregation emerging in the Bronx put too much demand on Guillermo Torres. His health was not good and his duties in Brooklyn precluded his taking this additional pastorate. Both congregations needed to be alert to "the desire of the younger generation for English." The Brooklyn church already had English-language Sunday school classes for the youth.[47]

Gladys Widmer had delayed her return to Puerto Rico by more than a year in order to build up the two congregations in New York City. "I really think it is time that she continue on to Puerto Rico to serve at the Summit Hills church who had invited her over a year ago," Lester Hershey wrote. She had been tireless in working for the two emerging churches, but her insistent prodding and challenging left little initiative for others. "I will not go into all the problems they have had in the Bronx, but Guillermo Torres feels that perhaps the work would not fail if she were to leave at this time. He feels that while she is still loved she should move on to Puerto Rico."[48]

On his stay in New York, Hershey contacted Nicolas Santos and discussed with him his interest in helping out in the Bronx. Santos was then working a night shift in a plastics factory to bring his wife and small children to the city. "The Bronx brethren and Torres were quite impressed with him, and are going to invite him to come to preach as often as he can go." Nelson Kauffman agreed with Hershey that it was best to let "the work develop as indigenously as possible" and see "the Bronx and Brooklyn brethren make decisions." Kauffman added that at the next Home Missions Council Steering Committee meeting he intended to raise the question of "an overall coordinator for the total Mennonite program in New York City." He saw this as "someone who could work as an overseer and serve any congregation that has problems of any kind" and "carry responsibility for assisting new churches to emerge—something comparable of what Gladys did." As Gladys Widmer's leadership role in the city was drawing to a close, Mennonite Board of Missions saw her as a role-model for what was needed in ministry.[49]

Gladys Widmer planned to return to her assignment in Puerto Rico in February 1966. Meanwhile, she continued to help with establishing the new church in the Bronx. They were still renting the Reformed church, which proved far from satisfactory, and they were combing the neighborhood for another location. "On the other hand, I have been impressed with the growth here in the Bronx and the many new people the new believers are contacting." The congregational leaders were not impressed with Nicolas Santos as a possible pastor. "They commented, first of all, on his dark skin; that he knows no English and could get nowhere with the youth; that he knows nothing about New York City life." Clearly any pastor for a Spanish-speaking congregation had to be bilingual, since the youth were growing up in New York speaking English and newcomers were coming from Puerto Rico knowing only Spanish.[50]

The Bronx Spanish congregation learned in January 1966 that they needed to move by the first of February. They had no pastor and Gladys

Widmer offered to stay longer to help them along. She reported an average attendance of 29 over the fall and winter, with five Sunday school classes taught by members of the church. They found a temporary place for worship in a nearby Holiness church, but the regular congregation met in an adjoining room on both Friday and Sunday and "the 'shouting' became quite annoying."[51]

Ron Collins remained a strong candidate for pastor of the Bronx Spanish congregation. He would be able to come every weekend for the immediate future and give leadership to the group.[52] By February 1966 Collins was driving every other weekend from Lansdale to work with the Bronx church.[53] When Samuel Miller visited in April, he found the Bronx congregation proposed to call Ron Collins as their pastor. Miller wrote: "I am frankly enthusiastic about the Spanish church in the Bronx. The fact of whole families attending is very encouraging. The openings into new homes and their eagerness to win others is also encouraging." The Bronx congregation found a more permanent place of meeting at the corner of Third and Brook Avenues. "The place is central, near the people and elevated train stop as well as main bus stops." The Bronx Spanish Mennonite Church met and unanimously called Ron Collins and his family to be their pastor.[54]

"Ron's bilingual ability also proved a real blessing to the other Mennonite churches of New York City," Paul Burkholder recalled. "It had

Ron and Betty Lou Collins family. Ron was pastor of the Bronx Spanish Church.

often been difficult for the English-speaking congregations to communicate effectively with their Spanish-speaking sister congregations. Ron Collins helped bridge this gap."

In the spring of 1967 the Bronx Spanish Mennonite Church had an opportunity to purchase an apartment house on the corner of East 160th Street and Elton Avenue, previously owned by the Salvation Army. The building already contained an adequate chapel and an apartment for the pastor. At last the congregation could really feel at home.[55]

Both congregations faced problems nonetheless. Puerto Ricans were highly mobile people, prepared to move to a new neighborhood that promised a better life for their families. This mobility took a toll on all the New York churches, especially First Mennonite of Brooklyn and Bronx Spanish. In the Bronx congregation, in January 1966, "several of the active members moved to Pennsylvania and to Manhattan so we here are without a treasurer, teachers, superintendent." In the Brooklyn church, Doña Aquilina Torres and Lucy Lopez did much of the visiting, "before moving out of the community, to Herkimer Street."[56]

The task of repairing and renovating their large new church building also proved burdensome to the Brooklyn congregation. Money was a problem. Treasurer Aurelio Rodriguez reported expenditures of $2,500 for repairs and $1,000 for roof repair in 1965. Painting the main auditorium, new windows and doors would cost an estimated $3,000, and classroom divisions, kitchen and nursery equipment had to wait indefinitely until the church could pay for them.[57] By February, repair work had stopped altogether and "there has been great discouragement there." The repairs which still needed to be made required professional skills. Nelson Kauffman contacted the Mennonite Disaster Service in Franconia Conference to help with the repairs. On March 8 the first MDS crew of five went to work on the former synagogue. Two men from Lancaster arrived on March 10 to help with roof repairs.[58] The building renovation remained a daunting problem for the congregation, even with outside help. It took all the time of the pastor and other leaders. "With Bro. Torres' additional task of going to the church building daily very little visiting gets done at Brooklyn." Would the building program prevent the building of the church?[59]

Gladys Widmer stayed in New York a few weeks longer helping with visitation. She finally left for Puerto Rico to work with the Summit Hills Mennonite Church there. Aquilina Torres and her daughter Ana Hilda continued to be active in First Mennonite of Brooklyn and to share with their neighbors the faith in Jesus Christ that Doña Aquilina had welcomed at her kitchen table in 1957. Ten years later two Mennonite congregations had grown from that first time of prayer that Aquilina Torres and Gladys Widmer held at the kitchen table.

NOTES

[1] Justus G. Holsinger, *Serving Rural Puerto Rico: A History of Eight Years of Service by the Mennonite Church*, (Scottdale, Pennsylvania, 1952), 29, 198-208.

[2] C. Wright Mills, Clarence Senior, and Rose Kohn Goldson, *The Puerto Rican Journey: New York's Newest Migrants*, (New York, 1950), 17-18.

[3] Virginia Sanchez Korrol, *From Colonia to Community: The History of Puerto Ricans in New York City 1917-1948*, (Westport, Connecticut, 1983), 22-23.

[4] Mills, Senior and Godson, *Puerto Rican Journey*, 18.

[5] Holsinger, *Serving Rural Puerto Rico*, 15.

[6] Joseph P. Fitzpatrick, *Puerto Rican Americans: The Meaning of Migration to the Mainland*, (Englewood Cliffs, N.J., 1987), 10, 38-39.

[7] Lawrence R. Chenault, *The Puerto Rican Migrant in New York City*, (New York, 1938), 94. Korrol, *From Colonia to Community*, 52-53.

[8] J. D. Graber to Paul Kraybill, Mar. 14, 1957, EMBMC-A.

[9] Holsinger, *Serving Rural Puerto Rico*, 215, 217.

[10] Interview with Aquilina Torres and Anna Hilda Pacheco, Apr. 12, 1991. Edna Beiler, "A Twelve Year Old Missionary," *Words of Cheer*, Aug. 2, 1963. Rhoda Ebersole, "A History of La Primera Iglesia Evangelica Menonita de Brooklyn," June 1, 1965.

[11] J. D. Graber to Paul Kraybill, March 14, 1957. Ebersole, "History," 3.

[12] Ebersole, "History," 2-3.

[13] J. D. Graber to Samuel E. Miller, June 7, 1957, MBM-AMC.

[14] J. D. Graber to Samuel E. Miller, Aug. 28, 1957, MBM-AMC.

[15] Samuel E. Miller to Nelson Kauffman, Sept. 24, 1957, MBM-AMC. Interview, Aquilina Torres. Ebersole, "History," 2.

[16] Samuel E. Miller to Nelson Kauffman, Oct. 25, 1957, MBM-AMC. Ebersole, "History," 3. Rafael Falcon, *The Hispanic Mennonite Church in North American 1932-1982*, (Scottdale, Pa., 1986), 89-90, 103.

[17] Ebersole, "History," 3-4.

[18] Samuel E. Miller to J. D. Graber, Mar. 20, 1958, MBM-AMC.

[19] Samuel E. Miller to J. D. Graber, Mar. 2, 1958, MBM-AMC.

[20] Paul Lauver to J. D. Graber, Apr. 22, 1958, MBM-AMC.

[21] Samuel Miller to J. D. Graber, May 6, 1958, MBM-AMC.

[22] J. D. Graber to Samuel E. Miller, May 27, 1958, MBM-AMC.

[23] Samuel E. Miller to J. D. Graber, July 28, 1958, MBM-AMC.

[24] Samuel E. Miller to J. D. Graber, June 16, 1958, July 28, 1958, MBM-AMC.

[25] Ebersole, "History," 4. J. D. Graber to Luci Lopez, Jan. 8, 1959. J. D. Graber to Paul Lauver, Oct. 21, 1958, MBM-AMC.

[26] Ebersole, "History," 5. Nelson E. Kauffman to Ernest Bennett, Oct. 9, 1961, MBM-AMC.

[27] Samuel E. Miller to J. D. Graber, May 2, 1960, MBM-AMC.

[28] Gladys Widmer to J. D. Graber, Aug. 3, 1960, MBM-AMC.

[29] Nelson E. Kauffman to Ernest Bennett, Sept. 12, 1960, MBM-AMC.

[30] Nelson Kauffman to Gladys Widmer, Nov. 30, 1960. Ebersole, "History," 6.

[31] Guillermo Torres, "La Primera Iglesia Evangelica Menonita de Brooklyn—Datos Historicos," 4. Nelson Kauffman to Ernest Bennett, Feb. 9, 1961, MBM-AMC.

[32] Nelson Kauffman to Ernest Bennett, Oct. 9, 1961, MBM-AMC.

[33] Samuel E. Miller to Nelson E. Kauffman, Jan. 8 1963, MBM-AMC. Ebersole, "History," 6.

[34] David W. Shenk to Donald Sensenig, Aug. 31, 1961. Mennonite Voluntary Service Center News Notes, Jan. 29, Feb. 11, 1962. Donald Sensenig to Paul Landis, Mar. 15, 1962, EMBMC-A. Ebersole, "History," 6.

[35] Ebersole, "History," 7. Samuel E. Miller to Nelson E. Kauffman, Jan. 8, 1963, MBM-AMC.

[36] Gladys Widmer, "Report of New York Visit, May 1 to June 9, 1964," MBM-AMC. Torres, "Datos Historicos," 4.

[37] Gladys Widmer to John Lehman, May 18, 1964. Gladys Widmer, "Report of New York Visit, May 1, to June 9, 1964." Paul Landis to Ray Horst, July 13, 1964, MBM-AMC. John H. Kraybill to Paul Landis, July 9, 1964. Paul Burkholder to Paul Landis, July 1, 1964, EMM.

[38] Samuel E. Miller to Nelson E. Kauffman, May 9, 1963, MBM-AMC.

[39] Falcon, *Hispanic Mennonite Church*, 106.

[40] John H. Kraybill to H. Howard Witmer, Nov. 11, 1964, EMM.

[41] Falcon, *Hispanic Mennonite Church*, 106.

[42] Nelson E. Kauffman to Guillermo Torres and John Smucker, Jan. 4, 1965, MBM-AMC.

[43] Gladys Widmer to Nelson Kauffman, Mar. 15, 1965, MBM-AMC.

[44] John I. Smucker to Nelson E. Kauffman, Mar. 19, 1965. Mennonite Board of Missions and Charities, Resolution, June 2, 1965. Ernest Bennett to Executive Committee, July 12, 1965. Nelson E. Kauffman, memorandum, Visit to Brooklyn, July 2, 1965. John I. Smucker to Shepherd Kole, July 21, 1965. John I. Smucker to Ernest Bennett, Aug. 1, 1965, MBM-AMC.

[45] Samuel Miller to Nelson Kauffman, Apr. 6, 1966, MBM-AMC.

[46] Lester T. Hershey to J. D. Graber, Dec. 1, 1965, MBM-AMC. Falcon, *Hispanic Mennonite Church*, 106.

[47] Addona Nissley to Nelson Kauffman, Aug. 5, 1965, MBM-AMC.

[48] Lester T. Hershey to J. D. Graber, Dec. 1, 1965, MBM-AMC.

[49] Lester T. Hershey to Nelson Kauffman, Dec. 1, 1965. Nelson Kauffman to Lester T. Hershey, Dec. 15, 1965, MBM-AMC.

[50] Gladys Widmer to Nelson Kauffman, Dec. 29, 1965, MBM-AMC.

[51] Gladys Widmer to Nelson E. Kauffman, Jan. 12, 1966, MBM-AMC.

[52] Dorsa J. Mishler to Nelson Kauffman, Jan. 12, 1966. Nelson Kauffman to Gladys Widmer, Jan. 17, 1966, MBM-AMC.

[53] Nelson Kauffman to Ronald Collins, Mar. 12, 1966, MBM-AMC.

[54] Samuel Miller to Nelson Kauffman, Apr. 6, 1966. Nelson Kauffman to Samuel Miller, Apr. 18, 1966, MBM-AMC.

[55] Paul Burkholder, "A History of the New York Mennonite Churches," *250 Years of Mellinger District 1717-1967* (Lancaster, Pa., 1967), F-7.

[56] Gladys Widmer to David Helmuth, Feb. 20. 1966. Samuel Miller to Nelson Kauffman, Apr. 6, 1966, MBM-AMC.

[57] Gladys Widmer to Nelson Kauffman, Jan. 12, 1966.

[58] Gladys Widmer to David Helmuth, Feb. 20, 1966. Ronald Collins to Nelson Kauffman, Mar. 10, 1966, MBM-AMC.

[59] Samuel Miller to Nelson Kauffman, Apr. 6, 1966.

CHAPTER EIGHT

A Dream Deferred

1964–1974

THE KILLING OF a fifteen-year-old boy by a New York City police lieutenant brought all the smoldering problems to a sudden flash of flame. On July 16, 1964, hundreds of the slain youth's classmates held a peaceful protest march. Two nights later there was a rally to demand the lieutenant's arrest and another march to the police station. As the police set up barricades to contain the marchers, pushing and scuffling began, the police arrested some demonstrators and others started throwing rocks and bottles at the policemen. The riot soon spread.[1]

Don and Elvira Schierling were working that summer with the East Harlem Protestant Parish as an internship from Mennonite Biblical Seminary. "The shooting of James Powell, one of many such incidents, forced the keg to blow. We were never actually involved although Pete Edigers and we drove through an area on West 125th Street which had just rioted a half hour earlier, but we could easily feel the empathy of all. They didn't agree with the few who looted, but they understood why."

Don Schierling was also beginning to understand why pent-up anger could lead some people to take to the streets. "I have no idea what it means to be enslaved for 400 years, to be taught, in various means, that I'm not human, or that I'm really not wanted but only tolerated or even hated by 'Christians.'" His summer schedule was much like that of other young Mennonites involved in urban mission. He directed the camping program, taught in the vacation church school, worked with junior and senior high school groups, and coached a softball team. He heard Martin Luther King Jr. preach and attended a James Baldwin play, "Blues for Mister Charlie." He visited families of the young people in the church programs. "On many occasions an intended five-minute call ended in a long discussion on the race problem and the failure of the church to meet the challenge. The response of many to my statement and belief that in Christ all are free was quite varied. Some hadn't witnessed or experienced the love of Christ which supposedly fills the lives of those who accept Him."[2]

The editor of *The East Harlem Protestant Parish Newsletter* commented on "The Long Hot Summer" of 1964. He spoke of "the genuine hopes inspired by the passage of the Civil Rights Bill" early in the summer and the dashing of those hopes in September when "Parents and Taxpayers, a white group, staged a two-day boycott in protest against the Board of Education's plan for school integration." The mood had changed. "Police brutality met overt anger rather than the customary apathy this summer." The editor observed "a greater sense of self-awareness in our neighborhood" which showed itself "sometimes in overt hostility, sometimes in unity and reconciliation."[3]

The Civil Rights Movement caught the imagination of many New Yorkers. A few picketed Woolworth and Kresge stores in support of lunch counter sit-ins and a handful went South to help with voter registration. The March on Washington in 1963 involved a larger number of city people, black and white. For the most part, New Yorkers saw the Civil Rights demonstrations as something remote and distant, something happening to other people. James Farmer, who headed the Congress of Racial Equality (CORE), put it succinctly: "The old way won us the right to eat hamburgers at lunch counters and is winning us the right to vote, but has not basically affected the lot of the average Negro."[4]

The Movement moved North and by 1964 began to grapple with issues that New Yorkers understood and faced every day. In November 1963 a wave of rent strikes began, with tenants refusing to pay rent until apartments received needed repairs and services. Rent strikers often found a sympathetic hearing in the courts where judges denounced slumlords. The strikes spread from Brooklyn to Harlem.[5] While the rent strikes were still making headlines, many Civil Rights groups began to focus on segregation in the New York City public schools. A city-wide boycott in February 1964 took nearly half a million students out of the classrooms for one day and a second boycott in March was almost as successful. The Rev. Milton Galamison of Brooklyn was the outspoken leader of the Committee for Integrated Schools. The House of Friendship Mennonite Church discussed the boycott and decided to let members be free to participate.[6]

Not all Mennonites empathized with black protest movements; some saw sit-ins and demonstrations as invitations to violence. A meeting at Glad Tidings in 1965 on race relations brought out concerns about marches and protests at City Hall. There were sometimes deeper causes of misunderstanding. As John Smucker noted in 1968:

> It is clear from the present Negro revolution that Mennonites are having a hard time understanding the blacks. Inasmuch as white Mennonites have been acculturated into American society, they find they are guilty of the same racism as any other whites.[7]

All the Mennonite and Brethren in Christ churches in the city were places where men and women of different racial and ethnic backgrounds joined together in worship and congregational life was fully integrated. It was tempting to see these churches as examples to the rest of the city. But, as older neighborhoods deteriorated, they were fast becoming commuter churches. One member at Seventh Avenue commented in 1965: "I don't know if the fact that the majority of the congregation lives away from the church and the community has any bearing on what the members feel about the church, but it sure tells what they feel about the community!" While they were aware their pastor John Kraybill participated in meetings of Harlem social action groups, members responding to a questionnaire generally identified community service and social action as areas "where a great deal more could be done."[8]

The New York World's Fair Witness

The spring of 1964 brought the opening day of the New York World's Fair and with it a protest demonstration by Civil Rights leaders. The civil rights revolution had brought down many racial barriers, but had little effect on economic barriers. Although most of the poor people in New York City and in the nation were not black, racial prejudice and poverty reinforced each other.[9] Protest took a new direction as the New York World's Fair prepared for its opening day. The contrast between the glittering promise of the world of tomorrow and the reality of exclusion of blacks and Hispanics from many union jobs connected with the World's Fair led Civil Rights activists to choose it for a major demonstration. The more militant groups proposed a massive "stall-in" to tie up traffic on all major highways and bridges leading to the Fair. A more traditional demonstration and the arrest of leaders made their point and the headlines.[10] Protest and behind-the-scenes negotiation resulted in making the World's Fair a self-proclaimed "showcase for civil rights, where Negroes and whites work together in virtually every phase of the operation."[11]

The World's Fair seemed a natural place for Christian witness. Early in 1963 John H. Kraybill and John I. Smucker contacted Fair officials about a Mennonite exhibit in the Protestant and Orthodox Center. Church leaders discussed their proposal at the MCC meeting in Chicago in May 1963 and decided against implementing it. A year later, with crowds pouring through the Fair gates at Flushing Meadow, John Smucker again pressed for opening a booth in the Protestant and Orthodox Center.[12]

In response to his appeal, H. Ernest Bennett of Mennonite Board of Missions and Walter Gering, moderator of the General Conference Mennonite Church, came from Elkhart to meet with city pastors. John H. Kraybill contrasted a Lancaster County information center and one at the World's Fair, where the witness would be separated from Mennonite culture "and the emphasis can be on the content of the message." Walter Gering suggested a peace emphasis. Ernest Bennett proposed "peace through Christian service." Paul Burkholder advised "Start with the Cross—and lead into every facet of life and service." Other questions brought out the advantage of certain locations, their comparative cost, the distribution of literature, and staffing problems. With local volunteers to staff the booth and the New York City pastors as an advisory council, they agreed to rent space in the Pavilion.[13]

Kenneth Hiebert, a Bethel College alumnus and professor of graphics at Carnegie Institute in Pittsburgh, agreed to design the panels for the exhibit. His design had as its theme "Jesus Christ is the Light of the World." He interpreted the texts "in a unique and modern way." Many visitors appreciated this approach. Some Mennonite and Brethren in Christ visitors—and most visitors came from the supporting churches—found it difficult to understand. Bishop Henry Ginder recognized Hiebert's "tremendous imagination" and willingness "to do something different from the other booths," but he wondered if the exhibit was not "so abstract that it is not sufficiently captivating to stop people for discussion."[14]

The volunteers staffing the exhibit and engaging visitors in discussion were crucial to its use in evangelism. Because they started planning so late, the Mennonite exhibit was only open in September and October 1964. For the second year of the World's Fair, the New York committee requested voluntary service personnel who would work at the Fair through the whole summer.[15] They would prefer students at Mennonite colleges, but recognized the difficulty of matching college schedules with the Fair reopening in April and continuing through October.[16]

The World's Fair VS Unit represented both Mennonite Church and General Conference constituencies. Edith Penner of Winnipeg, Manitoba, was a student at Canadian Mennonite Bible College. She had worked the previous summer on a VS assignment as receptionist at the MCC Peace Booth at the Canadian National Exhibition in Toronto. Eastern Mennonite College students James and Geraldine Rush came from Harrisonburg, Virginia. Titus Lehman, a psychiatric nurse in Lancaster, Pennsylvania, stayed only during the spring. Phyllis Lehman came from Johnstown, Pennsylvania. Mr. and Mrs. Newton S. Weber of West Liberty, Ohio, came in August.[17]

Some changes were made in the exhibit panels. The fourth panel was originally "almost solid black with a number of abstract symbols," but a panel of photographs of people replaced it, suggesting "that this message of light is directed toward people in need." The first panel presented the theme verse in an "eye-catching and striking way" since "the verse now covers the whole panel instead of a small portion at the bottom." Ken Hiebert came to the Bronx to orient the VSers so that they would understand the artist's intentions. Apparently some volunteers in 1964 "had no appreciation for the art itself."

Kenneth Seitz, VS director for Mennonite Board of Missions, attended the opening day ceremonies for the second year of the Fair on April 21, 1965 and was impressed with the opportunities the Fair provided for Christian witness. "After a few hours of attending the display myself, it seemed like this was the type of thing where we as a church ought to be involved." The Inter-Mennonite VS Unit at the New York World's Fair opened other new vistas for cooperation. Seitz initiated further discussions in Elkhart about voluntary service opportunities dealing with urban problems.[18]

Involvement in the Community

The New York City churches were in a time of transition. "The general character of our work is changing from Spanish to Negro," Home Missions director H. Howard Witmer noted. "There is increasing involvement in the community with various new wholesome and creative approaches." He believed that these "involvements in the community are not clear in their goals."[19]

By the spring of 1964 organizing the poor to deal with social problems was a major feature of the agenda of civil rights organizations like CORE. They hoped to work for "a much more cohesive and articulate black community" through building grass-roots organizations "around the expressed needs of slum dwellers." They began to talk about "the everyday needs of our people," decent housing, decent jobs at decent pay, and better schools. As James Farmer put it, "The real issue for them is getting the heel of oppression off their neck."[20]

President Lyndon Johnson submitted his specific recommendations for a War on Poverty to Congress in March 1964 and the Senate and the House of Representatives debated the bill that became the Economic Opportunity Act of 1964 over the next several months. The antipoverty bill faced a good deal of opposition in Congress, but Johnson made it the centerpiece of his program in an election year. In August, Congress gave the administration almost everything it asked. The act provided money for job training and community projects. Many of the new programs were intended to give the young more opportunities for education and training. Head Start was a program for preschoolers and Upward Bound offered bright high school students a chance at college. The Neighborhood Youth Corps provided inner city children with work experience and income. The Job Corps gave other young people intensive training and education. "Community Action and later the Model Cities program set up neighborhood health centers, provided legal services for the poor, and attempted to involve the poor in program development and leadership under the mandate to seek their 'maximum feasible participation.'"[21] This meant that poor people would make decisions about their own lives and their own neighborhoods. They would not simply be the recipients of programs designed for them by experts. In practice, with so many dollars and so many jobs involved, poverty programs became a political football, but representatives of disadvantaged groups still had to be heard. Neighborhood associations and churches came to the fore.

The churches did not do all they could in reaching out to a hurting world. Isaac Kanode and Wilmer Heisey of the Brethren in Christ Board for Missions recognized this in a statement on Brooklyn needs in 1969. "The rush of events in the past few years has caught the Church in a position where it appears that government and a secular society have greater concern and more relevance of perspective than those who claim allegiance to Christ and His message of hope for the world."[22]

Hopeful Signs

There were signs of hope throughout the city. Richard Pannell came to New York in 1961 to do his 1-W alternative service at New York University Hospital. He had grown up in the Coatesville Mennonite Church in Chester County, Pennsylvania, and attended Eastern Mennonite College, but like some other young Mennonite men, 1-W service in the city gave him an opportunity to kick off the traces. As a black man in an overwhelmingly white church, Dick Pannell had some unfinished business. For three years he fought God at every turn. He felt at that time, he said later, that God was "out to get blacks rather than help them." He turned his back on God, the Church, and everything other people had told him. He eventually realized that his life had become an empty, meaningless existence. "The answer came March 28, 1964, with Dick Pannell's Damascus Road being a small room in a New York City tenement house." With his reborn faith, Dick Pannell came to Seventh Avenue Mennonite Church and looked for ways to help other troubled young adults. He belonged to "a new, young generation of blacks who have love and respect for themselves, their heritage, for other human beings, and for God."[23]

Darrell Fast, a student at Mennonite Biblical Seminary in Elkhart, Indiana, spent the summer of 1965 as an intern with the East Harlem Protestant Parish. In his diary Fast asked:

> Why am I in East Harlem? I often wonder, yet I'm quite sure I know I did not want to sleep thru a revolution like Rip Van Winkle did. No Christian could afford to sleep through this revolution. Here are the poor; the gospel is for them. Here are the oppressed; the Christian is to set them free. Here are the captive and the blind; to them must come the proclamation of release and recovering of sight. (Luke 4:18f)[24]

In close contact with veteran parish ministers, he wrestled with ideas that challenged his Mennonite understanding of political action.

> The issue that we discussed tonight was that of politics and the clergy's relationship to this world. Two things that Norm Eddy said were helpful to me. The one (which I had realized before) is that politics is structured so that one exchanges votes for favors. This is not immoral, for that is the way democracy works. The other point which he made was the distinction between pressure and power politics. And most important of all, everyone is involved in a democratic society in politics, either negatively or positively. How do I, a Mennonite, assimilate this?[25]

He was learning all that summer, just as other young men and women in Voluntary Service learned from the city. On his last night in East Harlem, he wrote:

> I have to take a new look at my humanity, remind myself of what it means to be honest, to tell others when you feel mistrust or enmity or fear (?) or prejudice.[26]

Carl and Lois Good, and daughter Trudy.

Carl and Lois Good came to the city in 1964 for his 1-w service after graduation from Eastern Mennonite College. The Goods lived at the East 19th Street VS Center as unit leaders.

They soon became active at Fox Street Mennonite Church. In 1964 Lois Good spent time with children at the church on afternoons after school. The church had just moved to a new location, a half block from the original site, at the corner of Fox and Home Streets. The new building at 911 Home Street had been converted from a store to a church by another group and included an auditorium seating 125, classrooms, and a full basement. A Lutheran Church donated a pulpit, and the Northeast Bronx Baptist Church gave benches. John Silva and David Cotto painted the benches. Other volunteers painted the interior and laid carpet. Eddie Rivera painted a sign over the front door.[27]

Fox Street shared many problems with the other city churches. In 1965, as part of a self-study, Dorothy Freed, Lois Good and Carl Good sat together to consider these problems. Carl reported that, "A large percentage of the responsible church members and leaders commute to church from outside the geographical parish of Fox Street Church. These persons find it very difficult to relate to Fox Street community folks." Hispanic members had moved away to better neighborhoods in the Bronx and Queens. John Freed, the pastor, and others had discouraged the formation of "a Mennonite ghetto" with church members and VSers living in adjoining apartments "which would alienate the church from the community." The Fox Street neighborhood was shifting from Puerto Rican to black, and the church had moved "from a building at the predominantly Spanish end of the block to a building at the predominantly Negro end of the block." The congregation was still largely Spanish, but "those who have begun attending recently are Negro," so the church had "to adjust to the change and accommodate the new people."[28]

Evelyn (Groff) Hertzler taught in a New York City public school. "I spent half the day disciplining and the other half doing a little teaching." But she encouraged education majors at Eastern Mennonite College to apply for jobs in the city school system, and recruited short-term volunteers to help with vacation Bible school at Glad Tidings. Don and Evelyn Hertzler and their infant son lived next door to Glad Tidings and helped with the church in many ways. "That was the time of the African Revival Movement," Don Hertzler recalled, "a precious time of learning to know the Lord better." Paul and Miriam Burkholder and Glenn Zeager "helped us as young kids to learn to know more about Jesus, showing us to serve God where we are."[29]

Leon Stauffer, a young man from Lancaster County, confided to his diary in September 1964 that, "The city is becoming my home. The subway is becoming my friend." He found many signs of hope around New York.

Leon Stauffer.

Leon joined the VS unit at East 19th Street that summer. His assignment was to become familiar with existing youth programs across the metropolitan area, especially those working with young addicts and gang members. He began observing David Wilkerson's Teen Challenge Center as a staff member.[30]

Leon worked at the Teen Challenge Center on Mondays and Thursdays. He noticed "scars from needles and knife wounds on several fellows" on his first day. As his experience of the Center grew, he was sure it was "a work of the Lord, but it seems to border on brainwashing." He also had more positive reactions, noting in his diary in October that he was "more able to worship with them" now than at first. He learned that it took "six months to a year for an addict's body to return to normal after he stops."

Thursday evenings he worked with Bill Crawford and John Stanley at Youth Development, Inc. in Spanish Harlem. This was a follow-up program for boys who made decisions for Christ at a summer camp. He learned here how important the camping program could be. The leaders were feeling their way. They hoped to improve their "very meager" facilities with vocational training and a more disciplined program. Jim Vaus began this outreach ministry in 1949 centered on Camp Youth Development in Glen Spey, New Jersey.

Leon's reading that summer included Elizabeth O'Connor's *Call to Commitment*, the story of the Church of the Savior in Washington, D.C. and its new forms of urban ministry. It was a book many young Mennonites read in 1964.

Leon met Charles Rife, a VSer from Chambersburg, Pennsylvania, who ran the youth center at Fellowship Chapel in the Bronx. Rife had developed a small wood-working shop, physical fitness room and kitchenette for teenagers in the basement of the Brethren in Christ mission building. Stauffer also visited the crafts club program at the Church of the Ascension on East 106th Street, part of the East Harlem Protestant Parish. As he learned more about the Parish he commented favorably on their craft projects and their use of "simple, well-planned drama and acting to reinforce children's lessons," all made possible by much detailed planning and a large staff.

In October he talked with Paul Burkholder about "plans for a pilot project at Glad Tidings," but "neither one of us, at this point, feel definite direction in the youth project." Several Glad Tidings members saw possibilities for using the store at 342 Brook Avenue "for a sandwich or coffee shop, a room with facilities for studying and also recreation."

As weeks and months passed, Leon Stauffer wrote in his journal that "The task seems larger each day and the job greater." He was learning. He visited the Upper Park Avenue Baptist Church in Harlem, where the program included areas of social and political action, voter registration, elections, and race relations. He concluded that "social action is OK, if it can be Christ centered." After the congregation moved away, the Rev. Donald De Young, "a man of God," had done a remarkable job in rebuilding the Elmendorf Reformed Church on East 121st Street with a Spanish service, youth program, remedial reading and study hall programs with a full-time worker. "De Young gave me much courage." In October he met with Young Life workers, including Fred Alderfer, a Mennonite from Scottdale, Pennsylvania, who had been in VS in Denver, Colorado. Fred was a youth worker at St. Chrysostom's Chapel in the Hell's Kitchen section of Manhattan and directed a Young Life Club at the church.

Leon visited the Young Life Club and joined Fred Alderfer and others from Young Life and Youth Development in a "Life Lift" retreat in December. He also visited Wiltwyck School, "famous for its family therapy program," where Lucy Vance worked as personnel director. He learned about its program for boys between eight and ten years old committed by the courts as juvenile offenders.[31]

Glad Tidings began "a homework and recreational center in the church" in October. The only recreation provided was ping-pong "but there has been good interest shown in the homework center with as high as ten children present on one evening." Evelyn Hertzler and other adults from the congregation helped as volunteer tutors and staffed the center on Tuesday and Thursday evenings. "Suffice to say that the need for help in the area of reading especially is enormous."[32]

The Glad Tidings Sandwich Shop

Glad Tidings faced a problem common to urban Mennonite churches. The South Bronx was changing rapidly in the 1960s. Newton Beiler, a VSer at Glad Tidings, commented:

> Few people from the community attended the church and the members knew very little about the community. The majority of the members of the church were white and about one-half of them lived

> in the community but commuted to jobs outside of the community. About the only contact the church had with the community was kids attending summer Bible school and being an agent for the Fresh Air Fund.[33]

Paul and Miriam Burkholder owned the building next door to the church at 342 Brook Avenue with a store on the first floor and apartments above. The man who rented the store decided to give up his lease, and the possibility of a new kind of ministry opened for Glad Tidings. At the same time Esther Petersheim learned that she would need to get more schooling to hold her hospital job. A new kind of ministry was opening for her, too.[34]

On Election Day 1964, Leon Stauffer joined a group from Glad Tidings composed of Robert and Rose Rodriguez, Esther Petersheim, Esther Rivera, Don and Evelyn Hertzler, and Paul Burkholder for a trip to the Church of Our Savior in Washington, D.C. They met Carl and Lois Frey who had gone down the day before. Elizabeth O'Connor and Mrs. Gordon Cosby, the pastor's wife, showed them through the building. "We shared with them how we are thinking the Lord may be calling us to a new type of ministry to youth by utilizing a store next door to our church for a sandwich shop or luncheonette, homework facilities, and additional recreation areas. This gave them somewhere to start sharing with us what God has called them into."

Glad Tidings Community Center, 342 Brook Avenue, where the Sandwich Shop was located, right, and Glad Tidings Mennonite Church, left.

Esther Petersheim, serving a customer inside the Sandwich Shop.

They did not learn a great deal more about the Church of Our Savior and its Potter's House coffee house ministry than they had already read in *Call to Commitment*. "There was so much shared as we traveled, that we feel inadequate to put it on paper." They agreed on several points: "We will not be able to enter any kind of project unless we are committed first of all in loving, absolute obedience to Christ and secondly to his expression of

Robert and Rose Rodriguez family, members at Glad Tidings. Rose worked in the Sandwich Shop.

the church at Glad Tidings" and to each other as well. "We need to be sure of our aims and goals in any project prior to beginning." No less important, "We need to be willing to let the project drop or die, if it is no longer useful."[35]

Don and Evelyn Hertzler, and son Barry.

The Washington trip provided a catalyst for another development at Glad Tidings. Could the spirit of the East African Revival be institutionalized? Paul Burkholder shared the disciplines used by the Church of Our Savior with the Glad Tidings congregation.

> Our members after much discussion remained divided in feelings. Some feel we do need to have commitments first of all to Jesus Christ and also to each other. A fellowship and sharing of every day experiences and walk with Jesus Christ thus being an asset to each other. Some continued to feel our commitments must only be to Jesus Christ and not shared with the brethren.[36]

Glad Tidings members began talking about the sandwich and grocery store next to the church as "a point of witness for our congregation" in July 1964. Paul and Miriam Burkholder were concerned because "the proprietor of the store has been selling cigarettes and alcoholic beverages" and asked the advice of the congregation. At a members' meeting in September ideas became more focused and the church asked Paul Burkholder to investigate whether the city would require structural changes before the store could be used as a meeting place. After the trip to the Church of Our Savior, the congregation decided on November 11 "to move ahead and begin by opening a sandwich shop" and later to review "the possibilities of a coffee shop, study and recreation hall." Donald Hertzler, Rose Rodriguez, Esther Rivera and Esther Petersheim would begin preparations to open for business on December 1. They agreed the sandwich shop would be open from 7:30 in the morning until about 5:30 in the evening. Esther Petersheim would be the store manager and Rose Rodriguez would help her over the busy noon hour. On November 20 they settled with the former owner for the equipment, refrigerator, and cash register he had used. The Glad Tidings Sandwich Shop was nearly ready to open.[37]

They were unable to open for business on December 1, but met with the former proprietor for a final settlement. They changed the locks "and the place is now 'Glad Tidings Mennonite Church Sandwich Shop.'" Esther Petersheim wrote in the store diary, "Curiously we inspected our long-awaited store—the mice ran and the dirt looked at us." On December 3, "Accompanied by Tide, Mr. Clean, Ajax, Brillo pads, a pail, and plenty of old rags, I unlocked the store." She spent all day cleaning the soda refrigerator. Paul Burkholder knocked down unneeded shelves. "Joyce Edwards dropped in and cleaned the ice cream cabinet. After school Glenn Burkholder and Allan Rodriguez helped." Rose Rodriguez, Carl Frey, and Gloria Arroyo also pitched in. Gloria painted the wood pieces and brackets in the soda refrigerator. "I see the dawning of a new place," Esther wrote. "We listened to Gert Behenna's testimony at our evening fellowship, 'Lord, I want this place for you, what isn't from you keep us from having.'"[38]

After a week of cleaning, the sandwich shop opened on December 9, 1964. They only had thirty customers the first day. "The outstanding factor of our opening month was just getting to know the kids." Alexander Berger Junior High School was across the street and crowds of students began coming at lunchtime. "We were introduced to a number of 'hooky players' who found the shop warm from the outside cold December winds and a place to dodge Mike, the cop."[39]

The sandwich shop did not show a profit or meet expenses in the beginning, even with volunteer help. But the sandwich shop was becoming a recreation center for neighborhood youth. Jesus Constantin kept it open Saturday nights until eight o'clock. Leon Stauffer had charge of the pool room with Newton Beiler and Jay Lefever helping him. Pool was available two nights a week.[40]

Leon Stauffer wrote in June 1965, "Have you ever thought of using a pool table for mission work? The Mennonite Church in New York City has and is presently using it as a means of contact for the unreachable street kids." In the winter months pool attracted over a hundred youth to the sandwich shop. As warmer weather set in, the school playground became the point of contact. "Since the pool table is used less frequently in the summer, the need for outdoor activity and street work has to increase. Corner stores, doorways, playgrounds, and parks all offer good opportunities for 'shooting the breeze' with street kids who have nothing else to do." Leon Stauffer, Elmer Lapp, Newton Beiler, and Jay Lefever played handball, stickball, or shot baskets with neighborhood kids on the playground. "Sometimes it is too warm to do anything but to find a shady spot and sit and talk."[41]

The sandwich shop, the pool table, and the outdoor games brought almost all the neighborhood teenagers into casual contact with Glad Tidings, but about twenty black teenagers and a few Hispanics formed a core group who regularly hung out with their friends at Glad Tidings. Glenn Davis, Jr., called "Happy" because of "his high spirits and his constant smile," was one of the regulars. Happy spent much of Easter vacation talking with Esther in the sandwich shop.

> While doing a few odd clean-up jobs around the store, Happy initiated a conversation regarding membership at Glad Tidings Mennonite Church. Esther in her usual kind and tactful way tried to show Happy the importance of a relationship with Jesus Christ over and above church membership... The next day as I was momentarily tending the store counter, Happy, out of a clear blue sky said, "You know, Leon, I've been thinking about it, and I think I want to become a Christian." What did Happy mean? Was he aware of what he had said? What is the next step? Time will tell.[42]

The young VSers who made hero sandwiches and got to know the teenagers and the pre-teens on the playground or the street were part of a team. "The greatest thrill has been the team support and effort in this project." The youth work team was made up of eight members of Glad Tidings. They met in Don and Evelyn Hertzler's apartment on Brook Avenue and shared ideas from Elizabeth O'Connor's *Call to Commitment* and problems that emerged on the street. Esther Petersheim was not directly related to the youth work team, but "is probably more involved in the youth work than any of us." Paul Burkholder also had a major role in follow-up with the families.

Every story was different. Newton Beiler began working full time in the sandwich shop and youth team in June. On his first day Bobby, who had never given him any trouble before, was "using his mouth at me and a few of the smaller kids" and stole a few penny candies. He was pushing Newton to see how far he could go. Things escalated over the next few days until Bobby challenged Newton to a fight, which he refused. Bobby grabbed the sandwich slicing knife. He forgot it was chained to the wall and it gave his hand a deep gash. Newton offered to take him to the hospital for stitches, but Bobby refused. He came back to the store threatening Newton and telling Paul and Esther that he had cut him. Jerry Shenk talked with Bobby "and offered to take him to the hospital and to pay for it, but Bobby said no because it might make him cry and he didn't want anyone to see him cry." That night Bobby came back with his brother who offered to fight Newton, but he refused. A few days later Bobby came back and said "Let's forget about this whole thing."[43]

The Glad Tidings Rec Center had three purposes, according to a list of rules drafted by Elmer Lapp: "To present members with the claims of Christ always needs to be our primary aim; To seek to relate the members to the local church if they are not already attending another church; To keep the members out of trouble by getting them off the street into a good environment."[44]

Elmer Lapp arrived in the city on March 1, 1965 and moved into the 1-W apartment at Glad Tidings where five other young Mennonite men were living. He immediately became part of the team. Esther Petersheim recalled him as "a bit of a loner," but he "got out into the homes of city people like no one else" and "met up with more hard core kids than the rest of us did." Elmer developed a basketball team and ran Bible studies. He stayed on after his 1-W service term working with the Fresh Air program, remedial reading and youth programs at Glad Tidings for several years. He died of AIDS in Lancaster, Pennsylvania, in 1989. "Elmer was away from the Lord a number of years, but made a glorious comeback and a tremendous testimony."[45]

Jay Lefever described one of his typical days at the Sandwich Shop. "I help out over the rush hour in the store but my day really begins at 3:00 p.m., when the kids get out of school. From 3 to 5 or 6 we have a homework center set up. We are helping 4 or 5 fellows at the moment." On Mondays and Wednesdays he left at 5 for the East 19th Street Center to help Jerry Meck with his kids. "Tuesday and Friday I still put the pool table up. Thursday I try to play basketball with some of the fellows at Berger."[46]

Glad Tidings and Seventh Avenue Basketball Teams Honors Banquet held at Glad Tidings. VSer Jay Lefever, front left.

A transit strike that began on New Year's Day 1966 nearly paralyzed the city for two weeks. Jeanette Hershey, who worked in the Sandwich Shop during the day, had to stay at Glad Tidings until the strike was over. Jerry Meck joined the Sandwich Shop team in January 1966, but only worked through the spring of that year. Ray Siegrist took his place, working days behind the lunch counter and spending the evenings with neighborhood teenagers.[47] Ray Siegrist continued to work with the Sandwich Shop and the youth program after his Voluntary Service term ended. Erb's Mennonite Church provided partial support for him during this time. Robert and Rose Rodriguez returned to Puerto Rico in 1969. When Esther Petersheim resigned as manager of the Sandwich Shop, effective June 30, 1970, Ray took over management of the store.[48]

Ray Siegrist, Bob Keener and Jeanne Miller worked in the Sandwich Shop in Voluntary Service assignments. Jeanne completed her term in August 1971. Keener left at the end of the year. At this point, the Sandwich Shop had been losing money for several months because of increased wholesale food prices. The team decided to drop hero sandwiches and offer frankfurters and hamburgers instead. Eugene "Biggy" Davis joined the staff in 1971 as a Neighborhood Youth Corps employee.[49]

An electrical fire in January 1972 did serious damage to the store and led to another reappraisal of the Sandwich Shop ministry. The Glad Tidings congregation reaffirmed the Sandwich Shop and set to work repairing the store. The recreation program for neighborhood youth had first priority with the fast food operation taking a secondary role. Lorraine Weaver agreed to take over as manager of a scaled-down Sandwich Shop. Ray Siegrist continued to work in the store with full responsibility for the youth program. Marnetta Longenecker joined the staff in January 1972 on a one-year VS assignment. Eugene Davis remained on the store team in the reorganization.[50]

Ray Siegrist left the Sandwich Shop at the end of 1972, and Marnetta Longenecker completed VS in January 1973. Paul Beiler came in October 1972 on a VS assignment. Justine Branch, Eugene Davis, and Clarence Eldridge worked with Lorraine Weaver to staff the Sandwich Shop through the summer of 1973. Kirk Melvin and Eugene Oatman, who also came from the Glad Tidings community, worked there during the summer months. Rising wholesale food prices again pushed the operation into the red, and the only way to cut losses was to terminate the project. Glad Tidings Sandwich Shop closed its doors forever on August 31, 1973.[51]

In its nearly nine years of operation, the Glad Tidings Sandwich Shop built a bridge to the neighborhood. Parole officers met their clients there. Social workers found Glad Tidings people ready to help them find caring foster homes in Mennonite communities for troubled youngsters. The Sandwich Shop provided a place for recreation, remedial reading, and a base for outreach to South Bronx teenagers. The pilot project at Glad Tidings led to youth work on the city streets by all the Mennonite churches.

Street Work With Teenagers

In 1964 Frank King organized a boys club at Seventh Avenue for 8-to-12 year olds. "We met once or twice a week and worked on arts and crafts, trying to develop skills in the manual tasks as well as ability to work together." Frank took the boys on trips to the World's Fair and an auto show and often to the park. There were football games in the park in the fall, basketball in the winter in school gyms. The 1-ws and MYFers formed a softball team and joined a city-wide league that gave them real competition.[52]

Richard Pannell, Leon Stauffer, Frank King, Jeffrey Peggott, and Tom Allen began street work with youth in the church neighborhood in September 1965. They eventually set up a recreation center in the church basement.[53] "Leon and Dick did street work every Monday evening, going to places where the fellows were and meeting them on their own territory." They invited them to the youth center which was open at first on Friday evenings. "Some nights were pretty rough at the center." Leon turned the project over to Dick Pannell with Tom Allen and Frank King as his assistants.[54] The youth center involved 25 to 30 teens two nights a week by the end of 1965.[55]

Mel Thomas joined the youth work team at Seventh Avenue in 1966. Frank King left New York early in 1967 and Tom Allen moved away from Harlem. Leon Stauffer commented that it was difficult for anyone to be a youth worker in the inner-city without previous experience and "very difficult for a white person, regardless of his ability, to be a youth worker in Harlem." Without a black VSer to fill the job, Stauffer thought the best solution would be to have someone assist Pannell as chief youth worker, but relate full-time to the proposed day-care center. With Dick Pannell working full time, the project needed "someone to give time beyond the club hours for the continued developments of relationships with community youth."[56] Under Pannell's leadership, Seventh Avenue began a community day camp program in the summer of 1968, which evolved into a more elaborate plan for the Har-Menno Youth Center in 1969.

Jerry Meck arrived at the East 19th Street VS Center to begin his 1-w service in January 1966. Anna Mae Landis and other VSers ran an evening recreation program there for community children. As many as 25 youngsters came to the unit three evenings a week to play ping pong and other group games.[57] Jerry Meck worked at the Glad Tidings Sandwich Shop during the day and gave his evenings to teenagers in the VS Center neighborhood, especially a group known as The Knights. In April 1966

John W. Eby, director of Voluntary Service for Eastern Board, appointed Jerry as youth worker in the East 19th Street community. He gradually decreased his involvement with the team at Glad Tidings, leaving Jay Lefever responsible for youth work there. Leon Stauffer urged him to contact Fred Alderfer, Bill Milligan, and Bill Crawford of Young Life and "keep in close touch with Dick Pannell."[58]

Jerry Meck located a vacant loft at East 22nd Street and 2nd Avenue and rented it as a clubroom since facilities at the VS Center were so limited. As at the VS Center the kids could easily overstep the bounds, but they valued the program enough to keep the rules. He obtained community funds to buy softball uniforms for the Knights and had them playing Police Athletic League games. Jerry and Jay Lefever worked closely together and their teams regularly played each other. Jerry's softball team with teenagers from the VS Center neighborhood beat Jay's team in a five-game series. In November, as basketball season opened, Jerry got the use of the gymnasium at Friends' School on East 15th Street for his team.[59]

It was not all sports and club activities. Jerry Meck wrote Leon Stauffer that, "I have been in court with some of my fellows. They are having a rough time in the city."[60] He was also involved with the Religious Society of Friends at the East 15th Street Quaker Meeting House in a community project for homeless men.[61]

Jay Lefever made the basketball team at Glad Tidings the core group he worked with, especially after he became full-time youth worker at Glad Tidings in June 1966. "Since the job was new to me in a way, I spent a lot of time just sitting on stoops and talking. My main group became the 13-15-year-old kids." Jerry Meck had started a softball team, and Jay picked it up when Jerry began working downtown with youth in the East 19th Street neighborhood. Wayne Allen, Raymond Jones, Lenny Kitt, always known as "Funny," Ruben Padilla, and Ed "Go-Go" Gomez from the softball team became part of Jay's core group. In September 1966 Jay Lefever, Jerry Meck, and Dick Pannell planned to meet once a month "and all pull together in this work" with youth. They decided to have their own basketball league. Seventh Avenue won the league trophy with 8 wins and 2 losses, but Glad Tidings was a close second with 7 wins and 3 losses. "Although we did not win the trophy, things were accomplished. This became my core group that I work with." The kids practiced once a week and grew to working together and accepting each other. "We together have come a long way. The fellows quite often during the week come to see me in my apartment." Raymond Jones was the leader of the group and "probably the closest to us." He helped with the counter work at the Sandwich Shop when they were busy. Esther Petersheim recalled that Raymond assisted in opening the shop at six every weekday morning. With his basketball ability and Jay Lefever's encouragement, Raymond Jones won a college scholarship and became a public school administrator in North Dakota.[62] Ruben Padilla played for the EMC Flames. Ed Gomez went to Taylor University. One of the other team members died in a shooting on the street. The basketball team traveled to Pennsylvania for the wedding of Jay and Carol Lefever in 1967. The Lefevers stayed in New York through 1970 working with inner-city youth.[63]

The Fox Street congregation was slow in beginning youth work in their neighborhood. In the summer of 1967, Jerry Meck worked with Blair Seitz and Tom Spicher, EMC seniors, in beginning a youth program. They scouted around in the community and located a vacant lot across from the church suitable for a basketball court. Jerry was interested in continuing after the others left. Larry Nolt, the new unit leader at East 19th Street, reported the group there was willing to see him divide his time between Fox Street and East 19th Street. Jerry and Lynette Meck planned to move to Harrisonburg to complete his EMC degree in January 1968. Before they left the city, Robert Draper expressed interest in continuing Jerry Meck's work.[64]

Bob Draper worked with the Fox Street Falcons in the Mennonite basketball league and with neighborhood youth one-on-one. The Fox Street MYF had been moribund but became active again with Draper, Tom Villanueva and Pam McCarthy as leaders. Bob played basketball with some of the older kids at the P.S. 54 Center and softball with the kids in the schoolyard. He enrolled in an eleven-week seminar at Lincoln Hospital on East 141st Street to help social workers and youth workers like himself in short-term counseling situations. In April 1968 two of his teenagers accompanied him downtown to pick out a pool table, and the whole gang helped carry it in.[65]

The neighborhood in which these kids lived steadily deteriorated. The youth center was on the front lines. Bob Draper wrote in June 1968:

> Detectives have been raiding the Spanish hang-out catty corner from our center. At least five arrests have been made. The junkies have been hanging around our side of the street and near the center. They aren't even selling the stuff in the dark anymore but right out in the open where everyone can see them.

Fox Street sponsored a day camp program in the summer of 1968 for 25 children from six to ten years old. Dave Longacre, Bernell Switzer, and

Marvin Miller, summer VSers, made up the camp staff. Dave took his day camp boys to Crotona Park to play softball. "Two teenagers came up and put a knife in his back and walked off with his watch and $10." Five of Bob Draper's core group worked with the day camp and the youth center as a job assignment from Neighborhood Youth Corps. Summer jobs gave them more confidence.[66]

Camping trips to Camp Brookhaven, the softball league, outings to Coney Island or Central Park, and the give and take of the youth center created stronger relationships and sharing. Larry Ware began coming regularly to church and joined the MYF Bible quiz team. Other small victories encouraged the youth workers. Draper kept the center open every day during the school strike that began in September 1968. Teachers walked out in protest against an experiment in the Brownsville-Ocean Hill section of Brooklyn, where a local school board of black and Hispanic parents was given a free hand in curriculum and hiring. The United Federation of Teachers, led by Albert Shanker, charged the school board with anti-Semitism in the transfer of veteran teachers to other schools. In October 1968 the city caved in to the teachers' union and ended the experiment. Black and Hispanic parents across the school system felt betrayed. The teachers' strike polarized the city for a long time to come. It also threw ghetto youngsters back on the streets, with church youth centers as the only alternatives.[67]

Bob Draper ended his term as youth worker in December 1968, although he remained in the community working along with Dale Weaver and Amos Stoltzfus to keep the program—and the church—alive. They all had other jobs. Teenagers from 14 to 17 were their primary concern, then the 10- to 13-year-olds.

Much of the youth work related to teenaged males, but in 1969 Damaris Lugo, a member of the Glad Tidings congregation, began a summer program with neighborhood girls. She worked with them "in areas of cheerleading, in crafts and going places and has done an excellent job in gaining their confidence." The congregation found money to enable her to continue this program year round.[68]

Ray Siegrist and Dick Frey continued the tradition of basketball teams and pool at Glad Tidings as youth workers in 1969-1970.

Glad Tidings was a happy place for teenagers when Leonor Constantin was growing up there. Jesus Cruz led the MYF activities in 1968-1969. Leonor Constantin, Raymond Jones, Jay and Carol Lefever, and Dale and Doris Stoltzfus planned recreation. Siso Torres became assistant minister in 1970 with special responsibility for youth programs. The teenagers created a coffee house in the church basement which they called "The Rat Hole" as a place to hang out. City-wide MYF was very active in these years and young people from Glad Tidings, Fox Street, Friendship and Seventh Avenue did many things together. Damaris Lugo of Glad Tidings coordinated the city-wide activities. In 1971 the Glad Tidings Youth Council organized for ministry as "People on the Way." Members included Sis-Obed (Siso) Torres, Miriam Torres, Elmer Lapp, Ray Siegrist, Jose Rodriguez, Toni Rodriguez, Bob Keener, Jeanne Miller, Evelyn Buckwalter, Robert Santiago, and Minerva Figueroa. The Glad Tidings young people staffed the 1971 day camp. Ella Villanueva and Jesus Cruz taught the classes, Toni Rodriguez had responsibility for youth work, and Ruben Padilla was sports coordinator responsible for teams and tournaments.

In spite of all the activities, some young people, especially females, got involved in youth activities at other, larger churches. Leonor Constantin and her sister Gloria began attending Sunday evening services for youth at Calvary Baptist Church in Manhattan and invited their friends from Glad Tidings. The result was that Al and Dottie Kruse, who directed the youth ministry at Calvary, moved their membership to Glad Tidings and became an important part of the congregation.[69]

Jim King became the full-time youth worker at Fox Street in October 1969. Jerry Whyte joined him in January 1970. These two VSers held Fox Street together until Glenn Zeager came as mission superintendent.[70]

Jim King stayed on at Fox Street after his VS term ended in June 1971. He directed the day camp that summer, "running around trying to keep crafts, recreation and worship periods going smoothly for four teachers, their aides, and thirty-five kids." His new role in the fall involved coordinating youth work and clubs. "What I would like to do with twenty hours of my time is spend them at Fox Street, on the street, or inside, helping in craft and Bible clubs, discussion groups, MYF, and tutoring programs." Plans for a new building at Fox Street encouraged him, since the congregation had inadequate space for existing programs and a new building could have adequate facilities for church, recreation center, tutoring program, after-school center, and day nursery.

King had his own dreams, too. He hoped to go to college to major in preschool or elementary education, "so that I can be of service to our church and my community at Fox Street." His dreams might have to be deferred, along with hopes for the congregation and the neighborhood. "Sometimes it's not much use dreaming or planning for Fox Street if you know that other Mennonite churches can get more money to run a less needed program for the community."[71]

New Structures and New Leadership

During the summer, from early May to late August, Glad Tidings bustled with activity as an agency for the Herald-Tribune Fresh Air Fund. Registration of children who wanted to go to camp or visit one of the Friendly Town families began the first week of May. "At times we had four persons registering children—pushing pencils as rapidly as possible during those hours." By the middle of June registration had tapered off, but the actual assignments began. "This advances to a feverish pitch the last ten days of June" when departures began. "Children need to be located who have been reinvited [by host families] and have not yet registered." Then the children had to be taken by subway to bus and train stations. On a typical morning Paul Burkholder "was busy getting 91 children together on the sidewalk at 9 to go to Penn Station by subway." Late comers had to be called. Miriam Burkholder was getting sixteen children ready for medical examinations; others were late or decided not to keep this appointment with the doctor and substitutes had to be called. "Afternoons are a mad rush to write tags, nurses' sheets, information sheets, take new allotments, send out cards notifying children they are to go in two weeks, and many other things." In the summer of 1966 Glad Tidings sent 30 boys and 23 girls to the Fresh Air Camp and 159 boys and 237 girls to Friendly Towns. Almost half the children sent to Friendly Towns came from New York City Mennonite churches, and

Seventh Avenue Fresh Air Children ready to go to Lancaster County, Pennsylvania, for their summer vacation.

of the 396 children sent to Friendly Towns, 291 went to Mennonite homes. "Many children are invited to the same home year after year." In 1966 nearly 40 percent were returning to a family with whom they had stayed in 1965. Almost half the host families lived in Lancaster County and about a quarter in the Chambersburg area. Mennonite families in Harrisonburg, Virginia, Lowville, New York, and Beaver Run, Pennsylvania, also took part in the program. "Over the year this program has helped establish Glad Tidings as a church which is interested in doing practical things for people."[72]

The new summer program at Glad Tidings supplemented the Fresh Air Fund work, but had none of its numbers. The volunteers worked in very small groups, almost one-on-one, with the children. Teachers made every effort to get to know the children through smaller classes, a maximum of five children in any one class, visiting in their homes, afternoons helping in remedial reading or other interests, and once a week field trips to the zoo or a beach.[73]

Evelyn Hertzler took responsibility for the eight-week summer program at Glad Tidings from 1964 through 1968 and made changes in the summer Bible school format. "It operates more as a Bible day camp than the traditional Bible school. Time is spent in Bible classes, crafts, games, and educational trips. Some children return in the afternoon to review and drill in reading and arithmetic."[74]

A summer VS team of six young women came to the Bronx to staff the Bible day camp each year. The Sandwich Shop team selected children for the day camp. Each year there was a waiting list. Giving so much attention to thirty youngsters in a part of the city teeming with children was a deliberate strategy. Evelyn Hertzler planned the program around "this approach to the needs of these children" so that "we are able to give so much individual attention to each child." The tutoring program continued through the year under Evelyn Hertzler's direction. Eight Glad Tidings members tutored fifteen children in their homes twice a week for an hour. Some made progress, others did not. "It isn't so much that they want reading and arithmetic, but the companionship of being with someone who likes them," Evelyn Hertzler reported.[75]

She also served on a Christian Education Committee with representatives of Glad Tidings, Fox Street, Seventh Avenue, and the House of Friendship. In one meeting at Lucy Vance's apartment they discussed a wide range of topics.

> How can you keep a building from becoming an end? Relationship of facilities to Christian Education? How can you keep from creating barriers that keep out certain groups of people? Adults vs. children?

> Good kids vs. bad kids? Validity of vacation Bible school? What do these children need most? Responsibility of church to the community. When there is trouble what do you do? (Dope, etc.) Conflicts of experience of pupils with curriculum we tend to use. What cultural conflicts do we face? Language? Race? Out-of-Towners come in and assume leadership—indigenous church? Our relation to parent body.

The meetings of the Christian Education Committee led to a self-study by each congregation and a hard look at what urban ministry should mean in each congregational setting, as well as the role of Sunday school and vacation Bible school. John Freed, John Smucker, Lucy Vance, and Evelyn Hertzler took the lead in this self-study.[76] Professor Nile Harper of the Biblical Seminary became an enthusiastic participant in their meetings and made a major contribution to the effort. He was a key speaker at the Christian Education Conference sponsored by the Mennonite and Brethren in Christ churches of New York City in November 1965, together with Paul Lederach of the Mennonite Publishing House and Bernard Holliday of the Protestant Council. The conference met at Fox Street, Glad Tidings, Seventh Avenue, and the House of Friendship over a three-day weekend. Tours of Central Harlem, a visit to the East Harlem Protestant Parish Church of the Resurrection, and a tour of the South Bronx formed part of the program. Much of the time was spent in discussion of the theology of mission and mission strategy. "Should mission primarily focus on social changes through power blocs on a mass scale? How does one show love and be a 'good Samaritan' in the modern city? What does a ministry to the whole man mean in a city setting?"[77] The Christian Education Conference raised the question of the relationship of the church to social change and the relationship of the "good Samaritan" kind of ministry to that of an evangelistic ministry of salvation. They agreed that, "the church needs to be more helpful to our city congregations in providing resource to develop the theological base on which strategy is built."[78]

The Fox Street congregation made serious efforts to reach the neighboring families. In 1965 John Freed proposed a day nursery but city requirements appeared too stringent and he dropped the idea in favor of a study club like the Sherman Avenue Bible Club.[79]

The Fox Street congregation called Carl Good as assistant pastor and he was installed on June 6, 1965.[80] With an able assistant to take his place, John Freed proposed taking a year or two to finish his own college work at EMC or Goshen. Paul Landis believed it would be better for him to "stay in the city and take some work at one of the city colleges" so that "he would be able to maintain some of the very significant contacts he has in the Fox Street area." Eastern Board agreed to provide full support for the school year to free him from his cab-driving job and enable him to take summer courses at EMC and study through the year at Hunter College.[81]

Carl Good was scheduled to finish his Voluntary Service in August 1966. As early as November 1965 John H. Kraybill, John Freed, John Buckwalter, Mabel Herr, and Norma Brenner met with the Goods to discuss the possibility of Carl and Lois moving to Sherman Avenue. The Sherman Avenue Bible Club had loose ties to Fox Street, but was not really part of the congregation's outreach. Kraybill also highly recommended Carl as resource person for the New York churches, a role he declined himself since he would soon be leaving the city. Carl intended to enroll full-time in New York Biblical Seminary, but Carl and Lois agreed to move to an apartment near Sherman Avenue to work with the program there on his own time. John Buckwalter believed that "in the next few years we should be ready to allow a church to be born in that community."[82]

In February and March 1965 John H. Kraybill consulted with each member of Seventh Avenue Mennonite Church about an assistant pastor and, as he reported to a congregational meeting, "the feeling seems to be that Richard Pannell is the person to fill this role.[83] He was working at New York University full-time and taking courses to complete his college degree. He agreed to give up his job in August, after finishing his summer school classes, and would be available as part-time associate pastor in September. He asked to continue taking classes through the 1965-1966 academic year as that would enable him to graduate with a BA degree in May 1966. The committee felt that visitation and youth work should be the first areas for his attention.[84] Seventh Avenue held an installation service for Richard Pannell on October 3, 1965.[85]

With an associate pastor as gifted as Dick Pannell, John H. Kraybill began planning to leave Seventh Avenue Mennonite Church in his hands. In February 1966 Kraybill announced that he had accepted a call to the First Mennonite Church of Johnstown, Pennsylvania, and that he and his family would leave New York June 30. Richard Pannell would continue, at least for a time, as associate pastor. He would graduate from N.Y.U. that spring and his long-range plans had included medical school or other professional education. "Dick shared with the group that he is still uncertain about his call of God to the pastorate. He needs more time to find God's will in this."[86]

Richard and Ethel Pannell agreed to serve as pastor of the Seventh Avenue congregation. The decision was not an easy one for Richard

Pannell. He told the Administrative Council in January 1967 that he was "thinking seriously of medical school and taking steps toward acceptance." Although they counseled him to continue in the ministry, he still planned to apply for admission to medical school. After a long struggle, he gave up his own dreams and was ordained at Seventh Avenue on November 12, 1967.[87]

Ethel and Richard Pannell following their wedding ceremony at the Seventh Avenue Church. Paul Landis, bishop, left rear, and John Kraybill, pastor, right rear.

Eastern Board could help the autonomous Lancaster Conference congregations in the city with new administrative structures. The New York churches related to the Conference and the Mission Board through the bishop, the Home Missions director, the director of Voluntary Service and 1-w programs, and the Eastern Board treasurer. They had developed "a working relationship" with the House of Friendship and

First New York City Mennonite Administrative Council, (Lancaster Conference). Front row, left to right: John Kraybill, Paul Burkholder, Carl Good, Paul Landis, bishop. Back row, left to right: Bernie Spanier, Richard Pannell, Dale Stoltzfus, John Buckwalter, John Freed, and Glenn Zeager.

"a more tenuous relationship" with the other Mennonite and Brethren in Christ churches, largely through the Ministers' Fellowship chaired by John H. Kraybill. In December 1965 discussion of this situation led to the establishment of an administrative council for the Lancaster Conference churches. Each church would be represented by the pastor and another member, with the bishop, the VS Unit leader, and the 1-W sponsor, as council members ex officio.[88]

Dale and Doris Stoltzfus.

The New York City Administrative Council held its first meeting at Fox Street on February 27, 1966 with Paul Landis in the chair. Paul Burkholder, John Freed, John H. Kraybill, Richard Pannell, Carl Good, Jesus Constantin, John Buckwalter, Bernie Spanier, Dale Stoltzfus and Glenn Zeager attended. The transition of leadership at Seventh Avenue and the proposal to involve Carl Good in the program at Sherman Avenue formed the agenda.[89]

One of the first actions of the Administrative Council was to plan a retreat "for the group who are learning to work together in this council." The leaders suggested for the retreat—Don Jacobs, Elam Stauffer, John Leatherman, Festo Kivingere—all had direct involvement in the East African Revival.[90]

After the formation of the Administrative Council, Paul Landis continued to serve as bishop and area superintendent. He was the link to the Lancaster Conference Bishop Board and to the Conference generally. He also had the responsibility to negotiate with the Mission Board for funds for New York City programs and for the administration of those programs. Plans for future leadership in the district headed the agenda for the Administrative Council meeting on April 14, 1969. Paul Landis indicated that he would like to be released. "There was a feeling that the time is here for a change and that the position of leadership be here in New York City." The Council members explored two alternatives, an executive secretary of the Council and a bishop/overseer both living in the city, or a single person combining both roles.[91] At their May meeting, they chose the first option, appointing Monroe Yoder as executive secretary and asking Paul Landis to continue as bishop for the time being.[92]

The Council discussed this issue at meetings over the next year. In April 1970 Paul Landis reported that "The Bishop Board has responded with openness and approval on our request to call a resident bishop in the New York City District." The Council members then set up a procedure for involving congregations in the process of choosing a bishop. They would ask each congregation to nominate qualified persons and "hopefully through the power of the Holy Spirit the Council could arrive by consensus on one person." The resident bishop would also take the responsibility of executive secretary.[93]

John H. Kraybill, Monroe Yoder, Glenn Zeager, Dale Stoltzfus, Carl Good, and Harold Davenport were all nominated by one or more congregations. The Council added Richard Pannell and Eugene Shelly to the list of nominees.[94] At the June meeting Carl Good and Harold Davenport withdrew their names. The Council members had agreed in May to call a "local, minority, indigenous leader" and, with Harold Davenport's request to take his name out of consideration, only Richard Pannell met all qualifications. After again consulting with the members of the city congregations, the Council recommended a call to Richard Pannell.[95]

The members of Seventh Avenue Mennonite Church naturally expressed concern at losing their pastor, who had just accepted a full-time appointment.[96] Dick Pannell himself had grave doubts about taking on this new responsibility for all the New York churches, explaining that his heart was in Harlem. He finally asked to have his name withdrawn so that he could remain at Seventh Avenue. The Council members then returned to their earlier idea of a leadership team. In November 1970 they sent a letter to the congregations explaining the bishop-leadership team concept. As a result, Paul Landis continued to serve as non-resident bishop and a leadership team of local ministers was asked to "expedite the decisions of the Council, exert leadership in terms of strategy, and be sensitive to congregational needs."[97]

Glad Tidings and the other New York churches also began to develop a congregational discipline in 1965, working with Harold Bauman. A committee was asked to draw up a workable discipline and present it to the congregation. They began by exploring three questions, "What do I expect of church members?" "What is the purpose of our church?" and "How detailed should be our practical application?" Others raised questions about the relationships of a congregational discipline to the Lancaster Conference discipline. It soon became clear that each congregation would draw up its own discipline "because of the cultural differences" between Lancaster County and New York City and among the New York churches.

By 1965, the Conference *Rules and Discipline* had all but "ceased to exist for the Conference as a whole" and "individualism, of the congregations and of members" had replaced "an objective church standard." The committee accepted the reality of change. They quoted approvingly Harold Bauman's comment that "Leadership requires the quality of being firm and yet tentative in a world of rapid changes."[98]

The next meeting of the committee took its direction from Bauman's suggestion that "the less you write on paper the better." They questioned whether they might "be killing what God is doing" in the congregation "by trying to put all this on paper." They concluded that "as a congregation we must learn to know each other better, aiming to develop a fellowship of caring for each other." This could only happen as Jesus Christ becomes the center. "From a self-centered, self-willed, self-sufficient and hurtful people, we must become an open, healing, and Christ-centered people."[99]

Fox Street went through a similar process of determining where decisions are made and how to make congregational life more vital and disciplined. They concentrated on small group fellowships. "The congregation is attempting to find groups with a common mission and to provide a vehicle for these groups to meet together and also for their relationships to the larger congregational group."[100]

Richard Pannell and the Seventh Avenue Mennonite Church also had a vision for ministry to their community. In 1966 Bishop Paul Landis spent one weekend a month in Harlem to help with the pastoral transition. He noted that "Richard has a real burden to make this congregation a dynamic witness in the immediate community surrounding the church building and one can see that progress has been made in relating to the Harlem community."[101]

What shape would this witness take? That was up to the congregation and the neighborhood, Pannell wrote. "The group there must find out what the people need in their community, and plan to supply the need. Then, when the confidence of the community is won, the communication of the Gospel will be much easier."[102] Everything seemed to point to a day-care center. "The congregation is presently studying the possibilities of developing a child care program in order to relate more closely to the community and to get involved in more homes. Within the congregation we have persons with training in this field and a lady who is now working as a teacher in a pre-school child care center."[103]

While the day care project was still in the planning stage, Lucy Vance and others at Seventh Avenue explored the possibility of a Head Start

Lucy Vance with a Head Start Class at Seventh Avenue.

Program using federal anti-poverty funds, in addition to the proposed day care center.[104] Lucy Vance wrote the successful application for a Head Start Program at Seventh Avenue. It was a departure for New York City Mennonites to seek federal money to operate a program.

Lucy Vance left her job at Wiltwyck School in August 1967 to take charge of the Seventh Avenue Day Care Center. The Sewing Circles contributed sheets and bedding and Eastern Board provided a cash advance to begin the project.[105] It was a pioneering effort, too. This was the first Head Start Program approved for New York City. There were initially thirty children enrolled. When the grant came up for renewal in 1969, government authorities enthusiastically approved the application and doubled the number of children served by the Seventh Avenue Head Start Program.[106]

The Sherman Avenue program lost Bernard and Lillian Spanier, who moved to Lancaster County early in 1966. Mabel Herr also moved back to Pennsylvania to care for her ailing parents. The search for replacements was not easy. Wesley and Marian Newswanger had lived in the city for the two years of his 1-w service. They expressed interest in returning to New York as self-supporting mission workers. Wes was qualified to teach in the public schools. The members of the Administrative Council unanimously recommended them for Sherman Avenue. Ethel Horst and Alta Strite joined Norma Brenner in the Bible Club work in February 1967 with an agreement to stay through the summer or early autumn.[107]

There were changes at Glad Tidings, too. In a letter to the congregation dated August 16, 1966, Paul Burkholder announced his resignation as pastor, effective July 31, 1967. His immediate plans were to complete his undergraduate degree at Eastern Mennonite College in order to be better prepared for the pastoral ministry. With a year's lead time, the congregation could conduct a search for a successor. In January 1967 they voted to invite Eugene and Martine Shelly to Glad Tidings. He was ordained on July 18, 1968.[108]

Glad Tidings pastor Eugene and Martine Shelly, and son Michael.

When the Burkholders left, they were eager that the Glad Tidings congregation be able to use the building at 342 Brook Avenue where the Sandwich Shop was located.[109] In 1970 Paul and Miriam Burkholder donated the apartment building to Eastern Board for the use of Glad Tidings congregation.[110]

John Freed was the only one of the cab-driving pastors left in the city. He remained at his post, attempting to finish his college work at Hunter and EMC with summer courses. In 1968 the Fox Street congregation gave John and Dottie Freed a leave of absence for study at Eastern Mennonite College in the academic year 1968-1969, with the understanding that his resignation as pastor could take effect in June 1969.[111]

Hope in the South Bronx

The Fox Street neighborhood began to deteriorate through fires set by addicts trying to keep warm in a derelict apartments, tenants hoping to be moved to a better building by the city, and landlords eager to collect insurance. Anna Buckwalter who lived at 1128 Fox Street wrote, "The third fire here was September 9th. It started in a vacant house three doors from me." She took in an 89-year-old man and his 18-year-old grandson who were forced to move out of their damaged building. The firemen caused some water damage to her house. The building two doors away was vacant, "open to vandalism and a fire hazard." She hoped it would soon be demolished. She wrote that "It is dangerous living here," but she stayed.[112]

The South Bronx was rapidly deteriorating, as drugs spread over the city. In 1966 Paul Landis observed that, "The area of the Glad Tidings congregation is increasingly becoming a depressed area and is one of the narcotics centers of the city."[113] In 1967 John Freed talked with the Administrative Council about "the severe narcotics problem in the Fox Street community" and his own "relationship with four ex-addicts who have recently found the Lord and are presently in the Teen Challenge Program at Rehrersburg."[114] Teenagers came "high on dope" to the youth center at the House of Friendship and to the Glad Tidings Sandwich Shop.[115] By 1968 the sandwich shop staff faced the problem of "drug addicts hanging out at the store." The police and Narcotics Bureau encouraged the Glad Tidings people behind the counter "to work with these fellows." Eugene Shelly, pastor at Glad Tidings, sought the help of Samuel Santos.[116]

Santos, a recovering addict, had begun a ministry to others ensnared by drugs. Early in 1968 he began the Hope Christian Center at 1444 Bryant Avenue, about four blocks from the Fox Street church. John L. Freed gave him every encouragement in his difficult task. "I think I am groping for ways to slowly open up channels that can develop into long-term healthy relationships." Freed taught the only English-language Bible study at Hope Christian Center. He helped with fund-raising since "one of the immediate struggles for a ministry as it opens is its struggle for resources." John Freed, Paul Landis, Glenn Zeager, and Gene Shelly helped build bridges between Hope Christian Center and Lancaster Conference.[117] Mennonite involvement with Hope Christian Center's efforts to reach narcotics users increased to the point that Sammy Santos became a member of Friendship Mennonite Church and accepted a call as associate pastor.[118]

John Freed pointed out that the Fox Street neighborhood was not safe for a construction "team of outside, all-white personnel" to renovate the church building in 1968. "Fox Street community is a potential riot area. We have not had any difficulty up to this time; however everyone is predicting a difficult summer." Renovations at Fox Street had been delayed since 1966.[119] Other projects had taken precedence, such as enabling Seventh Avenue to meet federal standards for a Head Start center.[120] In March Chester Wenger, Eastern Board Home Missions Director, and Paul Landis met with the Fox Street Cabinet to discuss building plans. The relationship of Sherman Avenue to Fox Street emerged as a major concern. All agreed steps needed to be taken to clarify this relationship "for the health of both groups."[121]

The Fox Street community and the Sherman Avenue community each qualified for Neighborhood Youth Corps jobs. Bob Draper and Carl

Hope Christian Center, Bronx.

Good cooperated in identifying youngsters who could help in the summer day camp program as Youth Corps workers. The larger issue of the relationship between the two groups came to the fore as a possible site for a worship center became available in the Sherman Avenue area.[122] John Buckwalter had investigated various buildings in the neighborhood from the summer of 1967. He recommended purchase of the property at 1114 Sherman Avenue.[123] With a new congregation emerging there, John Freed pointed out that "The bulk of the contributing members of the team are more deeply committed to Sherman Avenue than to Fox Street." The older congregation was at a crucial point, needing to call a new pastor and complete a building program.[124] The impending separation of the Sherman Avenue group gave impetus to both identifying a new pastor to be in place when the Freeds left and to completing the renovations in the building. The Cabinet agreed on Dale Stoltzfus and Marvin Weaver as possibilities for the pastoral role.[125]

One solution would be to close Fox Street and concentrate efforts elsewhere. The community was "poverty-stricken and crime-ridden" with "inadequate housing" that put a severe strain on the pastor and his family. The Administrative Council nevertheless encouraged the continuance of Fox Street as a congregation.[126] Finding a pastor proved more difficult and a team ministry seemed the only solution. Until a pastor could be found, Carl Metzler agreed to serve as acting mission superintendent. John Freed tried to encourage Ralph and Esther Villanueva to move back to the Fox Street neighborhood; he had long believed Ralph Villanueva would make a good pastor for Fox Street.[127] They declined. Dale Stoltzfus also declined, when formally invited as pastor in January 1969.[128]

Carl and Marian Metzler, both full-time graduate students, faced a formidable challenge in keeping Fox Street alive. More members moved away in 1969, the Hodges family and the Woodleys to Brooklyn, the McKenzies to Queens, and Audrey Kriebel to the East Bronx. "Our attendance is considerably lower than a year ago."[129] By July, Fox Street members only came together for an informal Wednesday evening service, and youth work in the community was the only functioning part of the church program. MYF, Sunday school, and Sunday morning service had all become moribund. "The Wednesday evening group has become a back-up team for the ones who are working with the youth program." Some community teenagers attended the Wednesday service, too. "After the Wednesday evening fellowship senses the direction that God is leading them, they would like to open this fellowship up by inviting community people to participate with them," Monroe Yoder reported. "The group still feels that the youth work

Glenn Zeager pastor, with a baseball team at the entrance to the second Fox Street Mennonite Church building located at Fox and Home Streets, Bronx.

is its strongest point of contact and one of the greatest needs in the community."[130]

As 1969 drew to a close, the need for pastoral leadership at Fox Street remained a problem, but a solution emerged at the Administrative Council meeting. Glenn Zeager had sold his business, but continued "giving of himself and his time without any monetary consideration" to the programs of the New York City Mennonite churches, especially Hope Christian Center, Seventh Avenue Mennonite Church, and the camp. The Administrative Council members felt that they should not take advantage of Glenn and Florence in this way but offer him a job and salary. Monroe Yoder, Carl Metzler, and Carl Good were named a committee to explore possible options. Everything pointed toward Fox Street.[131]

Glenn Zeager agreed to accept the challenge. Chester Wenger wrote him: "Glenn, I can hardly tell you how happy I am to see you move into this tough spot... I am willing to respect your expressed desire to have the mission superintendent responsibility, but not the full pastor responsibility." He would be expected to function as pastor, leading worship and Bible study and giving counsel but, at his own request, as one of a team. The response from the Fox Street congregation was "enthusiastic about the possibilities of Glenn working with them," although Seventh Avenue members were "disappointed to see Glenn leave in light of his deep involvement" there.[132]

Glenn Zeager became mission superintendent at Fox Street in January 1970. During the year the Wednesday night fellowship grew so that in September Sunday morning worship services were resumed. On Sundays an average of 50 met for Sunday school and preaching. Membership of "the newly forming congregation" had not yet been sorted out. MYF revived and had 35 attending on the first Friday of every month. Chester Wenger observed: "Things are happening and there seems to be a new spirit developing at Fox Street. The group is concerned not to institutionalize the program but to keep it varied enough to meet the particular needs of community persons."

The Fox Street neighborhood faced an uncertain future. Zeager had checked with city authorities and found no plans for urban renewal for years to come. "Most people who settle in the area think of moving out, if and when they are able. The community needs something around which to rally, to build up its spirit, to lead the way."[133]

Zeager and the others at Fox Street proposed a major rehabilitation project. They proposed renovating buildings located at 1150, 1156 and 1160 Tiffany Street for low-cost housing. Two of the buildings were operational in 1970, in fair condition with no building code violations. The third five-story building could be altered to provide space for a day-care center, recreation center, after-school programs, and an infant-care nursery. The Fox Street Mennonite Church would relocate on a second or third floor of the building and the top floor would have apartments. Representatives of the New York City Department of Social Services encouraged the idea. They inspected the site and agreed to fund the proposed infant-care, day-care, and after-school programs and to pay rent for the facilities they used.[134]

Mennonite Disaster Service sent teams of volunteers to the South Bronx in 1970. Some MDS volunteers from Lancaster helped in the rehabilitation of Hope Christian Center for drug addicts and MDS continued to send teams there during the winter of 1970-1971. Dale Stoltzfus suggested using MDS for a large-scale rehabilitation project would make it more feasible for Fox Street. Richard Shertzer came from Pennsylvania to assess a possible role for MDS in the Tiffany Street project.[135]

Wally Hubert, a member of Good Shepherd Mennonite Church on Sherman Avenue, was an officer of First National City Bank. He sold bank officials on the Tiffany Street renovation as "the kind of inner-city project which the bank would like to engage in as a symbol of concern," thus making it probable Fox Street could obtain the needed loans.[136]

Another buyer had meanwhile signed a contract for the Tiffany Street property, but could not come up with adequate funds. He requested a three-week extension. Glenn Zeager and Dale Stoltzfus tied up as many loose ends as possible to be ready when the other buyer withdrew. In the end, the other buyer obtained the property and Glenn Zeager recognized the Tiffany Street project was "a dream of the past."[137]

The Sherman Avenue group had their first Sunday morning worship service on January 5, 1969, in the room used by the Bible club, with

A Sunday morning worship group at Good Shepherd Mennonite Church.

34 people present. They decided on Good Shepherd Mennonite Church as their official name since they planned to organize a congregation. There were several applicants for baptism in the believers class and it was agreed that at the time of their baptism the Mennonite members would transfer their membership to Good Shepherd.[138]

The Bible Club program continued. Norma Brenner, Ella Coffman, and Martha Charles taught the classes. Martha Charles was also making new contacts in the neighborhood.[139] The program continued through the summer with an emphasis on remedial reading.[140]

The transition to an autonomous congregation proceeded smoothly. Sixteen persons applied for membership in the Good Shepherd Mennonite Church and the congregation was formally organized on December 14, 1969. At the founding service three new members were baptized, three received on confession of faith, and ten as transfers from other Mennonite churches. The morning worship included a covenant of dedication and a communion service. The chairs in the chapel formed a semi-circle as everyone took part in the service where they were. In the afternoon they held their first member's meeting and chose Wesley Newswanger as congregational chairman, Ernestine Moir secretary, and John Buckwalter treasurer.[141]

Carl Good submitted his resignation as pastor at the second members' meeting on January 11, 1970. He told the congregation that his decision to leave New York for graduate school in clinical psychology had not been an easy one. "Carl and Lois have wrestled with this over a year and feel that God is leading them to make this move." Good Shepherd members reacted with disappointment at "seeing Carl leave them after putting in a lot of work and energy in building the congregation." They asked the Administrative Council to help them find another pastor.[142] While the search for a pastor went on, the Good Shepherd congregation held a dedication service for their new church building at 1126 Sherman Avenue on April 26, 1970.

Carl Good's resignation left the new congregation without a pastor at a time when Good Shepherd had not fully identified its purpose and mission. The church cabinet spent many frustrating weeks trying to find a pastor. By the summer of 1970, the search for leadership centered on the congregation. On August 9, 1970, they chose Wesley Newswanger as pastor and John Buckwalter as assistant pastor. Both Newswanger, the congregational chairman, and Buckwalter, the treasurer, had given leadership to the inchoate congregation in its transition from the Bible and crafts club work begun by Norma Brenner and Mabel Herr. Other leaders had emerged within the new congregation. Dr. Martin Bender had been invited to begin Mennonite Board of Missions outreach in New York City when he was still a student at Eastern Mennonite College. After graduating in 1957, Bender had earned a doctorate in education and developed a teaching machine that gave him recognition in academic circles and a substantial income. He moved to New York City with his family and became active in the House of Friendship. The Benders rented the house on Sherman Avenue vacated by Wesley and Marian Newswanger. Martin and Ethel Bender began holding weekly prayer meetings in their new home in the summer of 1970. Their charismatic emphasis appealed to many in the Good Shepherd community. Martha Charles recalled she did not attend the first meeting or two, but found the weekly meetings uplifting and inspiring. Because of his interests and gifts in evangelism, Bender was invited to

John and Miriam Buckwalter with their sons. From left: Timothy, Richard, and Robert.

Wes and Marian Newswanger family.
From left: Lynda, Daryl, Wes and Marian, Ryan.

take responsibility for evangelistic outreach. The prayer meeting became an outreach for evangelism when Norma Brenner and Martha Charles invited the group to visit the families of Bible club members and witness to them. Tension developed subsequently "between the church program and the evangelism program which had been under the leadership of Martin Bender."[143] Could Good Shepherd survive?

Other dreams were dying or set aside in those years. The war in Vietnam diverted money from the cities and reached into urban slums for a disproportionate number of young men to fight and die there. New York City Mennonites heard a good deal about the Vietnam war. James Metzler was the main speaker at a Peace Conference held in July 1967 at the Mennonite House of Friendship. He also spoke and showed slides at the Friends Meeting House on East 15th Street and met with the VS Unit at East 19th Street. The Glad Tidings congregation helped support Don Sensenig's work in Saigon. As the war became more destructive, New York Mennonites joined others in organizing the community to protest.[144]

NOTES

[1] August Meier and Elliott Rudwick, *CORE, A Study in the Civil Rights Movement*, (Urbana, Illinois, 1975), 301-302.

[2] Summer Student Pastoral Assistants, Report by Donald Schierling, East Harlem Protestant Parish, Church of the Resurrection," Sept. 21, 1964, MHLA.

[3] *East Harlem Protestant Parish Newsletter*, Oct. 1964.

[4] Meier and Rudwick, *CORE*, 330.

[5] *New York Times*, Dec. 1, Dec. 2, 1963. Michael Lipsky, "Protests in City Politics: Rent Strikes," *Housing and the Power of the Poor* (Chicago, 1970), 53-83. Meier and Rudwick, *CORE*, 244.

[6] *New York Times*, Feb. 3, Feb., 4, Feb. 28, Mar. 15, Mar. 16, 1964, Apr. 21, 1964. Smucker, "Reflections," 345.

[7] Anna Buckwalter to Paul Burkholder, Dec. 19, 1965. Burkholder Papers. John I. Smucker, "Blacks in the Mennonite Church," Term Paper, Union Theological Seminary, 1968, 11. MHL-Goshen.

[8] Seventh Avenue Mennonite Church, Self Analysis of Congregation, July-August 1965, EMM.

[9] *New York Times*, Apr. 23, 1964. David Chalmers, *And the Crooked Places Made Straight: The Struggle for Social Change in the 1960s*, (Baltimore, 1991), 55.

[10] *New York Times*, Apr. 11, 1964, Apr. 23, 1964, Apr. 24, 1964.

[11] *New York Times*, June 9, 1964.

[12] John I. Smucker to Mennonite and Brethren in Christ Ministers' Fellowship, May 19, 1964, MBM-AMC.

[13] Notes on Meeting at Mennonite House of Friendship, May 22, 1964, MBM-AMC.

[14] Henry A. Ginder to Paul Hill, October 15, 1964. Ginder Papers, BCA-MC.

[15] Ray Horst to Ken Seitz, Jan. 27, 1965. Kenneth Seitz to John Eby and Walter Paetkau, Jan. 28, 1965. Urie A. Bender to Ray Horst, Feb. 11, 1965, MBM-AMC.

[16] Kenneth Seitz to John Eby and Walter Paetkau, Feb. 15, 1965.

[17] Kenneth Seitz to John I. Smucker, Mar. 25, 1965. Kenneth Seitz, Summary of New York City Contacts during April 1965. Newton S. Weber to Kenneth Seitz, Sept. 13, 1965, MBM-AMC.

[18] Kenneth Seitz, Summary of New York City Contacts, Apr. 1965, MBM-AMC.

[19] H. Howard Witmer to Paul N. Kraybill, Jan. 10, 1966, EMM.

[20] Meier and Rudwick, *CORE*, 314-319.

[21] Chalmers, *And the Crooked Places*, 59-62. Dewey W. Grantham, *Recent America: The United States Since 1945* (Arlington Heights, Illinois, 1987), 271-273.

[22] "Recommendations from Directors Kanode and Heisey Regarding the Brooklyn Work, Feb. 27, 1969," BCA-MC.

[23] Richard Pannell Interview, Apr. 11, 1991. *Gospel Herald*, May 6, 1969, 414.

[24] Darrell Fast, Diary, June 12, 1965. Fast Papers.

[25] Darrell Fast, Diary, June 22, 1965. Fast Papers.

[26] Darrell Fast, Diary, Aug. 30, 1965. Fast Papers.

[27] "Fox Street, New York City," *Missionary Messenger*, (Oct. 1963), 2-3. Dorothy Freed, "Fox Street Revisited," *Missionary Messenger*, 40(Feb. 1964), 2-3. Fox Street Building Committee Minutes, July 29, 1963, EMM.

[28] John Freed and Carl Good comp. "Fox Street Mennonite," n.d. July-Aug. 1965. John L. Freed to Paul Landis, May 20, 1965, EMM.

[29] Evelyn Hertzler, form letter to Eastern Mennonite College students, 1964, EMM. Donald Hertzler, Interview, Aug. 18, 1990.

[30] Paul Landis to Don Wilkerson, July 27, 1964, EMM.

[31] Leon Stauffer, "New York City Youth Work Reports," September-December 1964, EMM.

[32] Paul Burkholder to H. Howard Witmer, Nov. 17, 1964, EMM.

[33] Newton Beiler, "The Glad Tidings Mennonite Church Discovers People in the Ghetto," Term Paper, 1970, Eastern Mennonite College, EMC-HL.

[34] Paul Burkholder to H. Howard Witmer, Nov. 17, 1964, EMM.

[35] "Report of Trip to Church of Our Savior in Washington, D.C.," Nov. 3, 1964, EMM.

[36] Glad Tidings members' Meeting Minutes, Nov. 11, 1964. Burkholder Papers.

[37] "Glad Tidings Store Developments," Nov. 27, 1964. Glad Tidings Members Meeting Minutes, July 23, 1964, Nov. 11, 1964. Burkholder Papers.

[38] Esther Petersheim, Sandwich Shop Diary, Dec. 1-3, 1964, LMHS.

[39] Petersheim, "Diary." Ruth Hoover, "Glad Tidings Sandwich Shop," *Missionary Messenger*, 40 (Dec. 1965), 10.

[40] Sandwich Shop Committee Minutes, Jan. 19, Feb. 9, 1965, LMHS.

[41] Leon Stauffer, "New York City Youth Work Project Special Report Glad Tidings Sandwich Shop", Apr., May, June 1965, EMM.

[42] Stauffer, "New York City Youth Work Project," Apr., May, June 1965, EMM.

[43] Beiler, "Glad Tidings Mennonite Church Discovers," Term Paper, 1970, Eastern Mennonite College, EMC-HL.

[44] Elmer Lapp, "Glad Tidings Rec Center," New York City Youth Work Project, Special Report Glad Tidings Sandwich Shop, April, May, June, 1965, EMM.

[45] Esther Petersheim, Interview, Aug. 16, 1990. Nancy Witmer, "Preparing for Death, Embracing Life," *Christian Living*, Mar. 1989.

[46] Jay Lefever to Leon Stauffer, Sept. 22, 1966, EMM.

[47] Youth Workers Council Minutes, Dec. 9, 1966, EMM.

[48] Glad Tidings Cabinet Minutes, May 1969, Apr. 1970, LMHS.

[49] Glad Tidings Cabinet Minutes, Aug. 25, 1971, Sept. 27, 1971, Oct. 12, 1971, Nov. 7, 1971, LMHS.

[50] Glad Tidings Cabinet Minutes, Feb. 9, 1972, Mar. 8, 1972, LMHS.

[51] Glad Tidings Cabinet Minutes, Oct. 15, 1972, Nov. 22, 1972, Aug. 13, 1973, LMHS.

[52] Frank King, "1-w in the Heart of Harlem," *The 1-w Mirror*, 14 (June 1966), 1-2.

[53] John I. Smucker, "Mennonites in Harlem: A Study of Seventh Avenue Mennonite Church," Term Paper, Union Theological Seminary, Jan. 1969, MHL-Goshen.

[54] New York City Youth Study Committee, Feb. 1968, EMM.

[55] New York Consultation, Dec. 28-29, 1965, EMM.

[56] Administrative Council Minutes, Feb. 11, 1967. Paul Landis to Leon Stauffer, June 14, 1967. Leon Stauffer to Paul Landis, June 16, 1967, EMM.

[57] Lois Good, VS Unit, New York, NY, Monthly Report, m.d.(January 1966), EMM.

[58] VS Center, Monthly Report, Jan. 29, 1966, Apr. 25, 1966. John W. Eby to Carl Good, Apr. 18, 1966, Apr. 29, 1966. Carl Good to John W. Eby, Apr. 29, 1966. Leon Stauffer to Jerry Meck, May 3, 1966, EMM.

[59] VS Center Monthly Report, June 25, 1966, July 29, 1966, Aug. 26, 1966, Sept. 26, 1966, Nov. 22, 1966. John W. Eby to Ira Buckwalter, Aug. 11, 1966. Jerry Meck to Leon Stauffer, Sept. 19, 1966, EMM.

[60] Gerald Meck to Leon Stauffer, Oct. 25, 1966, EMM.

[61] New York City Administrative Visit, Feb. 8, 1967, EMM.

[62] Jay Lefever, Glad Tidings Youth Work Project Report No. 2, June 1966, Apr. 1967, EMM. Esther Petersheim, Interview.

[63] Interview, Jay Lefever, Aug. 18, 1990. Jay Lefever, "Christmas with Our Basketball Team," Dec. 1967, EMM.

[64] Carl Good to Paul Landis, Aug. 11, 1967. Larry Nolt to Leon Stauffer, Sept. 20, 1967. John L. Freed to Leon Stauffer, Oct. 13, 1967. Dale Stoltzfus to Leon Stauffer, Nov. 30, 1967, EMM.

[65] Robert Draper, Fox Street Youth Work Report, Mar. 1968, Apr. 1968, EMM.

[66] Robert Draper, Fox Street Youth Work Reports, June 29, 1968, EMM.

[67] Robert Draper, Fox Street Youth Work Report, Sept. 21, 1968, Nov. 15, 1968, EMM.

[68] Eugene Shelly, Glad Tidings Mennonite Church 1969 Report, Feb. 20, 1970, EMM.

[69] Leonor Constantin Kennell, interview. Glad Tidings Cabinet Minutes, Dec. 1968, May 1969, Dec. 7, 1969, June 4, 1970, Sept. 30, 1970, Apr. 26, 1971, May 9, 1971, June 21, 1971, EMM.

[70] Administrative Council Minutes, Aug. 12, 1969, Nov. 10, 1969, Dec. 15, 1969, Mar. 3, 1970, EMM.

[71] Jim King to Mary Jean Kraybill, Aug. 14, 1971, EMM.

[72] Paul G. Burkholder, "Glad Tidings Mennonite Church Herald Tribune Fresh Air Fund Agency Report 1966," Mar. 17, 1967, EMM.

[73] Paul Burkholder to John Eby, Jan. 18, 1966. Paul Burkholder to John Eby, Mar. 8, 1966, EMM.

[74] Evelyn Hertzler, "A Report of Glad Tidings and Community," Aug. 1965, EMM.

[75] Loren Lind, "Four Hundred Heroes a Day," *Christian Living*, 14(Jan. 1967).

[76] Christian Education committee Meeting Minutes, May 20, 1965, June 7, 1965, EMM.

[77] Program, Christian Education Conference, Nov. 19-21, 1965. Kraybill Papers. John W. Eby, comp., New York consultation, Dec. 28-29, 1965, EMM.

[78] New York Consultation, Dec. 28-29, 1965, EMM.

[79] November Business Meeting, Fox Street Mennonite Church, Nov. 1964. John L. Freed to Paul Landis, May 20, 1965, EMM.

[80] John L. Freed to Paul G. Landis, May 13, 1965. Paul G. Landis to John L. Freed, May 17, 1965. John L. Freed to Paul Landis, May 20, 1965, EMM.

[81] Paul Landis to Howard Witmer, July 23, 1965. H. Howard Witmer to John L. Freed, Aug. 30, 1965. John L. Freed to Howard Witmer, Dec. 20, 1965, EMM.

[82] John H. Kraybill to H. Howard Witmer, Dec. 8, 1965. Administrative Council Minutes, Feb. 27, 1966, Mar. 26, 1966, EMM.

[83] Seventh Avenue Mennonite Church, Business Meeting Minutes, Mar. 17, 1965, EMM.

[84] John H. Kraybill to "Fellow Christians at Seventh Avenue," May 5, 1965, EMM.

[85] John H. Kraybill to Dear Friends, Sept. 24, 1965, EMM.

[86] Administrative Council Minutes, Lancaster Conference Mennonite Churches of New York City, Feb. 27, 1966, EMM.

[87] Administrative Council Minutes, Jan.5, 1967, Feb. 11, 1967, Sept. 28, 1967, EMM.

[88] H. Howard Witmer to Paul N. Kraybill, Jan. 10, 1966, EMM.

[89] Administrative Council Minutes, Feb. 27, 1966, EMM.

[90] Administrative Council Minutes, Mar. 26, 1966, EMM.

[91] Administrative Council Minutes, Apr. 14, 1969, EMM.

[92] Administrative Council Minutes, May 21, 1969, EMM.

[93] Administrative Council Minutes, Apr. 28, 1970, EMM.

[94] Kraybill, a pastor in Johnstown, Pennsylvania, was no longer resident in New York City and hence ineligible. Administrative Council Minutes, May 28, 1970, EMM.

[95] Administrative Council Minutes, June 3, 1970, June 11, 1970. Paul Landis to Dear Christian Friends, June 6, 1970, EMM.

[96] Administrative Council Minutes, June 29, 1970, EMM.

[97] Administrative Council Minutes, June 29, 1970, July 28, 1970, Sept. 3, 1970, Oct. 19, 1970, Nov. 10, 1970, EMM.

[98] Glad Tidings Discipline Committee Minutes, Sept. 19, 1965. Steven M. Nolt, "Church Discipline in the Lancaster Mennonite Conference," *Pennsylvania Mennonite Heritage*, XV(Oct. 1992), 11.

[99] Discipline Committee Meeting Minutes, Oct. 3, 1965. Margaret Huertas and Esther Petersheim, "Report of the Discipline Committee," Oct. 3, 1965, EMM.

[100] New York Consultation, Dec. 28-29, 1965, EMM.

[101] Paul Landis to H. Raymond Charles, Aug. 25, 1966, EMM.

[102] Richard Pannell, Oct. 31, 1966.

[103] Paul Landis to H. Raymond Charles, Aug. 25, 1966.

[104] Don Kraybill, Administrative Visit, Feb. 20-24, 1967.

[105] Chester Wenger to Lucy Vance, Aug. 22, 1967. Lucy Vance to Chester Wenger, Aug. 31, 1967.

[106] Administrative Council Minutes, June 19, 1967. Glenn Zeager to Paul Landis, Mar. 25, 1969. Lucy Vance, "On 24-Hour Duty," *Missionary Messenger*, May 1969, 8-10.

[107] Administrative Council Minutes, Mar. 26, 1966, Jan. 5, 1967, Feb. 11, 1967, EMBMC-A.

[108] Administrative Council Minutes, July 31, 1966, Aug. 25, 1966, Sept. 1, 1966, Jan. 5, 1967.

[109] Administrative Council Minutes, Oct. 1, 1966.

[110] Ira Buckwalter to Mr. and Mrs. Paul G. Burkholder, June 1, 1970. Norman Shenk to Ira Buckwalter, June 2, 1970, EMBMC-A.

[111] Administrative Council Minutes, June 26, 1968.

[112] Anna M. Buckwalter to Chester Wenger, Dec. 8, 1968, EMBMC-A.

[113] Paul Landis to H. Raymond Charles, Aug. 25, 1966, EMBMC-A.

[114] Administrative Council Minutes, Feb. 11, 1967, EMBMC-A.

[115] Bernard Rediger, Monthly Report, July 29, 1967, MBM-AMC.

[116] Administrative Council Minutes, Mar. 7, 1968, EMBMC-A.

[117] John L. Freed to Chester Wenger, Feb. 2, 1968. John L. Freed to Norman Shenk, Feb. 2, 1968. Administrative Council Minutes, Aug. 12, 1968, EMBMC-A.

[118] Smucker, "Reflections," 447.

119 John L. Freed to Paul G. Landis, Feb. 16, 1968, EMBMC-A.

120 Paul G. Landis to John L. Freed, Feb. 22, 1968, EMBMC-A.

121 Fox Street Cabinet Meeting Minutes, Mar. 10, 1968, Apr. 3, 1968, EMBMC-A.

122 Fox Street Cabinet Meeting Minutes, Apr. 3, 1968.

123 Carl Good to Paul Landis and Chester Wenger, Aug. 25, 1967. John Buckwalter to Chester Wenger, May 11, 1968.

124 John L. Freed to Chester Wenger, May 3, 1968, EMBMC-A.

125 Fox Street Cabinet Meeting Minutes, May 19, 1968, EMBMC-A.

126 Administrative Council Minutes, June 26, 1968, EMBMC-A.

127 John L. Freed to Paul Landis, Apr. 3, 1968. John L. Freed to Ralph and Esther Villanueva, n.d. Carl Metzler to Chester Wenger, Aug. 23, 1968, EMBMC-A.

128 Administrative Council Minutes, Jan. 13, 1969, EMBMC-A. Carl Metzler to Chester Wenger, Jan. 21, 1969. Paul Landis to Carl Metzler and Carl Good, Feb. 11, 1969. Carl Metzler to Chester Wenger and Paul Landis, Mar. 14, 1969, EMBMC-A.

129 Paul Landis to Carl Metzler, Mar. 20, 1969. Chester Wenger to Carl Metzler, Mar. 26, 1969. Carl Metzler to Paul Landis, Apr. 25, 1969, EMBMC-A.

130 Administrative Council Minutes, Aug. 12, 1969, EMBMC-A. Monroe Yoder to Chester Wenger, Aug. 20, 1969.

131 Administrative Council Minutes, Dec. 15, 1969, EMBMC-A.

132 Chester L. Wenger to Glenn Zeager, Dec. 19, 1969. Administrative Council Minutes, Jan. 12, 1970, EMBMC-A.

133 Chester Wenger to Executive Committee, Nov. 20, 1970.

134 Administrative Council Minutes, Jan. 11, 1971. Tiffany Street Renovation Project, Fox Street Mennonite Church, Dec. 21, 1970. Norman Shenk to Chester Wenger, De. 22, 1970. Chester L. Wenger to Norman Shenk, Dec. 23, 1970, EMBMC-A.

135 Mennonite Disaster Service Bulletin, Dec. 16, 1970. Chester Wenger to Dale Stoltzfus, Jan. 4, 1971. Dale Stoltzfus to Glenn Zeager, Jan. 7, 1971. Dale Stoltzfus to Richard Shertzer, Jan.8, 1971, EMBMC-A.

136 Chester L. Wenger to Norman Shenk, Feb. 17, 1971, EMBMC-A.

137 Chester Wenger to Norman Shenk, Mar. 3, 1971. Administrative Council Minutes, Feb. 23, 1971, Apr. 7, 1971, EMBMC-A.

138 Administrative Council Minutes, Jan. 13, 1969, EMBMC-A.

139 Carl Good to Paul Landis, Mar. 27, 1969. Carl Good to Chester Wenger, May 1, 1969, EMBMC-A.

140 Administrative Council Minutes, June 12, 1969, EMBMC-A.

141 Administrative Council Minutes, Nov. 10, 1969, Dec. 15, 1969, EMBMC-A. Good Shepherd Members' Meeting Minutes, Dec. 14, 1969, LMHS.

142 Good Shepherd Members' Meeting Minutes, Jan. 11, 1970, Feb. 1, 1970, LMHS. Administrative Council Minutes, Jan. 12, 1970, EMBMC-A.

143 Good Shepherd Members' Meeting Minutes, Mar. 1, 1970, Apr. 26, 1970, Aug. 9, 1970, LMHS. Dale Stoltzfus to Chester Wenger, Sept. 21, 1971, EMBMC-A.

144 New York City VS Unit Monthly Report, June 1967, July 1967. Don Kraybill, Administrative Visit, New York City, July 15-18, 1967, EMBMC-A. Hope Nisly, "Witness to the Way of Peace: The Vietnam War and the Evolving Mennonite View of this Relationship to the State," *Maryland Historian* 20 (1989), 7-23.

CHAPTER NINE

Organizing the Community
1968–1974

JUST BEFORE CHRISTMAS 1969, Millen Brand, a novelist and editor for a major publishing firm, came to the District Council meeting and shared some of his poems as a devotional reading.[1] Brand was a friend of Gene Shelly and the Glad Tidings congregation. As a poet, he caught the essence of what the Mennonites were doing in New York City and put it in words that might not have come so easily to them. He wrote of the difficult transformation of soft-spoken Lancaster farmers into advocates at City Hall for the poor and the first halting steps toward organizing community action.

The Glad Tidings Mennonite Church

Today being Sunday, the sandwich shop closed,
in the housefront church at 344 Brook Avenue, South Bronx,
in a room behind the altar
Pastor Eugene Shelly sits at a table end with six men and women
down one side and six down the other side
for Bible study.
Some are from the Service Unit on East Nineteenth Street.
VSers. Two are Puerto Rican.
On the women's heads, the Mennonite cap.
Nehemiah 8:
"(Ezra) before the water gate...read in the book in the law
of God distinctly, and gave the sense, and caused them
to understand the reading."
The people wept, but Ezra told them, 'The joy of the Lord is
your strength,' and told them not to weep."
Pastor Shelly says, "The Jews perhaps mourned for having broken
the law, but Ezra wanted them to rejoice that they had
the law. He wanted gladness, happiness."
"So they keep the law?" one asks.

"Yes. To be happy. Could the gods of the peoples around Jerusalem—Baal and those others—could they give happiness?"
"No." No.
"'Give me understanding, and I shall keep thy law; yea, I shall observe it with my whole heart.'"
Psalm 119.

At eleven thirty, church service begins.
Some members are "in retreat."
"We aren't many," Pastor Shelly says. "It's like the Coffee Hour, which we aren't having today. Let's come up around the organ and sing."
They gather at the organ, Puerto Ricans, blacks, VSers, four kids caressed by the grownups.
"Jesus, I my cross have taken,
All to leave and follow Thee:
Naked, poor, despised, forsaken,
Thou, from hence, my all shalt be-"
"Tranquil river, let me ever
Sit and sing by thee.
Tranquil river, let me ever
Sit and sing by thee."
After the singing, after the service and benediction, many go from church upstairs to see the pastor's wife, Martine, and the Shellys' newborn baby, Michael.
The baby sleeps on Martine's arm.
"Who does he look like?"
"Well, he has my forehead," Gene says, smiling and indicating his own receding hair.
One asks about "the robbery."
Gene says, "The church window's broken, we haven't had it fixed yet, and they stepped in that and got to the fire-escape ladder, and the window was open for air. So they came in while we slept."
The run-on and murmur of voices slackens until only an out-of-town visitor is left. Gene says,
"You think it's bad we had the TV stolen.
One night somebody called me at two o'clock in the morning. It was to tell me my car, that I keep parked outside, had one of the wheels gone.
I went down and found the car jacked up and no right rear wheel.
You can expect it in this street."

Gene was born in Lancaster, but was brought up in the "Deep South," absorbing there "the attitudes of my peers."
He went to the Eastern Mennonite College
in Harrisonburg, Virginia,
attended seminary there and from there, still from the South and inexperienced, not fully taught,
took over this church.
"You saw this street. It's unbelievable. At first I thought nothing could be done.
I still wonder.
I get help from the VSers here in this house
and from the brothers and sisters from the Unit House on Nineteenth Street,
but even so. Still
you have to do something.
I try not to let what I do and plan get too far ahead of the congregation,
but the need for local leadership is desperate. Two things:
Housing. Some tenants are organizing against the landlord, and need help. We're thinking, the church I mean, about 'adopting' one building, helping them get together.
Medical care. A woman, and maybe with kids, has to spend six hours now waiting in a clinic. What I'd like is a doctor to volunteer to work here.
But that isn't easy. They go abroad. And we so much need a doctor here.
Mennonites in the rural areas
don't know that work in the cities helps *them*, is important to them. Like,
there's a drug problem now in Lancaster County,
kids taking drugs. But it spreads from the city. Here in this block
nearly all the older teen-agers take drugs. They come in and talk with me, tell me how they steal, how the pushers push it, where they cut it.
They show me their arms.
We do what we can, work through certain ones to rehabilitate,
but the problem, like many others, is part political, isn't it? We Mennonites
haven't tended to join community groups.
It's considered dangerous and secular, and it is dangerous. But we, being under the lordship of Christ, must do it, must join with others,
if we're to accomplish something."[2]

The Glad Tidings congregation joined a coalition of South Bronx churches pressing the city authorities for decent housing. As the number of abandoned, burned-out and derelict buildings increased in sections like the South Bronx, the number of houses and apartments decreased for the first time in the city's history. The *New York Times* called attention to the problem in February 1970, noting "Housing Supply in City is Eroding."[3] Poor people found it harder to live as some landlords "milked" their buildings. Unable to overhaul the heating plant or make repairs needed to bring the building up to city code standards, they collected what rent they could while they paid no taxes and provided no services for tenants.[4] Eugene Shelly represented Glad Tidings on the Bronx Clergy Coalition for Housing Action. They took their concerns to the city authorities. As Millen Brand told the story—

A Litany of Housing

In early nineteen seventy,
thirty South Bronx clergy, seeing
not steeples, not churches
beside churchyard trees and protected bushes,
but never-ending blocks of poverty—these clergymen
prepared a statement on housing
in the form of a litany. On a certain day
all thirty went down to City Hall
to a City Council meeting-
such meetings are open to the public-
and took their places in the gallery.
"Then," Pastor Shelly says,
"something rather good happened,
an accident. The clergyman the Council was expecting
to open the meeting with prayer
didn't come. We suggested that one of us
give the prayer instead.
We were a cross section of the clergy-
Protestant, Catholic, Jewish—on the whole
conservative, and the Council President
Sanford D. Garelik and another councilman
stood reverently to hear us.
We gave our litany:

'O God the Father of all men,
HAVE MERCY UPON US

O God the Son, who suffered at the hand of governors and chief priests,

HAVE MERCY UPON US

O God the Holy Ghost who enlightens every man that comes into the world,

HAVE MERCY UPON US

Hear our prayer, O Lord, as we cry out for the homes in which Thy people dwell. In your compassion help those forced to live amid inhuman conditions, especially in the South Bronx.

LORD, HEAR OUR PRAYER

From ice on top of water in the kitchen; from the collapse of bathroom ceilings; from water running down the bedroom walls,

GOOD LORD, DELIVER US

From bits of paint and plaster in the babies' beds,

GOOD LORD, DELIVER US

From garbage in the hall and on the stairs; from garbage in the streets and in the cellar; from garbage on the sidewalk and the cars; from garbage in the courtyard and the alley, and in every other place,

GOOD LORD, DELIVER US

From the sicknesses of little children: from rat bite and lead poisoning; from colds, bronchitis, and pneumonia; from malnutrition and from starvation,

GOOD LORD, DELIVER US

From the abysmal hopelessness of families; from the rage of fathers; from the despair of mothers; from drunkenness and addiction, and from apathy,

GOOD LORD, DELIVER US

From a bureaucracy that cannot see; and seeing cannot act,

GOOD LORD, DELIVER US

From hearings that cannot comprehend,

GOOD LORD, DELIVER US

From all excuses, postponements, and delays; from redundant investigations, inquiries, studies, and reports; from referral and reconsideration, and from all subcommittees,

GOOD LORD, DELIVER US

From all emergency telephone numbers and emergency repairs that bring frustration faster,

GOOD LORD, DELIVER US

From promises that are made but never kept; from housing meetings that are dreamed up but never held,

GOOD LORD, DELIVER US

From the excuse that the City Council has no power, but only the Mayor; that the Mayor has no power, but only the State Legislature; that the Legislature has no power, but only the Governor; that the Governor has no power, but only the Congress; that the Congress has no power, but only the President; and from all buck passing,

GOOD LORD, DELIVER US

From attempts to belittle human dignity by labeling those who cry out for justice as anarchists, communists, troublemakers, and corrupters of youth,

GOOD LORD, DELIVER US

O God of Abraham, Isaac, and Jacob, protect this generation of Thy People.

LORD, HEAR OUR PRAYER

O God of Moses, deliver the oppressed from bondage.

LORD, HEAR OUR PRAYER

O God of the Prophets, confront the conscience and stir up the will of all in power and authority.

LORD, HEAR OUR PRAYER

Hear our prayer for the relief of human need.

LORD, HEAR OUR PRAYER

Remember the soul of the child living on East 138th Street who died because of no heat in the building.

LORD, HAVE MERCY

Christ, have mercy,

LORD, HAVE MERCY

O Lord, hear our prayer,

AND LET OUR CRY COME UNTO THEE.

AMEN.'"[5]

Glad Tidings joined with twelve other churches to provide affordable housing. Michael Gill of Bankers Trust provided the churches with the needed expertise to form the South Bronx Community Housing Development Corporation.[6] John Kreider, the congregational treasurer, volunteered to serve as the representative from Glad Tidings in the South Bronx Housing Development Fund. Through South Bronx Housing, Glad Tidings and the other churches sponsored St. Francis and George Hardy Houses.[7]

Social Ministry in Bedford-Stuyvesant

Brethren in Christ mission workers had also made a personal commitment to service ministry in the inner city. The Brooklyn Brethren in Christ Church at 958 Bedford Avenue was located in the deteriorating

Bedford-Stuyvesant section, easily the city's worst slum. Harold and Cathy Bowers, who had pastored the church since 1961, were both active in the community. They helped organize a local anti-poverty group, the United Block Association, which held its meetings in their apartment.

> Once a month, we open the parsonage door to all the adults of our block. The "Block Association" grapples with the real problems of a people trying desperately to walk "up the down escalator." I write graphic letters, knock on doors, and organize. The people know we are one of them. We've become involved, and this has hurt us. We bleed, as the Negro bleeds, internally.[8]

The United Block Association, open to residents of 15 adjoining blocks, developed a neighborhood playground on a vacant lot next to the church and set up a day-care project.

Lois and Lloyd Melhorn, Jr., newlyweds from Manheim, Pennsylvania, loaded her father's car with their worldly possessions and drove to Brooklyn in September 1965 to begin a VS unit at the Bedford Avenue church. Lloyd had spent the previous year in the VS unit at Fellowship Chapel in the Bronx. The Melhorns both worked full-time at New York University Medical Center. In addition, Lloyd served as assistant pastor and minister of music and Lois played the piano for worship. They both taught Sunday school and visited neighborhood families to invite them to church. Neighborhood children were always invited to the Sunday school and to the two-week vacation Bible school in the summer. Attendance at the summer program rose from 70 in 1963 to 104 in 1964 and 120 by 1967. Released Time Christian Education began in 1966 and crafts, refreshments, and outdoor play kept children long past the allotted hour.

In 1968 the Mission Board accepted a broader vision for ministry in Bedford-Stuyvesant. A Messiah College team supervised playground activities in cooperation with the Block Association on weekends in the spring and returned for the summer. The Mission Board recommended that "the Brooklyn church be the mission church upon which our efforts during the coming year will be concentrated in 'Operation Help.'" The Board reported to the 1968 General Conference that, "Plans are being developed for a stepped-up program of community relatedness and involvement."[9]

Unfortunately, these plans for an expanded community-related ministry coincided with a change of pastoral leadership. After seven years in the inner-city, the Bowers family planned to leave Brooklyn in the summer of 1968. Harold Bowers talked with Bishop Charlie B. Byers in November 1967 about "procuring the right pastor for the work here." By January 1968 he believed he had met the right man and urged Bishop Byers to contact Cecil Loney, a minister in the Church of the Nazarene. Loney had planted three churches in his native Trinidad and was looking for a pastorate in New York.[10]

Bishop Byers attempted to arrange a meeting with Loney in February, but he had returned to Trinidad. In the meantime, he proceeded with conversations with John Ebersole, who agreed to accept the Brooklyn pastorate. This news came as a shock to Bowers and the Brooklyn congregation, who had heard Loney preach and responded warmly to him as their next pastor.[11]

John Ebersole traveled from Messiah College to Brooklyn in April and Bowers gave him a tour of the mission and talked about the work there, "although we did not discuss any particulars, such as my coming or Brother Loney." It was Ebersole's first experience of Bedford-Stuyvesant. His meeting with Bowers gave Ebersole "some insights into the work of the mission and what to expect if I go to Brooklyn" as well as "a new appreciation for him" and his work.[12]

Bishop Byers, Harold Bowers, and Cecil Loney finally got together at the National Association of Evangelicals convention in April. Byers returned to Brooklyn the first weekend in May, when Loney again preached at the Bedford Avenue church. The bishop was impressed. "It was a sermon that reflected excellent training and preparation." After further conversations, Bishop Byers concluded that Cecil Loney should be invited as pastor, "but must not be given full charge of the Brooklyn work." He proposed changing John Ebersole's title and duties and making the two men co-pastors. Ebersole would be responsible for the VS Unit, buildings, grounds and finances, Loney for worship, evangelism and nurture.[13] By early June, Byers had drafted a tentative proposal for "a Working Relationship between Rev. Cecil Loney and the Brooklyn Congregation," stressing the division of the work between two pastors, "not one the pastor and the other the assistant, but equals." Ebersole and the VS Unit would occupy the mission building and the Loney family would live in a house nearby.[14]

The difficulty inherent in this arrangement would be further complicated by the fact that neither Loney nor Ebersole had ever lived in New York City before. In fact, the only person in the mission team with any prior experience was Nancy Charles, a Messiah student who had worked with neighborhood youth on spring weekends and remained for summer VS. "Nancy Charles seems to take the lead and is doing a superb job." The summer team of five college students, Sandra Burton, Nancy Charles, John Dean, David Mumma, and Jeanne O'Handley, staffed a two-month day camp for 80 children from the immediate community. They also began playing volleyball in the evenings with 30 teenagers. The summer team "built excellent community rapport." The Block Association fully supported the program and raised $72 for playground equipment. Frank and Diana Landis, who planned to spend a year in VS, arrived in August. When Harold and Cathy Bowers left after a farewell service on August 4, Nancy Charles was "given the responsibility of directing the program and leadership."[15]

The summer program worked out successfully and laid the groundwork for the incoming VS Unit, but no one remained in Brooklyn to link the new program with the old. Tensions began to develop immediately. By November 1968 Bishop Byers, Henry N. Hostetter, director of missions, David Climenhaga, and Isaac Kanode, director of mission churches, had to intervene. Kanode explained the board's expectation that the VS Unit would be actively involved in social ministries to the community and "work cooperatively with the pastor in church activities." The pastor and unit leader would need frequent consultation so that "the facilities at 958 Bedford Avenue shall be used for both the social and spiritual ministries of the church and unit on the basis of cooperative planning."[16]

Cecil Loney wanted to focus on the growth of the Brooklyn church through traditional evangelical methods. Worship services were dignified and his sermons well-prepared and well-delivered. He put all of his efforts into the church program, including evening services on weekdays. It did not help that attendance had dropped from the 47-55 of Harold Bower's pastorate to only 20-25. Fewer blacks were coming to church than a few months earlier when Bowers was pastor. Loney had no interest in social ministries to the community and wanted the VSers' assignment limited to Released Time classes and playground activities. As a West Indian immigrant, he had no empathy with the powerful movements shaping Black America in the 1960s and he belittled Civil Rights leaders from the pulpit.

John Ebersole, on his part, wondered if Brethren in Christ were ready to take the risks of an inner-city program and whether "we have people with the training and background for this type of work." With his co-pastor unwilling to consult with the unit leader or to allow the unit to function autonomously, Ebersole concluded that all they could do would be to put their energies into planning an effective program for the next summer.[17] Kanode encouraged Ebersole to look for a job as a substitute teacher in the city schools as one means of community involvement. Bishop Byers counseled the VSers "to go the second and third miles with patience as... we must try to help Brother Loney make whatever adjustments may be necessary and, at the same time, find meaningful services for the unit in this inner-city work."[18]

Both Loney and the VS unit were ready to leave Brooklyn in January 1969. Bishop Charlie Byers recognized, "The time has come when we must take a sharp new look at the situation in Brooklyn. To say the least the work is at a standstill." Further meetings with Loney and congregational leaders Dick Hilsher and Gideon Barnett ended in an impasse. "With these men, to say it frankly, we got nowhere," Kanode reported. The surprising conclusion was for the pastor and the church to relocate and leave the VS unit in Bedford-Stuyvesant. The Mission Board remained firm in its commitment to ministry that responded to the suffering of the inner city. They cited the radical discipleship of the Anabaptists and the social holiness of Wesley as precedent for this understanding of the gospel. They recognized that Cecil Loney had real gifts for pastoral ministry, but not as a pastor in the ghetto.[19]

Kanode and Heisey proposed restructuring the Brooklyn work so that the VS unit could "minister in the name and compassion of Christ to an inner-city community."[20] The Board insisted that the program be "community-related" and "committed to active participation with the Block Association which presently is organized to deal creatively with matters of local concern." The congregation was only incidental to this program. In a list of seven objectives, the seventh was, "To meet the needs for fellowship, worship and instruction of community people, religious services and activities shall be conducted."[21]

The Loney family moved out of the Bedford Avenue building, although the church remained there, at least for the immediate future. John Ebersole and the VS unit would have a free hand. As the dust settled, Isaac Kanode visited the unit and remained uncertain what the future would hold:

> I have a growing apprehension that at this point that the unit is pretty frustrated and they keep saying repeatedly, "Now just what are we supposed to do?" And I have real fear that even when Rev. Loney does move out, as far as the unit is concerned, nothing is going to happen and this may be partly because they are waiting for us to build program for them to operate.[22]

The search for a new location for the church was not easy. Bishop Byers, Henry Hostetter, and Cecil Loney looked at buildings, mainly in Flatbush and east of Prospect Park, south of Eastern Parkway, for several weeks before they finally found one at the corner of Rogers Avenue and Sterling Street. This became Pilgrim Chapel, at 403 Rogers Avenue, dedicated on Sunday, November 30, 1969.[23] The Brooklyn congregation, with key members like the Barnetts and Hilshers still active, began a slow growth. Byers recognized that "progress at Pilgrim Chapel will be difficult and slow." In spite of a week of evangelistic services in November 1970 and eight professions of faith and three baptisms in 1971, attendance on Sundays averaged 20-25. "The visible results did not come up to what was anticipated by Rev. Cecil Loney."[24]

Pilgrim Chapel, Brethren in Christ, 403 Rogers Avenue, Brooklyn. 2005 photo.

The program for the Brooklyn VS unit became almost by default the program of the United Block Association. The VS unit at Fellowship Chapel in the Bronx supported the work of the congregation with outreach in the community to neighborhood youth in addition to church activities. Without a nearby mission church, the young people at the Bedford Avenue unit had few settled points of reference. Lewis Miller joined the unit in 1969 as earning member with outside employment, making it possible for the Bedford unit to be financially self-sustaining. His wife, Joanne Engle Miller, as matron, hostess, and teacher made many person-to-person contacts in the neighborhood. When John Ebersole left in 1970, Lew Miller turned down an invitation to be unit leader. Eldon Sheffer took the responsibility of unit leader, but soon made it clear he would leave in May 1971. Norika Matsuura, a young Japanese woman, and David Frey, a 1970 Messiah graduate, joined the unit the same year.

The young VSers staffed "activities sponsored by the 15-block United Block Association at 958 Bedford Avenue," including a day-care center and recreation programs. They were also learning the facts of political life. Once the Block Association or any community organization had its program approved, anti-poverty funds flowed in with little or no supervision. The funds went to persons with connections on the Association's payroll, whose job performance was sub-standard and lacking in motivation. Although the Association claimed it represented the people, leaders quickly became hierarchical, with no interest in grass-roots democracy. It became evident that the arrangement with the United Block Association would not be renewed after May 1971.[25]

Other problems beset the VS unit. Leadership was lacking. Byers heard negative reports on an administrative visit in March 1971 to Pilgrim Chapel. Curtis Barnett, a Brooklyn College student who was active in Inter Varsity on his campus, lived in the neighborhood. "He said the parents of the community are very much disappointed that there is not more spiritual emphasis, no Bible class that involves the community." The VS unit had taken on the secular approach of the Block Association. Byers concluded after visiting the Bedford Avenue unit that, "The unit itself and work of the unit is badly in need of strong leadership. They need a well-defined program with better discipline on most levels." He was also concerned for a clearly defined purpose and the spiritual benefit to the community, "both for the youth and the homes of those open for help."

Charles and Ruth Rife seemed to Bishop Byers to provide "an answer to prayer and the first step for some improvements." Rife had had a good experience in VS at Fellowship Chapel where he developed a successful outreach to neighborhood youth. The Rifes were willing to become unit leaders in Brooklyn, but changed their minds when they had been there a short time. They explained to Byers that no one gave them a fair evaluation of Brooklyn and they assumed it would be "similar in living quarters to the Bronx." They found the mission house on Bedford Avenue "a genuine pig's mess." The regular VSers and the summer unit played rock and roll music until four in the morning and generally behaved like college students on spring break. The Rifes were shocked by the disorganization evident in the day-care center and other programs. The VSers lay in bed almost all morning. They seemed to be "wasting time, doing nothing." They agreed with Rife "that they are tired doing nothing."[26]

With the Rifes gone and the summer unit back in college in September 1971, Dana M. Crider remained at 958 Bedford Avenue as the lone VSer. His grandfather Rev. Harvey Musser moved in with him. The United Block Association wanted to lease the building with an option to buy. Dana pointed out that it would be nearly impossible to run any program with the Block Association in the building. "When UBA rented the chapel and the basement kitchen during the 1970-1971 school term, they spilled over into other space and hampered what little program the VSers tried to operate themselves." There had actually been no organized program for service and outreach since the summer of 1970 and no one in a money-earning capacity since the Millers left in the summer of 1971. The Mission Board could begin again with a newly-recruited unit or they could cut their losses and withdraw. Musser returned to Pennsylvania in November 1971 and Dana Crider was transferred to the VS unit at Fellowship Chapel in the Bronx. The United Block Association bought the building at 958 Bedford Avenue for $24,000 in May 1972. Another dream had died in Bedford-Stuyvesant.[27]

Organizing the Community

The congregation at the House of Friendship made do with an improvised chapel in the basement for the first few years, since the building was intended as a center, not a church. They began planning for larger facilities in 1960 and launched a building fund drive in 1963. By May 1965 they had obtained the necessary approval of the New York City Building Department and construction could proceed. As the new structure was rising, Pastor John Smucker reported: "The basic construction will cost $100,000. If we decided to use permanent benches and carpet it would cost another $5,000." The congregation had $35,000 on hand, including a $10,000 gift from the Mission Board.[28]

Excavation for the new church building at Mennonite House of Friendship on Southern Boulevard, Bronx. This is the only one of the Mennonite and Brethren in Christ congregations in New York City to erect a new building.

The new church was ready to be dedicated in February 1966. "We have completed our building and are using it," Smucker wrote. "The basic construction cost $107,000" and minimal furnishings added another $4,000.[29] The decision to use folding chairs had unexpected consequences. The building program had strained the resources of the congregation to the limit. Several families who had given sacrificially to the Church in money and time were disappointed that the new sanctuary still had the look of a temporary chapel. They wanted permanent benches and a carpet.[30] Smucker mused later, "Exhausted by the unusual energy the congregation just expended on completing the construction of the new building, they could not agree on how to furnish it. Was their problem benches or chairs, or was it a profound disagreement about mission to the community?"[31]

In the autumn of 1965, Protestant ministers in the area known as Bronx Park South, including John Smucker of the Mennonite House of Friendship, began talking about a common project. They decided to work with the East Tremont Neighborhood Association on a community summer recreation program. Smucker appealed to Mennonite Board of Missions for two or three Voluntary Service workers for the summer.[32]

They planned a full schedule from June 27 to the end of August with vacation church school in the mornings and recreation, arts, crafts, and music in the afternoons. "We are requesting poverty funds for the afternoon program."[33] Jesse Adams, Martin Brenneman, and Leonard Kilmer came to the Bronx to work in the summer program. Leonard and Martin worked with the House of Friendship and Jesse was assigned to Beck Presbyterian Church. They helped run seven vacation church schools for elementary pupils, a coffee house program, and helped with Bible distribution in the neighborhood.[34]

New church building for Mennonite House of Friendship, at 2281 Southern Boulevard, Bronx. 2005 photo.

Jesse Adams discovered the Mennonite Church as a student at Fort Wayne Bible College. A young African-American from Chattanooga, Tennessee, he remained in the Fort Wayne area after graduation and later worked in the Elkhart office of Mennonite Board of Missions. He returned to the House of Friendship in 1967 as director of the summer program. In 1968 the congregation called him as assistant pastor, but he did not accept until three years later.[35]

Kenneth Seitz, director of Voluntary Service, visited the House of Friendship to explore the need for long-term volunteers. He attended a meeting of the area pastors and others interested in "coordinated community action in making the area a better place in which to live and work." From his visit he had a clearer impression of the changing neighborhood and the problems endemic to it. "Juvenile delinquency, poor housing, more low income people are all a part of the neighborhood around the House of Friendship." The congregation was just beginning to reach out, "ministering to the community through club programs, release time Bible classes, and the regular worship services."[36]

Bernard and Emma Rediger from Kalona, Iowa, came to the House of Friendship in December 1966. Emma's assignment was as John Smucker's secretary. Bernard's job description was community youth worker. On one of his first days in the city he visited Jay Lefever at Glad Tidings and went with him to the Youth Workers Council meeting at Seventh Avenue. He could learn from the veterans and from relative newcomers.[37]

The Redigers set up a coffee-house recreation center in the basement of the House of Friendship where the original chapel had been. "The Cellar" opened in February 1967 with 30-40 kids, mostly boys. "I think it's going to be a great way to meet kids." Bernard was getting to know most of the neighborhood teenagers. He organized a basketball team and hung out with boys who had dropped out of an earlier boys' club. A core group was emerging. Hosea, 15, and Dennis, 13, would come to talk and began attending church with the Redigers. By late spring he could write "Softball, The Cellar, Boys' Club, Cleaning Church, etc. really keeps me busy. Emma and I are to the place where New York really seems like our home. We really enjoy being involved in this community and church. God has given us relationships with many kids."

The neighborhood had its dangerous moments, too. Walking with some visiting Christopher Dock students from the subway station, a block from Southern Boulevard, Bernard stopped to talk with some Puerto Rican friends. A few minutes later three other youths attacked Bernard and two of the visitors, warning them not to come into their territory again. Bernard's friends rescued them, explaining that they were not Italians. Gary Rumble, a Brethren in Christ 1-W man, was mistaken for an Italian, beaten up and left unconscious in the doorway of an apartment house, a block from the church. Dennis, Mike, and Jose found out who was responsible and confronted them in the pool room. Later that night they went back to East 180th Street with John Smucker and Bernard Rediger. "We talked with them a long time," Bernard reported. "They really were sorry that they got an innocent guy. So they agreed to come to the church the following Monday. So they did, about 15-20 guys. There we really got acquainted and they apologized to Gary." He gave his testimony of how Christ changed his heart. It was a significant moment in mission.[38]

Jesse Adams returned to the Bronx in July 1967 to direct the vacation Bible school at the House of Friendship and work with Bernard Rediger in taking 25 boys to Hunter College, where they could use all the athletic facilities including the swimming pool. Everyone agreed Jesse did a fabulous job. "There were nine decisions for Christ in our camp which he directed and we had an excellent day camp/vacation church school this summer." Friendship followed the pattern set by Evelyn Hertzler at Glad Tidings with an eight-week program of vacation Bible school in the morning and recreation and cultural activities in the afternoons under the Poverty Program.[39] Bernard Rediger had equal enthusiasm for Jesse Adams' contribution to the summer program. "Now that camp is over the kids themselves suggested meeting once a week as a group to discuss problems, have Bible study and prayer. We have met three times now and this meeting has proved to be very meaningful and helpful to the kids."[40] As a result of the summer camp, ten teenagers from the community became Christians. Ken Seitz noted, "These are youth that the church would not have been able to contact except through the efforts of the teen center where Bernard and Emma give a great deal of their time."[41] Leonard and Barbara Kilmer from Wooster, Ohio, took the Redigers' place. Leonard Kilmer already knew the community since he had spent the summer of 1966 helping with the House of Friendship day camp.

As the House of Friendship planned its summer program for 1968, they again invited Jesse Adams to return to the Bronx. Myrna Burkholder, who attended Mennonite House of Friendship, also volunteered to work with the summer program.[42]

The Redigers remained in New York after their two-year VS assignment ended in November 1968. Dan and Linda Hood, General Conference Mennonites who had graduated from Goshen in 1966, came as VSers that winter. The Hoods left the House of Friendship in 1969 but also stayed in the city.[43]

The House of Friendship began planning a day-care program in 1967. It opened in October 1968 with Mary Washington (later Mary Washington Davenport) as the director and a staff of ten part-time helpers. The New York City Department of Social Services paid nearly all the expenses of the program.[44]

By the late 1960s, Mennonite churches cooperated with churches of other denominations in running summer day camp programs. Glad Tidings shared the 1968 summer program with two neighboring churches, Willis Avenue Methodist and North Congregational. In 1969 and again in 1970 Glad Tidings participated in the South Bronx Community Day Camp with North Congregational, Willis Avenue Methodist, Mott Haven Reformed, and St. Ann's Episcopal churches. There were 200 children enrolled in the 1969 program, a few less the next year.[45] In 1971 they worked with North Congregational and St. Peter's Lutheran.[46] These large-scale community projects qualified for Neighborhood Youth Corps jobs providing summer employment for ghetto youth. They also paved the way for broader coalitions.

Churches cooperated in efforts at reversing urban blight. John Smucker took the lead in pushing for redevelopment of the House of Friendship neighborhood. Two members of the congregation, Hector Rosario and Harry Muller, also played major roles. Both men were leaders in the East Tremont Neighborhood Association and Muller served on the local antipoverty board and planning board. The newsletter of the East Tremont Neighborhood Association called *Twin Parks Neighborhood* suggested the name for a new coalition focused on rehabilitation of the area near the House of Friendship. They called it the Twin Parks Development Area.[47]

In September 1966 the New York City Board of Estimate approved a plan for construction of 800 low-income housing units and rehabilitation of some middle-income apartment buildings within a very large area bounded by Tremont Avenue, Southern Boulevard, Fordham Road, and Sedgwick Avenue. Construction of the Cross Bronx Expressway had destroyed the largely Jewish residential neighborhood north of Crotona Park. The predominantly Italian section bounded by East 179th Street, Belmont Avenue, East 183rd Street, and Southern Boulevard, known as Bronx Park West, needed rehabilitation of existing small houses and apartment buildings and demolition of some sub-standard housing to provide sites for parks and playgrounds. This plan had been indefinitely postponed by the city.

In October 1966 Smucker hosted a consultation at the House of Friendship on the needs of the East Tremont-Bronx Park South neighborhood, attended by Ministers and lay representatives from six nearby churches and representatives of the East Tremont Neighborhood Association. Thomas Bauer, rector of Grace Episcopal Church on Vyse Avenue, made a presentation on "The Community and the Anti-Poverty Program." He cited alarming statistics on the changes in the East Tremont area from 1962 to 1965. The number of welfare and Aid to Dependent Children cases rose from 7,000 to 17,000 in three years. Juvenile arrests jumped from 900 in 1962 to 1,600 in 1965. Bauer argued the need for programs for youth, especially job opportunities and recreation programs, and for the older people who held on in rent-controlled apartments. He noted the community planning group had been asked to sponsor the Poverty Program for the area. Harry Keifitz of the East Tremont Neighborhood Association discussed blight and deterioration in the area, despite zoning regulations, and claimed the urban renewal policy announced by Mayor John Lindsay had negative impact on three East Tremont renewal programs proposed earlier.

The city authorities did intend to implement a plan developed for the neighborhood identified as Bronx Park South, a fifteen-block section bounded by Boston Road, East Tremont, East 180th Street, Bronx Park South and Vyse Avenue. This immediately surrounded the House of Friendship. The city had already acquired 30 of the 174 parcels of land needed for the project. Plans called for rehabilitation of some tenement buildings as well as renewal and development, euphemisms for slum clearance. In the delay between announcement and implementation, this neighborhood had experienced more rapid deterioration and greater population shifts than any other neighborhood in East Tremont. Keifitz endorsed the proposal for economically integrated housing, a small "vest pocket" low-income Housing Authority project, a new shopping center and post office, community center, park and playgrounds, all adjoining the House of Friendship. This was the dream.[48]

The Twin Parks Association grew out of this 1966 meeting. John I. Smucker described it as an alliance of eight little Protestant churches and five big Catholic churches. They chose Smucker as their chairman. Intense negotiations brought the West Bronx Council and the Council of Tremont Organizations into the Twin Parks Association, giving it more Hispanic, black, and Jewish members. In March 1968 the Twin Parks Association requested the New York City Housing Authority to make it the sponsor for the Twin Parks Development Area. They proposed construction of 500 units of low-income housing around the House of Friendship. They later received authorization for the housing project and the New York Sate Urban Development Corporation agreed to provide all needed funds.[49]

John Smucker had become a community organizer. In April 1968 Mayor Lindsay created the Urban Action Task Force and named Smucker representative from the Fordham-East Tremont area.[50] Smucker described his own role in 1969 as "active on board of East Tremont Neighborhood Association to storm City Hall to approve Bronx Park South [and] Twin Parks Urban Renewal Project, to get better police protection, to get a narcotics program, to cooperate with Mayor's Urban Task Force, to work on extreme racial tension."[51]

Laura Kennell, a Goshen College senior from Roanoke Mennonite Church in Illinois, had come to New York to work in a city hospital and planned to return to Goshen to complete her undergraduate work in social welfare. While in the city she was active in the House of Friendship. She volunteered to survey the Twin Parks community and make contacts that would help the congregation in designing programs to meet the needs of the people.[52] Her survey confirmed the major population shift in the House of Friendship neighborhood. She found 34 percent of the residents were unemployed and 30 percent of the families lived below the poverty line in 1968 with an annual income under $4,000. Welfare cases had more than doubled in the three years since 1965.[53]

After completing her college work and graduating in the Goshen class of 1969, Laura Kennell returned to the House of Friendship. She worked with John Smucker in developing a proposal for an experimental VS team for the Tremont Anti-Poverty Program under Mennonite Central Committee. In response Paul Leatherman, MCC staff person, visited the Bronx in August 1969 to discuss the idea with John Smucker. The proposed team would include a community social worker and another in addiction services and one or more teachers in local public schools.[54]

Events in the immediate neighborhood underscored the need for some remedial action. On Sunday, April 27, 1969, about forty black and Hispanic youths ran up Crotona Avenue from East 182nd Street into the Italian neighborhood breaking windows in stores and houses. Several nights of confrontation followed. A month later a young black man was beaten by Italians and died of his injuries. On the night of June 3-4, the Mayor's Task Force held an open meeting at St. Martin of Tours Catholic Church trying to cool tempers, but violence continued through the night. The next night John Smucker and House of Friendship workers joined a hundred police, ministers and youth workers trying to calm the rock-throwing mob. That summer the House of Friendship had the biggest community program ever with 25 Neighborhood Youth Corps jobs to distribute and 150 neighborhood children enrolled in the House of Friendship day camp. The church sent 127 children to Camp Deerpark that year.[55]

Membership in the House of Friendship congregation grew steadily in those same years from 93 in 1968 to 96 in 1969 to reach a peak of 103 members in 1971. The ethnic Mennonites were mainly commuters from Long Island and New Jersey, but they made up the leadership of the congregation until 1970, John Smucker recalled.[56]

When Jerry Miller, assistant director of Voluntary Service for Mennonite Board of Missions, Elkhart, Indiana, visited the House of Friendship in 1969 Leonard and Barbara Kilmer told him that "the problems with the House of Friendship stem from the members of the congregation who live outside of the immediate church area but hold the purse strings to what goes on in the church." The internship program was not working out, they told him, because the members were not cooperating with Smucker. "Apparently part of the reason for this is that [one member of the proposed team] makes no profession whatsoever of being a Christian, but is concerned about youth." Smucker recalled that the interns had difficulty making "the adjustment to an urban evangelical congregation in a hostile community." He also remembered that the intern in question struggled with faith issues, but was always a Christian. Jerry Jantzi, the other team member, returned to the Bronx late in the year.[57]

Alongside the tensions created by violence in the community, new tensions were felt within the congregation after 1970, when Smucker and others became involved in the charismatic renewal movement. But the charismatic renewal also released new spiritual energy within the congregation. "Those who were touched by the Spirit were more discerning and could face the violence and problems in the community more creatively," Smucker recalled. In 1972, "when the church council suspended the youth team and closed the coffee house because of drugs and other off beat behavior, Wilma Bailey, a black youth leader from Friendship, established a more spiritual youth group with Bible studies and the youth group grew strong and large. They liked it better than the coffee house." Gangs clashed every night on Grote Street, next to the church, and in adjacent Twin Parks Mall, which had become a battleground between Italian and black and Hispanic teenagers, but inside the church other neighborhood youth were being converted and studying the Bible and praying.[58]

Completion of Twin Parks in 1972 did signal a new beginning of sorts for the neighborhood. Few local people moved in and many others had already moved away to escape the escalating violence. The new housing project brought new people from other parts of the city. Few Italians moved into the housing project but blacks and Hispanics did. The new housing shifted the ethnic boundary north a block or two into the Italian community. The Grote Street building had 100 of its 500 units vacant through the first year, but it slowly filled as problems in the building itself were solved and neighborhood violence decreased. With the construction completed, the Twin Parks Association, which created the housing, had a diminished role. "The community tended to organize along lines of self-interest and went back to old organizations," Smucker recalled.[59]

In the heady and challenging work of community activism, Mennonite pastors like Eugene Shelly and John Smucker and their congregations found a new dimension to urban mission as they worked side by side in attempting to make their neighborhoods places where people could live in decency and safety. They had to deal with the politics of urban renewal and poverty programs and the impersonal reality of economic and demographic change. Not every church member took the same activist stance, but they agreed that Christians could not close their eyes to the needs of God's children in the city.

NOTES

1 District Council Minutes, Dec. 15, 1969, EMM.

2 Millen Brand, "The Glad Tidings Mennonite Church," *Local Lives* (New York, 1975), 466-69.

3 *New York Times*, Feb. 9, 1970.

4 Jill Jonnes, *We're Still Here: The Rise, Fall, and Resurrection of the South Bronx*, (Boston, 1986), 199, 229.

5 Millen Brand, "A Litany of Housing," *Local Lives* (New York, 1975), 469-71.

6 *New York Times*, Jan. 15, 1972.

7 Glad Tidings Mennonite Church Cabinet Minutes, Sept. 22, 1972, Dec. 13, 1972. Burkholder Papers.

8 *The Evangelical Visitor*, Oct. 23, 1967.

9 Administrative Memo for Brooklyn, Mar. 11, 1969, BCA-MC.

10 Harold Bowers to Charlie B. Byers, Jan. 17, 1968. Byers Papers, BCA-MC.

11 Charlie B. Byers to Harold Bowers, Mar. 16, 1968. Catherine K. Bowers to Charlie B. Byers, Mar. 31, 1968. Nancy Charles to Charlie B. Byers, Apr. 3, 1968. Isaac S. Kanode to Nancy Charles, Apr. 16, 1968. Byers Papers, BCA-MC.

12 John Ebersole to Charlie B. Byers, Apr. 22, 1968. Byers Papers, BCA-MC.

13 C. B. Byers, "Memo on Rev. Cecil F. Loney," Apr. 23, 1968. "Report on C. B. Byers visit to Brooklyn, New York," May 2-5, 1958. Byers Papers, BCA-MC.

[14] C.B. Byers, "Tentative Proposition for a Working Relationship between Rev. Cecil Loney and the Brooklyn Congregation," June 5, 1968. Byers Papers, BCA-MC.

[15] Isaac S. Kanode to C. B. Byers, Aug. 5, 1968. Byers Papers, BCA-MC.

[16] Meeting regarding Brooklyn Church and VS Unit, Nov. 21, 1968. Administrative Guidelines, Nov. 21, 1968, BCA-MC.

[17] Henry N. Hostetter, Visit to Brooklyn Mission Center, Nov. 26, 1968. John Ebersole to Isaac Kanode, Dec. 10, 1968. Byers Papers, BCA-MC.

[18] Isaac Kanode to John Ebersole, Dec. 12, 1968. Charlie B. Byers to John Ebersole, Dec. 26, 1968. Byers Papers, BCA-MC.

[19] C. B. Byers, "Report to special setting of mission men January 16, 1969 on Brooklyn." Isaac S. Kanode, Memo: Brooklyn, Jan. 20, 1969, Jan. 23, 1969. Interview with Rev. Cecil F. Loney, Jan. 23, 1969. Memo: Brooklyn Jan. 31, 1969, BCA-MC.

[20] "Recommendations from Directors Kanode and Heisey Regarding the Brooklyn Work," Feb. 27, 1969, BCA-MC.

[21] C. B. Byers and Isaac Kanode, "Administrative Memo for Brooklyn," Mar. 11, 1969, BCA-MC.

[22] Isaac S. Kanode, Memo: Brooklyn, Mar. 13, 1969, BCA-MC.

[23] "Report by Bishop C. B. Byers on my visit with Rev. Cecil Loney, Brooklyn, NY," Apr. 24, 1969. C. B. Byers, "Report of my visit to Brooklyn," May 8, 1969. C. B. Byers, Memo, July 16, 1969. Byers Papers. Isaac Kanode, memo Re: 403 Rogers Avenue Property, Brooklyn, July 24, 1969. Pilgrim Chapel, Brooklyn. Dedication Programme, Sunday, Nov. 30, 1969, BCA-MC.

[24] Administrative Committee Minutes, June 22, 1970. C. B. Byers, Visit to Brooklyn, Mar. 10, 1971. Isaac Kanode, Memorandum, May 11, 1971, BCA-MC.

[25] J. Wilmer Heisey to C. B. Byers, Jan. 14, 1971. Byers Papers, BCA-MC.

[26] C. B. Byers, Visit to New York, Mar. 10-12, 1971. Memorandum, May 11, 1971. Report of My Visit with Charles and Ruth Rife, Aug. 3, 1971. Byers Papers, BCA-MC.

[27] Summary Memorandum, Brooklyn VS Unit, Oct. 29, 1971. Memorandum on New York (Brooklyn), Glen A. Pierce to J. Wilmer Heisey, Nov. 17, 1971. Brooklyn VS Report, Jan. 17, 1972, BCA-MC.

[28] John I. Smucker to Ernest Bennett, May 28, 1965. John I. Smucker to Ernest Bennett, Oct. 6, 1965, MBM-AMC.

[29] John I. Smucker to Ernest Bennett, Mar. 12, 1966, MBM-AMC. *Gospel Herald*, Apr. 19, 1966, 356.

[30] John I. Smucker, "The Dynamics of a Significant Decision in the Life of the Mennonite House of Friendship Congregation," 42-52. Smucker Papers.

[31] Smucker, *Reflections*, 72.

[32] John I. Smucker to Kenneth Seitz, Mar. 1, 1966, MBM-AMC.

[33] John I. Smucker to Kenneth Seitz, Apr. 11, 1966, MBM-AMC.

[34] Kenneth Seitz to John I. Smucker, Apr. 29, 1966. John I. Smucker to Ken Seitz, June 9, 1966. Kenneth Seitz to John I. Smucker, June 17, 1966. John I. Smucker to Ken Seitz, July 6, 1966, MBM-AMC. East Tremont-Bronx Park South Consultation, Oct. 23, 1966.

[35] Kenneth Seitz to John I. Smucker, Apr. 29, 1966, MBM-AMC. Smucker, "Urban Mennonite Mission," 448.

[36] Kenneth Seitz, Memorandum, Mennonite House of Friendship, Bronx, New York, Nov. 1, 1966, MBM-AMC.

[37] Kenneth Seitz to John I. Smucker, Nov. 15, 1966. "Agreement Between 1-w and VS Couple and Mennonite House of Friendship November 1966-October 1968," filed on December 9, 1966. Bernard Rediger to Ken Seitz, Dec. 10, 1966, MBM-AMC. Minutes of the Youth Workers Council, Dec. 9, 1966, EMM.

[38] Bernard Rediger to Ken Seitz, Jan. 18, 1967, Feb. 17, 1967, May 18, 1967. Kenneth Seitz, Administrative Visit to New York City, June 20, 1967. Bernard Rediger, Monthly Report, July 3, 1967, MBM-AMC.

[39] Bernard Rediger, Monthly Report, July 29, 1967. John I. Smucker to Ray Horst, Aug. 29, 1967, MBM-AMC.

[40] Bernard Rediger, Monthly Report, Sept. 5, 1967, MBM-AMC.

[41] Ken Seitz, Visit to New York City, Jan. 9, 1968.

[42] John I. Smucker to Ken Seitz, Mar. 12, 1968, MBM-AMC.

[43] Kenneth Seitz to Bernard and Emma Rediger, Oct. 22, 1968. Ken Seitz, Administrative Visit to New York City, Nov. 11, 1968. Jerry Miller to Mr. and Mrs. Dan Hood, Jan. 31, 1969. John I. Smucker to Jerry Miller, Mar. 12, 1969, MBM-AMC.

[44] Ken Seitz, Visit to New York City, Jan. 9, 1968. John I. Smucker to Ken Seitz, Mar. 12, 1968. Smucker, "Urban Mennonite Mission," 444.

[45] Glad Tidings Cabinet Minutes, June 16, 1968, Dec. 7, 1969, LMHS. Glad Tidings Mennonite Church Program Evaluations Fall of 1970. Glad Tidings Mennonite Church 1969 Report, EMM.

[46] Glad Tidings Cabinet Minutes, May 9, 1971, LMHS.

[47] Smucker, "Urban Mennonite Mission," 396, 409, 430.

[48] East Tremont-Bronx Park South Consultation, Oct. 23, 1966, MBM-AMC.

[49] Smucker, "Urban Mennonite Mission," 409-410, 446-447.

[50] Smucker, "Urban Mennonite Mission," 406.

[51] John Smucker and Laura Kennell, "Mennonite House of Friendship Proposal for Friendship Internship Program," Sept. 17, 1969, MBM-AMC.

[52] Ken Smith to John I. Smucker, June 14, 1968, MBM-AMC. Smucker, "Urban Mennonite Mission," 452.

[53] John I. Smucker, "Reflections and Implications of Urban Mennonite Mission in the South Bronx," Ph.D. dissertation, Union Graduate School, 1985, 386-387.

[54] Paul Leatherman to John I. Smucker, Sept. 5, 1969. Paul Leatherman to Roy Yoder, Sept. 5, 1969. John Smucker and Laura Kennell, "Mennonite House of Friendship Proposal for Friendship Internship Program," Sept. 17, 1969, MBM-AMC.

[55] John I. Smucker, "Reflections and Implications of Urban Mennonite Mission in the South Bronx," Ph.D. dissertation, Union Graduate School, 1985, 459-462.

[56] John I. Smucker, "Reflections and Implications of Urban Mennonite Mission in the South Bronx," Ph.D. dissertation, Union Graduate School, 1985, 463, 496, 502.

[57] Jerry Miller to Roy Yoder, Oct. 27, 1969, MBM-AMC.

[58] John I. Smucker, "Reflections and Implications of Urban Mennonite Mission in the South Bronx," Ph.D. dissertation, Union Graduate School, 1985, 513-14.

[59] John I. Smucker, "Reflections and Implications of Urban Mennonite Mission in the South Bronx," Ph.D. dissertation, Union Graduate School, 1985, 410-13.

CHAPTER TEN

Out of the Ashes

1971–1982

On October 21, 1974 fire destroyed the Seventh Avenue Mennonite Church. The fire began in a vacant apartment next door and swept through that building and the apartment building housing the church. The empty apartment was used by drug addicts who may have started the blaze. Four families were left homeless. Two days after the fire, Head Start classes resumed for 72 children in temporary quarters in the neighborhood day care center, and the congregation began meeting in the community room at Esplanade Gardens on the opposite side of Seventh Avenue. Mennonite Disaster Service volunteers helped clean up the damaged site, but before they arrived someone had ripped all the pipes out of the building and the resulting flood caused more damage.[1]

Richard Pannell, pastor, Celeste Jematt, and Evelyn Brown, Seventh Avenue members, survey the damage to the Seventh Avenue Mennonite Church building following the fire in 1974 that gutted the entire five story building.

Fires like this had become commonplace in many sections of New York City by 1974. Addicts shooting up in a vacant apartment caused some fires with their carelessness, but other fires were deliberately set by landlords, tenants, or neighborhood thrill seekers. Whatever the cause, "finishers" moved in before the embers cooled and stripped lead pipes, copper wire, anything and everything of value, for sale as scrap, and left the building a gutted ruin.[2]

The Seventh Avenue congregation called Monroe Yoder, a New York University staff member with an adjunct faculty appointment, as assistant pastor. His ordination took place on November 21, 1974, just a month after the fire. The Yoders stayed in the city after his graduate study and worked with the Seventh Avenue congregation from that time.

Monroe Yoder and Richard Pannell worked together on a plan to provide more adequate facilities for the church and decent housing for the community. They proposed purchasing the property at 2524 Seventh Avenue, next door to the burned-out church and the corner building at 201 West 146th Street, where a bar occupied the street level, and tying all three buildings together into church and Head Start facilities and renovated apartments.[3]

After the fire the Seventh Avenue Mennonite Church moved two buildings south on Seventh Avenue, (later named Adam Clayton Powell Boulevard). They renovated the building at 201 West 146th street, on the corner of 146th street and Seventh Avenue. This became the new home for the congregation. 2005 photo.

As negotiations proceeded on the 2524 Seventh Avenue building, they ran into a snag because of a cloud on the title; since the owner could not give the congregation a deed free of claims and potential litigation, they concentrated on the corner building alone. On May 5, 1975 Seventh Avenue Mennonite Church took title to the 201 West 146th Street building. The corner bar reopened under new management, but closed for good a few weeks later. Renovation of the building began that summer. Head Start moved into new quarters there in August 1975. The front room, the former bar room, was next in line for renovation as a meeting place for worship. The first worship service there was on Sunday, April 4, 1976.[4]

The city of New York eventually seized the fire-gutted building at 2524 Seventh Avenue for non-payment of taxes. Early in 1977 it became available for purchase from the city. Spurred on by Evelyn Brown, who had a vision for rehabilitating the apartments for older people, the congregation bought the building in May 1977.[5]

Rehabilitating the burned-out church building at 2526 Seventh Avenue and the newly-acquired building next door to provide 23 housing units would cost an estimated $644,000 and the project went on hold at least temporarily.[6] The cost of repairs was a major problem, precluding efforts at renovating most inner-city buildings damaged by fire. A typical three-

Rachel and Monroe Yoder, pastor at Seventh Avenue, and Theophilus Baptiste, Sunday school superintendent.

or four-story tenement in good repair in the South Bronx might have a market value of $20,000 or so, but require many times that to bring it up to building code specifications after a fire. As a result, damaged buildings stood derelict until they were reduced to mere shells by "finishers."

The fires in the South Bronx were on the increase all through the 1960s, but an epidemic of arson broke in 1969.[7] When Chester Wenger visited Fox Street with Paul Landis in May 1969, he observed

> There is a very rapid turnover of the total population of the area. Most people stay less than a year. More and more houses are standing empty. Some partly burned shells are also in evidence. It is reported that Model Cities plans to begin operations here within two or three years and that they pay for properties on their assessed value plus 20%. For this reason people are not ready to sell and there are some buyers who are investing in view of the Model Cities plans.[8]

If some landlords waited for Model Cities slum clearance to bail them out, others simply walked away from their buildings. More and more owners abandoned buildings in inner city neighborhoods. *The New York Times* reported that, "At a time of an acute housing shortage, with new residential construction at a virtual standstill, owners are abandoning sound but unprofitable buildings at a rate that the Mayor's Rent Control Committee, in a report issued in December [1969], called alarming." The city was losing apartments through owner abandonment at a rate of 30,000 apartments a year. Rent control laws were partly to blame. A landlord could increase rent only if rental income fell below the cost of maintaining the building *and* the landlord had lost money on the property for two successive years. This required a long complicated process of legal proof. The courts had created chaos in the landlord-tenant relationship by allowing rent strikers to withhold rent in buildings found to have building code violations. Municipal authorities encouraged tenants to find violations, not difficult in eighty-year-old buildings, and pay no rent at all. The rent control laws held the owner to a maximum 6 percent return on his property, but most buildings were mortgaged, often with second and third mortgages, and annual interest payments would normally exceed 6 percent of assessed value. The owner's net loss on debt service could not be counted as a loss to justify a rent increase. Tenants provided a critical factor, depending on how well they maintained the building. "A small number of destructive tenants can doom a building that could otherwise survive even with rental income well below the generally accepted standards of the amount needed for maintenance."[9]

Unscrupulous landlords learned how to "milk" a building. It took three years for the city to begin proceeding against tax delinquents to seize the building.[10] Arson allowed other landlords to collect insurance on unprofitable buildings. But derelict buildings attracted vandals, drug addicts, and professional building strippers, too.[11]

In 1970-1971 Glenn Zeager and the Fox Street Mennonite Church devoted many hours to planning the rehabilitation of blighted property on Tiffany Street with the help of Mennonite Disaster Service. In March 1971 another buyer signed a contract for the property, and Glenn Zeager reported Tiffany Street "a dream of the past."[12] At the same time, the city advanced $2.8 million for renovating nine four-story buildings on Fox Street. The work was completed within a year and families moved in. Nine months later seven of the buildings were vacant and burned out. The contractors were indicted for fraud, but not for the Fox Street project.[13] Early in 1972 the Fox Street congregation again looked at neighborhood rehabilitation. A building with eight stores and 32 apartments was seized by the city for $33,000 in delinquent taxes. The New York City District Council authorized Glenn Zeager to bid for the building and proceed with plans for rehabilitating it as a church and day-care center and low-income apartments. A $2,000 deposit would be needed and an estimated $40,000 to complete the purchase. As in the Tiffany Street project, another buyer had a prior claim. The law gave priority to tenants and the owner of a clothing store in the building was interested in buying it. Once again, Fox Street Mennonite Church failed to obtain the building it desperately needed.[14]

Deterioration of the South Bronx spread rapidly. A *New York Times* reporter estimated 3,000 to 5,000 abandoned buildings, many of them fire-charred ruins, in the area bounded by "Park Avenue on the west, the Cross Bronx Expressway on the north and the Bronx River on the east, encompassing such neighborhoods as Mott Haven, Morrisania, Bathgate and Hunts Point." A study by a local health center found 20 percent of the homes without water and 50 percent without heat at least half the time. "There's a total breakdown of services, looting is rampant, fires are everywhere."[15] Others described it as "a rubble-filled desert."[16]

Urban blight moved relentlessly, threatening Tremont and Fordham, and with it moved the geographic expression that said it all, the South Bronx. As Eugene Shelly wrote in 1977, "The South Bronx in 1968 was 149th Street and south, in 1972 it had grown to seven square miles from 161st Street and south, in 1975 it had grown to the Cross Bronx Expressway and south."[17]

John Smucker recalled that "the burning had reached Tremont by 1975" with many buildings abandoned and fires multiplying. By 1977 abandoned and burned-out buildings could be seen on Garden Street and Grote Street within a block of the Friendship Mennonite Church.[18] The spreading deterioration of the South Bronx was the setting for all the Mennonite and Brethren in Christ congregations in the 1970s.

Fox Street to Burnside

Anna Buckwalter was the only member of the Fox Street congregation who actually lived in the neighborhood in 1969 and, with fires in buildings adjoining hers, she was ready to move. The last two member families moved away that spring. The constant turnover among newcomers meant that youngsters involved in Fox Street teams and Bible clubs would likely leave the neighborhood within a year. Chester Wenger found the Fox Street neighborhood "crowded with children" on a visit in May 1969 and "a center of dope distribution and many other forms of vice." He could not think of "a more needy community."[19]

Jim King, a former VSer, from Cochranville, Pennsylvania, who "made a real contribution to the Fox Street congregation in the past," began working two afternoons and two evenings a week in September 1971 to expand the tutoring program and help Glenn Zeager in reaching out to the community. King was taking courses at NYU at the same time.[20] Zeager also invited Phebe Yoder, long-term missionary in Tanzania, to come out of retirement and develop a reading program at Fox Street. "Glenn has worked with his Church Cabinet and with the local school to see that everything is set up for her to begin a Remedial Reading Program and a Language Teaching Program." Her spiritual gifts were also needed in the South Bronx. She lived with the Zeagers as long as she worked in the Fox Street community, but her health eventually forced her to leave the city.[21]

The 1972 summer program went well under Jim King's direction with 25 children in regular attendance. "The Lord provided four good aides from the community," Zeager reported. "We were also able to operate a Playstreet and get one young fellow in with the local Police Athletic League to run a softball team." A young woman, about 20 years old, "has come to the Lord and is attending services."[22]

"God is still moving among us" and there was surely work to do in the Fox Street neighborhood, but by the summer of 1972 the congregation was ready to relocate. The search for a suitable building continued through the year. They looked at synagogues and churches, especially along the Grand Concourse. Once the prestigious main street of the Bronx, the

Concourse area collapsed in the late 1960s, leaving large synagogues and luxury apartments and stores as vacant relics. Moving the Fox Street Mennonite Church to more adequate facilities in a more stable neighborhood raised other possibilities. When Lancaster Mennonites first began mission work in New York in the 1940s, they talked about a center, preferably in Manhattan, and outlying preaching stations. Instead, independent congregations grew up in Harlem and the South Bronx. The new vision for Fox Street revived these older dreams. One central church with really adequate facilities could house many of the programs that each congregation attempted in remodeled store-fronts. At the least, the new center could provide office space for the District Council and encourage more joint activities among the churches.[23]

In February 1973 the search came to an end, when Glenn Zeager and Dale Stoltzfus led the Eastern Board executive committee through the West-side Jewish Center at Grand and Burnside Avenues in the West Bronx. The Mission Board made an offer, but there were delays and confusion. In April Zeager reported, "We still have not signed for the building because the Certificate of Occupancy was not properly filled out." In August the last obstacle fell and a closing date of October 1 was set. The building cost $120,000 financed at six percent. The Fox Street congregation held its first worship service in the new Burnside Center on Sunday morning October 14, 1973.[24]

2019 Grand Avenue, Bronx, the third location of the Fox Street Mennonite Church congregation. When they moved here they changed the name of the congregation to Burnside Mennonite Church, and then later to King of Glory Tabernacle. 2005 photo.

When the congregation moved into the former synagogue at 2019 Grand Avenue, Zeager got permission to block off the street. They showed a Billy Graham film and passed out leaflets and tracts "to let the community know who we are."[25]

One of the first events at Burnside Mennonite Church was Glenn Zeager's ordination. Although Glenn and Florence Zeager had worked faithfully in the urban mission field for nearly twenty years and he had served as pastor at Fox Street since 1969, he was never ordained a minister. Glenn Zeager was ordained at Burnside on October 28, 1973, after the congregation had called him as pastor for another three-year term.[26]

The Burnside congregation continued many of the outreach programs from Fox Street. They planned an eight-week day camp for July and August 1974. Nelson Shenk and Lorna Hodge directed the day camp which enrolled 18 children. They signed up Fresh Air children and organized clubs on Thursday nights. They also opened a day-care center for three and four-year-olds. In September 1974 posters advertising the new day-care center attracted inquiries, but few registrants. They soon had 15 children enrolled. Alice Hess directed the center with Esther Karpalla as her assistant.[27]

With the congregation established in a new location in the West Bronx, Glenn Zeager saw his task completed and declined to serve beyond his agreed term. A Pastor Replacement Committee began their search in April 1975, and learned that every candidate they solicited refused. In August 1975 Jane Hodge "shared her feelings of a call to ministry" but the committee "felt it was important to encourage her in her present calling and gifts," without suggesting her name as a potential pastor. She had been responsible for Sunday evening services. Jose Feliz of Bronx Spanish Mennonite Church agreed to help with visitation, but declined any consideration as Burnside pastor. In September 1975 the committee proposed a team as an interim solution. The congregation elected David Dyer, Steven Villanueva, Ed Hyman, Carl Metzler, Nathan Shenk, with Dale Weaver as chairman, to serve as a team until a pastor should be obtained.[28]

The pastoral search went on and on, with a long list of ministers contacted and their refusal recorded in the committee minutes. At last in January 1977 the committee proposed inviting Samuel Walters, pastor of First Mennonite Church in Kingston, Jamaica, and he agreed to visit Burnside. Walters, a seminary graduate, had served as pastor there since 1971 and worked with Mennonite Broadcasts and the Way of Life Committee. He had some hesitation about leaving the Jamaican church, but the congregation called him by consensus and he accepted. On Sunday, October 16, 1977, Sam and Shirley Walters were installed at Burnside Mennonite Church.[29]

Joe Garber, a VSer, ran the club programs. In 1978 the Burnside congregation began a Head Start program in addition to the day-care center.[30]

Samuel Walters, left, pastor at Burnside, speaking to Michael Banks who succeeded him as pastor.

The same year Michael and Addie Banks came to Burnside. Michael Banks, a native New Yorker, grew up on Washington Avenue in the Bronx and attended Catholic schools. The message of Black Power advocates attracted his enthusiastic support as a teenager. After service with the Navy during the Vietnam War, he returned to New York and worked as a counselor in a drug rehabilitation program. He began attending a Mosque of the Nation of Islam and drew his wife Addie reluctantly into the Muslim faith. Addie and their daughter Heidi had meanwhile become friendly with Irene Peters, a VSer assigned to Burnside. When Michael Banks experienced a dramatic conversion after a street brawl in June 1978, his wife introduced him to the Mennonites. Sam Walters recognized the young couple's gifts and nurtured them in the congregational setting. Michael and Addie Banks directed an after-school program for neighborhood children and took their turn in other roles in the congregation.[31]

Anna Buckwalter, one of the original members of the Fox Street congregation, remained active after the move to Burnside. She wrote in February 1980: "The fire in a large unoccupied building we witnessed after services the other Sunday is a common occurrence. We need to keep our eyes on Christ in the midst of violence and destruction."[32]

Glad Tidings: "A Healing Factor in the Community"

The fires had come close to Fox Street Mennonite Church as early as 1968. It did not take long for the fires to spread to the neighborhood of the Glad Tidings Mennonite Church at 344 Brook Avenue. The building next door at 342 Brook Avenue housed the Glad Tidings Sandwich Shop until it closed in 1973. The building next to it was a burned-out shell, finally demolished in 1975. On the other side of the church at 346 Brook Avenue was the building owned by Donald and Evelyn Hertzler. "The building is in good condition and maintains itself. However, a careless landlord could readily destroy its value" and it in turn would affect the value of the Mission Board property. The Hertzlers first offered 346 Brook Avenue to the church, then sold it to Martin Bender in December 1975.[33]

The devastation of South Bronx neighborhoods left the Glad Tidings area with a rapidly declining population. "Many can remember when there were 1,800 school children on East 141st Street between Brook and Willis," Eugene Shelly reminded the congregation in 1977. "Today there are only three apartment buildings remaining on the one side of the street." As the destruction spread, "our constituents have moved from one place to another" and many fled the South Bronx.[34]

The "constant movement of people from the South Bronx" was a topic of discussion at the annual business meeting in September 1976. Dottie Kruse, reporting for the Sunday school, said, "This past year we have had the unfortunate experience of having many families with about twenty children move away."[35]

On a visit to Glad Tidings in 1981, David Shenk noted the loss of population in the neighborhood. Alexander Berger Junior High School enrolled fewer than a third of the students it had in the 1960s. The Glad Tidings Mennonite Church had experienced a similar decline.

> Due to the economic decline and rapid change engulfing the area, the congregation has lost many members. Some of the apartment buildings in which most of the former members of Glad Tidings had lived are now uninhabitable. At present almost all the worshippers travel into the community from North Bronx. There is almost no local participation in the congregation.[36]

Other churches left the neighborhood. When the Missouri Synod Lutherans of St. John's Concordia Church at Brook Avenue and East 142nd Street prepared to close their church in 1973, Eugene Shelly talked with them about leasing or selling the building to Glad Tidings. A year later it was the Willis Avenue United Methodist Church that closed its doors and again Glad Tidings negotiated for the building without success.[37]

The Glad Tidings congregation sought to be relevant to its changing community in the South Bronx. To the other church projects and community activities, they added the Treasure Work Shoppe. In the autumn of 1971, Martine Shelly and a group of women from the neighborhood began meeting for candle-making and other craft projects. They sold the candles through local stores. "It wasn't really a big thing," Esther Petersheim recalled, "but it brought people in and gave us inroads into the mothers' lives." They used the park and playground behind Glad Tidings for some of their activities at the invitation of Hallie Brown, the park recreation director. Florence Yeboah, an MCC trainee from Ghana, led Bible studies during 1972-73 for 26 women.[38]

The Treasure Work Shoppe classes closed down for the summer each May, as Glad Tidings geared up for the summer program. They had no day camp of their own in 1973, joining instead with the North Congregational Church. Glad Tidings sponsored weekly beach trips, basketball tournaments, block parties, and a food cooperative.[39] In 1974 Paul Byler, Brenda Singleton, and Patty Dick staffed an eight-week day camp. In 1975 Glad Tidings operated two day-camps with Sue Eberly, Siso Torres, and Brenda Singleton as the staff persons. Brenda led the music. The kids spent time in El Barrio Museum and El Barrio Music workshops. Siso Torres and Tony Alexander offered to work with a summer remedial reading program. Berger Junior High School loaned materials from their reading lab. Paul Bates and Zoilo Carmona ran the summer athletic tournaments. Jim Martin, a new VSer, ran a handball tournament in People's Park. "I had never heard of handball before I came to the city but I enjoyed learning and playing it." The Rec Center at 342 Brook Avenue opened in April. Zoilo Carmona, a Youth Corps worker, helped Jim keep it open every night.[40]

Cynthia Carter, a Massachusetts Institute of Technology student from Seventh Avenue Mennonite Church, home for the summer, directed the 1976 day camp. Irving Blanks, senior counselor, was also a college student and duly noted in his report, "My boss was Miss Cynthia Grant Carter and she was pretty." As in previous summers, Neighborhood Youth Corps workers served as aides. Cynthia Carter wrote: "I had a difficult time with the staff. 'I got me a job so I didn't had to work.' That left me hang with the only three dependable persons, Eric [Richardson], Irving, and myself." The day camp proved successful, nonetheless, with "each of the kids taking something that was a part of them in the Glad Tidings

Summer Day Camp, especially the little creature who gave us the most trouble." Damaris Lugo Frey worked with the remedial reading program. Irving reported, "Damaris helped the kids in improving their reading and math which I thought was a very good idea." She had 35 children involved. Cynthia Carter added, "Damaris was a big help and very successful in developing a newspaper to take home to their parents."[41]

The summer program of 1977 added a sit-down lunch for 200 children each day provided by the city. Mim Cruz and LeRoy Moore helped with this. The day camp teachers that summer were Irving Blanks, Willie Myers, Patsy Musser, and Barb Kaufman. Eric Richardson, Karl Wallace, and Robert Williams worked as teacher aides under the Neighborhood Youth Corps.[42]

Glad Tidings continued to send children to Fresh Air camps and Friendly Towns each summer. In 1976 Glad Tidings arranged for 243 children to go to homes in Friendly Towns and sent 35 others to Fresh Air Camp at Fishkill, N.Y. Twenty others went to Camp Deerpark. Of these 278 youngsters, 29 came from Fellowship Chapel and 24 from Seventh Avenue Mennonite Church. Richard Frey handled the Fresh Air program with the help of Ronald Jenkins, a Youth Corps worker.[43]

A cooperative food-buying program was intended to help welfare recipients in the neighborhood get the most for their food dollar. VSer Jim Martin worked with pastor Eugene Shelly in getting it off the ground. Edward Scott became involved in 1975. "Steady Eddie has been a tremendous asset," Gene Shelly reported. "Jim is more relaxed and confident." In 1976 the congregation took a hard look at the program. Fifty families belonged to the food-buying club, but only five or six orders came in each week. Welfare clients, for whom the program was designed, did not participate. The need to pay in advance seemed to be an obstacle. When Jim Martin conducted a survey in October 1976, only ten families expressed any interest, and the program was dropped.[44]

The Cruz family. Left to right: Miriam, Christina, Daniel, and Jesus.

After the Glad Tidings Sandwich Shop closed in 1973, the congregation wondered what they could do with the vacant store to reach into the community in the same way. They decided on a Bible Club program. Dottie Kruse, Chris Benner, Paul Byler, and Elmer Lapp agreed to plan club activities. United Bronx Parents, a community-action group, asked to rent the first floor of 342 Brook Avenue where the sandwich shop had been located. The congregation agreed to let them use it part of the day with Bible Club and rec center activities there evenings. In 1974 Glad Tidings looked for a full-time female youth worker. Theda Siegrist, Janet Landis, and Leslie Murphy had organized activities for neighborhood girls. Edward "Steady Eddie" Scott, Wanda Wright, Karen Davis, and Kevin Rivera helped with the clubs. There were three clubs in 1975 for teenagers (13 to 15), another for 11-and-12 year olds, and another for 8-to-10 year olds, with a new club for small children. Lapp reported five clubs in 1976 with 30 children and teenagers participating in Bible study and crafts. The typical club was small, from three to ten students and a teacher, meeting for an hour and a half each week. Three boys between 12 and 14 made up one club. "All three fellows became Christians through the club program," Lapp wrote. Ten older teenagers were "really interested in studying and discussing the Bible." They also talked about death, sex, love, and drugs. The evening rec center program was in full swing. Jim Martin, Elmer Lapp, Ray Siegrist, Dick Frey, and Jesus Cruz each volunteered an evening a week from May to September 1975. From September Jim Martin and "Steady Eddie" Scott kept the center open three nights a week.[45]

Elmer Lapp continued to work with the Youth Council and the basketball teams while he attended Fordham University. He gave more time to basketball in the winter and dropped his club work. Jesus Cruz volunteered as Elmer's backup with the teams. Zoilo Carmona and Paul Bates ran the summer basketball tournaments. In 1976 church members questioned subsidizing Elmer Lapp's basketball teams "as a church function when he is so seldom present." But Elmer continued to coach Glad Tidings teams. Marvin Samuels also coached a team. James Bates and Eric Richardson, too old to play on the teams, became assistant coaches in 1976. Eric was working ten hours a week in the Glad Tidings youth program as a Youth Corps assignment. In 1977 Elmer's and Marvin's teams played and won a tournament with a Good Shepherd team coached by Mark Wenger and a Seventh Avenue team coached by Bernard Peterson. Gene Shelly, Jesus Cruz, Harold Davenport, Gary Rumble, and Bob Draper refereed.[46]

All of this activity and his own work with the Citizens Advisory Committee of the New York City Housing and Development Administration, South Bronx Housing Development Fund, and the Bronx Council of Churches, had a purpose, as Eugene Shelly put it, to be "a healing factor in the community."[47]

When the Glad Tidings congregation voted to renew Eugene and Martine Shelly's term for another two years in 1975, they promised to work at obtaining an assistant pastor. The annual meeting in September affirmed Jesus Cruz and Richard Frey as assistant pastors and the congregation installed them in a special service on November 2, 1975. That winter the Shellys moved to the Kingsbridge section of the northwest Bronx and Jesus and Miriam Cruz moved into the Shelly apartment at Glad Tidings. Jesus Cruz agreed to serve an additional year as assistant pastor, but Eugene Shelly made it clear he would only continue to June 30, 1977.[48]

The congregation expressed a preference for a full-time pastor with a team, composed of a community worker, youth worker, evangelist, and a program coordinator.[49] Jesus Cruz and Ray Siegrist, assistant pastors in 1977-78, kept the congregation going during the transition. "We are now able to expand our focus to more of an outreach to the community which is exciting," Siegrist reported.

John Bauman, pastor, left, Margaret Blanks, and Jesus Cruz in front of Glad Tidings.

The Pastoral Search Committee invited John and Susan Bauman to visit Glad Tidings. When the Baumans came to the church in December 1977 the consensus of the congregation was to invite them to take a leadership role. John Bauman was installed as pastor on June 18, 1978. In his report to the congregation in September, Bauman recognized the two assistant pastors. "The team ministry is especially helpful. Jesus and Ray shoulder responsibilities such as preaching once a month, helping to plan worship, and discussing outreach programs." They had initiated "a tutoring program for neighborhood children this fall."[50]

The remedial reading program was intended to provide a needed service "and gain contacts with families for the church." P.S. 139 (Berger Junior High) and P.S. 30 (elementary school) referred students who needed tutoring to improve their reading skills. Jim Robinson directed the program. He was working on his Master's degree and assisted the remedial reading teacher at Berger in reading classes. Doris Stoltzfus, a school psychologist in P.S. 30, Margaret Blanks and John Bauman did tutoring Tuesday, Wednesday, and Thursday. Michael Logan and Lori Kennel helped one day a week. Fifteen students, mostly from the Junior High, came twice a week for reading and vocabulary work, two to each tutor.[51]

The congregation wanted to reach more community people. "We have been doing home visitation of those families who sent children to our summer programs and inviting them to join us in Sunday morning activities."[52]

The depopulation of the South Bronx continued to be a problem. Once again Dottie Kruse reported, "This year has seen many children move away, so our Sunday school was small." The core group of young teenagers remained faithful. Jacqueline Buck, reporting on the youth council in September 1978, said "The majority of the participants were from the two basketball teams, cheerleaders, and Youth Council committee." She foresaw problems in keeping them active in the coming year. "As of September 1978 we have lost contact with the majority of the cheerleaders because Jackie has no time to teach them because she is in school now and has late classes. We may lose contact with Elmer's basketball team because he is not involved with Glad Tidings as much as he once was."[53]

Glad Tidings began to lose another constituency. Attendance fell off in 1979-1980. Some members no longer lived in the neighborhood but gave sacrificially of their time and energy to the church program. Monroe Yoder, as bishop, was aware of "a considerable number of persons who did not desire greater involvement" at Glad Tidings and who "did not find the Sunday morning worship that stimulating." They would like to have a Mennonite church closer to home. "Many of these persons live in the Northwest Bronx and had the desire to begin some type of worship in their community." About the same time, "a young enthusiastic believer" named Frankie Rodriguez came to Glad Tidings "with a desire to enter into a covenant-working relationship." He had been having Bible studies in his home with young people and wanted to bring these meetings into the church. His group began meeting with the congregation on Wednesday evenings and had a youth night on Saturdays that brought many young new Christians into the Glad Tidings fellowship by 1981.[54]

Developing Ministries at Fellowship Chapel

Fellowship Chapel on Tremont Avenue, just east of the Grand Concourse, and its immediate neighborhood, a section of the Bronx known as Mount Hope, escaped the devastation spreading over the South Bronx. The neighborhood was not without its own problems, as a survey made by Janet Hykes in 1976 demonstrated. In both church and community, most people had employment and the average family income was $6,000. But in the Mount Hope neighborhood welfare cases were on the increase from twenty percent to nearly thirty percent and retirees on Social Security made up another twenty percent of the community. In the congregation just five percent were on welfare and three percent depended on Social Security. As elsewhere in the Bronx the neighborhood had changed greatly in recent years. In 1976 half the people in Mount Hope were of Hispanic background and another forty percent African-Americans. The congregation reflected this, with Puerto Ricans comprising thirty five percent and blacks forty five percent of the members. Janet Hykes identified the major needs of the community as adequate housing, adequate employment, adequate health services, and adequate educational opportunities.[55]

Paul Hill, the founding pastor at Fellowship, resigned in 1969 to accept a call to the Life Line Mission in San Francisco. The Hills left the city at the end of July.[56] Bishop Charlie Byers thought of Charles Rife Jr., a former VSer in the Bronx who was studying at Fort Wayne Bible College, as Hill's successor, but Rife would not be available until 1971.[57] Hill had done all the administrative work of the Bronx mission himself, serving as pastor, VS director, camp director, and mission superintendent. Bishop Byers divided the responsibilities in making interim appointments. He asked Harold Paulus to be pastor of Fellowship Chapel and Kenneth Winger to serve as mission superintendent. Paulus, a retired pastor, had just left the Life Line Mission in San Francisco. The Wingers, an older couple, moved from rural Jarvis, Ontario, to the Bronx. Until Paulus and the Wingers could come to the city, Paul Espinosa, the deacon, would do the preaching and VS Unit leader Roy Shelly would be in charge of the mission.[58]

Harold Paulus resigned as pastor, effective November 8, 1970. Eldon Sheffer from the Brooklyn VS Unit assumed some of the pastoral duties. On a visit to the Bronx in January 1971, Bishop Byers found Sheffer "well accepted by everyone." He had concern for the Bronx VS Unit, however. He felt they needed "orientation on racial attitudes" and "to be involved with the religious and social life of the community." Eldon Sheffer had learned that youth involved in programs at Fellowship saw racism in the VSers' unthinking words.[59]

The congregation survived the change of personnel. In September 1969 attendance on Sundays averaged 76. In December 1970 Fellowship reported an average of 70 at worship, four baptisms and two received by letter. The congregation had had "a wonderful revival" with 19 seekers.

In January 1971 Bishop Byers invited Alvin and Thata Book, lately returned from mission work in Bulawayo, Zimbabwe, to consider the Bronx as their next mission field. Book accepted and the new pastor was installed on June 20, 1971. His job description included duties as mission superintendent, pastor, director of the VS Unit and of Camp Brookhaven. Book's own preference was his role as pastor of the congregation, but he worked wholeheartedly at administering the total program in the Bronx.[60]

Fellowship Chapel lost members as the neighborhood changed and people moved elsewhere in the city or suburbs. In 1969 Sunday school Superintendent Luther Schwartz noted, "The number in the register has dropped with the occasion of a number of families moving out of the community; in three families alone we lost eighteen members."[61] Despite this, Fellowship Chapel even grew significantly in the 1970s. In December 1972 Book reported an average attendance at worship of 74, six baptisms and five members received on confession of faith. The average attendance

Brethren in Christ Bishop Charlie Byers officiating at the Installation Service for pastor Alvin and Thata Book at Fellowship Chapel.

on Sunday mornings was 87 in December 1973. The congregation counted 51 members in December 1974. The report for June 1975 noted an average of 93 persons met for worship on Sundays.

The VS Unit helped the congregation in community outreach, although most VSers worked full-time at outside jobs. Joanne Kreider was Sunday school superintendent and directed Christ's Crusaders, a fellowship group for older teenagers. Gary Lebo was in charge of junior church and helped with the camp program. Daniel Knepper worked with the Shop Club, a group of boys from ten to fifteen years old. VSers also helped with vacation Bible school in the summer and Released Time classes during the year.[62]

In a rapidly changing community, with its share of urban problems, Fellowship Chapel demonstrated little interest in social ministries before 1974. Contacts with the neighborhood were limited to the church program, vacation Bible school, camp and Fresh Air programs, and the distribution of tracts door to door. Mary Lou Ruegg, the first Brethren in Christ VSer to come to the Bronx in 1961, remained in the city and she had a continuing role in the congregation. A small group of neighborhood youth met in her apartment on Tuesday evenings for Bible study and prayer.[63]

In 1974 the Bronx Administrative Committee, composed of Bishop Byers, Alvin Book, Glen Pierce, who was responsible for Home Missions and Voluntary Service in the Brethren in Christ Church, J. Wilmer Heisey, and Earl Musser, began to talk about new ministries for the congregation and the VS Unit. They expressed the need for "a Coffee House type of ministry" at a meeting in April. At the same time, they explored the possibility of calling an assistant pastor and determined to invite Premnath S. Dick, a Messiah graduate living in the city and relating to Fellowship Chapel. Dick came to New York as an intern for a year with Youth for Christ. He then worked with East Harlem Interfaith, the successor to the East Harlem Protestant Parish, initially with their prison committee, setting up bus trips for families of inmates and in a counselling program for ex-inmates. He found his work at Fellowship Chapel "challenging and exciting."[64]

Alvin Book, Premnath Dick, and Mary Lou Ruegg from Fellowship Chapel met in August with J. Wilmer Heisey, Earl Musser, and Glen Pierce, and with Kathryn Kreider and Wayne Cassel from Messiah College to discuss possible new ministries in New York. Kathryn Kreider, who taught Social Welfare at Messiah, had earlier suggested using college students in the city.[65]

"Al Book likened the program at Fellowship Chapel to a car with the rear wheels jacked up and the motor running—We've said that the

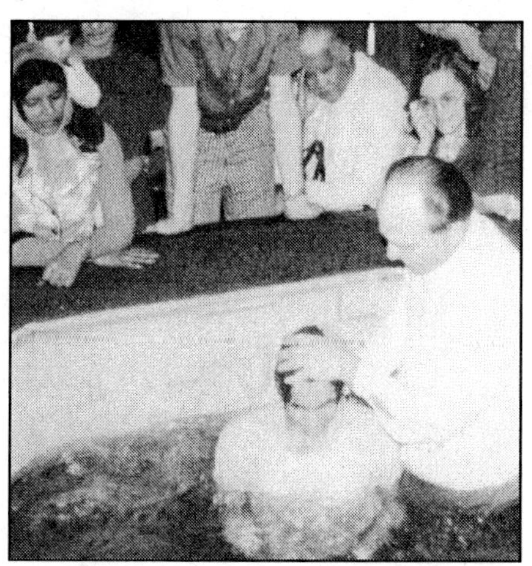

Alvin Book, pastor of Fellowship Chapel, officiating at a baptismal service.

focus of missions is on the city but we haven't gotten into gear." Discussion turned to the difficulties of using short-term personnel and relying on VSers to develop the congregational program. "Al agreed that it is hard to involve the city people if they see a 19-year-old coming to the city and immediately picking up responsibilities in the church. We have been making the city people bend our way; we need to bend their way."

Were there ministries for the Brethren in Christ in New York? Prem Dick urged closer contact with Mennonites and cooperation with what they were doing. He suggested a learning center to help young people at the Chapel prepare for college and to give them formal Bible training. The neighborhood could use homemakers and community nurses. He also suggested a job referral center or counselling center, especially for youngsters in trouble with the law. Mary Lou Ruegg proposed a day-care center and expanded youth clubs. Others proposed a coffee-house or Christian book store.[66]

The Bronx Administrative Committee drafted a "Bronx New Ministries Proposal" in October 1974, suggesting that a Service Ministries Coordinator be appointed to research and develop new service ministries in the area around Fellowship Chapel, help recruit personnel, and facilitate cooperative efforts with Messiah College. This individual would be self-supporting.[67]

In November 1975 the Bronx Administrative Committee asked Alvin Book, Premnath Dick, and Glen Pierce to produce a model and bring concrete recommendations to the committee. They also endorsed the idea of a Christian book store in the Bronx. But they recognized they lacked specific information about required services and services already provided by others in the community. Since Janet Hykes would be coming to the Bronx after the camp season, they suggested she conduct a six-week study of the Fellowship Chapel neighborhood. They asked Dale Stoltzfus to be a consultant for the study.[68]

Janet Hykes made her survey in August and September 1976. She found many areas of need, including housing, employment, and health services.

Alvin Book, pastor, preaching at Fellowship Chapel.

She recommended that a tutoring program to supplement existing public schools would be the place to start a community ministries program. Mary Cummings Bailey had tutored neighborhood children at Fellowship Chapel with some success. The Task Force reviewed her findings and recommended the initial focus be on an after-school tutoring program. They urged appointment of a Community Ministries Coordinator, but strongly recommended that the new program not be responsible to the congregation but to an overall New York City superintendent.[69]

In December 1976 Janet Hykes was appointed Community Ministries Coordinator. Alvin and Thata Book both expressed some misgivings on this appointment, feeling uncertain whether she shared their "concerns and priorities for the Community Ministries Program and whether she has the personal Christian commitment and spiritual resources." They feared the program could be divorced from the church program and take on more secular values. Wilmer Heisey made it clear that they were already committed to the program and to Janet Hykes and had to go ahead.[70]

The Little Lighthouse Learning Center opened November 30, 1977 at Fellowship Chapel. "This after-school tutoring program is a place where children may come to get extra help in reading and math skill," Janet Hykes wrote. She had fifteen volunteers from the church and the community who kept it staffed five afternoons a week. The staff worked closely with the neighborhood schools, and made home visits on each child tutored to involve the family. The Mission Board contributed $4,400 for the Learning Center in 1977-78 and $5,380 in 1978-79.[71]

The proposed Christian book store never came to be. The Publication Board gave a negative response in 1975 but agreed to further study the issue. Isaiah B. Harley made a positive recommendation to the Publication Board in August 1976, but the full board overruled it as too risky.[72]

Two other major concerns competed with the service ministries proposal and slowed implementation. In April 1975 the Bronx Administrative Committee decided to purchase the building at 240 East Tremont Avenue, next door to Fellowship Chapel, and remodel it for expanded facilities. In September Home Missions loaned $45,000 to the congregation for this purpose. Once the church took title, a stream of volunteers, 150 in all, came from Pennsylvania to help demolish old walls separating apartments and to help with construction of a new sanctuary. The new Fellowship Chapel was ready for dedication on June 20, 1977.[73]

The dedication of the renovated building marked the end of Alvin and Thata Book's ministry in the Bronx. When Bishop Byers met with Book and the Bronx Pastoral Committee, Premnath Dick, Anna Peachey, and Mary Lou Ruegg, in 1974, Alvin Book indicated that he planned to resign effective September 1, 1975. Byers felt that too much administrative pressure was Book's only reason for wanting to leave Fellowship Chapel and he remedied this by taking responsibility for the camp out of Book's hands. He recognized that Book was doing an excellent job and there was no need to move him.[74]

Fellowship Chapel had emerged as a strong enough congregation to no longer need nurturing as a mission outpost. In January 1976 the church board determined the need for an assistant pastor who could speak Spanish. At the same time Book announced his decision to stay in the Bronx only through June 1977. Over the next few months everyone concerned began looking for an assistant pastor who might also succeed Book. The church board developed a job description for the assistant pastor that made explicit the requirement that he be bilingual and from the city. On this basis several candidates suggested by Bishop Byers were ruled out. Alvin Book himself came up with a solution to the dilemma after many months. Eddie Gonzalez, a member of the congregation, would become assistant minister. He was a young married man who worked as manager of a shoe store and who was at home in both English and Spanish. Gonzalez wrote in August 1976 of his own pilgrimage:

> I've been a Christian since last November. Fellowship Chapel is the only church that I've attended regularly since I accepted Christ. I am just a born-again believer seeking to work for Christ and serve my brothers. I love to help in church, teaching classes, going to the Bowery or whatever I can do.

Eddie and Naomi Gonzalez moved to one of the apartments at 246 East Tremont Avenue.[75]

As 1976 drew to a close, Bishop Byers assured the congregation that, "We are working as fast as we can to get a successor," but two promising candidates declined. In June 1977, just four Sundays before the Books left the city, Glen Pierce from the Home Missions office agreed to serve as interim pastor for ninety days. Mary Lou Ruegg continued as church coordinator.[76]

The pastoral search went on without success, until Glen Pierce identified a candidate within the congregation. Dan Farina grew up in an Italian Protestant family in the Bronx and, after attending Bible School, went to work for the New York Bible Society. His continuing employment with the Bible Society precluded a full-time pastorate, but he could give two days a week to the congregation in addition to leading worship on Sundays. Bishop Byers endorsed Pierce's choice. "Dan Farina sounds like a good person to do weekend work for Fellowship Chapel." Byers met with the pastoral committee in September to discuss Farina and all agreed to invite him. He was called as a part-time pastor, with Eddie Gonzalez "as his Timothy" in the assistant pastor post. Since both men were young and new to the Brethren in Christ Church, Byers asked Samuel Minter to join "the staff on an interim basis, serving in the capacity of superintendent." The Minters, an older couple, came to the Bronx in October.[77]

Ruth Minter tutoring a young girl at Fellowship Chapel.

Although Mary Lou Ruegg carried "a heavy burden" as congregational coordinator during the transition, Fellowship Chapel had a supportive and involved congregation. Mary Lou led a women's Bible study in her apartment at 240 East

Tremont. Eddie Gonzalez led Bible studies in the church on Wednesday nights through the fall and winter months. Vacation Bible school teachers in the summer of 1977 included Pat Gobin, Jan Hykes, Naomi Gonzalez, Beverly DaCosta, Lee Mylin, Felicita Fuentes, Millie Jones, Jesse Wolgemuth, Ina Taylor, Anna Peachey, Colron Powery, Eddie Gonzalez, Nancy Mann, Dan Farina, Eric Kronawetter, Bill Martin, and Mary Lou Ruegg, a good mix of Pennsylvanians and New Yorkers.[78]

Dan Farina proved to be a good match for Fellowship Chapel. After a dip in the average attendance during the summer and autumn, Sunday morning worship drew an average of 102 in March 1978. New Christians were coming to the baptismal waters. "Already this year we have seen eight new souls confess Jesus as Savior." Eddie Gonzalez resigned as assistant to the pastor in 1978, but he continued as a lay minister in Fellowship Chapel. When Bishop Byers visited the Bronx in February, he offered Dan Farina a three-year pastoral contract on a part-time basis beginning July 1, 1978. Farina would continue working for the Bible Society while serving as pastor. Dan Farina remained as pastor at Fellowship Chapel until 1982.[79]

Renewal at Friendship Community Church

The charismatic renewal spread through many denominations in the late 1960s, touching both Catholics and Protestants. As in earlier renewal movements, non-denominational fellowships, conferences, and weekly prayer meetings allowed Spirit-filled Christians from different backgrounds to meet and encourage one another. The Full Gospel Business Men International sponsored dinner meetings with a speaker, opportunities for prayer and laying on of hands, as well as displays of tapes and books. The open atmosphere of these events provided easy access to the movement for inquirers or friends or coworkers invited by a regular attender. Some of the earliest contacts of New York City Mennonites with the renewal came through the FGBMI meetings.

In January 1970 a psychiatric nurse who was a member of the Mennonite House of Friendship congregation telephoned Irene Smucker, the pastor's wife, to share her experience of baptism with the Holy Spirit at a Full Gospel Businessmen's meeting. She invited others in the congregation to join her at these meetings and they had the same experience as she did. In April 1970 John and Irene Smucker had their own baptism.[80]

John and Irene Smucker were away from the Bronx during the school year 1969-1970 while John completed a Master's degree at Union Theological Seminary. During his absence Nelson Kauffman had pastoral care of the Friendship Community Church. Kauffman, a veteran urban missionary, was himself on sabbatical from his duties as Director of Home Missions of the Mennonite Board of Missions. He was no mere caretaker in this interim pastorate, but a vigorous and dynamic leader in congregational evangelism.

The Friendship pastor and congregation were both worn out by efforts at community activism and internal divisions as neighborhood concerns pressed on church members faster than they could absorb them. The charismatic emphasis could be a path to renewal and reconciliation or it could further divide the congregation. Services became longer with longer sermons and livelier music and Scripture songs. Enthusiastic personal testimonies became common in worship. Services ended with an altar call and opportunities for the elders to lay on hands and pray for those with needs. In October 1970 the church council meeting became an extended prayer meeting lasting until one in the morning. Sometimes individual charismatic members seemed to push things too far. At the Thanksgiving Day service in November a woman fell on the floor and screamed while other members tried to pray the demon out of her.[81]

Mennonites had taken a dim view of speaking in tongues and divine healing when Gerald Derstine led a charismatic revival in his Minnesota congregation. North Central Mennonite Conference revoked Derstine's ministerial credentials in 1955 and he began a non-denominational revival ministry in Florida.[82] At the request of a few members Smucker reluctantly invited Derstine to come to have meetings. In February, and again in April 1971, Derstine held weekend conferences at the House of Friendship and in the summer of 1971 the Smuckers attended Derstine's School of the Spirit at Ogema, Minnesota. The whole congregation was impressed with Derstine's love and gentleness in ministry.[83]

Samuel Santos, associate pastor at Friendship, shared Smucker's openness to the work of the Holy Spirit in the charismatic revival. Not all church members held this view. Smucker estimated that half the 103 members in 1971 did not participate in the charismatic movement.[84] Jesse Adams, the other associate pastor, was ready to take on greater pastoral responsibility and concerned about raising his children in the violence of the South Bronx. He left Friendship in 1971 to become pastor of Garden Chapel Mennonite Church in Dover, New Jersey.[85]

The charismatic movement had a major impact on the Mennonite Church by 1971. Eastern Mennonite College and Goshen College experienced a Holy Spirit revival that autumn and many local churches had an outpouring of the Spirit.[86] The New York City VS Unit also felt the charismatic renewal. Dale Stoltzfus reported, "At the VS Center some things are developing which I would relate to the earlier experiences some had with the charismatic movement." Two VSers intended to leave the unit. Stoltzfus believed they were "very mixed up in terms of what the Bible is teaching us about the way the Spirit works in our lives." He concluded:

> This situation at the VS Center, along with the earlier relationship problems we had at Good Shepherd and the constant tensions we have been having with the brother at the House of Friendship, makes it clear that we need to hang together and somehow not let these different movements and experiences be divisive to us.[87]

As in other renewal movements, tensions developed between those who embraced the new measures and those who did not. John Smucker wrote:

> It was difficult for me as pastor to keep the charismatics and non-charismatics working and worshiping together constructively. Some wanted to make changes faster toward the traditional Pentecostal way. Others wanted to go slow, and still others were completely turned off by the new charismatic worship expressions in the body. The zealous charismatics tended to lack patience for the non-charismatics and wanted their own group experiences. The non-charismatics considered the charismatic expressions an intrusion to what they were used to in an orderly, evangelical type church.[88]

Other tensions in the Friendship Community Church had little to do with the renewal movement. On his first Sunday back in the Bronx in June 1970, the youth of the congregation presented Smucker with a list of seven demands for greater control of the youth program and representation in the church council. The council and congregation went through a series of meetings, making more room for young people to participate in decision-making, but falling short of what they asked.[89] John Smucker's involvement with community organizations—he mentioned 68 such meetings in his 1971 report—and his extensive outside speaking engagements raised some questions. A church council member wondered about "church money spent in telephone and transportation," but did not question outside meetings.

The New York Mennonite churches related to different mission boards and belonged to different conferences. They moved closer in 1966 when they formed the Council of Mennonite Churches, but relations did not always go smoothly. This had nothing to do with charismatic renewal. It had a great deal to do with the high standards new Christians expected of themselves and others. Because of a lack of equal representation from

Lancaster and Atlantic Coast Conferences on the Camp Deerpark Board and because Friendship leaders felt a Lancaster leader was not disciplined sufficiently for an indiscreet incident at camp, Friendship leaders decided not to use Camp Deerpark for one season to register their displeasure. Friendship sent campers to Spruce Lake Camp and did not participate in MYF or other city-wide activities. Mennonite Board of Missions and Eastern Board leaders intervened with a conflict resolution expert to heal the breach.[90]

John I. Smucker resigned as vice-chairman and as a member of the Council of Mennonite Churches in New York City in October 1971. "My reason for resignation is that the Council has not been able or willing to practice true Christian brotherhood and fairness to all its members." He saw them as "farther apart spiritually then we were five years ago" when the Council began. "Unless this Council cleans house and practices true Christian brotherhood and lets Christ be its Lord, how can I or anyone else in good conscience back its work?" Assistant Pastor Sammy Santos resigned at the same time.[91] On October 31, 1971, the Friendship Community Church held a congregational meeting and determined to "back our leaders fully and completely." The congregation withdrew its membership "unless and until full reconciliation and unity is restored among our leaders under the power of the Holy Spirit."[92]

In April 1972 Lupe DeLeon, of the Minority Ministries Council of Mennonite Board of Missions, discussed the situation with Paul Landis. They recognized two separate, but intertwined issues, "the incident at camp two years ago and the persistent accusations" and "the struggle for leadership and political power." The only way to resolve them was to work at them separately. They set up a meeting in May "to look at the matter of the camp incident and the accusations."[93]

As a result, Martin Bender, Hubert Brown, Lupe DeLeon, Simon Gingerich, Richard Pannell, Sammy Santos, John Smucker, Dale Stoltzfus, Chester Wenger, and Monroe Yoder met at the Protestant Center on Riverside Drive on May 8, 1972. Paul G. Landis, Ray Pacheco, Richard Pannell, and Gordon Zook joined the group later in the day. They agreed "to resolve the conflict over the incident that happened two years ago at camp."

Sammy Santos and Martin Bender expressed concern about staff at Camp Deerpark. "It was clear that they feel the camp management has not required high enough standards for staff in the past." The group agreed that this was not a central issue. "Martin said he is concerned about what is being taught our youth, that sin doesn't matter, that the church allows most anything to happen without discipline." After considerable discussion everyone present "expressed himself willing to forgive" and forget the incident. Martin Bender asked for a private meeting with another brother "and reached an agreement and reconciliation." John Smucker had left early to take Hubert Brown to the airport and missed the final stage of the meeting although he had been a leader in efforts of reconciliation leading up this point. He brought the two Friendship leaders, Bender and Santos, together later.[94]

A week after the meeting, on May 13, 1972, the Mennonite House of Friendship Church Council decided "that we will withdraw from using Camp Deerpark facilities for the rest of 1972" and sent their October 1971 letter of withdrawal to the Mennonite Council of Churches. The Church Council members who signed the letter included only one ethnic Mennonite. Chester Wenger told Lupe DeLeon about "their course of disassociating themselves from the other churches of New York" and hoped they could keep "channels of communication open and our spirit of love and unity pure in the sight of the Lord."[95]

The Council of Mennonite Churches discussed the withdrawal from Camp Deerpark at its May meeting. The next month they received Smucker's letter of resignation. Smucker worked for reconciliation in Christ even as he made this gesture. By September 1972 John Smucker was back at the Council meeting and in October the Friendship congregation formally returned to the Council.[96]

At this same time the Friendship congregation brought its membership lists up to date. So many families had moved away that thirty-eight inactive and absent members were purged from the roll.[97] In March 1972 increasing violence in the community led the church to call for a day of prayer and fasting for the urban violence, drugs, gangs, and crime, threatening their children. In April the church council suspended the youth choir and the youth team and closed the coffee house because of "drugs and other off-beat behavior."[98] The charismatic renewal strengthened the church in the crisis. A revitalized youth group grew into a strong spiritual Bible study under black leader Wilma Bailey.[99]

The congregation renewed John Smucker's call as their pastor and allowed him outside preaching engagements fifteen Sundays a year. In 1973 and 1974 he preached at Friendship 37 times, with an altar call for prayer, ministry, and counseling after each sermon. "Many times I would, with a team of persons, counsel persons for hours after a charismatic service."[100] In August 1974 John and Irene Smucker visited the Church of the Redeemer in Houston, Texas, and experimented with reproducing their vision for an urban church organized as a network of "households" or house churches.[101] At the end of the same year, Smucker accepted an appointment as Protestant Chaplain at Fordham Hospital and began work there in February 1975. The Friendship congregation allowed him to correspondingly reduce his obligations to the church and his financial support from the church. They wholeheartedly supported his chaplain work as an extension of the congregation's mission, with twenty volunteers from Friendship going regularly to the hospital to visit patients with him.[102] When the city closed Fordham Hospital in July 1976, Smucker became chaplain at North Central Bronx Hospital. Because of the greater distance, Friendship members did not participate in his new chaplaincy, nor support it to the same extent.[103]

"At the time of the closing of Fordham Hospital, the charismatic movement turned inward and cooled at Friendship," Smucker recalled later. One elder resigned, urging others to go to more spiritual churches. Divisions surfaced and financial problems continued to plague the congregation. The effort to create discipleship groups on the Church of the Redeemer model had to be abandoned. Smucker himself began a Doctor of Ministry program at New York Theological Seminary, which some members saw as a distraction from the congregational commitment. The church council left it to Pastor Smucker whether he wanted to have his call to ministry renewed, but the congregation voted over 90 percent for him to continue as pastor. Smucker agreed to serve as pastor only a year at a time from 1977, and in 1979 John and Irene Smucker left the Bronx after almost a quarter century of urban ministry.[104] After four years of study and teaching the Smuckers were invited by the New York City Council of Mennonite Churches and the Atlantic Coast Conference to return to New York City to start a new church in Queens, the sixteenth Mennonite church in New York City. Looking back, the Smuckers say that it was because of the deep moving of the Spirit at Friendship that it was possible for them to return to start the new church.

Evangelistic Outreach at Good Shepherd

Good Shepherd Mennonite Church absorbed the shock of the resignation of their new pastor, Carl Good, and in August 1970 voted unanimously to call Wesley Newswanger as pastor and John Buckwalter as assistant pastor. Newswanger had full-time employment as a New York City public school teacher, so the congregation recognized he could give no more than one-fourth time to Good Shepherd, even if he should negotiate a reduced teaching load with the Board of Education. As it turned out, he was unable to cut back on his classroom duties and served as pastor only on marginal time.[105]

As congregational chairman, Wes Newswanger had led the search for a replacement for Carl Good. The congregation invited John H. Kraybill to return to the city as their pastor, but he saw no good reason to leave his Johnstown congregation.[106] By July, with the situation "reaching a desperate point," Paul Landis suggested veteran African missionary Clyde Shenk as pastor for Good Shepherd and added that, "There has also been some discussion about Martin Bender from the House of Friendship or Wesley Newswanger giving leadership to the congregation, but there are also some who have some uncertainties about this."[107] The congregational vote made this point moot. Good Shepherd members selected Jerome Yates to succeed Newswanger as congregational chairman. Monroe Yoder reported:

> They will also be in conversation with Martin Benders, a family that is interested in moving into the area. Martin is interested in evangelism, developing some of the techniques that Nelson Kauffman introduced.[108]

Good Shepherd Mennonite Church building, at 1126 Sherman Avenue, Bronx, later used by the Ebenezer Mennonite congregation. 2005 photo.

Martin Bender accepted the invitation to work with Good Shepherd in neighborhood evangelism. Martha Charles had responsibility for the club program.

A year later, after Good Shepherd had experienced serious division, Monroe Yoder, Richard Pannell, and Dale Stoltzfus met with each member of the congregation and presented their findings to a congregational meeting. Yoder reported "numerous expressions of appreciation for Wesley, John, Martha, and Martin" as well as "appreciation for the Sunday morning worship together." There was general agreement, however, that the team had not been too effective, as there had been some differences between the regular church program and the evangelism program, which had been under Martin Bender's leadership. Members felt a need for "more coordination and communication between various leaders" and "involvement in community activities to spread the presence and program of the church and to exchange with community residents."

> The concern of the congregation was that the entire church be involved in these projects together... There was concern that the evangelistic outreach in the community be tied in with the life of the congregation, including the Sunday morning program.[109]

Wes Newswanger announced in September 1971 that he would serve as pastor for only one year. He continued to be employed full-time by the city school system and planned to stay with his teaching job beyond 1972. Although Wes did not feel he had "the training or experience to continue being in charge of the nurture and guidance programs of a developing inner-city congregation," both Wes and Marian wanted to help out at Good Shepherd and would consider being part of a team after September 1972.[110] Meanwhile, the search for a long-term pastor began.

Verneice, Rachelle, and Harold Davenport, pastor at Good Shepherd Mennonite Church.

By the spring of 1972, Harold Davenport emerged as the logical choice for Good Shepherd. He had been active at Seventh Avenue before going to college and seminary and, when he and his wife Verneice returned to the city in 1971, Richard Pannell wanted Harold to help him and perhaps succeed him. Since he was one of the few African-American Mennonite pastors, Chester Wenger hoped he might relate to other predominantly black churches. Davenport sometimes preached at Glad Tidings, but he primarily worked with the Seventh Avenue congregation. "We will need to work out a number of details with Seventh Avenue before we could feel free to have Harold and Verneice assist Wes for one year," Dale Stoltzfus reported in April.[111]

The Good Shepherd congregation remained divided, mirroring the attitudes of Friendship over the incident at camp and the need for greater discipline. In April 1972 Dale Stoltzfus heard from several members about "some of the feelings at Good Shepherd concerning camp and the leadership in New York." Paul Landis and the District Leadership Team met again with each member at Good Shepherd in May 1972. "Plans are being made for Harold to meet the congregation and then a congregational meeting will be held to discuss further plans." The congregation received the proposal for Harold Davenport as pastor and Wes Newswanger as assistant pastor "with a good positive vote" and "Church reorganization and club program will be discussed at a future members' meeting." Harold Davenport began his new assignment in October 1972.[112]

Division had progressed to a split in 1972 with several members, including Norma Brenner, going with Martin Bender to an independent fellowship. Samuel Santos, the charismatic assistant pastor at Friendship, worked with this group. This fellowship experienced its own division a year later. On a Sunday morning in April, Dale Stoltzfus again visited Good Shepherd:

> Norma Brenner was there on Sunday morning and she had been relating in the past Sundays to the congregation. I had a chat with Norma and she has some bad feelings about what happened a year ago.... She regrets what happened then and stated that she would like to come back to Good Shepherd again. In the business meeting Norma apologized to the group for some of the things that were said and the feelings that were expressed at that time and stated that she would be giving up her activities at the other center and would again be relating to Good Shepherd....[113]

Attendance at the Bible clubs increased early in 1973. "They appreciate the leadership of Wes and Marian," Harold Davenport said. In September Rhoda Ehst, who had worked in VS assignments in New York and in Atlanta, came back to the Bronx to help with the club program, and continued more than two years. Diane Freeman directed the Good Shepherd day camp in the summer with five staff persons.[114]

The Bible Club program involved 250 children in 1972-1973. Three classes of 25 children each met on Monday and Wednesday afternoons and two classes of the same size met Tuesday, Thursday, and Friday afternoons. Older girls met Monday evenings and older boys on Tuesday evenings. Wesley and Marian Newswanger worked with Harold and Verneice Davenport in directing the program, with twenty volunteers, church members, parents, and youth, helping them. The clubs followed the pattern of flannelgraph Bible stories and crafts projects for the youngsters and woodworking, cooking and sewing, recreation, and more serious Bible study for the teenagers.[115]

The congregation called Harold and Verneice Davenport for an additional two years in 1974, and renewed their call in 1976.[116] At the end of that year, Good Shepherd planned to re-evaluate the church cabinet, pastor and congregational life. The three components of the Good Shepherd outreach program, Bible clubs, summer day camp, and monthly ladies' group, needed a close look, too. Davenport also proposed a three-day revival meeting and a new emphasis on stewardship.[117] In the spring of 1977, Paul Landis and Dale Stoltzfus worked with Ken McGhie, the congregational chairman, on leadership evaluation.[118]

The congregation had 28 members in 1977 and three preparing for baptism. Good Shepherd again sponsored a day camp for 21 children and sent 20 boys and girls to Fresh Air vacations in 1977. Clubs and summer program continued in 1978. Young people took the initiative in planning Friday night youth meetings. The congregation opened a used clothing outlet. In the early autumn of 1978, Harold Davenport announced his intention of getting a divorce from his wife. They expected this to be final in January. The pastoral study group began meeting early in 1979 to prepare for a transition in leadership. Eugene Shelly, who was serving as coordinator of special projects in the District since he left Glad Tidings, preached a Lenten series at Good Shepherd. He took over as interim pastor in May 1979 when Harold Davenport left Good Shepherd to become a full-time hospital chaplain.[119]

Changes in Voluntary Service

In 1974 the Voluntary Service Center moved from 314 East 19th Street in Manhattan to the Good Shepherd neighborhood at 1114 Sherman

Avenue in the Bronx. With the end of the Vietnam War and the military draft, young men and young married couples no longer came to the city for two years of alternative service. The VS Unit had nine members in December 1973 but, with scheduled terminations, it would be down to four VSers in January 1974.[120] The building on East 19th Street had many empty rooms. The Unit opened some of them to mothers with children undergoing plastic surgery at NYU Medical Center. In March 1973 the District Council looked at another aspect of the same issue: "Due to a large number of VSers working in the Bronx, there has been an active discussion of moving the VS Center to the Bronx."[121]

Dale Stoltzfus, as VS administrator, had noticed other changes in a report he drafted in 1969 for Eastern Board. Stoltzfus contrasted the typical VSer of 1959 with those coming to the city a decade later: "Many of the youth are more independent in the way they relate to the church and church groups. They no longer feel the need to belong to a Mennonite community and they find apartments on their own." They had a higher

Uptown Voluntary Service Center building at 1114 Sherman Avenue, Bronx. 2005 photo.

level of education, nine of ten coming from college or university, "and thus have different ideas about the city and city culture than the fellows of ten years ago." Many came to New York for more advanced study or more challenging jobs.[122]

The city churches had also changed. A study in 1973 agreed "that we still do need VSers but we need to challenge our own community people to serve and to encourage the youth of our congregations to work in training with the VSers, so that VS as we now know it can be phasing out and community VS will take hold." There was also consensus on moving the VS Center uptown, nearer the churches.[123]

In October 1973 Sid and Sue Hyman moved into the VS Center to begin the Morning Star Community, an intentional community of Christians who would live together. They started a Wednesday evening prayer group fellowship soon afterwards.[124] Sid Hyman had a profound interest in Jewish evangelism and worked with the Metro Messianic Fellowship.[125]

Dale Stoltzfus and Alvin Book explored the possibility of merging the Brethren in Christ and Mennonite VS Center at Fellowship Chapel on East Tremont Avenue. The District Council decided instead to encourage Eastern Board to purchase the Wesley Newswanger building at 1114 Sherman Avenue for relocation of the VS program. Unit leader Warren Heller agreed to the possibility of the unit moving to the Bronx, and Sid Hyman expressed his willingness to begin community outreach and develop the Morning Star Community as successor to the VS Center at the East 19th Street location.[126]

The Newswanger family moved out on the 4th of July 1974, returning to Strasburg, Pennsylvania, so Wesley could begin teaching at Lancaster Mennonite High School in the fall. The VS Unit moved in two days later.[127]

Warren Heller, youth worker at Seventh Avenue, and Chris Benner, VSer first at Glad Tidings and then at the Staten Island Girls' Home, married in 1974 and served as the first unit leaders at the Sherman Avenue VS Center. After they completed their term in 1975, they remained in the city as associate VSers. Mark Wenger became unit leader in August 1975.[128]

LaVern Yutzy, director of the VS program in the Salunga office, told the New York District Council that Eastern Board would like to sell the East 19th Street property, "but is seeking guidance from the New York City churches on the best solution for disposition of the property." Yutzy brought them up to date on the state of voluntary service in New York. The role of the VSers had "shifted from crucial ministry to auxiliary work." The response of the city churches had changed as a result, Yutzy said. The cost of maintaining a VS worker in New York amounted to $300 a month. Eastern Board would prefer that the unit become self-supporting with more VSers earning salaries.[129]

The Morning Star Community began in 1974 and counted four adults and three children in January 1975. "It was agreed that the program will be self-supporting. We have faith that God will bless the program so that this goal may be reached."[130] Morning Star Community had four residential members in addition to the Hyman family. Rayetta Martin and Alice Hess were both Mennonites. Ralph Murphy and Chuck Winsitt, a Quaker and a Catholic, retained their membership in their own churches. A larger group of non-residents "covenanted to seek to grow into a more intensive and comprehensive Christian life together than is found in normal church life." The community sought to develop "a sense of Christian fellowship and community for people who feel the alienation of urban living." Bible study meetings on Tuesday evenings offered their major effort to accomplish this. The Tuesday night meetings for seekers attracted 20 to 25 each week. The Thursday night in-depth Bible study for believers drew an average of twenty, as did Sunday morning worship. As individuals, the residents worked with alcoholics, the deaf, children, and the poor. They hoped the community could work as a group with these concerns. The Hymans had a heart for Jewish evangelism.[131]

By September 1975 Morning Star members decided to disband the residential community. Sue Hyman was the one who pressed to dissolve the community, the other four thought it still viable. Alice Hess, who was director of the day care center at Burnside Mennonite Church, asked to move to the Sherman Avenue VS Center. The Morning Star Community planned to focus on deaf children. They proposed using the upper floors as a guest house to make the community more self-supporting. The District Leadership Team offered to rent the building to them for $425 a month, to be raised to $500 a month the next year. Sid and Sue Hyman moved to their own apartment in lower Manhattan, but met with the intentional community. Only Chuck Winsitt and Rayetta Martin continued to live at the East 19th Street building. With three more people in the residential community, it might yet succeed.[132]

Morning Star Community did not long survive. In May 1976 the District Council discussed plans to sell the former VS Center on East 19th Street. Eugene Shelly proposed other options. One possibility was for Morning Star to enlarge its residential community, but "Gene did not feel the prospects of Morning Star continuing were very good." He had talked with Jim King about an International Student Center at East 19th

Street. A VS couple would serve as host and hostess. "It was proposed as a place for lonely and needy students to come. A reading room would be provided." Since Jim King was not interested in pursuing the idea, it might not be feasible either. Another possible use would be as a guest house for Mennonites visiting in New York. The most promising suggestion came from Richard Russo, who proposed developing the Morning Star interest in deaf children into a center for deaf children with a professional staff and the support of foundation grants and public money.[133]

Myrna Burkholder moved into the Morning Star Community in August 1976. She had lived in a university dormitory when working on a master's degree in remedial reading and learning disabilities at NYU. She moved out of the dormitory and needed temporary housing while job hunting. When she moved to East 19th Street "it was explained to me that the building will soon be sold or that it might be leased to a program for the deaf." She had another idea. One Sunday after church at Glad Tidings she talked with Gene Shelly and Dale Stoltzfus about her suggestion "that the Morning Star residence be used in the future as a residence for Mennonite graduate students." This would enable the church to reach out to "young people of Mennonite persuasion and heritage" and encourage them "to keep their ties with the church." The graduate student residence could also provide overnight accommodations for Mennonite visitors to New York.[134]

Gene Shelly presented proposals from both Richard Russo and Myrna Burkholder to the District Council in September.[135]

The New York churches were already reaching some graduate students. Mel Lehman coordinated a revived Mennonite Graduate Student Fellowship. They held a pot-luck supper at Burnside, for instance, in October 1975 with "a good cross-section of students and NYU people represented" and went caroling at Bellevue Hospital before Christmas. Other events followed through the year.[136]

With only Rayetta Martin and Chuck Winsitt left in the residential group, the District Council terminated Morning Star Community in October 1976. The Council then endorsed development of a Mennonite Student Center at 314 East 19th Street. They appointed Myrna Burkholder, Mel Lehman, chair of the Mennonite Young Adult and Student Fellowship, David and Ruth Wenger, and Dale Stoltzfus as a committee to draw up a budget, work with the other persons then in the house, decide on a hostess, and develop a program for the Student Center.[137]

In January 1977 the committee submitted a formal proposal to Eastern Board. The Executive Committee of Eastern Board approved the committee proposal for a Mennonite student and young adult center at East

19th Street and arranged a loan to finance renovating of the building. Myrna Burkholder agreed to serve as house manager and David Wenger as program coordinator. In the first six months of operation, Menno House sponsored a variety of programs, discussion on women's issues, a lecture by theologian Gordon Kaufman, an open house, Christmas caroling, and a seminar on professionalism directed by Rick Mojonnier and Arden Shank of Mennonite Student and Young Adult Services, a new ministry of the Mennonite Church. In May 1977 J. Lawrence Burkholder led a theological discussion. "The group of twenty-five persons grappled with Mel Lehman's thesis that the Schleitheim Confession is offensive on all counts, except, possibly in its statement on non-participation in war."[138]

Original plans for the residence called for rooms for six resident students and for up to ten temporary residents, who might include participants in an inner-city seminar, college or seminary students involved in short-term internships in the city, or VSers on temporary assignment. It would be a meeting place for Mennonite students and young adults in the city and a natural location for the Student Services Coordinator. Gene Shelly added a new dimension, offering to be the spiritual shepherd and to develop fellowships attractive to scattered Mennonites. He was already doing some of this out of Glad Tidings.[139] The committee did not pursue his idea in the early days of Menno House.

J. Lawrence Burkholder, left, President of Goshen College, Indiana, guest speaker at the Mennonite Student and Young Adult Fellowship held at Menno House.

As renovation of the building neared completion in the spring of 1977, the advisory committee determined to use more of Menno House for long-term residents without totally eliminating space for guests. David and Ruth Wenger moved into Menno House in March. As program coordinator, he continued "the monthly fellowship meetings Mel Lehman has been planning for almost two years" and thought of "perhaps developing a small, frequently-meeting group." Mel Lehman continued to be involved in planning programs. Myrna Burkholder, a strong personality, "tended to become involved in certain program details beyond the specifics of her job description" as house manager.[140] Early in her work at Menno House, she proposed publishing *Menno News* ten times a year as a newsletter for scattered Mennonites in the city. It included a calendar of events at the New York City churches and at Menno House and provided a forum for discussing "relevant religious and social issues facing young Mennonites." Publication began in 1978 with an original mailing list of 200 people.[141]

Myrna Burkholder, director of Menno House at 314 East 19th Street, Manhattan, (former VS Center) welcoming a new resident, Ben Karamata.

Development of Student and Young Adult Services as an outreach of both the Mennonite Church and the General Conference Mennonite Church naturally impacted Menno House. Myrna Burkholder became New York City director for Student and Young Adult Services in 1977. She became national director of Student and Young Adult Services under Mennonite Board of Missions in 1981 and moved to Elkhart, Indiana, the following year.[142] When Myrna left New York in 1982, the Menno House Committee asked the New York City Council of Mennonite Churches to take full responsibility for Menno House. The Council did not immediately act on this suggestion. At the end of the year, David W. Shenk, Eastern Mennonite Board Home Missions Director, asked the Council to develop appropriate accountability for the project, so that "the administrative accountability for Menno House not fall through the cracks."

Myrna Burkholder had proposed John Bauman as the administrative link between the Menno House Committee and the Council.[143]

Menno House was self-supporting. In its first five years of operation, over one hundred young adults lived at Menno House for periods of time ranging from one month to four years. A fourth of the residents were graduate students and a fourth of them non-Mennonite. Menno House was almost always filled to capacity. Two rooms were reserved as guest rooms for Mennonites and others passing through the city. In 1982 rents ranged from $140 to $292 a month. Jewel Van Ord, a nursery school teacher, was house manager. Her husband, Marty, a student, took care of repairs. Yohanna Kawira, a student from Tanzania, served as host for guests.

Menno House had functioned well as a meeting place for urban Mennonites and demonstrated a sense of community among its residents. "Attempts have been made at various times to incorporate worship or Bible study into the life of the house, but residents have to date resisted the idea. Many are 'in search' and want the freedom to choose spiritual and worship options for themselves."[144]

Staten Island Girls' Home (SIGH)

Although the concept of Voluntary Service was changing in the 1970s, Mennonites had the reputation in evangelical circles of drawing on an almost unlimited supply of volunteers for mission work in the city. They had also demonstrated an ability to work with inner-city youth and to administer programs on a limited budget. As a result, Eastern Board was offered new ministries by long-established agencies.

A Christian radio station owned an old mansion on Woodrow Road in a rural section of Staten Island. They offered to lease it at a merely nominal rent to a Christian social agency and approached the McAuley Mission on the Lower East Side. Paul Shirk was associated with the McAuley Mission in 1971 and proposed the house be used as a group home for troubled girls. He and his wife intended to be on the staff at the home and approached Eastern Board for support as VS workers. The District Council felt that Mission Board money should be used for Mennonite projects but authorized Dale Stoltzfus to explore the girls'

Staten Island Girls' Home, 1117 Woodrow Road, Staten Island.

home idea with McAuley Mission and the Shirks. They were open to a partnership with Eastern Board. Dale requested a detailed proposal from McAuley with goals, objectives, and budget clearly spelled out.[145]

Eastern Board responded favorably to the proposal and recommended that the local representative look into this project and test the idea with District Council members. The Executive Committee of Eastern Board approved the project with a budget of $6,000 for the first year. They agreed on an administrative committee with nine members, five Mennonites and four from McAuley, to oversee the project. It only remained for the District Council to give its approval. At its January 17, 1972 meeting, the District Council went on record "as supporting two people from the Council to start this project" and elected Harold Davenport and Esther Petersheim to the administrative committee. The McAuley Mission declined any administrative role and asked Eastern Board and the New York churches to take it over completely. Dale Stoltzfus met with the McAuley board and they agreed to nominate two of their board members to the Staten Island oversight committee.[146]

The Paul Shirks withdrew from the proposed home in January. The possibility of Paul and Miriam Burkholder returning to the city led to an invitation to them to head the girls' home. The Burkholders informed the Council that Paul had taken another job, but they were willing to help in Staten Island.[147]

While these negotiations were going on, another New York City mission was offered to Eastern Board. *The Christian Herald* magazine had taken responsibility for a halfway house for young felons released from Rikers Island penitentiary. *The Christian Herald* contributed twenty-five percent of the operating budget for Bridge House, the remainder came from grants from the City of New York. The magazine wanted to withdraw its support and this loss of funds threatened to close the halfway house. Hilda Regier, a General Conference Mennonite living in New York, invited the Home Mission Board in Newton, Kansas, to help salvage the project. Harold Regier of the General Conference Mission Board wrote to Eastern Board, indicating his own reading was that "it is not clear if the program can be salvaged." Dale Stoltzfus met with Hilda Regier and with Bill Peck, director of the halfway house, and concluded the program would need a major commitment of money by Mennonites to survive. The District Council concluded, "Since they would maintain complete administrative responsibility it is not likely that we could find it practical to become involved." Mennonite Central Committee, willing enough to assist or support a Mission Board effort, declined taking the halfway house as its own project. The decision, reached by Eastern Board after careful study, indicated Mennonites were not anxious to take on any and all work in New York City.[148]

In November 1972 Peter and LeAnna Gerber Dunn moved to the thirty-room Woodrow Mansion at 1117 Woodrow Road as the first step toward opening the Staten Island Girls' Home. Peter and LeAnna had been married less than a year. Peter, a Canadian, was a biology graduate of the University of Alberta, LeAnna, who came from Kidron, Ohio, was a mathematics graduate of Eastern Mennonite College.[149] Neither Peter nor LeAnna had previously worked with a group home. Two years later, Peter Dunn would write about volunteers "as inexperienced and naive as were LeAnna and myself when we arrived."[150]

Explaining the purpose of the home in December, the Dunns said they intended "to provide an atmosphere in which girls can meet God, and through this encounter have their lives changed." They did not intend to impose cultural changes. "We feel it is important *not* to attempt to change the cultural mores of each girl." In an interview with *The Staten Island Advance* soon after the home opened in February 1973, Peter Dunn explained:

> We are not emphasizing psychological readjustment, but rather a spiritual one. We feel if people get their hearts right with God, if their relationship with God is taken care of, their relationship with others will fall in line... Mind you, there are special issues on peace and war we're going to be strong about, because this is one of the basic tenets of our faith, but we're not saying, "Become Mennonites."[151]

Peter and LeAnna Dunn, left and center, and Dorcas Miller, right, staff persons at Staten Island Girls Home.

The Staten Island Girls' Home welcomed young women from 16 to 21 years old who needed housing for any reason. Some stayed only for two or three weeks. Others, like Kathy spent eight months at the home. Most were high school dropouts who had left home because of turmoil in the family. Linda, who came from a wealthy home in a Chicago suburb, had taken to a wandering life as a painter to find herself. Cynthia was a lesbian and had to be asked to leave the home soon after she came there.[152]

Dorcas Miller from Grantsville, Maryland, joined the Dunns in 1973 as a staff member. She eventually became associate director. As the first year drew to a close, Chris Benner, a VSer at Glad Tidings from Souderton, Pennsylvania, joined the team. She remained at the home until September 1974 when she left to get married and work with her husband at the Sherman Avenue VS Center. Sue Eberly, a VSer from Lancaster County, was also on the staff in 1974. Nancy Sosna, an artist from Champaign, Illinois, worked with the girls to develop their abilities in arts and crafts projects.[153]

The Girls' Home held an open house for the community in February 1974 to mark the first year of operation. Dale Stoltzfus reported to the District Council on interest in beginning a Mennonite fellowship. "Since the open house, they've had contacts with community people and wish to relate to them through a fellowship." Peter Dunn was also considering Bible clubs for children in the neighborhood.[154]

The cost of operating the home amounted to $22,280 in its first year. The Kidron Mennonite Church contributed $500 a month, Mellingers Mennonite Church in Lancaster $50 a month, and Maple Glen Mennonite Church in Grantsville, Maryland, $25 a month. Eastern Board had responsibility for the rest. Peter Dunn wondered about other sources of money and shared his thinking with the District Council. "Funding the Home continues to be a question. Should work be funded by the church? Is it wise stewardship for the church or should the Home be under state certification?" He thought they should seek state certification, which would make the Home eligible for public funding, although it would limit their clientele to girls under sixteen. Dunn also recognized the need for a professional counselor to provide five to ten hours a week of counseling for the girls and to be a consultant for the whole program.[155]

Once begun, the process of getting state certification moved rapidly and took much of their time. Dunn reported a positive reaction to both Eastern Board and the Staten Island Girls' Home from representatives of the New York State Department of Public Welfare. He waited for state action. Chester Wenger thought Dunn's proposal "a masterpiece," but a meeting with Louise Murray of the New York City Bureau of Child Welfare was not encouraging. At the end of the year, they were still anticipating certification and the release of city money.[156]

The Staten Island Girls' Home had opened with the conviction that sincere and motivated Christians, with no special preparation or training, could have a positive influence on the lives of deeply troubled young women. After a year of operation, the staff concluded that they needed people with professional training in counseling and social work. Dorcas Miller influenced that change of attitude. She was interested in taking courses leading to a Master's in Social Work and explained how this would better enable her to do her work. Eastern Board agreed with her, but they authorized Peter Dunn to take graduate courses in social work. Despite this setback, she became familiar with the operations of other group homes, including those run by the Jewish Child Care Association, Catholic Charities, and the Florence Crittenton League. She learned that these group homes were always part of a larger child-caring institution and invariably had psychiatrists and counselors on call as well as house parents. She also noticed that these social agencies were totally accepting of her as a professional colleague. In contrast, she observed that in the Eastern Board offices at Salunga the women were all secretaries and the men worked behind closed doors in offices. Peter Dunn acknowledged, but could not understand her attitude. "We discussed the biblically based perspective of the role of a woman in the Church and ultimately in society and Dorcas admitted she was confused as to how this applied to the Church's ministry today." Chester Wenger and the executive committee appreciated her report on group homes and the need for professional staff and prepared to act on it.[157]

Staffing of any kind was proving to be a problem. Peter and LeAnna Dunn moved to their own apartment in June. Bob Petersheim, from Morgantown, Pennsylvania, and Rachel Gerber, LeAnna's sister, from Kidron, Ohio, arrived as summer VSers at the same time. Having a male resident at all times was a condition of the lease. Young men hanging around, looking for the girls, were prime suspects in a break-in at the adjacent broadcasting studio. The radio station wanted someone at the home who could protect their property. Carl and Nancy Hess moved to the home in September. They asked to be released from their full-time commitment in November, although they continued to help out on weekends. Warren and Chris Benner Heller also gave two days a week at the home.[158]

Eight young women lived at the Girls' Home in November 1974 and seven in December. The need for money to cover operating expenses was so great that Dunn solicited donations of food from the New York and Lancaster churches and invited the New York churches to send volunteers to cut wood during the winter. The girls had worked at different crafts projects and at Christmas time these articles went on sale in a store in the Staten Island Mall. Bob Petersheim and Chuck Gerber staffed the crafts shop.[159]

The search for professional models led the Girls' Home staff to the Heartsease Home at 216 East 70th Street in Manhattan, a facility begun in 1899 and operated for 75 years as a home for unwed mothers. Peter Dunn and Dorcas Miller initiated conversations which led to an invitation in January 1975 to merge the two institutions. The SIGH staff met with Monroe Yoder, Dale Stoltzfus, Dick Pannell, and Harold Davenport at the end of January to discuss taking over Heartsease. They decided the Heartsease building could serve as headquarters for the child care program, with the Staten Island facility as an extension. In February, the Heartsease board of directors considered this proposal from the Staten Island Girls' Home. They accepted it and both boards met in joint session with lawyers to work out implications of the transfer. The Executive Committee of Eastern Board recommended acceptance and the full Mission Board ratified the agreement on March 21, 1975.[160]

The Staten Island Girls' Home continued to operate through 1975. Rowland Shank of Philhaven spent three days in February evaluating the program. He noted that it had developed backwards, first a facility, then a program, and only later a purpose and philosophy. He also observed that "an unapologetic evangelical Christian stance has been central from the time the program was conceived."[161]

The Staten Island Advance carried a news story in October 1975 about the on-going effort to get state approval for the Staten Island Girls' Home, but Peter Dunn's report to his own board a few days later made it clear that, with the Heartsease program already approved by both city and state, they would be looking for "proper placements for the girls presently in the Staten Island facility" and close it as soon as possible.[162]

Staten Island residents attended in large numbers to support the Girls' Home at a public hearing by Community Board 4 in January 1976. Fiorello Cicero, vice-chairman of the board, had recommended unconditional endorsement of the home's request for state approval, but other board members requested an open hearing. Board members noted that "never has the community backed an issue so overwhelmingly" and that they had not heard "one negative word" about it. The news report mentioned that Staten Island Girls' Home was in the process of merging with Heartsease and temporarily closed. It had, in fact, officially terminated in December 1975.[163]

The owners of the Woodrow Mansion wanted Eastern Board to continue leasing the property and offered a three-to-five-year term automatically renewable. Eastern Board agreed. Over the next few years the building was used by students from Eastern Mennonite College and Seminary for urban seminars and as a guest house. Eastern Board sublet it to the American Board of Missions to the Jews for six months in 1977. The Woodrow property again became the center for Mennonite outreach on Staten Island in 1980.[164]

Heartsease

As soon as the agreement transferring responsibility for Heartsease Home was signed, Eastern Board began looking for qualified personnel. Chester Wenger approached Daniel Yutzy indicating he wanted someone with a Ph.D. in psychology to head the Heartsease program. Yutzy declined. Philhaven provided in-service training for the staff and James E. Johnson of Philhaven was clinical director for Heartsease from April 1975 through January 1976. At the same time, Dorcas Miller was working on her Master's in Social Work at Columbia University. In his first report to the board of directors in April 1975, Dr. Johnson explained that Heartsease could not have selective intake, but had to accept all referrals to qualify for public funding. The city would pay from $36 to $51 a day for each client. In the combined program, Staten Island would be a halfway house.[165]

Heartsease Home, 216 East 70th street, Manhattan, 1975-2004, now rented to Bowery Mission for Bowery Mission Womens Center at Heartsease Home.

The New York State Department of Social Welfare approved the amended charter for Heartsease Home in August 1975, permitting Heartsease to operate as a state-approved group home. Heartsease thereby became eligible to receive public money to cover nearly all its operating expenses. In September, Heartsease was still recruiting a housekeeper, cooks, maintenance workers, and social workers. Pam Leggett was the only staff member to link the old and new Heartsease. A 1971 graduate of Gordon College with credits towards her Master's in Social Work at Columbia, she had been a caseworker at Heartsease Home in 1973-74 and continued as supervisor of child care workers. Omar Zook, staff social worker, became acting clinical director in October 1975, when Johnson returned to Philhaven temporarily.[166]

Bowery Mission, 227 Bowery, Manhattan. For 125 years this mission has served homeless men, who come in from the street, with gospel services, food, shelter, and recovery programs. Throughout the years many persons from the New York City Mennonite and Brethren in Christ congregations have assisted with the gospel services at Bowery Mission. 2005 photo.

Heartsease reopened January 19, 1976 with six girls in residence. There were ten girls in mid-May and twelve by the end of the month. In February 1976 Robert Brinckerhoff succeeded James Johnson as clinical director. He remained only six months. Peter Dunn continued as assistant director until May 1976, when Peter and LeAnna went back to Ohio. Pam Leggett succeeded him. Dorcas Miller was both coordinator and teacher in the mini-school until July, when she left to complete her graduate school work. Ruth Wenger was her assistant as a volunteer, but joined the staff full-time in June. Two young VSers, Lanny Millette and Dan Brubaker, worked in child care with Debra Lehman and Nancy Yunginger, practical nurses from Philhaven, Roberta Kennedy, an older black woman, and Rosa Colon, a Brooklyn College student.[167]

As a publicly funded agency, Heartsease had to bring its vision into line with the determinedly secular policies of the New York City Bureau of Child Welfare. In March 1976, Peter Dunn, Omar Zook, and Bob Brinckerhoff met with department representatives to be lectured on not using religious criteria in the selection of staff, no religious proselytizing of the children, and no inappropriate emphasis on religion to the detriment of a sound psychological approach. "I had them read our staff's statement of religious policy," Brinckerhoff reported. He pointed out that a teacher assigned by the Board of Education was of Jewish heritage and a volunteer from Brooklyn College was non-religious. He agreed to end staff prayer.[168]

In July Brinckerhoff, Pam Leggett, and board members Dale Stoltzfus, Lou Ann Hyder, and Harold Davenport had another meeting with Harriet Schurf of the Bureau of Child Welfare. She criticized the religious emphasis and commented on reports of staff dissension and complaints by neighbors about the resident girls. Brinckerhoff and Anna Geoghan, his assistant director, solved the problems with the neighbors and three disgruntled employees, hired in April, left in July.[169]

Anna Geoghan succeeded Brinckerhoff as director in September 1976 and continued through May 1978. Cynthia Lyman agreed to serve as interim director for the rest of that year. In January 1979 Jerry Meck became director of Heartsease and continued until June 1983.[170]

The journey from Staten Island to East 70th Street in Manhattan was more than moving from one part of the city to another. The Staten Island Girls' Home represented the type of social service that Mennonites had undertaken and done well in the past. Young inexperienced Christian men and women came to the city, reached out to other young people in trouble or in danger from an unwholesome environment, much as Jerry Meck did with kids on the streets of the South Bronx or the East Side of Manhattan,

Heartsease Home Board of Directors, 1994. Left to right: Nancy Keefer, Jesus Cruz, Mary Jane Wilkie, Victor Huebner, Ruth Ann Stauffer, Daniel Ness, Janet Guerin, Debra Bontrager, Ruth Yoder Wenger, and Patricia Rath.

and made up program and goals as they needed them. Heartsease was a new kind of social service in which Mennonite professionals in psychology and social work cared for the same sort of troubled or at risk teenagers according to the best methods, programs, and goals developed and tested by their peers. Only the motivation remained the same.

NOTES

[1] District Council Minutes, November 4, 1974, EMM. *Gospel Herald*, November 2, 1974, 870, 883. *Missionary Messenger*, January 1975, 16.

[2] Herbert E. Meyer, "How Government Helped Ruin the South Bronx," *Fortune*, November 1975, 146-147.

[3] Monroe Yoder and Richard Pannell to Chester W. Wenger, December 19, 1974. Monroe Yoder, Memorandum, January 9, 1975. District Council Minutes, December 6, 1974, EMM.

[4] Monroe Yoder to Dear Friends, July 26, 1976. District Council Minutes, Feb. 10, 1975, Mar. 10, 1975, May 16, 1975, EMM. *Gospel Herald*, Feb. 11, 1975, 103, Apr. 27, 1975, 376. *Missionary Messenger*, Mar. 1975, 23.

[5] District Council Minutes, Mar. 14, 1977, May 12, 1977, EMM.

[6] District Council Minutes, Jan. 31, 1978, EMM.

[7] Jill Jonnes, *We're Still Here: The Rise, Fall, and Resurrection of the South Bronx* (Boston, 1986), 7, 233.

[8] Chester W. Wenger to Executive Committee, May 23, 1969, EMM.

[9] Alan S. Oser, "Housing Supply in City Eroding Amid Construction Standstill," *New York Times*, February 8, 1970.

[10] Jonnes, *We're Still Here*, 229.

[11] Nathan Glazer, "The South Bronx Story: An Extreme Case of Neighborhood Decline," *Policy Studies Journal* 16(1987), 269-276.

[12] District Council Minutes, January 25, 1971, February 23, 1971, March 23, 1971, April 26, 1971, EMM.

[13] Martin Tolchin, "The South Bronx: A Jungle Stalked by Fear, Seized by Rage," *New York Times*, January 15, 1972.

[14] Dale Stoltzfus to Chester Wenger, February 17, 1972; Dale Stoltzfus to Norman Shenk and Ira Buckwalter, February 28, 1972; Dale Stoltzfus to Chester Wenger, April 10, 1972. District Council Minutes, January 17, 1972, February 27, 1972, March 28, 1972, EMM.

[15] *New York Times*, January 15, 1972.

[16] Stewart Alsop, "The City Disease," *Newsweek*, February 28, 1972.

[17] Pastor's Report, Glad Tidings Cabinet Minutes, September 18, 1977, Petersheim Papers.

[18] Smucker, *Urban Mennonite Mission in South Bronx*, (4/24/85, double spaced edition) p.550 and 619.

[19] Chester Wenger to Executive Committee, May 23, 1969, EMM.

[20] Proposal for Jim King, June 30, 1971. Glenn Zeager to Chester Wenger, Aug. 31, 1971. Jim King to Mary Jean Kraybill, Aug. 14, 1971, EMM.

[21] Chester Wenger to Glenn Zeager, Sept. 24, 1971. Glenn Zeager to Phoebe Yoder, Oct. 8, 1971. Glenn Zeager to Chester Wenger, Nov. 1, 1971. Dale Stoltzfus to Chester Wenger, Nov. 11, 1971, EMM.

[22] Glenn Zeager to Chester Wenger, Aug. 24, 1972, EMM.

[23] Chester Wenger to Glenn Zeager, Aug. 8, 1972. Glenn Zeager to Chester Wenger, Aug. 24, 1972. Dale Stoltzfus to Chester Wenger, Nov. 29, 1972. Chester Wenger to Dale Stoltzfus, Dec. 12, 1972. District Council Minutes, Sept. 14, 1972, Sept. 20, 1972, Jan. 23, 1973, EMM.

[24] Chester Wenger to Glenn Zeager, Feb. 26, 1973. Glenn Zeager to Chester Wenger, Apr. 16, 1973. Glenn Zeager to Norman Shenk, Aug. 14, 1973. Chester Wenger, Memorandum, Oct. 29, 1973. District Council Minutes, Feb. 20, 1973, Mar, 27, 1973, Sept. 11, 1973, Nov. 1, 1973, EMM.

[25] *Missionary Messenger*, July 1975, 21.

[26] District Council Minutes, May 8, 1973, June 12, 1973. District Council Leadership Team Minutes, Dec. 18, 1972, Apr. 23, 1973. Glenn Zeager to Chester Wenger, Dec. 27, 1973, EMM.

[27] Burnside Mennonite Church Cabinet Minutes, Feb. 5, 1974, Report, Sept. 1, 1974. *Missionary Messenger*, July 1975, 21.

[28] Burnside Mennonite Church Pastor Replacement Committee Minutes, Apr. 18, 1975, May 12, 1975, May 18, 1975, July 3, 1975, July 8, 1975, July 17, 1975, Aug. 28, 1975, Sept. 11, 1975. Business Meeting Minutes, Sept. 22, 1975, EMM.

[29] Pastoral Replacement Committee Minutes, Jan. 6, 1977, Feb. 18, 1977, Feb. 20, 1977, EMM.

[30] Jerry Meck to Chester Wenger, Mar. 2, 1978, EMM.

[31] Mel Lehman, "The Spiritual Journey of Michael and Addie Banks," *Missionary Messenger*, July 1984, 2-4.

[32] *Missionary Messenger*, July 1980, 20.

[33] Anna M. Buckwalter to Chester Wenger, Dec. 8, 1968, EMM. Glad Tidings Cabinet Minutes, Aug. 12, 1975, Sept. 17, 1975, Dec. 15, 1975, Petersheim Papers.

[34] Eugene Shelly, Report, Sept. 18, 1977, EMM.

[35] Glad Tidings Cabinet Minutes, Sept. 16, 1976, Petersheim Papers.

[36] Report of Visit to new York City by Howard and Miriam Witmer and David and Grace Shenk, Mar. 30-31, 1981, EMM.

[37] Glad Tidings Cabinet Minutes, Apr. 23, 1973, May 24, 1973, Oct. 22, 1973, Dec. 23, 1974, Feb. 13, 1975. Petersheim Papers. Eugene Shelly to Ed Ruen, Oct. 24, 1973, EMM.

[38] Glad Tidings Church Cabinet Minutes, Mar. 28, 1973, May 24, 1973. Esther Petersheim, Interview. Esther Petersheim to Eastern Board, Dec. 20, 1973, EMM.

[39] Glad Tidings Cabinet Minutes, Apr. 23, 1973, June 27, 1973, July 1, 1973.

[40] Glad Tidings Cabinet Minutes, Apr. 30, 1974, May 6, 1975, May 27, 1975, June 17, 1975, July 8, 1975, July 22, 1975, Aug. 12, 1975, Petersheim Papers.

[41] Glad Tidings Cabinet Minutes, May 26, 1976, June 24, 1976, Sept, 19, 1976, Petersheim Papers.

[42] Glad Tidings Cabinet Minutes, Sept. 18, 1977, Petersheim papers.

[43] Glad Tidings Cabinet Minutes, Sept. 19, 1976, Petersheim Papers.

[44] Glad Tidings Cabinet Minutes, June 27, 1973, July 1, 1973, May 27, 1975, Oct. 13, 1975, Feb. 4, 1976, Mar. 30, 1976, Sept. 19, 1976, Oct. 21, 1976, Petersheim Papers.

45 Glad Tidings Cabinet Minutes, Sept. 16, 1973, Nov. 15, 1973, Feb. 1974, Nov. 2, 1974, Jan. 15, 1975, Mar. 14, 1975, July 22, 1975, Sept. 17, 1975, Sept. 21, 1975, Petersheim Papers.

46 Glad Tidings Cabinet Minutes, Feb. 28, 1973, Sept. 16, 1973, Dec. 23, 1974, July 22, 1975, Nov. 11, 1975, July 21, 1976, Oct. 21, 1976, Feb. 1, 1977, Petersheim Papers.

47 Glad Tidings Cabinet Minutes, Mar. 10, 1974, Petersheim Papers.

48 Glad Tidings Cabinet Minutes, May 4, 1975, Sept. 21, 1975, Nov. 11, 1975, Sept. 19, 1976, Oct. 21, 1976, Petersheim Papers.

49 Dale Stoltzfus to Chester Wenger, March 29, 1977, EMM.

50 Glad Tidings Mennonite Church, Annual Report, September 1978 EMM.

51 John Bauman to Chester Wenger, October 5, 1978. John Bauman to Chester Wenger, February 6, 1979. enc. Funding Proposal for the Glad Tidings Church Tutoring Center, n.d., EMM.

52 John Bauman to Chester Wenger, October 5, 1978, EMM.

53 Glad Tidings Mennonite Church, Annual Report, September 1978, EMM.

54 Monroe Yoder to David Shenk, October 28, 1981, EMM.

55 Report to Bronx Administrative Committee from Special Task Force on Service Models, October 14, 1976, BCA-MC.

56 Isaac Kanode to Charlie B. Byers, February 7, 1969. Paul Hill to Charlie B. Byers, February 14, 1969. Memorandum, June 6, 1969, BCA-MC.

57 Charlie B. Byers to Charles Rife Jr. June 11, 1969. Charles Rife Jr. to CBB to CRVR April 7, 1970. CBB to CRVR August 24, 1970, BCA-MC.

58 Charlie B. Byers to Bronx congregation, July 13, 1969. Charlie B. Byers to Roy Shelly, July 30, 1969. Charlie B. Byers to Harold Paulus, July 15, 1969. Charlie B. Byers to Harold Paulus, July 30, 1969. Harold Paulus to Charlie B. Byers, Aug. 4, 1969. Harold Paulus to Charlie B. Byers, Nov. 2, 1969, BCA-MC.

59 Charlie B. Byers to Harold Paulus, Nov. 26, 1970. Charlie B. Byers to Fellowship Chapel Congregation, Oct. 26, 1970. J. Wilmer Heisey to Charlie B. Byers, Jan. 14, 1971. Charlie B. Byers Memorandum, Visit to New York City January 18-20, 1971, BCA-MC.

60 Charlie B. Byers to Alvin Book, Jan. 28, 1971. Job Description for Rev. Alvin Book, n.d. (1971). Installation Service Program, June 20, 1971, BCA-MC.

61 Isaac Kanode to Charlie B. Byers, Feb. 7, 1969, BCA-MC.

62 Fellowship Chapel Council Meeting, Jan. 6, 1972. Fellowship Chapel Council Meeting, Feb. 13, 1975, BCA-MC.

63 Thata Book, Profile of Fellowship Chapel, 1975, BCA-MC.

64 Bronx Administrative Committee Minutes, Apr. 9, 1974. Premnath S. Dick, form letter, July 1974, Sept. 1977, BCA-MC.

65 Consultation in Developing Ministries in New York City, Aug. 26, 1974. Bronx Administrative Committee Minutes, Aug. 15, 1974, BCA-MC.

66 Consultation on Developing Ministries in New York City, Aug. 26, 1974, BCA-MC.

67 Bronx New Ministries Proposal, n.d. (October 1974), BCA-MC.

68 Bronx Administrative Committee Minutes, Nov. 5, 1975. Report to Bronx Administrative Committee, n.d., BMC-MC.

69 Report to Bronx Administrative Committee, Oct. 14, 1976, BCA-MC.

70 Glen Pierce to Alvin J. Book, Dec. 16, 1976. J. Wilmer Heisey to Alvin J. Book, Jan. 22, 1977, BCA-MC.

71 *Echoes from Fellowship Chapel* 13(March 1978), BCA-MC.

[72] Bronx Administrative Committee Minutes, Oct. 31, 1975. J. Wilmer Heisey to I. B. Hartley, Nov. 12, 1975. Isaiah B. Hartley to Alvin J. Book, Feb. 10, 1977, BCA-MC.

[73] Bronx Administrative Committee Minutes, Apr. 16, 1975, Sept. 18, 1975, BCA-MC.

[74] Charlie B. Byers, Memo of My Visit with Rev. Alvin Book, May 21, 1974, BCA-MC.

[75] Charlie B. Byers, Meeting with Alvin Book and Fellowship Chapel Church Board, Jan. 5, 1976. Church Board Minutes, Mar. 4, 1976. Charlie B. Byers to Wilmer Heisey and Earl Musser, Mar. 30, 1976. Alvin J. Book to J. Wilmer Heisey and Earl Musser, June 18, 1976. Mary Lou Ruegg to J. Wilmer Heisey, June 22, 1976. Charlie B. Byers to Fellowship Chapel Church Board, July 20, 1976. Alvin J. Book to Charlie B. Byers, Oct. 9, 1976. Heriberto Gonzalez, Pastoral Resume Form, Aug. 26, 1976, BCA-MC.

[76] Charlie B. Byers to Alvin Book and Mary Lou Ruegg, Dec. 1, 1976. Charlie B. Byers to Heriberto Gonzalez, Dec. 1, 1976. Charlie B. Byers, Memorandum, Jan. 5, 1977. Charlie B. Byers to H. Frank Kipe, Mar. 15, 1977. Charlie B. Byers to Mary Lou Ruegg, Mar. 15, 1976. H. Frank Kipe to Charlie B. Byers, May 14, 977. Bronx Administrative Committee Minutes, June 1, 1977. Charlie B. Byers to Mary Lou Ruegg, June 24, 1977. Charlie B. Byers to Mary Lou Ruegg, July 6, 1977, BCA-MC.

[77] Charlie B. Byers to Glen Pierce, Aug. 1, 1977. Glen Pierce to Charlie B. Byers, Aug. 20, 1977. Charlie B. Byers to Mary Lou Ruegg, Aug. 29, 1977. Glen Pierce to Dan Farina, Sept. 8, 1977. Charlie B. Byers to Daniel Farina, Sept. 12, 1977. Charlie B. Byers to Mary Lou Ruegg, Sept. 12, 1977. *Echoes of New York*, Dec. 1977, BCA-MC.

[78] Vacation Bible School Report, Aug. 26, 1977. Dan Farina to Charlie B. Byers, Oct. 26, 1977, BCA-MC.

[79] Dan Farina to Charlie B. Byers, Jan. 24, 1978. Bronx Administrative Committee Minutes, Feb. 24, 1978. Charlie B. Byers, Memorandum of Bishop's Visit to the Bronx, Feb. 24-26, 1978. Charlie B. Byers to Mary Lou Ruegg, Mar. 14, 1978, BCA-MC.

[80] Smucker, "Urban Mennonite Mission," (4/24/85 double spaced edition) p.148, 470-6.

[81] Smucker, "Urban Mennonite Mission," ibid., 479-82.

[82] Smucker, "Urban Mennonite Mission," ibid., 108-18.

[83] Smucker, "Urban Mennonite Mission," ibid., 150-1.

[84] Smucker, "Urban Mennonite Mission," ibid., 494-5, 518.

[85] Smucker, "Urban Mennonite Mission," ibid., 499.

[86] *Gospel Herald*, Aug. 24, 1971, 695, Oct. 26, 1971, 896, Nov. 16, 1971.

[87] Dale Stoltzfus to Chester Wenger, Nov. 11, 1971, EMM.

[88] Smucker, "Reflections," (11/15/85 double spaced edition) 126-127.

[89] Smucker, "Reflections," ibid., 123.

[90] John I. Smucker, Interview, June 19, 1990, "Mennonite Urban Mission," 494.

[91] John I. Smucker to Council of Mennonite Churches in NYC, Oct. 9, 1971, EMM.

[92] Mennonite House of Friendship to the Council of Mennonite Churches in NYC, n.d. (ca. October 31, 1971), enclosed with Mennonite House of Friendship to Council of Mennonite Churches in NYC, May 15, 1972, EMM.

[93] Paul G. Landis to Lupe DeLeon, Apr. 19, 1972, EMM.

[94] Simon Gingerich, Resume Consultation in New York, May 8, 1972. Lupe DeLeon to Chester Wenger, May 12, 1972, EMM.

[95] Mennonite House of Friendship to Council of Mennonite Churches in NYC, May 15, 1972. Chester L. Wenger to Lupe DeLeon, May 22, 1972, EMM.

[96] Council of Mennonite Churches in New York City Minutes, May 22, 1972, June 5, 1972, Sept. 4, 1972, Oct. 30, 1972, EMM.

[97] Smucker, "Mennonite Urban Mission," (4/24/85 double spaced edition), 502.

[98] Smucker, "Mennonite Urban Mission," 513.

[99] Smucker, "Mennonite Urban Mission," loc. cit.

[100] Smucker, "Reflections," (11/15/85 double spaced edition), 130-131.

[101] Smucker, "Mennonite Urban Mission," (4/24/85 double spaced edition), 173-174.

[102] Smucker, "Mennonite Urban Mission," 556, 572-573, "Reflections," 134-135.

[103] Smucker, "Mennonite Urban Mission," 569, 585.

[104] Smucker, "Urban Mennonite Mission," 585-599, 617.

[105] Recommendation for Leadership of the Good Shepherd Mennonite Church, Aug. 9, 1970. Monroe Yoder to Chester Wenger, Aug. 17, 1970. Chester Wenger to Monroe Yoder, Aug. 19, 1970, EMM.

[106] Wesley Newswanger to John H. Kraybill, May 13, 1970. John H. Kraybill to Wesley Newswanger, May 18, 1970, EMM.

[107] Since Paul Landis offered three names, there is ambiguity in Chester Wenger's reply. He found the first acceptable, but thought the second might not be suitable. Paul Landis to Chester Wenger, July 29, 1970. Chester Wenger to Paul Landis, Aug. 3, 1970, EMM.

[108] Monroe Yoder to Chester L. Wenger, Aug. 17, 1970, EMM.

[109] Monroe Yoder, Summary Report of Interviews, Sept. 12, 1971. Dale Stoltzfus to Chester Wenger, Sept. 21, 1971, EMM.

[110] Dale Stoltzfus to Chester Wenger, Sept. 21, 1971, Nov. 11, 1971, EMM.

[111] Dale Stoltzfus to Chester Wenger, Apr. 3, 1971, May 18, 1971, June 14, 1971. Chester Wenger to Dale Stoltzfus, June 24, 1971. Dale Stoltzfus to Chester Wenger, Jan. 31, 1972, Apr. 10, 1972, EMM.

[112] Dale Stoltzfus to Chester Wenger, Apr. 10, 1972. District Council Minutes, May 30, 1972, July 17, 1972, EMM.

[113] Dale Stoltzfus to Chester Wenger, Mar. 6, 1973, Apr. 13, 1973, EMM.

[114] Dale Stoltzfus to Chester Wenger, Sept. 11, 1973. District Council Minutes, Mar. 27, 1973, Apr. 15, 1974, Jan. 10, 1975, EMM.

[115] Marian H. Landis, "Good Times at Good Shepherd," *Missionary Messenger*, Oct. 1973, 8-9.

[116] District Council Minutes, June 11, 1974, EMM.

[117] District Council Minutes, Dec. 6, 1976, EMM.

[118] District Council Minutes, Apr. 12, 1977, EMM.

[119] Harold Davenport, Report, Jan. 11, 1977, Apr. 5, 1977. District Council Minutes, July 12, 1977, Sept. 19, 1977, Dec. 5, 1977, Dec. 4, 1978, Apr. 10, 1979, June 11, 1979, EMM.

[120] District Council Minutes, Dec. 11, 1973, EMM.

[121] District Council Minutes, Mar. 27, 1973, EMM.

[122] Dale Stoltzfus, VS Study, June 1969, EMM.

[123] District Council Minutes, Sept. 11, 1973, EMM.

[124] District Council Minutes, Jan. 29, 1974, EMM.

[125] District Council Minutes, Mar. 19, 1974, EMM.

[126] Dale Stoltzfus to Alvin Book, Mar. 11, 1974, BCA-MC. District Council Minutes, Mar. 19, 1974, Apr. 15, 1974, EMM.

[127] Dale Stoltzfus to Jerry Meck, May 16, 1974. District Council Minutes, May 20, 1974, June 11, 1974, July 15, 1974, EMM.

[128] District Council Minutes, Jan. 10, 1975, Aug. 26, 1975, EMM.

[129] District Council Minutes, Apr. 10, 1975, EMM.

[130] Dale Stoltzfus to Sid Hyman, June 7, 1974. Dale Stoltzfus to Norman G. Shenk, July 16, 1974, EMM.

[131] Members Covenant of Morning Star Community, n.d. Morning Star Residential Proposal, n.d., Chester L. Wenger, Memo, June 12, 1975, EMM.

[132] Alice Hess to Laverne Yutzy, Sept. 22, 1975. District Council Minutes, Oct. 20, 1975, Nov. 14, 1975, EMM.

[133] District Council Minutes, May 20, 1976, July 27, 1976, EMM.

[134] Myrna Burkholder to Gene Shelly, Sept. 9, 1976, EMM.

[135] District Council Minutes, Sept. 13, 1976, EMM.

[136] District Council Minutes, Oct. 20, 1975, EMM.

[137] District Council Minutes, Oct. 11, 1976, EMM.

[138] District Council Minutes, Feb. 3, 1977, Dec. 5, 1977. Mennonite Student Center Program Development Committee to Chester Wenger, Jan. 15, 1977. David A. Wenger to Hubert Brown, June 27, 1977, EMM.

[139] Nate Showalter to Chester Wenger, Dec. 10, 1976, EMM.

[140] David Wenger to Hubert Brown, June 27, 1977. Nate Showalter to Dale Stoltzfus, Sept. 22, 1977, EMM.

[141] General Description of Purposes, n.d., EMM.

[142] Myrna Burkholder to Gerry Keener, Sept. 29, 1982, EMM.

[143] David W. Shenk to Gerry Keener, Dec. 27, 1982, EMM.

[144] Myrna Burkholder to Gerry Keener, Sept. 29, 1982, EMM.

[145] Dale Stoltzfus to Chester Wenger, July 20, 1971. District Council Minutes, July 26, 1971, Sept. 20, 1971, EMM.

[146] Chester L. Wenger to Dale Stoltzfus, Dec. 17, 1971. District Council Minutes, Jan. 17, 1972, Feb. 27, 1972, Mar. 28, 1972, May 2, 1972, EMM.

[147] Dale Stoltzfus to Chester Wenger, Apr. 10, 1972. District Council Minutes, Mar. 28, 1972, May 2, 1972, EMM.

[148] Chester L. Wenger to Dale Stoltzfus, Dec. 17, 1971. Harold Regier to Chester Wenger, Dec. 27, 1971. Dale Stoltzfus to Chester Wenger, Jan. 31, 1972. District Council minutes, Feb. 27, 1972. Paul Leatherman to Leon Stauffer, Feb. 25, 1972. Clipping, *Chelsea-Clinton News*, Dec. 23, 1971, EMM.

[149] District Council Minutes, Dec. 11, 1972, Jan. 23, 1973. Dale Stoltzfus to Chester Wenger, Nov. 29, 1972. *The Staten Island Advance*, Feb. 25, 1973, EMM.

[150] Peter Dunn to Chester Wenger, Jan. 18, 1975, EMM.

[151] Peter and LeAnna Dunn, Statement, Dec. 17, 1972. *Staten Island Advance*, Feb. 25, 1973, EMM.

[152] Sketch Descriptions of Girls at SIGH, Jan. 5, 1974, EMM.

[153] SIGH Newsletter, Feb. 1974, EMM.

[154] District Council Minutes, Mar. 19, 1974. Peter Dunn to John R. Linstra, Apr. 5, 1974, EMM.

[155] Peter Dunn to Chester Wenger, May 20, 1974. SIGH Board Meeting Minutes, Dec. 20, 1973. District Council Minutes, May 20, 1974, EMM.

[156] Peter Dunn to Chester Wenger, June 25, 1974. Chester Wenger to Peter Dunn, June 25, 1974. Peter Dunn to Chester Wenger, July 17, 1974. SIGH Board Meeting Minutes, July 22, 1974. Chester Wenger to Peter Dunn, Aug. 29, 1974. Peter Dunn to Chester Wenger, Oct. 22, 1974. District Council Minutes, Dec. 6, 1974, EMM.

[157] Chester Wenger to Peter Dunn, June 25, 1974. Peter Dunn to Chester Wenger, June 25, 1974, July 5, 1974. Chester Wenger to Dorcas Miller, July 25, 1974, EMM.

[158] Peter Dunn to SIGH Committee Members, June 5, 1974. Peter Dunn to Chester Wenger, Mar. 19, 1974. Ed Smith to Chester Wenger, June 13, 1974. Peter Dunn to Larry Newswanger, June 12, 1974, June 14, 1974. Peter Dunn to Chester Wenger, June 17, 1974, Oct. 22, 1974. District Council Minutes, Nov. 4, 1974. Chester Wenger to Carl and Nancy Hess, Nov. 14, 1974. Peter Dunn to Chester Wenger, Jan. 18, 1975, EMM.

[159] Chester Wenger to Mildred Steffy and Janet Kreider, Jan. 15, 1975. Peter Dunn to Chester Wenger, Jan. 18, 1975. District Council Minutes, Nov. 4, 1974, Dec. 6, 1974, Jan. 10, 1975, EMM.

[160] Peter Dunn to Elvin Horst, Jan. 30, 1975. Peter Dunn to Chester Wenger, Feb. 13, 1975. Chester Wenger to SIGH Board, Feb. 14, 1975. Chester Wenger to Executive Committee, Mar. 5, 1975. District Council Minutes, Feb. 10, 1975, Mar. 10, 1975, EMM. Chester Wenger, "The Road from Staten Island," *Heartsease*, Spring 1990.

[161] Rowland Shank, Consultation Summary, Mar. 1975, EMM.

[162] The Staten Island Advance, Oct. 11, 1975. SIGH Report, Oct. 14, 1975, EMM.

[163] *The Staten Island Advance*, Jan. 13, 1976.

[164] John Linstra to Chester Wenger, Feb. 11, 1976. Ed Smith to Dale Stoltzfus, Aug. 24, 1977, EMM.

[165] Chester Wenger to Harold Reed, May 21, 1975. Chester Wenger to Daniel Yutzy, May 29, 1975. James E. Johnson, Report to the Board of Directors, Apr. 15-16, 1975. Report on In-Service Training, July 13, 1975. SIGH Report, Apr. 10, 1975, July 8, 1975, EMM.

[166] James E. Johnson to Board of Directors, Oct. 1975. Johnson, Interview Notes, [n.d. 1975]. District Council Minutes, Sept. 22, 1975. Robert Brinckerhoff, Report, Feb. 10, 1976, EMM.

[167] Robert Brinckerhoff, Report, Feb. 10, 1976, July 14, 1976, EMM.

[168] Robert Brinckerhoff, Report, Mar. 10, 1976, EMM.

[169] Robert Brinckerhoff, Report, July 14, 1976, EMM.

[170] Chester Wenger, "The Road from Staten Island," *Heartsease*, Spring 1990.

CHAPTER ELEVEN

A Missionary Church
1967–1984

THE DECADE OF the 1970s brought growth and new maturity to the Spanish-speaking Mennonite churches of New York City. Reflecting changes on the national scene, Hispanic Mennonites had an increased self-awareness and a readiness to take on responsibility for local outreach and for church-wide ministries. The formation of the Council of Hispanic Mennonite Churches, initially as part of the new Minority Ministries Council in 1970, then as a separate body in 1973, was a major step.[1] New York City pastors attended the first Workers Retreat in 1973 and set basic priorities for the development of the Hispanic Mennonite churches. Representatives from the New York City churches also attended the first meeting of the Hispanic Mennonite Women's Conference in 1973. Cecilia Robinson of Friendship Mennonite Church in the Bronx was named to the steering committee to coordinate future activities.[2]

New York City attracted Spanish-speaking people from many different countries. Immigrants from Spain, Cuba, the Dominican Republic, Guatemala, Mexico, Venezuela, Colombia, and many other countries of Central and South America had created their own economic and cultural and religious institutions in the city, but for many years their numbers were few in the urban melting pot. The migration of American citizens from Puerto Rico to the continental United States in the 1940s and 1950s focused almost entirely on New York City. Nearly all the Puerto Ricans on the mainland lived in New York in 1950. To New Yorkers at that time Hispanic meant Puerto Rican. In the 1970s and 1980s migration from Central America and the Dominican Republic far surpassed movement from Puerto Rico. At the same time, New Yorkers of Puerto Rican origin had moved up the economic ladder as skilled workers, business people, and professionals. Like other Americans, they were increasingly mobile and moved away from the old urban neighborhoods, often away from the city altogether.

Two New York churches, Primera Iglesia Evangelica Menonita in Brooklyn and Bronx Spanish, were largely Puerto Rican in their membership and part of the Puerto Rican Convention of the Mennonite Church until 1969. Hispanic members of the other Mennonite and Brethren in Christ churches in the city were also generally of Puerto Rican background. In the 1970s Spanish-speaking immigrants from the Dominican Republic, Honduras, and other Latin American countries joined the Mennonite Church and brought a fresh diversity to the New York City churches.

The Spanish-speaking churches in Brooklyn and the Bronx affiliated with the Ohio and Eastern Conference (later Atlantic Coast Conference) in 1969. The following year the Ohio and Eastern Conference welcomed another Spanish-speaking congregation into membership as a part of the Mennonite Church. This Evangelical Spanish Church had its beginnings in 1953 and met in the French Presbyterian Pilgrim Temple at 216 West 16th Street in Manhattan. It was also known as Templo el Peregrino as a result.

The leader of the congregation was Mario de Orive who was editor of the Spanish language newspaper, *Ecos de Nueva York.* De Orive, a journalist in his native Spain, came to New York in 1952. Within a few months, he began to hold Bible studies and worship services for other Spanish-speaking New Yorkers, buying Bibles and hymnals for them himself. In Spain, at that time, Protestants had to meet for worship in private and could not publicly organize congregations or evangelize. The "Evangelical Spanish Church "had no denominational connection and met in different church buildings, the 23rd Street YWCA, and a hotel on West 82nd Street.

In October 1958 Juan Isais of the *Editorial Caribe* bookshop introduced de Orive to the Mennonites. He visited the First Mennonite Church of Brooklyn and became friendly with Guillermo Torres, the pastor, and other members of the church. "From this moment a relationship was established that culminated in the affiliation of the group with the Mennonite Church in 1970."[3] The congregation had found a permanent home in the French Temple on West 16th Street before they united with the Mennonite Church. In 1971 the Evangelical Spanish Church had 24 members and by 1973 membership had risen to 33.

The death of Mario de Orive in September 1975 left the small congregation leaderless and membership dwindled. Guillermo Torres took responsibility for the church, which was seen as related to the Brooklyn church. There were now only seven members, including Dolores de Orive, widow of the founding pastor. Torres was in poor health and in 1980 Aurelio Rodriguez took his place. Pilgrim Temple struggled along as a mission outreach of the Brooklyn church through the next few years with only ten members. In 1985 the Pilgrim Temple congregation merged with Ephesians Mennonite Church.

Ephesians Mennonite Church began in 1975 with 12 members. The congregation met in different rented rooms in Manhattan, starting out at 21 Eighth Avenue and moving to 243 West 15th Street the next year. Solomon Arrias, the founding pastor, lived in Queens. Ephesians was still a small congregation at the time of the merger, with just twenty members, but it acquired a permanent meeting place at 218 West 16th Street about the same time and began steady growth over the next few years.

Guillermo Torres suffered from poor health during much of his time as pastor of First Evangelical Mennonite Church of Brooklyn. In 1967 John Smucker recognized the need for Mennonite Board of Missions "to help Brother Torres and the congregation work at the problems that are emerging there." These problems stemmed from the pastor's inability to put as much energy into the church program as he once had, but "misunderstandings" had created "tensions within the group that is there."[4]

Ronald Lehman, a former VSer who remained in the city, attended the Brooklyn church. He believed "the existing problems are the result of Pastor Torres' failing health." The congregation was no longer growing. "There has been no significant increase in membership and attendance and several members have left to attend other churches. No serious attempt was made to try and find out why these people left or to try and bring them back into fellowship." Torres might have become used to a small church where the pastor did not need assistance. "Bro. Torres does not favor the idea of allowing members to participate in worship services and would rather take charge of everything himself, including the congregational singing." The small First Mennonite congregation wanted "to get more involved," Lehman believed. The congregation included natural leaders, notably Aurelio Rodriguez, the first baptized member.[5]

The Brooklyn church added ten members by baptism in the course of 1967—Jose Adorno, Felicita Briones, Rosita Diaz, Elicer Monserrate, Eufemia Carrazona, Consuelo Inesta, Raquel Inesta, Pedro Lugo, Edwin Lopez, and Siso Torres, the pastor's son.[6] The congregation was very much alive.

While Elkhart looked for a Spanish-speaking couple to help with the work in Brooklyn, they were also concerned to find VS assistance for Ron Collins and the Bronx Spanish congregation. Ken Seitz gave priority to these two congregations in assigning personnel to New York. He proposed that a couple could relate to both congregations. Ray Horst explored possible leads in Puerto Rico and the States for persons to contact.[7] Addona Nissley, general secretary of the Puerto Rican Convention, visited the Bronx and Brooklyn churches in the summer of 1968. He was concerned about Ron Collins' heavy schedule as a full-time teacher and full-time pastor. He encouraged Elkhart to find a VS couple to help the Bronx Spanish church.[8] In September 1968, Leonard and Barbara Kilmer from Wooster, Ohio, came to the Bronx to help in the Spanish congregation there. Leonard had earlier done voluntary service with the House of Friendship and knew the city to some extent. The Kilmers both spoke Spanish. Work with teens got top priority and teaching piano to youngsters fitted their own talents.[9] They worked one day a week with the Brooklyn church, teaching piano and helping with Siso Torres' basketball team. But Brooklyn still needed a full-time VS couple. The Atlantic States District of Ohio and Eastern Conference set aside $3600 towards the support of a Brooklyn VS couple and the women of WMSA (now MW) gave $750 for youth work in Brooklyn.[10]

Mennonite Board of Missions was ready to do "something to help Brother Torres or his lay leaders or both in this situation." Simon Gingerich and Ken Seitz of the Elkhart VS office had talked in 1967 with the Lupe DeLeon family about helping with the program in Brooklyn.[11] This did not work out.

The churches relating to Mennonite Board of Missions and Charities in Elkhart, Indiana, formed their own Council, made up of Friendship, First Mennonite of Brooklyn, and Bronx Spanish. Although the last two belonged to the Puerto Rican convention administratively and had personal ties with Mennonites in Virgina and Iowa, they naturally looked to the Atlantic States District of Ohio and Eastern Conference to which the Friendship Church belonged. This relationship began to be formalized in October 1968 in the meeting of the Council of MBMC Churches of New York City:

> If we are agreed to work together no matter what Conference we belong to, then the conferences should let the Council make the decisions.... Our relationship with the Puerto Rican Conference is fraternal and spiritual and not financial. It is too far away. It cannot possibly do what the Council can and should do.[12]

After visiting the Brooklyn church in the summer of 1968, Addona Nissley of the Puerto Rican Convention had serious reservations.

> As for the work in Brooklyn one hardly knows what to say. We here are of the opinion that it will hardly keep its own under the present pastor. The adults appreciate and respect him highly there and don't want to say anything that might hurt his feelings. There is nothing for the youth and it would be extremely difficult for a VS couple to fit in the present program.[13]

After a lengthy search for a VS couple for Brooklyn had located no promising candidates, Nissley came up with a different solution. Mateo and Luz Cubilete went to Puerto Rico from the Dominican Republic because of political disturbances there. She had worked with the Mennonite Church in the Domincan Republic as a Sunday school teacher and home missionary. They became members of the Mennonite congregation at Bayamon. Later, they moved to the Bronx and became part of the Bronx Spanish congregation. Gladys Widmer had suggested Luz Cubilete be appointed a missionary by Mennonite Board of Missions to facilitate their return to Puerto Rico on a permanent residential visa. Nissley thought of the needs of the Brooklyn church. He wrote Guillermo Torres proposing that Luz Cubilete help him in the Brooklyn congregation on a short-term VS basis.[14] Torres endorsed the idea with enthusiasm and the congregation also seemed happy. Ohio and Eastern Conference pledged $50 a week for the support of Luz Cubilete. The Brooklyn congregation found an apartment for the Cubiletes. The MBMC Council worked with Luz and Pastor Torres on a job description.[15]

The need for a pastoral change in Brooklyn was still evident to the conference leadership in Puerto Rico. Membership dropped from 27 in 1967 to 20 in 1968 and attendance fell from an average 53 on Sundays in 1967 to 45 in 1968. Guillermo Torres was "one fine wonderful servant of the Lord" who was "consecrated to the Lord and zealous for the cause of Christ's Church." He preached "very good sermons." Addona Nissley was nonetheless convinced that "his paternalistic approach" had become an obstacle in Brooklyn. In November 1968 Nissley urged Torres to consider a change, offering him a rural pastorate in Puerto Rico where he could recuperate his health.[16]

Leadership came from within the congregation. Aurelio Rodriguez served as co-pastor at the Brooklyn church, as well as taking responsibility for the Pilgrim Temple congregation. This arrangement continued until the death of Guillermo Torres in 1980. Ray Pacheco took responsibility for the Brooklyn congregation in that year. Families who had long taken an active role in Primera Eglesia Menonita were continually moving away, some further out on Long Island, others to Florida and, despite some growth, membership remained small with only 32 members in 1980. The Brooklyn church called Bolivar Colberg from Puerto Rico as pastor in 1982, and the congregation began a new spurt of growth with 59 members by the end of 1983.

The Bronx Spanish Mennonite Church had a different history. The congregation reached a plateau with 16 members and never increased their numbers. With such a small base, they lacked the ability to obtain a permanent meeting place. The congregation called Jose Feliz, an able man in his mid-30s, originally from the Dominican Republic, as their pastor in 1973 and he was ordained in 1974. He began a new Mennonite congregation, the Revival Temple, located at 126 Willis Avenue in the Bronx, in 1979, which was not listed in the *Mennonite Yearbook* after 1981. When Pastor Feliz moved to Pennsylvania, Bronx Spanish and the Morris Heights Mennonite Church merged to become Ebenezer Mennonite Church in 1984. This is still a flourishing congregation at the time of this writing.

Several Spanish-language churches had a similar story. The Morris Heights Mennonite Church began in 1978 as an outreach to newcomers from the Dominican Republic. Juan Suero was ordained the same year as pastor. The Morris Heights section of the South Bronx was a neighborhood in transition. By 1982 the Spanish-language church was surrounded by African-American neighbors and most of its members lived at a distance. As a commuter church, Morris Heights faced the same problems that other city churches had faced earlier. Outreach in the immediate neighborhood was impossible because of language barriers and members would inevitably find churches closer to home. Membership dwindled each year from 24 members in 1978 to 17 members in 1982. Two years later they became part of the Ebenezer Mennonite congregation.

A Mennonite congregation began in Staten Island in 1978. Julio Rodriguez, pastor of a Puerto Rican evangelical church, was personally attracted to the Mennonite Church and encouraged his congregation to affiliate with Lancaster Conference. In April 1979 the congregation moved to a larger building at 153 Bay Street, capable of seating 250 persons. They held a farewell service the same month for Julio Rodriguez on his return to Puerto Rico. The congregation called Ramon Vargas as pastor in May, but Vargas was more at home with a Pentecostal emphasis, and the church severed its ties with the Mennonites soon afterwards.[17]

The General Conference Mennonite Church has had close links with the Evangelical Mennonite Church in Colombia since 1947 when the first Mennonites began mission work there, so it was natural for a congregation of Colombians in New York City to look to the General Conference Mennonites for fellowship. Iglesia Cristiana Menonita Cuerpo de Cristo began in January 1979 when a group of Colombian believers met together in the apartment of Julio Duenas and his family at 83rd Street and 37th Avenue in the Jackson Heights section of Queens. They later moved to the barbershop owned by Duenas. The congregation found a more permanent home in a former Plymouth Brethren church at 99-10 37th Avenue in the

Corona section. Through contact with Antonio Arevalo, pastor of a Mennonite Church in Bogota, the congregation began discussions later the same year with the General Conference Home Missions office in Newton, Kansas. In 1980 Hector Valencia and Ernest Harder visited them. A year later, on May 5, 1981, the congregation requested membership in the General Conference Mennonite Church in a letter signed by 24 members. Duenas was the first pastor.[18]

Mary Ann Zehr, a VSer assigned as secretary for the New York City Council of Mennonite Churches, became an active member of Cuerpo de Cristo in January 1982 and taught the youth class there. "The language sometimes causes difficulties, as some persons in her class do not speak any English." She was also involved in their after-school tutoring program. Some of the Cuerpo de Cristo youth participated in the MYF retreat at Camp Deerpark in March. In August 1982 she reported "a spiritually renewing time at a baptismal service on the beach" and "with a Colombian family from her church."[19]

The Cuerpo de Cristo congregation was "well integrated into the denomination" and promised to be "a source of leaders." Pastor Duenas left in 1982 and Henry Ortiz succeeded him as pastor. Ortiz remained only a year. Alberto Hurtado was the pastor in 1983. Luis Adames took his place in 1984. The rapid turnover in leadership contributed to a drop in attendance and in 1986 the remaining members voted to disband.[20]

Other Spanish-language churches flourished and nurtured new churches. One Mennonite congregation in Brooklyn is an outstanding example. Although the Lancaster Conference churches in the Bronx always included many Spanish-speaking members, no Spanish-language congregation in New York City related to Lancaster Conference until 1978. In that year, the United Revival Mennonite Church of Brooklyn asked to be transferred from the Spanish Council to Lancaster Conference.[21] Cesar Segura, a gifted minister from the Dominican Republic, organized the United Mennonite Church of Revival in the Bushwick section of Brooklyn in 1974. The congregation had 34 members at its beginning.[22] A year later Segura left the city to become a pastor in Pennsylvania and executive secretary of the Spanish Mennonite Council. Baino Mateo, also from the Dominican Republic, became pastor at United Revival in 1975.[23] The congregation found a suitable building at 169 Knickerbocker Avenue with ample space for a sanctuary, Sunday school classes, and church office. Pastor Mateo reported 46 members in 1980. Dinorah Mateo, Pastor Mateo's wife, Mercedes Gonzalez, her mother, and Jose Polanco gave leadership in the congregation.[24]

Mercedes Gonzalez, a gifted preacher and Bible teacher, visited families and taught Bible studies in home settings as a church-appointed missionary. In 1979, with the blessing of the United Revival congregation, she accepted an invitation to serve as interim pastor for a Pentecostal congregation a few blocks away. Many members of the Pentecostal congregation appreciated her leadership and wanted her to continue as pastor. In 1982, with the guidance of Bishop Monroe Yoder, they became a Mennonite church. The Valle de Jesus congregation had 21 members in 1983 and 25 members in 1987. They experienced considerable growth in the 1990s and nearly 100 people participate in worship each Sunday.[25]

Mercedes Gonzalez, pastor, in front of the Valley of Jesus Mennonite Church in Brooklyn.

Pastor Mateo accepted an assignment as District Superintendent for the New York City Mennonite churches in 1980, succeeding Dale Stoltzfus, and resigned as pastor in 1981. Continuity of leadership allowed the United Revival congregation to develop steadily. Nicholas Angustia, an active leader in the congregation, became pastor of the United Revival Mennonite Church in February 1981. He remains the pastor at the time of this writing. Dinorah Mateo, Hilda La Salle, Dominga Jimenez, Dionisio Arias, Carlos Perez, Rosa Aviles, and Mercedes Gonzalez served on the church board in September 1981. Hilda La Salle was secretary, Antonio Carrasco treasurer, and Carlos Perez, Thelma Puello, Martha Moreno, and Daniel Bouret board members in 1983.[26]

Members of the United Revival Mennonite Church gave sacrificially to support the work of the church. Eastern Board was impressed enough to halt the process of reducing the mission board's subsidy in order to match the congregation's generosity. Children from the United Revival Mennonite Church attended the Little Learners Academy, a private school sponsored by Eastern Board and Mennonite Central Committee. Pastor Angustia drove the school bus.[27]

A Sunday morning worship service at the United Revival Mennonite Church in Brooklyn.

The neighborhood around United Revival Mennonite Church deteriorated in the 1980s. It was possible to see drug deals being made in broad daylight just outside the church door in 1991. The church is there to stay as a lively witness to God's love for the city and its people.

In 1984 Pastor Mateo began a new congregation to reach into the Hispanic community in Queens. The Mennonite Evangelistic Tabernacle church grew slowly. In May 1985 Pastor Mateo reported a membership of 20 and an average attendance of 40. A year later the congregation counted 25 members and an average of 55 persons at services. The Mennonite Evangelistic Tabernacle had difficulty locating an appropriate meeting place, however. After several false starts, they settled on rented quarters at 981 Broadway in Brooklyn in November 1987. The church moved to 623 Wilson Avenue, at the corner of Decatur, and had 49 members in 1991.

Naftali DeLeon and Elias Paulino, pastor, preaching at the Mennonite Evangelistic Tabernacle in Brooklyn.

Pastor Mateo invited Elias Paulino to come to Brooklyn from the Dominican Republic in 1987. He was trained as a clinical psychologist and had served as pastor of seven churches in his native land. At Pastor Mateo's request he became lead pastor. The congregation is comprised predominantly of people who have come from the Dominican Republic and services are in Spanish. The neighborhood is largely African-American, but the congregation reaches out in a friendly way to its neighbors.

Camping Outreach

A different kind of ministry began for the city churches in 1961. The New York City Brethren in Christ and Mennonite churches joined together to provide summer camping for their young members and a retreat center for all of the congregations to use as part of their evangelistic program. John Kraybill recalled the first discussion of a possible summer camp at a meeting of the pastors on November 5, 1961. Things moved quickly after that.

Church camps as mission outreach became popular in the Mennonite world in the 1950s. Tel-Hai Camp began in 1950 and was the first to welcome children from the New York City churches. Black Rock opened in 1954 and Camp Hebron in 1957. City children from the New York City missions used these camps, too.

Paul Hill, pastor of the Brethren in Christ Fellowship Chapel in the Bronx, found a suitable location about 75 miles northwest of the city in the Catskill area. He visited an established camp near Wertzboro, New York, located on a 55-acre tract, and improved with two dormitories and three double-cabin units, an auditorium, ball fields and other recreational facilities. A dam on a creek provided a natural swimming hole. The owners wanted $18,000 for the property.

Hill shared his dream with the other New York pastors and they soon caught his enthusiasm. They agreed with him that the Mennonite churches should chip in for the purchase price and share the camp with the two Brethren in Christ missions in the city. Norman Shenk of Eastern Board talked over the proposal and raised questions they had not anticipated. In letters to John Kraybill and John I. Smucker, Shenk asked about their long-range goals in considering operation of a camp. "Can we build our church best by enlarging the summer program?" If more elaborate summer programs were needed, was a camping association the answer? If the city churches operated a summer camp, would this open the door to another type of witness to vacationers in a summer resort setting? Did the churches know what they were getting into? "Is financial planning on a commercial basis a good approach to adult evangelism?" Shenk's bottom line was that the Lancaster Conference mission outposts could continue to enjoy the facilities at Camp Hebron in Dauphin County, Pennsylvania, at less cost than developing and maintaining a camp of their own. He believed the General Conference Camp Men-O-Lan and the Brethren in Christ Camp Kenbrook would also serve the city churches. Eastern Board representatives had less enthusiasm for another real estate investment. Ira Buckwalter and Norman Shenk recommended that the New York City churches think in terms of renting facilities and defer purchasing a camp.[28]

In spite of Shenk's counsel for hesitation, the pastors moved ahead. "The New York City workers have continued to have interest in a retreat center somewhere not too far from New York City," Paul Landis reported. A year later they were ready to buy a share in the Fellowship Chapel camp. On February 13, 1963, John Kraybill, Paul Burkholder, Don Sensenig, John Freed, Glenn Zeager, Curtis Godshall, and John Smucker toured the camp and approved the purchase of one or more of the cabin units, which would give them use of the entire facility. This time Eastern Board supported their plan with a grant of $3,000 to buy one of the double cabin units. John Smucker arranged for the Mennonite House of Friendship to acquire half of the other cabin unit for $1,500. The Brethren in Christ Mission Board provided an outright gift of $1,500 and a loan of $3,000. The camp owners had agreed to a cash payment of $8,000 with the remainder raised by a mortgage. In May 1963 a camp board comprised of Bishop Henry Ginder, Isaac Kanode, Paul Hill, Roy Mann, Mark Peachey, John H. Kraybill, and Paul Espinosa made final arrangements for purchasing Camp Brookhaven. They appointed Mark Peachey as camp director and Paul Hill as manager. Camp Brookhaven opened for its first season as a Brethren in Christ and Mennonite church camp with a formal service of dedication on June 27, 1963.[29]

Mark and Faye Peachey directed Camp Brookhaven in its first years. Naomi Breckbill taught crafts. Evelyn Hill and Carolyn Gilbert were the cooks. Charles and Ruth Rife and Mary Lou Ruegg from Fellowship Chapel each gave a week as camp volunteers. Peachey reported "a good spirit" between the Brethren in Christ and Mennonite churches in arranging for one-week camps and providing volunteer help on work days. The Lancaster Conference churches still sent their campers to Camp Hebron in the 1960s and used Camp Brookhaven primarily as a retreat center. In the 1964 season, the House of Friendship had two week-long camp sessions, along with shorter stays by groups from Fox Street and Fellowship Chapel and weekend retreats from the other churches. The camp board approved plans for enlarging the lake and acquiring a boat and for four weeks of children's camps in 1965.[30]

In order to subsidize the camping program, Paul Hill and the camp board opened a store at 4142 Third Avenue in November 1966. After a four-month trial the store netted $600 for the camp treasury. The following year store profits brought in $1,200 for Camp Brookhaven and VSers at Fellowship Chapel earned another $2,009 for the camp. The store raised a net profit of $1,536 in its operation during 1969-70, but the store lost $170 the following year and the camp closed its books in the red in 1970-71. The camp relied more on outright gifts in the later 1960s. A promotional dinner in 1968 raised $4,115 for Camp Brookhaven and this became the preferred mode of fund-raising.

Jacob and Rhoda Stern of Chambersburg, Pennsylvania, moved to Camp Brookhaven in April 1967 as resident manager and hostess. They worked at the camp each summer for several years. Ray Shelly, youth worker at Fellowship Chapel, was camp director in 1968, when 140 youngsters came to Brookhaven for one of its four week-long camps. According to that year's report, Friday night was always Decision Night and the camp staff aimed at bringing young campers to a personal relationship with the Lord during their stay.

Changes came for Camp Brookhaven in 1969, when Paul Hill left the city and the Mennonite churches bought a new camp of their own. The camp board approved John Ebersole's suggestion for construction of a basketball court in 1969. Jay Poe took over as camp director with Norman Mowery as his assistant for the 1970 season. Poe continued the following year and Gary Lebo joined the camp staff as athletic director for 1971. Lebo became camp director in 1972, assisted by the Ken Wingers and Hazen Cronks as resident managers. Camp Brookhaven built a new swimming pool in 1971 and the board pondered its possible use as a drug rehabilitation center in 1972.[31]

The Atlantic Conference Commission on Camping began to look at a new site for a Brethren in Christ Church camp in 1972. Dale Stoltzfus, a member of the board of Camp Brookhaven, gave helpful advice based on his experience in developing the new Mennonite Camp Deerpark. He suggested a 15-year plan for camping and retreat needs. The board decided these needs could no longer be met at Brookhaven and investigated other sites. In May 1973 the board authorized appraisal of Camp Brookhaven and Camp St. Agnes Villa, which seemed best suited to their expanded needs. The appraiser set $75,000 as a fair market price for Camp Brookhaven and $150,000 for St. Agnes Villa. In July 1973 Isaac Kanode and Alvin Book, pastor at Fellowship Chapel, met with Mrs. Watson, the owner of Camp St. Agnes Villa. She agreed to sell her camp for $145,000. By October,

Mennonite Action Program board, MAP, representing the New York City Mennonite Churches, was formed to oversee various citywide ministries. Their first project was Camp Deerpark. Seated left to right: Nelson Kauffman, Dale Stoltzfus, and Glenn Zeager. Standing left to right: Carl Metzler, Ron Collins, Eugene Shelly, John Buckwalter, and Aurelio Rodriguez.

Camp Brookhaven sold for $90,000 and the board took title to Camp St. Agnes Villa in November.[32]

The Mennonite churches in the city decided for the first time to send their children to the same camp with the purchase of Camp Deerpark in 1969. Glenn Zeager and Dale Stoltzfus took the lead in buying the new camp and selling the Brookhaven cabin back to the Camp Brookhaven board.[33]

The new Mennonite camp was ready for dedication on May 31, 1969. This service made it clear that Camp Deerpark would be "a Christian camp and will be used to point individuals to Jesus Christ." In its first season Ron Collins brought 109 adults and children for a Spanish-language family retreat and Carl Good led a weekend retreat for 75 people from Good Shepherd. The Youth Workers and MYF made good use of the Deerpark facilities in July, with several weekend congregational retreats also scheduled. Children's camps filled the schedule in the month

Camp Deerpark administration building at Westbrookville, New York.

of August 1969. Dale Stoltzfus commented on a deliberate policy in the camp's first season: "Camp Deerpark attempts to involve the members and youth affiliated with the Mennonite churches in New York City to establish its program. This helps to break down the image of the white establishment dictating a program."[34]

Dale Stoltzfus continued as program director for Camp Deerpark from the beginning through the 1970s. Jerry Kennell, a VSer from Illinois, and Leonor Constantin, who grew up in the Glad Tidings congregation, met at Goshen College and were married. They came back to Camp Deerpark for a summer and stayed as camp managers for six years until they returned to Goshen College in August 1979 to complete their degrees. James and Arlene Stauffer, just returned from EMM service in Vietnam, served as camp pastors in 1975. Eugene Davis and Harlan (Lannie) Millette were camp directors that summer. An average of 55 children attended the week-long camp sessions in the summer of 1975, but in 1976 New York City's economic crunch dropped the average to 35 a week. Maynard Shirk and Lowell

Glad Tidings pastor Eugene Shelly officiating at a baptismal service in the lake at Camp Deerpark.

Jantzi assisted Dale Stoltzfus and Jerry and Leonor Kennell in running the camp that year. Jerry Kennell became program director when Dale Stoltzfus left for other duties and the board invited him to continue on a permanent basis, but Kennell wanted to finish his college work.

Miriam Cruz took over as program director at Camp Deerpark in 1979. Mark Wenger and Kevin Phillips ran two summer sessions of youth camps. Harlan Millette and Ray Siegrist served as camp pastors. Phil and Bonnie Detweiler had responsibility for food and grounds in 1979 and 1980. Mim Cruz continued as director with Herb and Debbie Graff as her assistants through 1981.

NOTES

[1] Rafael Falcon, *The Hispanic Mennonite Church in North America 1932-1982* (Scottdale, PA, 1986), 45-49.

[2] Falcon, *Hispanic Mennonite Church*, 143-144.

[3] Falcon, *Hispanic Mennonite Church*, 108-109.

[4] Simon Gingerich to Lester T. Hershey, June 27, 1967, MBM-AMC.

[5] Ronald Lehman to Lester T. Hershey, June 28, 1967, MBM-AMC.

[6] Guillermo Torres, "La Primera Iglesia Evangelica Menonita de Brooklyn, Datos Historicos," 1974, 4-5.

[7] Ken Seitz to Ron Collins, Jan. 16, 1968, MBM-AMC.

[8] Addona Nissley to Nelson Kauffman, Aug. 6, 1968, MBM-AMC.

[9] Ron Collins to Leonard and Barbara Kilmer, Aug. 9, 1968, MBM-AMC.

[10] Council of MBMC Churches of NYC, Oct. 28, 1968, MBM-AMC.

[11] Simon Gingerich to Lester Hershey, June 27, 1967, MBM-AMC.

[12] Council of MBMC Churches of NYC, Oct. 28, 1968, MBM-AMC.

[13] Addona Nissley to Nelson Kauffman, Aug. 6, 1968, MBM-AMC.

[14] Addona Nissley to Simon Gingerich, Jan. 3, 1969. Addona Nissley to Simon Gingerich, Jan. 29, 1969, MBM-AMC.

[15] Council of MBMC Churches in NYC, Feb 20, 1969, MBM-AMC.

[16] Addona Nissley to Simon Gingerich, Jan. 31969. Addona Nissley to Simon Gingerich, Jan. 29, 1969, MBM-AMC.

[17] New York City District Council Minutes, April 10, 1979, May 10, 1979, EMBMC-A.

[18] Falcon, *Hispanic Mennonite Church*, 196-197. General Conference Mennonite Church Handbook, 1981-1982.

[19] Monthly Report to VS Director, Jan. 1982, Feb. 1982, Mar. 1982, June 1982, Aug. 1982. John Wert, Annual Administrative Report, Apr. 16, 1982, EMM.

[20] *General Conference Mennonite Church Handbook* 1981-1982, 1982-1983, 1983-1984, 1984-1985, 1986, 1987.

[21] Cesar Segura to Dale Stoltzfus, July 20, 1978, EMM.

[22] New York District Council Minutes, April 15, 1974.

[23] New York District Council Minutes, July 1, 1975, EMM.

[24] New York District Council Minutes, April 16, 1980, EMM.

[25] Steve Kriss and Jewel Showalter, "A Stalwart in the Church," *Missionary Messenger*, May 1995, 6-7.

[26] Nicholas Angustia to David W. Shenk, September 1, 1981. Nicholas Angustia to Eastern Board, February 16, 1983, EMM.

[27] David W. Shenk to Monroe Yoder, Pastor Mateo, and Nicholas Angustia, Sept. 20, 1982, EMM.

[28] Norman Shenk to John H. Kraybill, January 8, 1962. John H. Kraybill to Executive Committee, February 20, 1962. Ira Buckwalter to John H. Kraybill, February 21, 1962. Norman Shenk, Memorandum of NYC Investigative Trip, March 5, 1962. Norman Shenk to H. Raymond Charles, March 5, 1962. Paul Landis to H. Raymond Charles, February 14, 1963, EMM.

[29] Paul G. Landis to H. Raymond Charles. February 14, 1963, EMM. Camp Brookhaven Board Minutes, May 14, 1963, October 1, 1963. Atlantic Conference Commission on Camping, BCA-MC.

[30] Camp Brookhaven Report, 1964. Camp Brookhaven Board Minutes, May 22, 1964, October 9, 1964, May 7, 1965, October 22, 1965. Ginder Papers, BCA-MC.

[31] Camp Brookhaven Board Minutes, October 15, 1966, May 5, 1967, October 7, 1967,May 3, 1968, October 8, 1968, May 2, 1969, October 4, 1969, September 22, 1970, May 14, 1971, October 12, 1971. Ginder Papers, BCA-MC.

[32] Camp Brookhaven Board Minutes, May 12,1972, October 12, 1972, May 11, 1973, June 11, 1973, July 13, 1973, October 30, 1973. Atlantic Conference Commission on Camping, BCA-MC.

[33] Ira Buckwalter to Paul G. Landis, February 27, 1969. Monroe Yoder to Glenn Zeager, August 29, 1969, EMM.

[34] Camp Deerpark Newsletter, 1969. Dale Stoltzfus, "Inner City Youth at Camp," Mennonite Camping Association Newsletter, June 1970.

CHAPTER TWELVE

Planting Churches

1979–1994

The Mennonite churches of New York City began without a great deal of planning or application of theoretical models. The mission boards hoped they would eventually become "self-propagating, self-governing, and self-supporting," a goal common to missionaries at home and overseas since the nineteenth century. As a result, they encouraged the development of indigenous leadership, although there was always a tendency to rely on VSers and other born-Mennonites in the city.

A new theory, formulated by Donald McGavran and the Institute of Church Growth at Fuller Theological Seminary, shaped some Mennonite thinking about missions in the 1970s and 1980s. With this shift to a new paradigm came a new emphasis on church planting and outreach to specific groups of people.

Donald McGavran and Bishop J. Waskom Pickett made pioneering studies in the 1930s of their own missions in central India. They concluded that "people movements" played a more important role in the growth of the church than individual conversions. McGavran applied what he had learned in India to a general theory of church growth in *The Bridges of God*, published in 1955. He believed that "people like to become Christians without crossing racial, linguistic, or class barriers" and that "the great obstacles to conversion are social, not theological." In his books, *How Churches Grow* (1959) and *Understanding Church Growth* (1970), McGavran stressed the "homogenous unit," where all members have some characteristic in common, as the key to church planting and church growth. C. Peter Wagner, Paul G. Hiebert, and other Fuller professors addressed the individualistic American society in the 1970s. The homogenous unit approach meant that no one needed "to adapt to the culture of another homogenous unit in order to become an authentic Christian."[1] As Mennonites G. Edwin Bontrager and Nathan D. Showalter put it:

> Church planting is an effective response to cultural diversity. People are different, and no one congregation can meet the needs of all persons and cultures, especially in an urban community. New churches can focus on particular groups of persons in a community who are yet unreached by the good news of Jesus.[2]

McGavran and his colleagues made a distinction between discipling and perfecting that was equally important to their theory. In inviting "entire cohesive social groups" to an encounter with Jesus Christ and in nurturing these new Christians, "a bare minimum of simple moral demands" would be made with "perfecting" later on as they grew in the faith.[3] For Mennonite churches in the city, the implication would not only be that cultural norms were irrelevant, but that the Gospel message should be presented in stages.

Mennonites did not adopt prevailing ideas about church growth without questioning them. Discussions in Mennonite mission circles stressed the weakness of its scriptural grounding and its assumptions drawn from American evangelicalism. Church Growth theorists seemed to accept a privatized, socially irrelevant Christian faith. "It is one thing to have a homogenous church where other kinds of people are absent or far away; it is a quite different thing to maintain such a church in a heterogeneous community," like a modern American city. Multiplying congregations and increasing numbers in each one seemed the central goal.[4] David W. Shenk, who assumed responsibility for home missions at Eastern Board in 1979, commented:

> The overall assumptions of Church Growth theory seem to be anchored on the premise that correct missiology will produce church growth. However, is it not true that from a kingdom perspective, faithfulness, not success, is the only valid criterion of authentic mission?

Shenk was also critical of "strategies that see people as objects to be manipulated into the church."[5]

David and Grace Shenk.

Church Growth gave Mennonites a new strategy and a set of priorities for mission. The renewed emphasis on church planting as the central concern of mission was a needed corrective, in veteran missionary Stanley Friesen's view.[6] The appointment of Nathan D.

Showalter, who had studied Church Growth at Fuller, as director of Church Growth Training, in 1979 and the later appointment of David W. Shenk as the Home Missions director marked a new era at Eastern Board.

Eastern Board sponsored a meeting on church growth in March 1979 with Wilbert Shenk as resource person. Dale Stoltzfus, Monroe Yoder, and John Bauman helped plan the meeting. They hoped "to come up with concrete proposals and guidelines in the area of church growth."[7]

Paul Landis became president of the mission board in 1980. Chester Wenger, who had long had responsibility for Home Missions, resigned as he was of retirement age. In April, Paul Landis met with the District Council to discuss replacing Chester Wenger and restructuring the office. After a lengthy discussion it became clear that David Shenk had already been appointed. The Council found it difficult to "justify the haste in which the decision was taken" and the fact that the new appointee was waiting outside to meet with them.[8] The child of missionaries in Tanzania, he had spent his adult life in East Africa as an Eastern Board missionary. He seemed a logical choice to direct overseas missions, but his experience of American cities was limited. Shenk had lived in New York as a VSer for two years and taught at Lancaster Mennonite High School for two years after that.

Church Plantings in Staten Island and Queens

In October 1979 Nate Showalter informed the Council that he was working with a person interested in planting a church in the Borough of Queens. Roger Lehman, a graduate of Elim Bible Institute, had proposed a church planting in either the Rego Park or College Point sections. Lehman had worked for two years with Robert Johannsson, pastor of the Community Gospel Church in Astoria, directing a young adult fellowship and helping with preaching and visitation. In November, Dale Stoltzfus presented Roger's proposal, now directed to church planting in Staten Island, to the Council. They wanted "to be involved in church planting activities in a brotherly manner with the Eastern Board" and asked the Home Missions staff to "work with us in

Roger and Cheryl Lehman and daughter Jennifer, pastor of New Life Fellowship on Staten Island, which later became Redeeming Grace Fellowship.

establishing a church in this District, whether it be in Staten Island or another area."[9]

Nathan Showalter, Dale Stoltzfus, and Gerry Keener met with Roger and Cherry Lehman in December and explored the Queens neighborhoods they had targeted. Over Christmas the Lehmans visited the Staten Island Girls' Home and got a sense of the Huguenot section of Staten Island. They seemed comfortable with a church planting in Staten Island. In February 1980 Chester Wenger, Nathan Showalter, and Dale Stoltzfus again met with the Lehmans. They agreed that Roger and Cherry would move to the Woodrow Road mansion and get acquainted with people in the neighborhood. Eastern Board would provide financial support for the project, but the New York City District Council would take responsibility for administration. As soon as the new Council of Mennonite Churches was ready, they would administer church planting in Staten Island.[10]

The Lehmans spent their first months in Staten Island remodeling the Woodrow Road mansion. They began a neighborhood Bible study with two other couples. By October 1980 they had Bible studies on Sunday and Wednesday evenings with three couples attending regularly and a few others dropping in occasionally. A leaflet from this time advertised neighborhood Bible Study with baby-sitting available and identified the group as the New Life Fellowship. They began Sunday morning services in January 1981. The Bible studies had enough regular members by the spring to divide into two groups meeting at the same time. A leaflet advertising New Life Fellowship, "a new church in the Huguenot area," listed Sunday worship at 11, a Tim LaHaye film Sunday night, and neighborhood Bible studies at 7:30 Tuesday and Thursday evenings.[11]

The New Life Fellowship continued to grow in 1981. That summer the vacation Bible school registered 70 children. They added two more week night Bible studies in the autumn. Mary Ann Jacobs, an Elim graduate, moved to the Woodrow Road mansion to help with the emerging church. In December they had a youth group, an adult fellowship, and counted 50 people in attendance one Sunday morning.[12]

The new church experienced "less than anticipated increase in attendance" during 1982. They had apparently leveled off at 50 or below, as the goals for 1983 set a "100 percent increase to 100 people." They were reaching needy people, however, as David Shenk found on a visit in October. "We greatly enjoyed the Bible fellowship experience and the time of sharing with you as a team," he wrote, particularly "the testimonies of people who have recently found Jesus." But the house on Woodrow Road was too big and heating too costly for the little group. They were looking for a place to rent for worship services. Roger and Cherry Lehman bought a home of their own about a mile away.[13]

The Lehmans experienced some problems in the first year of the fellowship. A discipleship group of five men began meetings centered on "New Life Studies." Before long, one of the group split from the fellowship over the ministry of the Holy Spirit and other families followed him. Roger recognized later on that "programs started at this time tended to fold."[14]

Most of the fifteen members of New Life Fellowship were of Italian background and had moved to Staten Island from Brooklyn. In May 1983 the congregation rented a Baptist church and held their Sunday services in the early afternoon. Attendance ranged from 50 to 70.[15]

Stan Sutter, another Elim graduate, joined the Staten Island team. His parents, Lester and Marietta Sutter, Mennonite church planters, had pastored Crown Hill and other Ohio Conference churches. Stan and Cathy Pike Sutter, newly married, were commissioned in June as associate church planters. They would work with the Staten Island fellowship for a time and then plant a new church.

Eastern Board looked to begin other Mennonite churches in New York City. Among the newer immigrants in the city were the Garifuna, decendants of intermarriage of escaped and liberated slaves and American Indians and who had settled their own communities in Spanish and British Honduras (now Belize) and maintained their own languages. David Shenk asked Roger Lehman to help reach them. "Paul Landis keeps reminding me that there is a large community of Garifuna people from Belize living in the Brooklyn area." Steve Shank, recently returned from Belize, was interested in church planting among them. Could Roger Lehman study the demographics and come up with some specific recommendations?[16]

John and Irene Smucker returned to New York in 1983 and began to work on planting a church, the Queens Mennonite Church, in the Murray Hill section of Flushing. They rented a house at 149th Place and Beech Avenue and there the church held its first service on November 13, 1983. The Smuckers came back to the city in response to an invitation in 1982 from the New York City Council of Mennonite Churches to plant an urban congregation. Mennonite Board of Missions provided a subsidy for the first five years. First Baptist Church in Flushing and Community Gospel Church in Astoria encouraged them to target Flushing. Before they rented a place for public worship, the Smuckers visited other churches in the area to learn what they were doing, so as not to duplicate programs. Wayne D. and Clara King joined them in August 1983 as church planters, moving from Ohio to a house on 149th Place. King had been a Mennonite pastor since 1959 and most recently of Living Word Fellowship in Dalton, Ohio. Lester and Marietta Sutter also moved to New York in 1983 to join the church-planting team. Both couples initially lived at the New York School of Urban Ministry in Long Island City. The three veteran missionary couples attended the annual week of prayer at Elim Bible Institute in January 1984.[17]

The growth of New Life Fellowship in Staten Island slowed in 1983. David Shenk noted that, after a rapid start, attendance leveled off at 40-50. In November 1983 the average attendance on Sunday was still 35-40. He urged Roger Lehman and his elders to pray for additional growth, as "something begins to happen" once attendance is in the 80-100 range. He shared with them the covenants of the Hopewell and Washington Community Fellowships and the Mennonite Confession of Faith.[18]

From the beginning New Life Fellowship had closer ties with the Community Gospel Church in Astoria and with Elim Bible Institute than with any Mennonite churches. Both Roger Lehman and Stan Sutter counseled with Bob Johannsson, the Community pastor, rather than with Monroe Yoder. Lehman had worked for two years with Johannsson, whose brother was Elim's dean, and Mennonite contacts had been limited to Nate Showalter and Dale Stoltzfus. Not surprisingly, New Life wore its Mennonite affiliation lightly. In January 1984 Roger and Stan told David Shenk the church would remain identified with the Mennonite Church, but they wanted to be accountable to the Vineyard Churches. They had found a kindred spirit, Lance Pittluck, pastor of a rapidly growing church in suburban Hempstead, Long Island, a Vineyard affiliate. There was a growing Vineyard influence, especially in Roger's small group.

The Vineyard churches developed from the ideas of John Wimber, "a revivalist healer and inspiring worship leader." After pastoring an Evangelical Quaker church, Wimber began working in 1975 with the Fuller Evangelistic Association as a lecturer on church growth. He served on "a team that traveled widely, consulting, analyzing local churches and offering advice on how to foster growth." During this time, the Quaker congregation dismissed a group of 125 who formed Calvary Chapel, Yorba Linda, California, and called Wimber as pastor. The congregation grew rapidly and became more charismatic. Wimber emphasized miraculous healings and exorcisms. In 1981 Peter Wagner, Donald McGavran's successor as professor of church growth at Fuller, invited Wimber to teach a course "Signs and Wonders and Church Growth." Calvary Chapel became the first Vineyard Church in 1982. Within three years 120 other congregations joined the Vineyard movement "in the expectation of experiencing revival." Wimber and close associates like Lance Pittluck taught "Signs and Wonders" seminars across the country and the world. Roger Lehman drew from the Vineyard movement a more spontaneous and freer worship and an emphasis on "training people for spiritual gift ministry." Roger Lehman wrote at the time, "I was moving more toward a style of ministry which I had learned at the Vineyard Seminars. Stan did not attend them." The immediate result of this tension was that Stan and Cathy Sutter moved to Flushing in 1984 to help with the Queens Mennonite Church.[19]

The long-term effect was a concern shared by Lehman and his elders to "more clearly define our relationship with Lancaster Conference." In a doctrinal statement drawn up in 1985, they said, "Although we are a Mennonite Church, the community sees us as a non-denominational church. New Life Fellowship looks and functions more like an urban charismatic church."[20] The congregation "has a small group feeling," David Shenk observed. The elders had strongly positive things to say about Roger and Cherry and the church. Some people had left the fellowship for a variety of reasons, such as the lack of programs for children and teenagers, or the closeness of the group. Newcomers might sometimes be put off because "the Lord gives a word of knowledge geared to visitors' needs." The congregation rented a Moravian church and held worship services on Saturday nights. Seminars were held on Sunday evenings and Thursday night was for Kinship, a small group. Roger Lehman worked four days a week as a carpenter in addition to his pastoral duties.[21]

On a visit to Staten Island in November 1985, David Shenk sensed "a renewed commitment of the congregation to reaching out in evangelistic commitment to others, working with more intentionality at absorbing new people happily into the congregation, and developing a plan for the multiplication of small groups." The greatest obstacle to growth was the need to rent a church building available only on Saturdays. A year later, he noted that Roger Lehman was "fully self supporting, working in construction." The congregation would need no further Eastern Board support until they attempted to purchase a church building.[22]

The Eastern Board subsidy came to an end in January 1986, but the New Life Fellowship struggled along. In June 1987 Roger Lehman resigned as pastor. Some members continued to meet for prayer and fellowship on Thursday evenings. In September, Monroe Yoder asked Lester and Marietta Sutter and Stan and Cathy Sutter to help the New Life Fellowship survive. Many members were uncertain about continuing or had negative feelings about the Mennonite Church. The Mennonite presence in Staten Island needed a fresh start. On December 2, 1987 New Life Fellowship disbanded.[23]

The second effort at church planting in Staten Island began in January 1988 when Lester and Marietta Sutter moved to a two-family house in Richmondtown. They met at first in the home of Nick and Louise Marzella with from seven to fifteen people each time. In February they obtained the use of the community room at the Staten Island Community Service building at 11 Sampsay Street in Great Kills as a meeting place. The small group organized as Redeeming Grace Fellowship and adopted a Statement of Faith. On March 20, 1988 there was a commissioning service and a week later, on Palm Sunday, Redeeming Grace Fellowship held its first Sunday worship service. By May attendance on Sundays averaged 31. About half the group had belonged to New Life Fellowship, so there was a real continuity with the earlier church planting.[24]

Stan and Cathy Sutter moved to Staten Island on the 4th of July. Youth activities and a men's fellowship developed over the summer. Mary Lynn Erigo, who had been part of the New Life Fellowship, had a Bible study in her home. Frank Marzella and Debbie James were married at Redeeming Grace.[25] The new congregation grew slowly. In 1990 an average of 35 people attended Sunday services.[26] They found more permanent quarters at 539 Greeley Avenue.

The church planting in Flushing had taken root. They began with Bible study in the Smuckers' living room on 149th Place with several Queens College students attending. Other Bible studies met in other homes. On Sunday afternoons about 20 gathered for worship service at Smuckers'

Cathy, Stanley, Lester, and Marietta Sutter, pastors of Redeeming Grace Fellowship on Staten Island.

home.[27] In May 1984 the congregation obtained use of the historic Quaker Meeting House on Northern Boulevard, near Main Street, in Flushing. The Meeting House, built in 1694, was the oldest house of worship in the city. "The Friends are more than eager to share their large old facilities with us." The youngest congregation in the city met for worship and Sunday school from 5 to 7 on Sunday evenings. In the first few months the attendance averaged 35. Lester and Marietta Sutter moved to Roosevelt Avenue, a few blocks from the Smuckers and Kings, in April. "Clara King is teaching English to foreigners at the First Baptist Church of Flushing. We are all meeting new persons in our neighborhood."[28]

A sign in front of the First Baptist Church, on Sanford Avenue almost a mile from the Smuckers' home, suggested the changes taking place in Flushing in the 1970s and 1980s. It announced services in Chinese, Korean, Japanese, Hindi, Tamil, Spanish, and English. This old middle-class community was largely Protestant, with many Catholics and some Jews, until the 1940s. Sprawling Victorian houses on acre or half-acre lots along Sanford Avenue, Northern Boulevard and other main roads were replaced by apartment houses in the 1950s and 1960s and old estates were developed as new high-rise cities like Mitchell Gardens. The Jewish population soared with many sections of both new apartment houses and single-family homes solidly Jewish. The Catholic population also grew with many Hispanic and Italian Catholics joining Catholics of Irish and German descent. The newer immigrants to New York in the 1970s came from Asia and they gravitated to Flushing as a desirable area with little street crime. Within a short time signs in Korean and Japanese outnumbered English signs on Main Street and other shopping areas. Hindu and Buddhist temples, a Sikh community center, Korean Presbyterian churches, and a Chinese Methodist church opened on tree-lined residential streets. The Mennonites had moved into an international crossroads. The Smuckers began to know their neighbors in Murray Hill, a fifteen-minute walk from downtown Flushing. "This is an integrated area with Korean, Chinese, German, Irish, Italian, Hispanic, Russian, Swiss, Indian, and black living within a few blocks of us." The Tuesday evening Bible study at Smuckers' drew a few people from the neighborhood. They planned a block party, "so that we can get to know more of our neighbors."

A Mennonite enclave also developed. Ed and Millie Mullen, who had been involved with evangelism in the House of Friendship in the 1960s, moved to Murray Hill. Mark and Anabelle Perri, newlywed Queens College students, found an apartment near the Smuckers. The team members and these couples saw each other every day and formed the backbone of the weekly Bible study. The team met every Tuesday and Thursday for prayer and decision-making.

By the summer of 1984 they had reached "consensus about our new name—The Redeemer Community Church, affiliated with the NYC Council of Mennonite Churches and supported by the Atlantic Coast Conference of the Mennonite Church."[29]

Immanuel Community Church, Flushing, Queens. The congregation meets in the educational building of a Presbyterian Church. 2005 photo.

They had also developed "A Vision for Ministry in New York City," agreeing that, "This new congregation will seek to be New Testament in theology, charismatic in nature, evangelistic in thrust, and Anabaptist in orientation." The Church of the Redeemer in Houston, Texas might serve as a model in their efforts to express "Christian community in some form, which could include intentional community for those desiring it." They wanted the new congregation to became indigenous, defined as "self-governing, self-supporting, and self-propagating." Reflecting John Smucker's own involvement in teaching urban mission courses at Elim Bible Institute and the New York School of Urban Ministry, programs in leadership training and evangelism had an important part in their thinking.[30]

Discipleship groups, emphasizing "Worshipping and Sharing the Word with each other and Witnessing," began in August 1984. These small groups met regularly for prayer, sharing, developing gifts, and evangelism. "We are hoping that the congregation can grow indefinitely by the Spirit's direction through this simple Jesus way."[31]

The congregation grew steadily, reflecting the community in that fifteen different ethnic groups were represented. Membership reached 51 in 1990. They eventually outgrew the Quaker Meeting House and moved their worship services and Sunday School to St. John's Episcopal Church at Sanford Avenue and 149th Place. Redeemer also rented space in the parish hall for a church office and for "Global Village," a project directed by Mark Perri to sell MCC Self Help Crafts (now Ten Thousand Villages).

Redeemer took a new direction in 1990 when Elim Tabernacle Church in Bayside, a community just three miles east of Flushing, called John

Smucker as their pastor. Elim, a non-denominational charismatic church, was affiliated with Elim Fellowship of Lima, New York, an outreach of Elim Bible Institute. Smucker was installed as pastor at Elim Tabernacle in August 1990. This congregation met Sunday mornings and Redeemer continued to meet on Sunday evenings. On January 6, 1991 the two congregations began to worship together in the Masonic Temple on Bell Boulevard in Bayside. Merger of the two congregations was completed in March 1991. The emerging congregation would have dual affiliation with Elim Fellowship and with Atlantic Coast Conference and the New York City Council of Mennonite Churches. In April members chose a new name, Immanuel Community Church. The combined congregation had a membership of 105 with as many as 180 people attending services.[32]

Church Growth and the Older Churches

The fresh emphasis on church planting had an impact on the churches planted in Manhattan and the Bronx in the 1950s. All the churches had been crowded to capacity on Sunday mornings in the days of the cab-driving pastors. They had maintained difficult schedules, balancing the need to earn a living for their families with pastoral duties, but they managed to visit people in their neighborhoods on a regular basis. Then visitation and friendship evangelism no longer had the same priority in the churches, and numbers remained static. The city changed in 60s and 70s years. Once crowded neighborhoods lost population as burned-out shells took the place of bustling apartment houses and stores. The spread of drugs brought crime and fear to the streets. City neighborhoods bristled with barbed wire and metal bars. People didn't respond to a stranger's knock as they had when Harold Thomas hauled children to Sunday school.[33]

When Chester Wenger visited the New York churches in March 1979, he talked with the pastors "about church growth principles as they may apply to the inner city." He observed that:

> The congregations are not presently in a growth stage. The pastors are deeply concerned and wonder how they can lead on from the caring ministries in which they are involved to a harvest of new believers and Christian disciples. Memberships in the seven congregations range from 10 to 42 with an average membership of 30 per congregation.

Was it possible for such small congregations to become self-supporting and self-propagating?

A shift in population in "this very depressed South Bronx area" made the Glad Tidings neighborhood "largely Spanish" in 1979. John Bauman, the new pastor there, was considering "regular separate Spanish services." The after-school tutoring program provided the major outreach into the community.[34] Two years later, David Shenk found "almost no local participation in the congregation," with nearly all who came to worship at Glad Tidings traveling from the North Bronx. With the "challenge of a rapidly changing neighborhood," Glad Tidings reassessed its involvement in the community.[35]

VSer Ulli Klemm assists with the Aluminum Can Drive at Glad Tidings.

Glad Tidings dropped their after-school tutoring program in 1981, "to give themselves to more home visitation." Both Jim Robinson and Dennis Witmer served as community workers at Glad Tidings, giving much of their time to the reading-tutoring program. Jim Robinson completed his VS year in September 1980. Ulli Klemm began at Glad Tidings as Dennis terminated. He continued with the tutoring program. In addition, the Glad Tidings youth worker "directs Bible Clubs, directs the Sunday school program, is on the Church Cabinet, is in charge of the Fresh Air Program which means registering students, getting them to have physicals and taking them to buses at the right time, running the summer lunch program, helping in youth activities, doing preaching, supervising recreation at the center, helping in youth Bible study, building relationships and visiting in the community, helping organize games for the basketball team and generally being at the Community Center when it is open." Tony Miller and Dale Hershey helped him with the Bible Clubs. During the summer months, Tom Baker, an EMC student, also helped out. Ulli Klemm found time for other activities, including an aluminum can drive.

> He got a grocery cart and a couple times a week they would walk around blocks in the city looking for tin cans. There were many, many cans, and the children had fun finding them and smashing them. These were loaded into the grocery cart and wheeled back to the church where they were dumped into a large box and once a month taken to a recycling center. The money collected was used to buy new pool sticks and other equipment for the Community Center. Ulli tried

> something new this year by keeping the Center open Tuesday and Friday evenings until nine o'clock.[36]

Ulli Klemm came at a low point in morale at Glad Tidings. VS Administrator Jeryl Hollinger said in his 1981 report:

> At Glad Tidings, I feel that Ulli may very well be holding the church together. He works along with John Bauman the pastor very, very closely. Ulli is a good leadership person and has an unlimited amount of ideas. However, he has felt pretty much alone in this, and at times has dealt with the depressed feeling that if anything is to be done, it depends on him.[37]

Young professionals who had grown up at Glad Tidings no longer came to church there. John Bauman was discouraged and looking for other options. Monroe Yoder observed a different spirit at Glad Tidings in October 1981. "John, Ulli, and Jesus Cruz developed a much tighter bond and the church cabinet took on an entirely different cast." Jesus Cruz believed that "Glad Tidings is now on the right track... and developing an effective witness." On a Sunday morning Bishop Yoder noticed "about 30 persons with a good mixture of young adults and adults" at Glad Tidings.[38]

Pastor Mateo, an energetic church planter, joined the team at Glad Tidings. Hispanic youth used English, but their parents were more comfortable in Spanish. Pastor Mateo began visiting the families of teenagers involved in youth programs. "Their parents have begun to respond to Pastor and we want to develop that." He also helped with Wednesday evening prayer meeting and Spanish-speaking adults began to attend. He worked with Frankie Rodriguez "in the Saturday evening fellowship meetings and outreach." About 30 young people participated. "Frankie Rodriguez has brought persons into the church through the Saturday fellowship." Elmer Lapp's basketball teams involved another 40 teenagers and about 60 youngsters came to the Community Center programs, so there were many families to visit. Pastor Mateo and John Bauman each preached twice a month.[39]

John Bauman continued at Glad Tidings as half-time associate pastor after September 1, 1982, when he began studies in clinical psychology. He reported "an increase in attendance, offerings, spiritual maturity, and enthusiasm" during 1982. Two new Christians were baptized during the summer.[40] Ulli Klemm kept his many jobs as youth worker at Glad Tidings until September 1982 when he completed two years of voluntary service. He was "seen by many as a person of strength and stability in the church." Wes Nolt arrived in May 1982 to eventually take his place, allowing Ulli to introduce him to his work and the people he worked with in the neighborhood. Wes Nolt continued through September 1983. John Stahl-Wert, VS Administrator, noted that, "Because John Bauman is in school and Pastor Mateo is on temporary leave, a good bit of work falls back onto the lap of the VSer." Although this could be "overwhelming at times," Ulli Klemm and Wes Nolt both made outstanding contributions in a job that included "doing visitation in the community and occasional preaching." Glad Tidings did not ask for a new VSer in 1983, but "identified and commissioned persons from their congregation to pick up many of the responsibilities."[41]

Late in 1983 the Glad Tidings congregation elected Vicente Martinez from First Mennonite Church of Brooklyn as associate pastor with John Bauman, each giving half-time to the church.[42]

A better day seemed to be dawning for Glad Tidings and for the South Bronx. On a visit in October 1984, David Shenk wrote: "It was encouraging to see the way the community is being upgraded with new housing and apparently there is a pretty good spirit in the community." Glad Tidings continued to distribute food and clothing to needy people in the neighborhood.[43] Vicente Martinez and Jesus Cruz worked with the congregation to make "some careful assessment of long-term goals" and invited David Shenk to join them in this process. Shenk found "a freedom of the Holy Spirit in that fellowship which refreshed and enriched us as we met Jesus Christ" in a worship service at Glad Tidings.

Eastern Board's new policy planned to eliminate all financial subsidies within ten years. The vision was for churches to be weaned from dependence on mission board money, so that they could be self-sufficient. David Shenk wanted to do this in such a way as to "provide a long-term undergirding for viable and thriving congregational life in the South Bronx." Inevitably numbers mattered.

> How many people does God plan to entrust to the Glad Tidings congregation? If in His providence He is entrusting 30 people to your congregation, we will praise Him! But obviously a congregation of 30 does not need a full-time pastor, and in that case steps need to be taken rather expeditiously to contracting the external subsidies for the Glad Tidings congregation commensurate to the number of people whom God is entrusting to your congregational care.[44]

Glad Tidings' numbers were not impressive. The congregation had 37 members, but the average attendance on the Sundays in May 1984 was 27 and in May 1985 only 20. There were two baptisms and two conversions in 1983-1984, none in 1984-1985.[45]

Shenk was nonetheless hopeful when he visited Glad Tidings in November 1985. The congregation had experienced "healthy growth during the past year, with particular growth in the number of youth attending" and Bauman, Cruz, and Martinez worked well as a pastoral team. He recommended a $15,000 contribution from Eastern Board to renovating the building to provide more Sunday school rooms and nursery.[46] David Shenk hoped John Bauman would continue on the pastoral team, but he resigned.

Shenk was still optimistic when he again visited Glad Tidings in October 1986. Vicente Martinez served as half-time pastor at Glad Tidings and half time as Church Administrator for New York City Council of Mennonite Churches. "The demand for administration sometimes sabotages pastoral commitment" and Glad Tidings had suffered during the year as a result. "Vicente and Evangeline continue to have a vision and sense of call for the Glad Tidings congregation" and Shenk remained confident that there would be renewed growth, "as Vicente and the congregation focus more time in prayer, evangelistic outreach, and pastoral ministry."[47]

Glad Tidings Mennonite Church never regained its momentum. In May 1988 Monroe Yoder reported that "they are closing down Glad Tidings for the summer" but the congregation hoped "to reopen this fall, if possible." In September Glad Tidings Mennonite Church disbanded.[48] After thirty-seven years of ministry in the South Bronx, a sentence in *Lancaster Conference News* announced the end. In one sense, Glad Tidings survived in the North Bronx Mennonite Church.

Good Shepherd Mennonite Church closed its doors two years before Glad Tidings. After Harold Davenport left Good Shepherd in 1979, Eugene Shelly accepted a call as interim pastor. He remained at Good Shepherd until February 1981 when Raymond Bell came from Chicago to take responsibility for the congregation. At this time Good Shepherd had 28 members, and 40-45 people attended worship services on Sundays.[49]

With a new pastor in residence, congregational morale was high. "Raymond has a keen sense of vision for effective evangelism and outreach" and "ideas as to how the congregation can become more attractive in the community." This part of the Bronx had escaped the urban blight of the Glad Tidings neighborhood. The more solid economic base gave a good possibility for "developing a vigorous self-supporting congregation" at Good Shepherd.[50]

Since the VS Center was near the church, Gene Shelly made himself available to the VSers. "There were some hassles in personal relationships and Gene met with the unit on Sunday evenings to work on helping them develop ways of open communication." Kim Rathman, one of the VSers, worked at Good Shepherd running Bible Clubs, helping with the summer day camp, and organizing a youth group. She worked well with Pastor Shelly. "Gene understood Kim very well and helped her develop herself in certain areas." When he left and Raymond Bell took his place, things changed. "Raymond had a very different approach to church life and evangelism than either Kim or Gene did." As a result, "Kim suddenly felt she was not appreciated nor wanted there." Jeryl Hollinger added, "I think she had the situation rather correctly understood." Kim Rathman completed her VS at Inwood House, a home for pregnant girls. She was then hired as a permanent staff member there.[51]

Evidently others had difficulty adjusting to the new pastor's methods. As Bell's first year at Good Shepherd drew to a close, David Shenk met with him and the Church Council. Shenk observed, "It is taking a bit of time for the congregation to become accustomed to the changes in leadership style that have taken place over the last year." But the congregation was beginning to demonstrate "a greater sense of mutual trust" and, as that trust deepened, the congregation could begin to think "in terms of its ministry to the community." The greatest need was for more visitation, both of church members and of people in the neighborhood. The Bible clubs provided a ready opening in the community, but these contacts had to be followed up with home visits. The congregation needed to "find ways to joyously reach out to the neighbors," and Bell needed "to listen to some of the concerns expressed by members of the congregation who are somewhat alienated at this time." There had been a growth in membership, through a membership drive, but the congregational report still showed 28 members in May 1982 and an average of 15 attending services.[52]

In September 1982 the Bells announced that they would be leaving Good Shepherd. They left in March 1983 and the congregation was again searching for a pastor.[53]

Emmanuel and Doris Okorley accepted a call to pastor Good Shepherd in May 1983. They were from Nigeria and they needed to clarify their status with the U.S. Immigration and Naturalization Service. A year later their immigration problem remained an issue.[54] In his first year at Good Shepherd, Okorley reported 15 conversions. Membership remained at 28 in May 1984 but an average of 50 attended services. A number of West Africans became part of the Good Shepherd fellowship. The congregation was growing again.[55]

Good Shepherd operated on a growing deficit. Gerry Keener, as property manager for the New York churches, informed Emmanuel Okorley in November 1985 that, "Good Shepherd is in arrears on rent by $11,378.54 and about $7,500 from other sources was needed to sustain 1126 Sherman Avenue in this one year." Okorley had found a teaching position which reduced some budget pressure.[56]

The financial crisis and other related problems paralyzed the congregation. The number of active members and attenders dwindled to ten. Bishop Monroe Yoder held a congregational meeting on April 13, 1986 with Emmanuel and Doris Okorley, Carol Bedward, Faith Bryant, Annie Farmer, Bettye Johnson, Gladys Mitchell, Rhonda Mitchell, Ayo Ojo, Isaacs Oyebode, Gloria and Enid Welch. "We now are all aware that some very deep problems exist, but by God's grace and prayerful obedience to the Holy Spirit this can be resolved!" The small group committed themselves to "search for guidance through prayer and fasting."[57]

Good Shepherd Mennonite Church closed permanently in September 1986. David Shenk explained:

> The reason for the closure is that this congregation has suffered from a pastoral crisis for a good many years, and finally the congregation has become exhausted. Yet there is a core group who will continue to meet for prayer fellowship, and this core group are praying that the congregation will be revived again.[58]

Ironically, Joy Fellowship, a non-denominational charismatic church, dedicated their new church center in October 1986. After being part of the Good Shepherd Mennonite Church, Martin Bender and his family "felt led to begin their own outreach in an area not far distant from Good Shepherd." The fellowship grew steadily in the 1970s and early 1980s. "They will have now renovated a spacious theater which will seat 500 people." Their new church was "about two-thirds full" for the dedication service in which John and Irene Smucker and David Shenk participated. "The quality of Christian commitment and the vitality and vigorous outreach of this congregation" impressed Shenk. He encouraged the New York City Council of Mennonite Churches to develop a fraternal relationship with Joy Fellowship, "the semi-independent congregation pastored by Martin Bender." Shenk and his successor Freeman Miller maintained contact with Bender and his congregation. Miller expressed special interest in learning about Bender's methods of financing urban ministry. "I understand you have been very creative and successful" and Eastern Board might have a great deal to learn from Bender's example.[59]

Friendship Mennonite Church celebrated its 24th anniversary in January 1981. Faith Mennonite High School choir from Lancaster sang on Friday night. Some of the men from Hope Christian Center shared their testimony and Ike McKinnon from King's Full Gospel Tabernacle in New Jersey preached on Saturday night on "Visits, Visions, and Visitations," and Sunday night Herb Zwickel was the speaker with Hebrew Christian music by a group from Hurt's Christian Assembly. Ruth Burkholder, one of the original members, noted that

> Attendance has increased markedly in the last year and a half, needs are being met, more men are attending and becoming members, and the home Bible study groups represent good outreach and spiritual nourishment of new believers... If attendance continues to grow, we may have to have two Sunday morning services or divide to form another church.

Friendship counted 84 members in 1981, approaching the peak membership ten years earlier.[60]

Friendship Mennonite Church, like the other South Bronx churches, lost members in the next decade. The 1983 *Mennonite Yearbook* counted 61 members at Friendship and the 1984 *Yearbook* reported 55 members. The congregation had 53 members in 1991. Billie Thompson came to Friendship as pastor in 1990. He and his family were long-time members of the congregation. His wife began attending before he did, but he eventually joined the church and began giving more time to it, as an usher at first, then Sunday School teacher, and finally as pastor.

The neighborhood around Fellowship Chapel of the Brethren in Christ Church was also changing. The area became poorer with many more people on welfare and many single-parent families. In the early 1980s drugs and street crime increased sharply. The area had its share of abandoned buildings where landlords walked away or torched their own building. Some were rehabilitated, but the cost was prohibitive. It took over one million dollars to provide fifteen apartments.

Dan Farina served as pastor until the autumn of 1982. Terry Brensinger, a doctoral candidate at Drew, came to Fellowship early in 1983 and left in the summer of 1984. Henry N. Miller arrived as pastor in January 1985 and remained at Fellowship into the 1990s. Fellowship continued to reflect the cultural diversity of the Bronx. The multi-racial church board included Hispanics, African-Americans, West Indians, whites, and an Indian from Guyana. The worship expression also reflected the different ethnic backgrounds of the congregation. While the content was always "basic Brethren in Christ," the expression was fairly free with lots of Scripture choruses and tambourines.

The tutorial program continued with Jan Hykes and Premnath Dick taking responsibility for organizing volunteers. Fellowship Chapel had a recreation program for neighborhood children and a game room open several nights a week. In the summer they sent children to Camp Kenbrook and operated a Vacation Bible School.

The VS Unit also remained active, but VSers did not work in the regular church program. They were generally recent graduates of Messiah College and found outside employment in a variety of jobs as nurses, engineers, even an actuary, or with social service agencies. The VSers shared facilities with the congregation and took part in congregational life and worship. After their term of service ended, several VSers stayed on in the neighborhood or in upper Manhattan, all relating to Fellowship Chapel.[61]

Seventh Avenue Mennonite Church had earned the respect and friendship of the Harlem community over the years. The Head Start program, with 65 children enrolled in 1981, enjoyed enthusiastic community support. Over $60,000 came in voluntary contributions from Harlem residents to support Head Start. Paradoxically, Seventh Avenue was the only Harlem church with a white pastor and a congregation with about 75 percent of the people on the church roll black and 25 percent white. The large number of high school and college age young people comprised an active youth group and youth choir. Seventh Avenue had clubs to provide after-school activities for older children and operated a day camp and Fresh Air program in the summer.[62]

Richard Pannell's resignation as pastor in 1976 and the break-up of his marriage came as a blow to the congregation less than two years after the fire that destroyed their church.[63] Seventh Avenue had purchased the corner building in 1975 and renovated it for church, Head Start, and club facilities and held their first worship service there in April 1976. As they had the new building renovated, Seventh Avenue members joined together to give the church a new beginning. Olivia Peterson gave the club program a fresh start. Evelyn Brown organized the youth fellowship group. The congregation began holding weekly community meetings to get neighborhood action on deteriorating housing conditions, unemployment, and drug traffic.[64] The community program continued in 1981 as Harlem Against Lost Togetherness (HALT), a group of community residents and church members committed to improving conditions in housing, safety, education in Harlem. The Seventh Avenue Mennonite

Mennonite bishop Monroe and Rachel Yoder, front.
Rear, left to right: daughter Naomi, son Keith and wife Lisa.

Church helped establish contacts, encourage participation, and generally support these initiatives.

Monroe Yoder provided leadership as pastor at Seventh Avenue in this period of transition. When he was called to be the resident bishop for the New York City District, the congregation invited Gerald Keener, an energetic young man completing work at Eastern Mennonite Seminary. Gerry Keener became the Seventh Avenue pastor and part-time director of city-wide youth work in July 1978.[65] Gerry and Donna Zehr Keener initially lived on Mosholu Parkway in a middle-class section of the Bronx, but moved to an apartment in Harlem, four blocks from the church.

Gerry Keener picked up the concern for decent housing, especially for senior citizens, raised by Evelyn Brown and other Seventh Avenue members. He began looking for funding sources to rehabilitate the two five-story tenement buildings abandoned after the 1974 fire. He had been able to serve as catalyst in obtaining funds for an 85-apartment condominium complex, but funding for a half million dollar rehabilitation project was more elusive. "The deepening freeze of federal funding for further housing development in the community" was a keen disappointment to the Seventh Avenue congregation. Loan funds for reconstruction of the two buildings would have come through a federal program Section

Gerry Keener in his office at Heartsease Home at 216 East 70th street, Manhattan.

312, but "the present administration's policy of vastly accelerating military expenditures" and rapidly decreasing "programs related to the cause of the poor" eliminated the program. The Reagan Revolution had impacted Harlem within two months of the new president's inauguration.[66]

David Shenk thought the project "barely feasible financially and certainly a challenge for a 34-member congregation." He attempted to interest Habitat for Humanity, Mennonite Economic Development Association (MEDA) and individual Mennonite businessmen in the proposal.[67] In the spring of 1982 the Seventh Avenue congregation spent a weekend in prayer and fasting to decide what should be done and appointed a building committee. Eastern Board promised $100,000 in loans. The congregation would have to raise the rest. The committee looked at two options. They could raze the two existing buildings and construct a new chapel and commercial office space for $250,000 or they could rehabilitate the two buildings providing fifteen low-income apartments in addition to chapel and office space, for $600,000. They favored the second option. Was it even feasible? Dale Witmer, comptroller for the Horst Group, and Richard Martin, director of Menno Housing, helped them with financial questions.[68]

Projected costs rose rapidly. In July 1983 their architect estimated a cost of $659,510. Another estimate put the total cost of rebuilding at $791,510 plus $12,510 a year to maintain the two buildings. Eastern Board rounded it off to $800,000 for construction costs. The mission board could still loan no more than $100,000 and challenged Seventh Avenue to raise $50,000 locally. The rest would have to come from foundations, corporations, and individuals.[69]

Sylvia Horst headed the building fund drive and prepared a brochure, published in March 1984. Gerry Keener and Ponzella Peterson made a presentation on the building project at a Seventh Avenue Youth Choir concert at Good's Mennonite Church in December 1983. Ruth Yoder Wenger and Sherry Strong directed the choir, with David Wenger as accompanist. *The Mennonite Weekly Review* published an article, "Small New York Church Has Big Visions."[70]

The Harlem community and friends of the congregation contributed $13,000 in the first six months of the drive. This was a great deal for a congregation with 31 members and an average attendance of 35 in May 1983, increased a year later to 32 members and an average attendance of 40 in May 1984. For a project of this size it was only a gesture. Lindsey Robinson, Eastern Board Home Missions Secretary, commented, "Look around at this community and you see countless burned out and gutted buildings. No one is building in Harlem and we want to build so that people will realize there is hope."[71]

The project was scaled down somewhat. A 1985 proposal talked of renovating the two burned-out buildings by demolishing the upper three stories and turning the basement, street level and second floor into a community center. Fund raising strapped the resources of the congregation but the large-scale donations needed had not materialized. In September 1985 Gerry Keener had an offer of $70,000 for each of the buildings. He presented it to the congregation in October and Seventh Avenue agreed to sell, but this offer was later withdrawn.[72]

Donna Keener in her office at Heartsease Home.

A more modest effort in those same years proved more successful. Donna Zehr Keener worked at Heartsease Home. In May 1982 she was asked to design and direct a new residence for girls in Harlem, where six girls could learn independent living. The city and state would meet most costs of the program.

She located a suitable house at 463 West 143rd Street, a few blocks from Seventh Avenue Church, and on October 24 the Keeners moved to Rehoboth House to begin a new ministry.[73]

Rehoboth House, 463 West 143rd Street, Manhattan.

Congregational life is more than buildings and outreach to the community. Gerry Keener preached three times a month at Seventh Avenue. The worship and evangelism committee made the other Sundays available to "all persons in the Seventh Avenue congregation with the interest and gifts," as they wanted the people to share in the preaching. Seventh Avenue had a prayer and praise service one Friday evening a month. The committee, comprised of Jean Pierce, Ross Bender, Gerry Keener, Ken Brown, Lucy Vance, and Sylvia Horst in 1982, selected a series on "The People of God in Community" for Sunday worship services. The informal worship style in 1985 included praise, intercession, testimony, prayer, teaching, and inspiration. Renewal of the church school program and leadership development headed Seventh Avenue's goals in 1985.

The congregation included twenty family units in its 32 members. About 60 people attended worship more or less regularly. The church touched about 250 people in the community through the club program, with 15 children, day camp, with 40 children, and Head Start, with 60 children. A congregational meeting in 1985 rated evangelism "very poor" and saw a need for more work with youth and young adults.[74]

Seventh Avenue's next pastor, Jimmy Johnson, was expected to begin an evangelism explosion. The new pastor came from Philadelphia where he had been associate pastor with Willie Richardson of Christian Stronghold Baptist Church in West Philadelphia. His background included training in evangelism and church growth. Freeman Miller noted that Johnson "is used to a more centralized, aggressive, single pastor leadership style than Seventh Avenue" had experienced. He felt that "more black male leadership" was needed in the church to attract men from the Harlem community. The Seventh Avenue congregation was reluctant to accept this new approach at first. The Martin Luther King commemoration service at Seventh Avenue in January 1987 "seemed to pull old and new members, including the pastor and his family, together in a new way" and to suggest the congregation was ready to work with Johnson. "I certainly hope the congregation can support Jimmy long enough to give him a chance to get settled and to exercise some of his gifts in leadership."[75]

To some members Johnson's leadership spelled "turmoil and badgering within the congregation." As an example, one member told Freeman Miller, "Jimmy Johnson wants to have Sunday evening services so he plans to have baptism, communion, and the Easter program on Sunday evenings." Rather than growing, "the congregation is diminishing" and some long-term members were "close to leaving."[76] In 1988 Johnson resigned as pastor and left Seventh Avenue.[77] Monroe Yoder returned to the congregation as interim pastor.

Seventh Avenue, like the other Lancaster churches, saw a steady reduction in the subsidy from Eastern Board from 1981 on. At the end of the decade the congregation was self-supporting. Its survival with only 32 members was a mark of its strength and its place in the Harlem community.

Burnside Mennonite Church committed itself to the block by block evangelization of the immediate neighborhood in the 1980s. The congregation grew steadily through the decade. Like the other New York churches, Burnside had to become totally self-supporting as Eastern Board gradually reduced its subsidy.

Lunch time at Head Start Program at Seventh Avenue Mennonite Church.

The Head Start program, begun in 1978, gave Burnside outreach into the community. Lori Kennel was the first VSer assigned to the new program. Charlene Landis Hoover divided her time between Seventh Avenue and Burnside Head Start in 1979-1980. One group of children from three to five years old came in the morning and another in the afternoon. Parents worked with the program, filling half the staff positions. They also had a speech specialist, social worker, and psychologist as staff persons. Lucy Vance directed both programs. Tony Miller helped the following year as a Head Start aide. Irene Peters, the VSer who helped Addie and Michael Banks find the Mennonite Church, also worked with the Burnside Head Start during her term of service in New York from September 1978 to June 1981.

Glenn Zeager talks to two Head Start pupils at Burnside.

Alfred Yoder worked with the Burnside and Seventh Avenue Head Start. Lucy Vance believed both Tony and Alfred strengthened the program, "because many of the children do not have strong male role models in their lives." Ken Bontrager succeeded Alfred Yoder, working two days a week at Seventh Avenue and three days a week at Burnside.[78]

Darryl Wenger and Irene Peters were both involved in youth work at Burnside and assisted Sam Walters, the pastor, in visitation in the community. They ran the children's clubs and the summer day camp program. Darryl did some after school tutoring as well.[79]

In September 1982 Burnside Mennonite Church began a new After School Program. Sharon Kuhns, a VSer, gave continuity by being there every afternoon and helping to organize the events. The 25 neighborhood children had help in completing homework assignments, or if they had no homework, received help in going over lessons. They spent time in a Bible class and had a nutritious meal each afternoon. Some mothers volunteered to help. John Stahl-Wert, Eastern Board VS Administrator, saw the program in action and saw a need for more mothers to help "with all those kids."[80]

On a visit with Samuel Walters in 1982, David Shenk noted: "The Burnside congregation is committing itself to community outreach" and experienced both "growth in attendance" and "people coming to faith in

Christ."[81] The congregation had 30 members in May 1982 and an average attendance of 43.

A congregational meeting in May 1982 affirmed two of their own members Michael and Addie Banks "for pursuit of further training" for Christian ministry and anticipated their return to Burnside. They hoped to spend "a year in a Bible institute to sharpen their tools for evangelism." David Shenk pledged to support the congregation in this effort. Eastern Board paid for their year at Elim Bible Institute in Lima, New York and arranged for them to spend the summer of 1983 with John Perkins at the Voice of Calvary in Mendenhall, Mississippi.[82]

The Burnside congregation provided an internship in the summer of 1982 for Desmond Miller, a student at Eastern Mennonite Seminary. When Michael and Addie Banks returned from Mississippi in 1983, Samuel Walters proposed a similar internship for them. Walters and elder Lowell Jantzi reported Mike's interest in working with Burnside to David Shenk. They would talk with him to determine in what specific areas he could best be employed. They requested a subsidy of $800 a month for four months from Eastern Board for his family's support enabling him to give full-time to the internship. David Shenk agreed and arranged with Eastern Mennonite Seminary for reading assignments during the internship. Walters and Jantzi proposed that Michael Banks preach once a month and teach the Wednesday night Bible study. Mike and Addie together would be responsible for youth ministry. They would direct the tutoring program and include black and Hispanic studies to help students develop a positive image and affirmative goals. In addition, Mike would relate to senior citizens in a nearby nursing home. David Shenk approved all of this, but added

> There is one area of ministry which I believe is very close to Michael and Addie Banks, but which is not specifically mentioned in your job description. This has to do with evangelism. So often in the life of a congregation, we do get programmatically involved, and the work of evangelism can be neglected. I feel deeply about that when a leadership couple has specific gifts for evangelism.

He recommended an assignment for "evangelistic outreach, which may include such things as street meetings and visitation."[83]

After nurturing Michael Banks' gifts for ministry, Samuel Walters was ready to turn the Burnside Mennonite Church over to him as pastor. Walters asked to be released from the Burnside pastorate in June 1984, and Samuel and Shirley Walters moved to Lancaster in August. Michael Banks became Burnside pastor on September 1, 1984.[84]

Burnside Mennonite Church had a group committed to street ministry in 1984 with on-going door to door evangelism, primarily within the immediate neighborhood. Members of the congregation led Bible studies and trained for evangelism in the fall and winter, moving out to street meetings in the spring and summer. Michael and Addie Banks had returned from their work at Voice of Calvary Ministries with a vision for community. "We hoped to bring about a kingdom community via evangelization of the neighborhoods, block by block for Christ!" They "encountered sobering realities as we shared our vision for community," both from church members and from the neighborhoods to whom "the idea of Christian community evoked something foreign and cultic."[85]

The other goals of the congregation, as Banks described them in 1984, included preparing "the local body to effectively minister a holistic gospel," a preparation that demanded Bible literacy, identification and cultivation of spiritual gifts, and "a close ongoing examination of accountability and commitment as it relates to this church's call to be a prophetic voice in the Bronx," developing the interior life, and supporting and developing Christian family.[86]

The homeless and those suffering from mental breakdowns attracted Michael and Addie Banks' concern. "His family has taken in some homeless people and the church is ministering to homeless people regularly." He had a vision for the building next door, moving in his own family, a few others, and providing community for some homeless people. "Michael would like to open a special home just for them," Freeman Miller wrote, "but I am concerned that he and his family might pour too much energy into that one important ministry to the neglect of both family and congregation."

The Burnside neighborhood experienced a renaissance in the late 1980s with new housing and new families moving in. The drastic reduction in Eastern Board subsidy, on the other hand, seemed too sudden. Burnside was making a fresh start, but "a continuous subsidy reduction that is already in the sixth year" threatened the church's rebirth. Eastern Board's formula needed to be modified to better match the congregation's effort at this time with a goal of self-support.[87]

The Burnside church had 38 members and an average attendance of 54 in May 1984. Two years later the congregation counted 50 members and an average attendance of 70 in May 1986. There were 7 baptisms and 10 conversions in 1986.[88] Burnside had 63 members by 1990.

The tutoring program expanded. Michael Banks directed the program with Elizabeth Weaver, a recent Goshen graduate, as assistant director in

1988 when it grew into "Project Charisma." The program proposed to do more than prepare youngsters from ten to fourteen for the next day's classroom assignments. "Through Project Charisma we intend to provide them with new role models and to promote a new peer group with new values." Volunteers from the community and professionals worked with the children "to rechannel their energies and abilities into new constructive directions." The program would involve Bronx colleges, social service agencies, and network of arts and culture groups as well as public school teachers and principals in the effort to "empower children by helping them identify their skills and talents" and build their confidence "with a curriculum that stresses creative expression." The program operated Monday through Thursday afternoons from 3 to 6 during the school year, with one day a week for cultural enrichment. The summer program, with day camp and trips, kept the youngsters interested when school was out.[89]

As Project Charisma took off, changes in the Voluntary Service program enabled Michael and Addie Banks to link the congregation and the VS Unit with an intentional community. The Banks family would move to 1114 Sherman Avenue as household pastors. All VSers would participate in the Burnside congregation and two VSers would be assigned full-time to Project Charisma, beginning in 1989.[90] This was the beginning of Pilgrim's Way, an intentional Christian Community sponsored by Discipleship Ministries of Eastern Board as a vital part of the Burnside ministry.[91]

Voluntary Service and Discipleship

The concept of voluntary service changed in the 1980s as church agencies put less emphasis on the service VSers could do and more on how the service experience could train the young people who signed on for it. Eastern Board developed Summer Training Action Team (STAT) and Youth Evangelism Service (YES) in addition to traditional long-term voluntary service. Since the city churches did not seem to want help as they once did, Eastern Board asked a committee of New York City pastors and congregational leaders to explore what new approaches would better meet urban needs. Michael Banks advised the committee, "We need to build communities. This is the strength of Mennonite Anabaptist theology. With community and unity is power."[92] Voluntary service assignments reflected some of these new approaches, responding to initiatives from New York.

John Elmer and Alfred Yoder joined Ulli Klemm at the Sherman Avenue VS Unit in September 1981. Sylvia Horst moved into the unit in November to begin work at the Peace Center. In January 1982 Mary Ann

Zehr completed the group. Sylvia and Ulli, as the older members of the unit, by two or three years, smiled tolerantly at the youthful antics of the others.

> In January 1982 a co-ed subgroup of the VS Unit ("we bad") "boothopped" cars. While the unit leader was absent from the vicinity, they loitered on the street corners grabbing bumpers of cars as the cars slowed down for red lights and accelerated again. The ice-covered street provided a slick course on which the adventurous trio slid for as long as they could hold onto a car. The members of this VS subgroup had moderate success in boothopping a limousine. They all felt daring and clever, but arrived home cold and wet. Sylvia and Ulli had nothing to do with the winter sport.

Mary Ann Zehr worked as secretary in the Mennonite Church office at Burnside. Mary Ann and John took Spanish classes at Lehman College and they both tutored youngsters after school. Mary Ann helped with Good Shepherd Bible clubs, but she found a church home at Cuerpo de Cristo Mennonite Church in the Corona section of Queens, where she taught a youth Sunday school class. "The language sometimes causes difficulties, as some persons in her class do not speak any English."

John Elmer worked full-time at the Morris Heights Mennonite Church, a Spanish-speaking church in a Bronx neighborhood with "many kids and youth who do not have positive outlets for their activity needs." John's main assignment was to develop a community center in the church building. "Each day he has 15-25 neighborhood kids come by to play games, become involved in athletic activities, or take field trips with him." He had regular Bible studies with the kids and worked hard at building relationships between the church and the neighborhood. He taught a Sunday school class and taught English to some of the adults in the Morris Heights congregation. He also organized a food pantry at the church.[93]

John continued teaching English to church members three nights a week. His basketball ministry was in full swing. He took twenty kids to a Yankees game and planned a block party at the Morris Heights Church.[94]

The Morris Heights Mennonite Church was a Spanish-speaking church, made up primarily of recent immigrants from the Dominican Republic. Church members drove in from other areas and did not live in the immediate neighborhood of the church. The children and teenagers John Elmer contacted were English-speaking African-Americans. John kept the center open every afternoon. He had Bible studies for different age groups and learned to know many parents. "The work that John has developed at Morris Heights is very much community-based in that he is touching the lives of families in the immediate Morris Heights community, but it is not founded on the Morris Heights Mennonite Church because of the language difference." Juan Suero, the pastor, was open at first to this community outreach, but it became clear that a community center in a predominantly African-American neighborhood could not relate to a Spanish-speaking church. John Elmer hoped to develop a church-planting project in the Morris Heights neighborhood, "maintaining the contacts he has built with kids and families."[95]

Two of John's Messiah College classmates helped him in his ministry. Tom Hale worked for the Sudan Interior Mission office in New York as a computer programmer. Gwen Lomakin was employed by Columbia Presbyterian Medical Center as a pediatric nurse. The three of them led Bible studies and worked with the Bible Club program at Morris Heights. John's college roommate, Dan Drawbaugh, completed his studies at Temple University and went to work as a bio-medical engineer in Philadelphia after graduation. Brian Fulmer, a member of the Neffsville Mennonite Church, worked in Lancaster in investment management. The five friends had talked and prayed about planting a church in the Bronx and believed the Lord was leading them to build a body of believers there. Joe Blaise also helped with the community center.

In the spring of 1983 they approached the New York City Council of Mennonite Churches, asking "for your permission and blessing to continue in our effort to follow the Lord's calling to plant a new church in the Bronx for the advancement of God's Kingdom." John Elmer conducted

Citywide Council of New York City Mennonite Churches. Left to right: Ray Morales, Cecilia Robinson, Anna Kuhns, John Smucker, Herb Zwickel, Monroe Yoder.

"his first English service at Morris Heights with contacts he has made through his community center."[96]

John had served as unit leader at the VS house and every report spoke highly of his work there and in the Morris Heights community. But the Morris Heights congregation was unhappy with his work with neighborhood people who had no connection with their church. Except for occasional conversations, John Elmer and Juan Suero, the pastor, did not communicate or attempt to keep each other informed. Ross Goldfus, Atlantic Coast Conference overseer, and Monroe Yoder, Lancaster Conference bishop, advised termination. "John ended his VS assignment in profound frustration and disappointment" in September 1983. VS administrator John Stahl-Wert saw it as "the logical conclusion of a VS assignment which is not held accountable to a congregational base of leadership" and dashed the hopes of community people who were being ministered to by him. "This should give us great pause when thinking about ways that we can develop program and furnish leadership outside the context of a partnership with a local congregation."[97]

Another new mission opportunity opened with the placement of a VSer with the Council of Churches of the City of New York. Dan Shenk, a Lancaster Mennonite and a staff member in Pastoral Care Ministries, opened conversation between CCCNY and Eastern Board. The Department of Christian Social Relations, which addressed broadly defined justice issues in the city, was understaffed and welcomed a VS appointment. Mark Bullock, the first VSer at the Council of Churches office, began in October 1983 working in Pastoral Care Ministries under Dan Shenk's supervision. His assignment was the growing problem of homelessness in the city and finding ways to involve churches in responding to this need. Financial problems and deep staff cuts resulted in Shenk's reduction to half-time and Bullock being given sole responsibility for the entire program of Christian Social Relations.[98]

In March 1980 eight young Mennonites from the city took part in a New Call to Peacemaking seminar. One of the topics under discussion was the possibility of establishing local centers for peacemaking. After returning home, they formed the New York City Committee for New Call to Peacemaking and designated Sylvia Horst as chair. Ardis Grosjean, Myrna Burkholder, David Wenger, and John Bauman attended the initial meeting. Prem Dick of East Harlem Interfaith joined the committee at its second meeting. They proposed "a Center for Peacemaking as a visible peace witness in New York City" to help congregations promote peacemaking and to serve as a resource on peace issues. They thought a full-time voluntary service worker should direct the activities of the center and approached John K. Stoner of the MCC Peace Section about staffing. The committee continued meeting for about a year before they were ready to begin. John Bauman, Myrna Burkholder, Prem Dick, Ardis Grosjean, Sylvia Horst, and David Wenger were the original committee members. Evelyn Brown and Henry Muller became active later on. Early in their planning, Sylvia Horst offered to be a self-supporting VSer under Eastern Board, working part-time to provide income and giving the rest of her time to the project.[99]

Sylvia Horst, a graduate of Eastern Mennonite College, had moved to New York as a social worker and became active in Seventh Avenue Mennonite Church. She was bilingual, speaking and writing Spanish with ease. The committee recognized her as the ideal person for the job and asked her to apply to Eastern Board for a one-year commitment with the possibility of extending it to two years.

Pastor Mateo offered the Mennonite Church office at Burnside as the location for the Peace Center.[100] After Sylvia met with Richard Thomas, the Lancaster Commission on Peace and Social Concerns contributed $800 for the 1982 Peace Center budget. She was accountable to Pastor Mateo for her management of time and her peace-related activities. She trained with the Central Committee on Conscientious Objection as a draft counselor and worked with each of the New York churches.

Sylvia began her year with orientation at Salunga. Eastern Board representatives met with her while she was at Salunga to help focus the vision. "It was affirmed that peace education is important in the congregation, as some youth in New York City congregations do not see peace as the heart of the Gospel." In developing plans for a longer-term ministry, they advised the New York committee to explore a Victim Offender Program or mediation service since "theological understanding of peace happens in the context of peacemaking rather than in abstract discussion groups." Richard Thomas, for Lancaster Conference, and Urbane Peachey, for Atlantic Coast Conference, would work with Horst to provide resources and support for "this important project in New York City."[101]

The Peace Center program initially concentrated on peace education in the congregation. Sylvia spoke to youth in each of the churches and made a list of recommended readings. She was particularly effective in Spanish-speaking congregations and translated peace materials for their use. She also became the local contact person for two new MCC programs, a community development project for urban minority college students and IMPACT, the Inter-Mennonite Program for Alternatives in Career

Training, which provided opportunities for urban youth to take advanced occupational training and gain work experience. Sylvia supervised Juan Peters' urban community development project and arranged for a Seventh Avenue member, Junior Brock, to be enrolled in a technical school in the IMPACT program. She coordinated Mennonite activities connected with the Disarmament Campaign in June 1982. All of this was time consuming, but the need to fund the Peace Center for its second year took even more of her time.[102]

The New York City Council of Mennonite Churches submitted a proposal to Eastern Board for a permanent Peace Center with a part-time director. With limited funds, and a need to reduce the budget below 1982 levels, Eastern Board could contribute only $1,000.[103] New York City congregations came up with $775. MCC donated $1,133. Victor F. Weaver contributed $1,000 and so did the General Conference Mennonite Church.[104]

As a VSer, Sylvia Horst participated in the life of the unit, worked with the after-school clubs at Seventh Avenue, and taught Sunday school there. Sylvia Horst married Ross Bender in October 1982 and completed her VS year in November. She continued with the Peace Center as a volunteer for another year. In her second year she gave considerable time to the Urban Community Development Program and IMPACT. She developed a seminar on conflict resolution with Ron Kraybill as resource person. She began working to develop church sanctuaries for immigrants from Central America. Her committee thought the latter too time-consuming and she passed this concern on to others. She continued her task of translating peacemaking materials into Spanish. Sylvia and David Wenger worked with the Coalition Against Militarism to end Junior ROTC and provide draft counseling in high schools.

In her two years, Sylvia Horst spoke to every New York Mennonite congregation at least once. "Messages (in English or Spanish) dealt with peacemaking themes in the Old and New Testaments. Week-night presentations, especially to youth groups, have centered on conscientious objection and alternatives to the military. City-wide programs featured such themes as 'Conscientious Objection and War Taxes,' 'Peace and Justice,' and 'Conflict Resolution.'"[105]

Ross Bender and Sylvia Horst moved to Elkhart in December 1983 to enroll at Associated Mennonite Biblical Seminary. Sylvia proposed that Wanda Santini, a member of First Mennonite Church of Brooklyn, and a student at Hunter College, take her place. She had been involved in Peace Center activities and had asked about working there. Wanda continued the work of the Peace Center in 1984.[106]

Restructuring voluntary service in New York City made it more responsive to urban needs and emphasized the strengths that Mennonites brought to the city. In 1987 the New York City Council of Mennonite Churches appointed Michael and Addie Banks, Ken Bontrager, Gerry Keener, and Vincente Martinez to a committee to evaluate VS. The committee discovered "a great deal of stress in their day-to-day ministries" as well as "a great deal of in-house conflict" within the unit. Michael Banks led a series of Bible studies on "Becoming a Healing Community" with the VSers.

In 1988 Discipleship Ministries again looked at VS in New York City with termination as one option. After completing a survey of VSers who had served the city in the previous ten years and discussions with a new New York City Discipleship Commission, composed of Ken Bontrager, Addie Banks, Michael Banks, Gerry Keener, and Elizabeth Weaver, the NYC VS administrator Brian Ebersole decided to make a fresh start.

Michael and Addie Banks moved into the VS Unit at 1114 Sherman Avenue in October 1988 as household pastors to begin an intentional Christian Community. In time the community chose the name Pilgrim's Way. The VSers who became part of Pilgrim's Way were Clarke Bell, who worked with "We Can," a redemption center that helped the homeless to earn money through recycling aluminum cans, and three workers in the Project Charisma after-school program at Burnside, Doug Olson, Tim Miller, and Deb Sharp. Later, Clarke Bell began a ministry to homeless people, living with them in the streets and in shelters.

Michael Banks described Pilgrim's Way Community as seeking to "express the principles of kingdom living, through an urban relevant prophetic community, committed to service, hospitality, and the declaration of the good news."[107]

Growing Churches in Manhattan and the Bronx

In 1985 David W. Shenk, as director of home missions for Eastern Board, sketched a vision for church growth in New York City. Existing congregations would expand to 150-200 in each worship community. One or two new congregations would begin every year, including "one flourishing center city congregation which is particularly attuned to young professionals," "at least one flourishing congregation in every major language group in New York City," with priority to Chinese, Haitian Creole, Ethiopian, Garifuna, and Vietnamese church plantings, and "six flourishing suburban congregations on the city fringes."[108]

Urban Mennonites had been aware of the new immigration changing the ethnic composition of the city. Church growth theory targeted homogeneous groups like these for proclamation of the Gospel. Shenk recognized an equal need to plant churches among groups already Mennonite—young professionals moving to the city and young professionals displaced by the continuing deterioration of the city neighborhoods where they formerly lived. For them, as for the newcomers from Central America or East Asia, the Gospel needed to be contextualized. Traditional patterns were not enough.

About 150 students and young professionals of Mennonite background lived and worked in New York City in the 1980s, but only one in six attended any of the Mennonite churches in the city. They either did not participate in any church or attended churches of other denominations. Myrna Burkholder was one of those who sensed the need for "a congregation in New York City that would relate to the interests and spiritual needs of some of these persons, and which would provide a congregational setting to which these persons can bring their peers."[109] In 1978 some of these young adults expressed interest in meaningful worship and Bible study. Gene Shelly began a fellowship group at Menno House for them, but it did not develop as hoped. Myrna proposed a Sunday morning service at Menno House once a month in 1979-1980 school year, but this did not work out either.[110]

Peace Mennonite Fellowship met the needs of some young New Yorkers. Mel Lehman, Ardis Grosjean, Gloria Leinbach, Lin Garber, and Arthur Berk were among the "Anabaptist radicals" who began meeting for fellowship in the late 1970s. Arthur Berk, a Quaker activist, had belonged to the Morning Star Community. Mel Lehman was responsible for revitalizing the Mennonite graduate student meetings and later developing programs at Menno House under Student and Young Adult Services. Others in the group organized seminars for young Mennonite professionals. Artists Erma Martin Yost, Ardis Grosjean, and Susan Ebersole planned the May 1979 arts seminar. In the early 1980s John Bauman, pastor at Glad Tidings, and his wife Susan Ebersole, Columbia graduate students Daniel and Mary Lemons, and Daniel and Mary Classen Born played a leading part in the informal fellowship.[111]

Peace Mennonite Fellowship took formal shape by 1981. Michael and Alice Bender were the contact persons. "This group of believers, most of whom are young adults, meet on the first four Sunday evenings of each month. Meetings consist of worship, Bible study, and sharing of spiritual pilgrimages. About 15-20 persons attend each meeting." Fellowship members met in each other's homes at five o'clock. A monthly mailing went out to interested persons describing the next month's meeting. Although several key members were also active in Lancaster Conference churches, Seventh Avenue and Glad Tidings, Peace Mennonite Fellowship affiliated with Eastern District of the General Conference Mennonite Church. It was listed in the 1981-82 and 1982-83 General Conference *Handbook* with Ross Bender designated as leader.[112] One member recalled, "Nobody funded Peace Mennonite Fellowship. You just had to bring wine and cheese."[113]

Informality characterized the fellowship. There were "ten or fifteen young adults" meeting regularly in each other's homes in 1982. Myrna Burkholder wrote of Lin Garber and Mel Lehman as "both active in giving leadership to Peace Mennonite Fellowship this year." Susan Ebersole and John Bauman were involved in leadership, too.[114] Ross Bender was the designated leader in the *Handbook*, but they were all leaders. Asked what were the dynamics that made Peace Mennonite Fellowship worthwhile, Erma Martin Yost stressed that it was "not institutionalized or organized." Many fellowship members were consciously fleeing a church "where all believe and all do exactly the same." Another member recalled, "You didn't have to prove yourself." At Peace Mennonite Fellowship, "the group was open and inclusive enough" that he felt comfortable and "I assumed people felt comfortable with me." He knew that his identity as a gay man would be an issue if he were to "formalize his connection with the Mennonite Church." One member remembered that "others left in the early days because of an incapacity to agree on anything." The group was a "meeting of minds," another said, and they preferred discussion to singing. "We didn't sing all that much." The group included "people with a positive Mennonite Church experience in Virginia" who wanted worship services as well as "people escaping that kind of church."[115]

Most members of the fellowship went regularly to other churches. Ross Bender and Sylvia Horst were involved in Seventh Avenue. John Bauman had obligations at Glad Tidings. Caroline Little attended a Presbyterian church for a while, then went to Grace Episcopal. Eric Alderfer sang in the choir at St. Ann's Episcopal Church. Susan Ebersole attended St. John the Divine. Myrna Burkholder and Dan Shenk went to Judson Memorial Baptist Church.[116]

When Myrna Burkholder left New York for Elkhart, Susan Ebersole succeeded her as director of Student and Young Adult Services in the city. She edited *The Menno News* from 1981. Other active members of the Peace Mennonite Fellowship left the city about the same time. The Fellowship began to change. Susan Ebersole "played a pivotal role" in the changes, one member recalled. "Susan had a lot to do with reorganization around

Fifteenth Street Friends Meeting House, 15 Rutherford Place, Manhattan, the meeting place of the Manhattan Mennonite Fellowship. 2005 photo.

1983," another remembered, through *The Menno News* and the Menno Committee.

A new fellowship, "the 'Upper-West-Side-Manhattan' fellowship (presently unnamed)," had its first monthly meeting on September 12, 1982 with about forty people in attendance. They shared a pot-luck supper in the basement of the Broadway Presbyterian Church at 114th Street and Broadway. "Beth Heisey was worship leader for the evening, David Bishop song leader, and Dan Shenk gave a very eloquent meditation on the theme of 'waiting for God' using the illustration of the harlot who anointed Christ's feet." Families with children were pleased that child care was provided. The group agreed that "the main purpose of the group was to worship together given our disparate positions and interests." The Menno Committee planned themes of meetings and selected speakers.[117]

The Manhattan Mennonite Fellowship organized in 1983. The emerging congregation looked to Mary Classen Born and Mel Lehman for pastoral leadership. They maintained Peace Mennonite Fellowship's link with Eastern District of the General Conference Mennonite Church, but affiliated with the Mennonite Church through the New York City Council of Mennonite Churches.

After meeting for some time in the Broadway Presbyterian Church, the small cluster of "about 20 core participants" moved their evening worship service and shared meal to the Fifteenth Street Meeting House of the Religious Society of Friends. The Quaker Meeting House is located only a short walk from Menno House. David Shenk observed in 1985 that:

> The Midtown Manhattan Fellowship is blessed with a strong and committed leadership who work in complementarity and consultation... The fellowship has been discussing what the nature of its mission should be in the city and whether they should move towards more regular meetings with increased church and urban mission intentionality.[118]

The Manhattan fellowship seemed a natural vehicle for a ministry that had long concerned David Shenk. In 1985 he talked with Mary Classen Born about a Mennonite presence at the United Nations. He had initiated conversations with John A. Lapp, Executive Secretary, and others at MCC and they responded favorably. "Mennonite Central Committee is prepared to provide half time support for a missioner assigned to the United Nations, providing such a missioner is also actively involved in the life and ministry of a local New York City church."[119]

The Mennonite Central Committee Ecumenical Peace Project came together in 1986 with the appointment of J. R. Burkholder as United Nations missioner. One of his first activities was a retreat with the Manhattan Fellowship. David Shenk was encouraged by "what is happening in that congregation" but felt they might need Burkholder's help to move "in the direction of more church and ministry intentionality."[120] The Manhattan Mennonite Fellowship took initiative in developing United Nations contacts. In October 1986 Mel Lehman spoke to wives of U.N. ambassadors. Shenk urged him to see the Manhattan fellowship as "the spiritual home for a ministry to the United Nations" and encourage the congregation to develop the vision, philosophy and purpose of such a mission.[121]

During 1986 the congregation scrutinized the link with Menno House and its ministry and became "more intentional in their church and mission commitment."[122] As a result the Manhattan Mennonite Fellowship "agreed to organize into a formal church and to call a pastor to give leadership to the congregation." Freeman Miller, who succeeded David Shenk at Eastern Board Home Missions, visited the group soon afterwards for a Sunday evening service. "They had 23 people present and nice worship service of Scripture readings, prayers, hymns, and a very good sermon by John Smucker.... He gave a clear call to remain focused and unashamed in our urban ministry and encouraged us to recapture some of the early Anabaptist fever for urban evangelization." Mel Lehman and Merv Stoltzfus led the worship.[123]

The search for a pastor moved slowly. Becky Kurtz, chair of the pastoral search committee, reported that the congregation called John D. Rempel as pastor on a three-quarter time basis in May 1989. He had served as chaplain at Conrad Grebel College in Waterloo, Ontario, for the previous fifteen years. A graduate of AMBS with a doctorate in theology from Toronto, "John will be an excellent pastor and church-builder for Manhattan Mennonite Fellowship and also an important resource for the Mennonite churches in New York City."[124]

John Rempel joined Manhattan Mennonite Fellowship as their minister in October 1989. The elders at that time were Gloria Leinbach, Deb Augsburger, and Ruth Ann Stauffer. Becky Kurtz was administrative chair and Ruth Ann Stauffer treasurer of the congregation.[125] Although Manhattan Mennonite Fellowship has no Mennonite Church conference affiliation, Eastern Board contributed $6,000 toward their expenses in 1990.[126] On a visit in March 1990 Freeman Miller found the congregation "off to a new start with the arrival of their new pastor, John Rempel." Miller had "several meetings with the pastor and several letters from members of this young church" and recommended that Eastern Board "respond warmly to their overtures for ongoing fraternal relationships in our work in New York."[127]

In 1991 Manhattan Mennonite Fellowship counted 34 members and 8 "friends of MMF" in its membership directory. Nancy Benignus and Gloria Leinbach were elders. Steve Troyer was administrative chair and Merv Horst treasurer. The members included "a few couples, one child, one baby, and a lot of singles."[128]

Another emerging fellowship, the North Bronx Mennonite Church, followed a similar pattern. In this case, the mostly young professionals had moved from deteriorating neighborhoods. They continued to give freely of their time and talent to one of the inner-city Mennonite churches, but by the mid-1980s these churches were in crisis. As early as 1981 Bishop Monroe Yoder related that a "group of persons from Glad Tidings" and "other Mennonites who live in the Northwest Bronx" had formed a fellowship.

> After Gene Shelly was no longer responsible for Good Shepherd, they [the Shellys] began to have Sunday School and worship in their home for their children and their friends. This grew to a number that Gene felt he needed some help. Others were interested in having something in the community in which they live. So they combined the groups and the fellowship involves several families with children and several single persons. The group will soon need to decide whether they continue as a fellowship or if they can grow into a church.[129]

This fellowship continued to meet for a time, but did not grow into a church.

The North Bronx Mennonite had its beginning in the summer of 1986 when "a group of Mennonite professionals" began to "meet together for prayer" on a regular schedule. "The indications are that this core group will be taking steps during the coming year to form a new congregation in the North Bronx."[130] These people had participated in the Mennonite churches of the city "for periods of time ranging from fifteen to twenty years or more." During this time they had "experienced excitement, encouragement, and a sense that they were a part of God's purpose in New York." For a variety of reasons they saw the need for "a church with a somewhat different character, focus, ministry, and agenda" from the Mennonite churches they had known in the city. They met at first just to discuss church, then turned to planning for a new church. In the process, they lost a few, added a few.[131]

Jesus and Miriam Cruz from Glad Tidings, David and Ruth Wenger and Marian Sauder from Seventh Avenue formed the core group. Monroe and Rachel Yoder, as bishop couple, also met with the group. In the summer of 1987 the core group drew up a statement of purpose and formed committees to select leadership and determine a location for the new church. The statement of purpose spelled out their intention to be a church that is intergenerational, educating its members toward mature Christian living, serving the local community and the world-wide community, a church where people with a variety of backgrounds and experience will feel welcomed, a church that encourages freedom and creativity in formal and informal worship services, and a church that offers small group fellowship. Above all, it was to be a church obedient to Christ, with the Bible as the final rule for faith and practice, and interpreting Scripture in the Anabaptist perspective. They listed the characteristics of Anabaptism drawn from J. C. Wenger's *How Mennonites Came to Be.*[132] They knew that such a church would draw others. They were sure they could have twenty if they began that fall, but they didn't want to be hasty. They wanted to challenge the church's colleges "to send one of their best to the North Bronx," suggesting Don Augsburger, J. R. Burkholder, or Ray Gingerich. The four couples and one single adult met with Freeman Miller, who encouraged them "to press vigorously ahead toward their dream." He responded to the suggestion that one of the church institutions send a theologian on sabbatical "to give birth to this new style of New York congregation."[133]

Marian Sauder speaks to Tom Finger, pastor of North Bronx Mennonite Church.

Thomas N. Finger, a Mennonite theologian, spent several weeks in the Bronx in November 1987. He left his wife and children in Chicago and lived in a Catholic religious community during his stay in the Bronx. The congregation called him as their pastor in December. Tom Finger returned in mid-January 1988 to work with the congregation in planting a church. They chose the Norwood section, a diverse but stable neighborhood. "They have decided that they do not want to start as a house fellowship but have the goal of becoming a church from the word go." The group chose North Bronx Mennonite Church as their name.

North Bronx Mennonite Church met initially in a Lutheran church on Sunday afternoons. In February 1988 Rev. Paul Brandt, S. J., campus chaplain at Fordham University, invited the new Mennonite fellowship to hold services in the university chapel. Father Brandt encouraged them to invite Protestant students. *The Ram*, the Fordham newspaper, published an article about the Mennonite church meeting in historic St. John's Chapel. The Sunday morning schedule there began with coffee and doughnuts at nine, followed by a Christian educational hour with two separate classes. The children studied a Bible story which they presented as a skit during the worship service. One member of the fellowship commented: "It is wonderful to go to church and know that when Tom stands up to preach the sermon will be good."[134]

The core group expanded to include Lorraine Weaver, Marty and Jewel Van Ord, and "a number of people from the neighborhood." There continued to be some confusion about their role as guests of the Fordham campus ministry and what was appropriate outreach to students. Father Brant encouraged them to make surveys in the summer and plan on campus outreach the following year, but the president of the university overruled him and asked the fellowship to leave the campus at the end of the summer.[135]

North Bronx Mennonite Church migrated to St. Stephen's Episcopal Church Parish House in Woodlawn in September. The congregation there was friendly, urging the small Mennonite group to join them each Sunday morning for their coffee hour. The Mennonites were able to have Sunday school and worship on the same schedule as at Fordham, but instead of free facilities they had to pay $250 a month rent. They were guaranteed use through March 1989, but they were intrigued by the possibility of using Holy Nativity Episcopal Church in Norwood, since that was the neighborhood they had chosen as a permanent location for the new church. Attendance remained constant in the 20s and 30s and the congregation recognized outreach as their most important priority. They depended on friendship evangelism rather than newspaper advertisements or telemarketing the church. Growth was depressingly slow. About 20 people were "ready to commit to this church, but some were not interested and withdrew." A mailing in the fall did not bring any additional people. Joseph and Carol Kotva and Margaret Blanks were the only new names on the visionary committee in January 1989.[136]

Tom Finger planned to return to teaching at Eastern Mennonite Seminary in the fall of 1989. In beginning the pastoral search process, congregational leaders assessed their progress so far. They recognized that there had been little growth in numbers. "Growth takes time, but perhaps numbers are not the most important aspect." They reaffirmed the progress they had made in outreach and ruled out any major shift in focus. They thought it possible they had put "too much emphasis on a building rather than location." After targeting the Norwood section, they had used churches of other denominations at some distance from Norwood. They raised other questions. "Are we too intense a group to be open to outsiders? Are we mission oriented? Are we doing this for ourselves? Are we pressuring people to be either in or out?"[137]

In July 1989, when Tom Finger left for Eastern Mennonite Seminary, the congregation designated Jesus Cruz and Joseph Kotva as associate ministers. The search for a permanent pastor continued. North Bronx Mennonite

North Bronx Mennonite Church met at the Lutheran Church of the Epiphany, East 206th street, Bronx. 2005 photo.

Church "came home" in July 1989, when they began meeting for worship at Epiphany Lutheran Church in the hub of Norwood. "The fall and winter of 1989 represented another stage in the development of our congregation, a stage in which the current participants banded together to do the work of the church." The congregation reached out to people in the community and found this a time "of vibrancy and of growth in relationships." They had a Thanksgiving dinner with 50 participants, "half of whom do not attend church with us regularly but could well become members of the congregation." A friendship Sunday enabled them to invite others to join them for worship. Only 17 adults and 12 children attended services regularly.[138] In November 1989 one of their own, Beth Gingrich, was ordained to the ministry as chaplain at Calvary Hospital in the Bronx.[139]

In April 1990 Duncan Smith and his wife Charlene Epp, graduates of Associated Mennonite Biblical Seminaries, accepted an invitation to visit the North Bronx group. The congregation responded warmly to them. Financial support remained a problem with so small a group. Eastern Board allowed only three months full-time support as a transition, but it would be difficult for them to find part-time employment in the Bronx. While these negotiations were going on at Salunga, Duncan Smith moved to New York in September 1990. Charlene needed to complete her seminary credits and followed in December. Duncan Smith came originally from Spokane, Washington, and Charlene was from South Dakota. They soon became acclimated to city life and "glad to be a part of the church and the alternative of real life we have to offer people in what can often be a hostile and violent environment." Hostility and violence did not characterize their Norwood neighborhood where they saw "people greeting each other on the street, and kids playing football on 'the green' in the middle of the boulevard near our apartment." With a resident pastor to lead them in their ministry, North Bronx Mennonite Church was ready to grow.[140]

Newcomers in the City

The Garifuna are descendants of African slaves who escaped from slavery, intermarried with the Carib Indians, and developed a unique language and culture. Their communities are found near the coast of the Gulf of Honduras in Belize, Guatemala, and Honduras, where they form a close-knit society of fishermen and farmers. They retain many African customs and speak a language with West African grammar, vocabulary, and idiom. Traditionally, the Garifuna practice a form of African animism. Roman Catholic missionaries brought many Garifuna to the Catholic faith. Elements of traditional religion often survived alongside their Christian practice. Later, Wesleyan missionaries planted a number of churches there.

Mennonites first related to the Garifuna as a result of "The Way to Life" radio broadcast and inquiries sent by some Garifuna who heard the program. In 1980 Steve and Rose Shenk began a ministry among Garifuna in Belize under Eastern Board. Duane and Nancy Leatherman followed them in church planting.

Large numbers of Garifuna came to the United States in the 1970s and 1980s, settling primarily in Los Angeles, New York, and Chicago. There was no Garifuna church anywhere in the States, however.

Stephen and Evelyn Garcia left Belize for Los Angeles in 1979. He obtained employment as an accountant and the Garcias found a church home at Family Mennonite Church in Los Angeles. Stephen Garcia became part of the ministry team and developed his strong evangelistic and preaching gifts. In September 1984, at the request of Eastern Board, the Garcias visited New York and made contacts in the Garifuna community in Brooklyn. They agreed to accept the challenge of planting a church among the Garifuna. "Stephen envisions a church that will be focused on the Garifuna community, but will be able to encompass West Indian and American blacks also." In February 1985 Eastern Board authorized Home Ministries to plant a church among the Garifuna in New York City and affirmed Stephen and Evelyn Garcia in their calling by commissioning them as church planters.[141] They were much like the mission workers who came to New York from Lancaster County thirty-five years earlier, a young couple in their early 20s with two small children beginning a church in an unfamiliar city.

"We arrived in Brooklyn on May 8, 1985 with great anticipation to be used of God, primarily among the Garifuna people, who are bound with some beliefs and practices that are not biblical. Most of them do not go to any church, and the majority are not born again."[142] They found a place to live on Strauss Street and began at once to invite people to worship with them. "On May 27, 1985, God made it possible for us to start a fellowship. During the first two Sundays we met, three souls have come to the Father by accepting Jesus Christ as their Lord and Savior." Before June was out, Garcia could report, "Currently there are six souls that have given their hearts to Jesus our Lord." One of the new converts was ready to be baptized at a swimming pool. Garcia was working with the others. "On June 30, 1985 we voted on a name for the group out here. The name chosen was 'Believers Mennonite Fellowship.'"[143]

Fellowship at the Evangelical Garifuna Church, 344 Brook Avenue, Bronx, the former Glad Tidings building.

Stephen and Evelyn Garcia witnessed around the Garifuna community and visited in homes. The congregation steadily grew. They rented a dance hall in the center of the Belizean neighborhood for public worship. By the end of their second summer in Brooklyn, 31 persons had accepted Christ and 18 of these new Christians were active in the church. Three home Bible studies met each week. Believers Mennonite Fellowship had organized a church council. The congregation had distributed 12,000 tracts during a summer outreach thrust. They had begun a new outreach in the East New York section of Brooklyn with Friday evening worship in the Garifuna language attended by 15 to 25 people each week. There was a possibility that Believers and United Revival Mennonite Church would jointly acquire a church building.[144]

A year later the Garifuna ministry had three preaching stations. Believers Mennonite Fellowship met on Sunday morning with worship in English and Garifuna attended by 40-45 people each week. They had an active youth group, too. The East New York Fellowship continued to meet on Friday evenings with 15-20 people participating. A third fellowship had emerged in the Bronx among Garifuna from Honduras. Their second language was Spanish, in contrast to those from Belize whose second language was English. Celso Jaime was the leader of this group.

During the summer of 1987 eleven members of Youth With a Mission spent a month working with Believers Mennonite Fellowship. The YES team from Baltimore also spent two weekends with the congregation. One young woman from Believers joined Youth With a Mission for overseas service.[145]

Believers Mennonite Fellowship lost part of the space they rented in the dance hall and began to look for a new location in January 1988. They located a suitable building, an older three-story structure on a corner, at 4 Ralph Avenue in Brooklyn to rent as both a church and a residence. Later the congregation bought a building at 36 Malcolm X Avenue with help from Eastern Board. The building carried a mortgage with monthly payments of $2,100 offset by monthly rental income of $1,150. The congregation began renovating and refurbishing the building in February 1989, with most of the work done by church members.[146]

With a permanent location, only six blocks from the original site, attendance began to rise steadily. Believers Mennonite Fellowship had services on Sunday morning and evening and on Monday, Wednesday, and Friday evenings. The church had taken a new direction, reaching out to all neighborhood residents and not just to Garifuna immigrants from Belize. By 1989 all services were in English and only about half of those who participated in Sunday worship or home Bible studies were of Garifuna background. The others were West Indians and Africans. This shift in emphasis caused some division in the congregation. One leader withdrew and attendance dropped from 40 to 20, but seven new people began attending regularly. Stephen Garcia visited those who had stopped coming to church as well as newcomers.[147]

Andrew Nunez, one of the congregational leaders, succeeded Stephen Garcia as pastor in 1991. At that time Believers Mennonite Fellowship counted 35 members.

The work in the Bronx among Spanish-speaking Garifuna from Honduras began in 1987. Celso Jaime was licensed as their pastor and the congregation obtained use of the former Glad Tidings Mennonite Church at 344 Brook Avenue when they dissolved in September 1988. Services are conducted primarily in Garifuna, but also in Spanish. The Evangelical Garifuna Church counted 16 members in 1990 with an average attendance of 70 at worship.[148]

In 1985 David Shenk arranged for a church planter from the Meserete Kristos Church in Ethiopia to begin a congregation among Ethiopians living in New York City. The difficulty of obtaining visas delayed this plan.[149] Mulugeta Abate and his family moved from Kenya to the United States as refugees. He had been a pastor in Ethiopia and worked with Eastern Board. "After numerous meetings, prayers, and visits, the Abate family united in answering God's call to Newark, New Jersey, to pastor a group of Ethiopian believers."[150] He did not go to Newark, however.

Ethiopians in New York City had their own Orthodox churches, but there were no Ethiopian evangelical churches. The Ethiopian Christian Fellowship of New York came into being in the early 1980s to meet that need. According to Solomon H. S. Mekonnen, one of the leaders of the group, several Ethiopians began to meet once a month for Bible study and fellowship. Since many of them were students, the International Student Ministry helped them organize. Steve Hartley, a furloughed missionary under Sudan Interior Mission, knew several Ethiopian refugees in the city and brought them to the meetings. Their original meeting place in Astoria, Queens, was inconvenient, and in July 1985 the group moved to the Broadway Presbyterian Church at Broadway and 79th Street in Manhattan. About 30 people attended their meeting. They quickly moved to meeting twice a month and in September 1985 agreed to meet weekly. They attracted more people, with attendance ranging from 30 to 50, and hoped to grow into a church. Most of them were either students or refugees working at minimum-wage jobs.

In January 1989 Mulugeta Abate was invited to preach and lead worship for the group at the suggestion of the Ethiopian pastor in Washington, D. C. The congregation saw him as the leader they needed. Monroe Yoder and Freeman Miller met with Solomon Mekonnen, Daniel Haile-Mariam, Yetbarik Desta and Alemayehu Seifu Mekuria, the four leaders of the Ethiopian Christian Fellowship. They knew the Mennonites in Ethiopia and thought it a good idea to be linked with an American denomination. Yoder and Miller also talked with Carl Rosenblum, pastor of the Broadway Presbyterian Church, who would continue to welcome the Ethiopian fellowship as a Mennonite congregation.[151]

Mulugeta Abate, pastor of Ethiopian Evangelical Church.

Mulugeta Abate, his wife Tihute, and their children moved to the North Bronx in April 1989. David and Ruth Wenger offered them the third floor apartment in their new house. They continued at that address for three years, moving to New Jersey in 1992. Broadway Presbyterian Church continued to offer the congregation a meeting room at the token rent of $300 a year. There was no space there for a church office, but Monroe Yoder requested office space at Church World Service headquarters next door.[152]

The fellowship grew rapidly. About 50 people, many of them new to the group, attended each week. Five people came to know the Lord in June, 1989. They had Bible study groups, led by the pastor, meeting weekly in the Bronx, in Flushing and in Lefrak City, Queens. Mulugeta conducted a weekly Bible study for the group leaders. The fellowship held a prayer meeting Friday nights at a member's home in Manhattan from seven o'clock to midnight. There was a church choir with seven members.[153]

In September the Ethiopian Evangelical Church moved from the Broadway Presbyterian Church to the First Baptist Church at 79th Street and Broadway. They were able to use the new church for the Friday evening prayer meeting, discipleship classes on Saturday morning, choir

Emmanuel Worship Center, 2407 East Tremont Avenue, Bronx, formerly Ethiopian Evangelical Church. 2005 photo.

practice Saturday afternoon and Sunday afternoon worship from three to half-past six. About 45 adults and many children attended worship. The congregation was scattered all over the city, so visitation was time-consuming. The Flushing Bible study had its own leader-teacher, and Mulugeta was looking for a teacher to take his place in the Lefrak City Bible study. He continued to lead the Bronx group and had started a new group in downtown Manhattan.[154]

By the end of 1989 regular attendance averaged 50-60 adults plus children and six persons were ready for baptism. Attendance held steady in the first months of 1990. By June the congregation counted 40 members and an average attendance of 80-90 each week. More than 40 people participated in the Friday evening prayer meetings.[155]

On a visit to the church in March 1990, Freeman Miller found it "a warm, dynamic, vibrant, young fellowship" and "was humbled to be asked to preach to this Ethiopian group that normally worships in the Amharic language for the entire service." He wrote that, "The chapel filled up and there was much enthusiastic worship, as well as a spirit of reverent joy pervading the audience." After the service was over, the congregation lingered for over an hour in the basement fellowship room drinking coffee

Ethiopian worship at Emmanuel Worship Center.

and talking. "Again, the warmth and closeness of this growing fellowship was very evident."[156]

The congregation had to find a new meeting place by September 1990 and moved to Central Baptist Church at 92nd Street and Amsterdam Avenue in Manhattan. The rent for facilities had risen from $300 a year at their original location to $700 a month at Central Baptist. They continue to meet for worship at this location.

As the congregation took more and more responsibility for ministering to one another, Mulugeta Abate was able to give his full attention to pastoring. A social committee had formed to help meet physical needs and also to organize fellowship meals. They chose a building committee. The church officers handled most of the financial and administrative detail. The most striking characteristic of the Ethiopian Evangelical Church was its prayerfulness, which involved the church leaders, too. "There is a monthly meeting of all those involved in ministry in the church, all night long (from 8:00 PM until 4:00 AM) to seriously pray about church matters, and God has been supplying needs marvelously. This is the key to the whole church."[157] Perhaps it was the key to all the mission work in New York City.

NOTES

[1] Wilbert R. Shenk, ed., *The Challenge of Church Growth* (Scottdale, PA, 1973), 7-8, 15-17. Wilbert R. Shenk, ed., *Exploring Church Growth* (Grand Rapids, MI, 1983), 79-80, 293.

[2] G. Edwin Bontrager and Nathan D. Showalter, *It Can Happen Today!* (Scottdale, PA, 1986), 67.

[3] Charles Taber, "Contextualization," Shenk, ed., *Exploring Church Growth*, 118.

[4] Taber, loc. cit.

[5] David W. Shenk, "The Muslim Umma and the Growth of the Church," Shenk, ed., *Exploring Church Growth*, 154.

[6] J. Stanley Friesen, "The Significance of Indigenous Movements for the Study of Church Growth," Shenk, ed., *Challenge of Church Growth*, 103.

[7] District Council Minutes, Feb. 1, 1979, Apr. 10, 1979, EMM.

[8] District Council Minutes, Apr. 16, 1980, EMM.

[9] District Council Minutes, Oct. 8, 1979, Nov. 13, 1979. Roger Lehman, Proposal, n.d. (1979), EMM.

[10] Roger Lehman, Proposal, n.d. (1979), Meeting with Cherry and Roger Lehman, Feb. 7, 1980. Dale Stoltzfus to District Council Members, Mar. 1980, EMM.

[11] Nate Showalter, Dale Stoltzfus, Roger and Cherry Lehman, Meeting, Oct. 29, 1980. Lehman Christmas letter, Dec. 1981. Leaflets, n.d., June 1981, EMM.

[12] Roger, Cherry, Jennifer and Jenelle Lehman, Christmas letter, Dec. 1981, EMM.

[13] New Life Fellowship, Planning for Resource Sharing, Sept. 28, 1982. David W. Shenk to Roger and Cherry Lehman, Oct. 28, 1982. David W. Shenk to Pastor Mateo, Oct. 28, 1982, EMM.

[14] New Life Fellowship, Five Year Review, May 14, 1985, EMM.

[15] David Shenk, Paul Landis, Roger and Cherry Lehman, Stan Sutter, Meeting, May 9, 1983, EMM.

[16] David W. Shenk to Roger Lehman, Nov. 15, 1983, EMM.

[17] John and Irene Smucker to New York City Council of Mennonite Churches, Feb. 10, 1984. EMBMC-A. Smucker, "Reflections," 176-190.

[18] David W. Shenk to Roger Lehman, Nov. 15, 1983, EMM.

[19] David W. Shenk, Notes on Staten Island, Jan. 19, 1984, EMM. James R. Coggins and Paul G. Hiebert, *Wonders and the Word* (Winnipeg, 1989), 15-20.

[20] "A Stone in God's House: A statement of New Life Fellowship's relationship to the larger body of Christ," n.d., 1985, EMM.

[21] Roger Lehman to Ervin Stutzman, Mar. 27, 1985, Five Year Review, May 14, 1985, EMM.

[22] David W. Shenk, New York City Report, Nov. 6-8, 1985. David W. Shenk to Executive Committee, Oct. 28, 1986, EMM.

[23] David W. Shenk to Roger and Cherry Lehman, Nov. 18, 1985. Monroe Yoder to Lester and Marietta Sutter, Sept. 19, 1987. Support Group for Staten Island Church Planters, 1988, EMM.

[24] Support Group Meeting, Feb. 25, 1988, May 20, 1988, EMM.

[25] Support Group Meeting, Sept. 7, 1988, EMM.

[26] *Missionary Messenger*, Jan. 1991, 6.

[27] John and Irene Smucker to NYC Council of Mennonite Churches, Feb. 10, 1984, EMM.

[28] John and Irene Smucker to NYC Council of Mennonite Churches, May 15, 1984, EMM.

[29] John and Irene Smucker to NYC Council of Mennonite Churches, July 15, 1984, EMM.

[30] Wayne King, "A Vision for Ministry in New York City," Dec. 7, 1982, revised Mar. 16, 1984, EMM.

[31] John and Irene Smucker to NYC Council of Mennonite Churches, July 15, 1984. Marian Sauder, "Queens—A Borough of Houses," *Camp Deerpark Newsletter*, spring 1991, EMM.

[32] Irene Smucker, "NYC Church Merger Forms Immanuel Community Church," *Atlantic Coast Conference Currents* 12(Sept.-Oct. 1991), 1-2.

[33] David W. Shenk, Interview, Aug. 18, 1990.

[34] Chester Wenger, A New York City Visit, Mar. 27-29, 1979, EMM.

[35] David W. Shenk, Report of Visit to New York City, Mar. 30-31, 1981, EMM.

[36] Jeryl Holinger, Annual Administrative Report, New York City, Apr. 18, 1980, Annual Administrative Report, New York City, July 31, 1981, EMM.

[37] Jeryl Holinger, Annual Administrative Report, New York City, July 31, 1981, EMM.

[38] Monroe Yoder to David Shenk, Oct. 28, 1981, EMM.

[39] John Bauman, Jesus Cruz, Pastor Mateo to Home Ministries Department, EMBMC, Apr. 2, 1982. David W. Shenk, A Visit to New York City and Connecticut, Apr. 13-14, 1982, EMM.

[40] John Bauman, Planning for Resource Sharing, Nov. 12, 1982, EMM.

[41] John Stahl-Wert, Annual Administrative Report, New York City, Apr. 16, 1982, Apr. 8. 1983, Apr. 27, 1984, EMM.

[42] Pastor Mateo to David W. Shenk, Jan. 3, 1984. Pastor Mateo to Sally Jo Hess, Feb. 2, 1984, EMM.

[43] David W. Shenk to John Bauman, Oct. 10, 1984, EMM.

[44] David W. Shenk to Jesus Cruz, Dec. 10, 1984, EMM.

[45] Glad Tidings, Reports, July 1984, July 1985, EMM.

[46] David W. Shenk, New York City Report, Nov. 6-8, 1985, EMM.

[47] David W. Shenk, to Executive committee, Oct. 28, 1986, EMM.

[48] Freeman J. Miller to Ruth Zimmerman, May 25, 1988. Roger Ledyard to John H. Kraybill, Aug. 28, 1989, EMM. *Missionary Messenger*, Nov. 1988, 6.

[49] David Shenk to Rev. and Mrs. Raymond Bell, Feb. 10, 1981, EMM.

[50] David Shenk, Report of Visit to New York City, Mar. 30-31, 1981, EMM.

[51] Jeryl Hollinger, Annual Administrative Report, July 31, 1981, EMM.

[52] David Shenk to Raymond Bell, Feb. 1, 1982. Resource Sharing Report, Sept. 20, 1982, EMM.

[53] David W. Shenk to Monroe Yoder, Sept. 28, 1982. Ruth Zimmerman to Good Shepherd Mennonite Church, Feb. 10, 1983, EMM.

[54] Monroe J. Yoder to David Shenk, May 9, 1983. Monroe J. Yoder to Emmanuel Okorley, May 9, 1983. David W. Shenk to Emmanuel and Doris Okorley, May 11, 1984, EMM.

[55] Report, July 1, 1983-June 30, 1984, EMM.

[56] Gerry Keener to Emmanuel Okorley, Nov. 14, 1985, EMM.

[57] Monroe J. Yoder to Emmanuel and Doris Okorley, Apr. 16, 1986, EMM.

[58] David W. Shenk to Executive Committee, Oct. 28, 1986, EMM.

[59] David W. Shenk to Executive Committee, Oct. 28, 1986. Freeman J. Miller to Martin Bender, June 2, 1988, EMM.

[60] *Friendship News*, 1(April 1981), 3, MBM-AMC.

[61] Henry Miller, Interview, Apr. 19, 1991.

[62] David W. Shenk, Report of Visit to New York City, Mar. 30-31, 1981, EMM.

[63] District Council Minutes, June 21, 1976, EMM.

[64] Monroe Yoder to Dear Friends, July 26, 1976. District Council Minutes, Dec. 6, 1976, Jan. 11, 1977, EMM.

[65] District Council Minutes, Nov. 17, 1977, July 11, 1978, Sept. 12, 1978. David Wenger to Gerald Keener, May 3, 1978. EMBMC Minutes, July 6, 1978, EMM.

[66] Gerry Keener to Jeryl Hollinger, Jan. 21, 1981. David Shenk to Gerry Keener, Jan. 20, 1981. EMBMC Meeting, Seventh Avenue, Feb. 13, 1981. David W. Shenk, Report of Visit to New York, Feb. 13, 1981. David W. Shenk Report of Visit to New York City, Mar. 30-31, 1981. EMBMC-A. There were political aspects to the project. The director of the Ministerial Interfaith Association, who also headed a construction company, indicated federal Section 312 funds would be forthcoming *with his encouragement* and his company as a limited partner in the project.

[67] David W. Shenk to Bob Stevens, Sept. 10, 1981. Bob Stevens to David W. Shenk, Nov. 18, 1981. David W. Shenk to Gerry Keener, Mar. 3, 1982. David W. Shenk to Abe Hallman, May 23, 1982, EMM.

[68] David W. Shenk to Abe Hallman, May 23, 1982. Paul Derstine to Neil Janzen, June 16, 1982, EMM.

69 Harry Simmons Jr. to Gerry Keener, July 20, 1983. Seventh Avenue Building Project Meeting, Salunga, Sept. 28, 1983, EMM.

70 Brochure, Mar. 1984. Youth Choir in Concert, Dec. 3, 1983, EMM. *Mennonite Weekly Review*, Dec. 1, 1983.

71 Lindsey Robinson to Executive Committee, EMBMC, Aug. 27, 1984, EMM.

72 Norman Shenk to Executive Committee, Oct. 2, 1985, EMM.

73 Donna Zehr Keener to Friends of Heartsease, Oct. 1982, EMM.

74 Worship and Evangelism Committee Minutes, Nov. 15, 1982. Lindsey Robinson to Gerry Keener, Feb. 4, 1985. Proposal for Resourcing Seventh Avenue Mennonite Church, Feb. 1985. Congregational Meeting Minutes, July 10, 1985, EMM.

75 David W. Shenk, Notes on Jimmy Johnson, Jan. 1, 1986. Freeman Miller, Administrative Trip to New York City, Jan. 16-18, 1987, EMM.

76 Marian Landis to Freeman Miller, Mar. 5, 1988, EMM.

77 Lindsey Robinson to Jimmy and Karen Johnson, Dec. 22, 1988, EMM.

78 John Stahl-Wert, Annual Administrative Report, Apr. 16, 1982, Apr. 8, 1983, EMM.

79 Jeryl Hollinger, Annual Administrative Report, Apr. 18, 1980, July 31, 1981, EMM.

80 John Wert to Samuel Walters, Apr. 24, 1983. John Wert, Annual Administrative Report, Apr. 8, 1983, EMM.

81 David W. Shenk, A Visit to New York City and Connecticut, Apr. 13-14, 1982, EMM.

82 Congregational Meeting Minutes, May 12, 1982. Steve Villanueva to Chester Wenger, June 1, 1982. David W. Shenk, A Visit to New York City and Connecticut, Apr. 13-14, 1982, EMM.

83 Samuel Walters and Lowell Jantzi to David W. Shenk, Aug. 24, 1983. David W. Shenk to Samuel Walters and Lowell Jantzi, Sept. 8, 1983. Samuel Walters and Lowell Jantzi to David W. Shenk, Sept. 19, 1983. David W. Shenk to Samuel Walters and Lowell Jantzi, Sept. 28, 1983, EMM.

84 David W. Shenk to Ralph Villanueva, June 20, 1984, EMM.

85 Goal Statement for 1985, Dec. 21, 1984. Michael and Addie Banks, "Pilgrim's Way—a Christian community," *Missionary Messenger*, Mar. 1990, 18-19.

86 Goal Statement for 1985, Dec. 21, 1984, EMM.

87 Freeman J. Miller, Administrative Trip to New York City, Jan. 16-18, 1987. Freeman J. Miller, Notes, Jan. 16-18, 1987, EMM.

88 Resource Sharing, July 1984, July 1986, EMM.

89 Michael Banks to Dear Friend, n.d. Project Charisma brochure, n.d. (1988), EMM.

90 Brian Ebersole to Executive Committee, Aug. 5, 1988, EMM.

91 Michael and Addie Banks, "Pilgrim's Way," *Missionary Messenger* Mar. 1990, 18-19.

92 Report on the Special Meeting to Discuss the Future of Voluntary Service, June 23, 1981, EMM.

93 New York City Unit, Monthly Report to VS Director, Jan. 25, 1982, Feb. 24, 1982. John Wert, Annual Administrative Report, Apr. 16, 1982, EMM.

94 New York City Unit, Monthly Report to VS Director, June 30, 1982, Aug. 30, 1982, EMM.

95 John Wert, Annual Administrative Report, Apr. 8, 1983, EMM.

96 Dan Drawbaugh, John Elmer, Brian Fulmer, Tom Hale, Gwen Lomakin, Proposal, n.d. (April 1983), EMM.

[97] John Stahl-Wert, Annual Administrative Report, Apr. 27, 1984, EMM. John Elmer became active in the Pittsburgh Mennonite Fellowship after he left New York.

[98] John Stahl-Wert, Annual Administrative Report, Apr. 8, 1983, Apr. 27, 1984, EMM.

[99] Proposed Peace Center for NYC, Sept. 5, 1980, EMM.

[100] Minutes of the Ad Hoc Committee for New Call to Peacemaking, Sept. 10, 1981, EMM.

[101] New York City Mennonite Peace Center Advisory Committee Meeting, Nov. 30, 1981. New York City Peace Center Meeting, Jan. 8, 1982, EMM.

[102] NYC Mennonite Peace Center Advisory Committee Minutes, Mar. 25, 1982, July 12, 1982. Report of Peace Center Activities, Jan. 30-Mar. 24, 1982, May 7-July 12, 1982, EMM.

[103] Pastor Mateo, Gerry H. Keener, John P. Bauman to David W. Shenk, Aug. 17, 1982, with enclosure. David W. Shenk to Sylvia Horst, Oct. 12, 1982, EMM.

[104] NYC Mennonite Peace Center Advisory Committee Minutes, Sept. 27, 1982, Jan. 25, 1983. Sylvia Horst to Victor F. Weaver, Jan. 17, 1983, EMM.

[105] NYC Mennonite Peace Center Advisory Committee Minutes, Jan. 25, 1983, Apr. 4, 1983, June 27, 1983, Sept. 26, 1983. Report of Peace Center Activities, Nov. 16, 1982-Jan. 24, 1983, Jan. 25-Apr. 11, 1983, Apr. 12-June 25, 1983. *Mennonite Peace Center Bulletin*, Mar. 1983, Aug. 1983, EMM. *Missionary Messenger*, Feb. 1984, 20.

[106] Peace Center Advisory Committee Meeting, Sept. 26, 1983, Nov. 28, 1983. *Missionary Messenger*, Feb. 1984, 20.

[107] Brian Ebersole to NYC Council of Mennonite Churches, Aug. 5, 1988, EMM. Michael Banks, "Pilgrim's Way," *Missionary Messenger*, Mar. 1990, 18-19; Apr. 1990, 18.

[108] Vision for the New York City Area Mennonite Churches—the year 2000 AD n.d. (1985), EMM.

[109] Myrna Burkholder to Galen Burkholder and Melville Nafziger, June 4, 1982, EMM.

[110] Richard Mojonnier to H. Ernest Bennett, Jan. 19, 1979. MBM-AMC. Myrna Burkholder to Nate Showalter, May 23, 1979, EMM.

[111] Manhattan Mennonite Fellowship Interviews. Menno House. In March 1991 John Rempel taped reminiscences by persons involved in the Manhattan Mennonite Fellowship and in Peace Mennonite Fellowship.

[112] New York City Council of Mennonite Churches, 1981 Directory of Congregations. General Conference Mennonite Church, *Handbook*, 1981-82, 1982-83.

[113] Manhattan Mennonite Fellowship Interviews, MH

[114] Myrna Burkholder to Galen Burkholder and Melville Nafziger, June 4, 1982, EMM.

[115] Manhattan Mennonite Fellowship Interviews, MH

[116] Manhattan Mennonite Fellowship Interviews, MH.

[117] Susan Ebersole Application to SYAS for Fiscal Year 1983—NYC, Sept. 30, 1982. Myrna Burkholder to Ross Goldfus, Oct. 11, 1982. Myrna Burkholder to Susan Ebersole, Oct. 11, 1982, EMM.

[118] David W. Shenk, New York City Report, Nov. 6-8, 1985, EMM.

[119] David W. Shenk to Mary Klassen (sic), Oct. 3, 1985. David W. Shenk, New York City Report, Nov. 6-8, 1985, EMM.

[120] David W. Shenk to J. R. Burkholder, Sept. 29, 1986, EMM.

[121] David W. Shenk to Mel Lehman, Oct. 30, 1986, EMM.

[122] David W. Shenk to Executive Committee, Oct. 28, 1986, EMM.

[123] Freeman J. Miller, Administrative Trip to new York City, Jan. 16-18, 1987. Manhattan Mennonite Fellowship, Jan. 18, 1987 (order of worship), EMM.

[124] Becky Kurtz to Joint Committee, May 7, 1989, EMM.

[125] Becky Kurtz to Freeman Miller, Dec. 6, 1989, EMM.

[126] Becky Kurtz to Freeman Miller, Feb. 2, 1990, EMM.

[127] Freeman Miller to Executive Committee, Mar. 7, 1990, EMM.

[128] Manhattan Mennonite Fellowship Interview, MH.

[129] Monroe Yoder to David Shenk, Oct. 28, 1981, EMM.

[130] David W. Shenk to Executive Committee, Oct. 28, 1986, EMM.

[131] Freeman Miller, Notes on North Bronx Group, June 13, 1987.The North Bronx Mennonite Church: Profile of a Developing Congregation, n.d. 1990, EMM.

[132] Freeman Miller, Notes on North Bronx Group, June 13, 1987. The North Bronx Mennonite Church: Profile of a Developing Congregation, n.d. 1990, EMM.

[133] Freeman J. Miller to Executive Committee, June 16, 1987, EMM.

[134] Marian Sauder to Freeman Miller, Mar. 5, 1988. North Bronx Support Group Meeting Minutes, Feb. 5, 1988, Apr. 25, 1988, EMBMC-A.

[135] North Bronx Support Group, Apr. 25, 1988, July 9, 1988, EMBMC-A.

[136] North Bronx Mennonite Church Evaluation, Sept. 1988. North Bronx Support Group, Oct. 17, 1988. North Bronx Mennonite Church, Church Council Meeting, Jan. 19, 1989. Visionary Meeting, Jan. 22, 1989.

[137] Pastoral Search Committee Minutes, Jan. 26, 1989, Feb. 8, 1989, EMBMC-A.

[138] The North Bronx Mennonite Church: Profile of a Developing Congregation, Feb. 1990, EMBMC-A.

[139] *Missionary Guide*, Feb. 1990, 4.

[140] Freeman J. Miller to Duncan Smith and Charlene Epp, Apr. 26, 1990. Frank Peachey to Freeman Miller, May 17, 1990, EMBMC-A. Duncan Smith and Charlene Epp, "Spreading the good news in the Bronx," *Missionary Messenger* July-Aug. 1991, 7.

[141] Lindsey A. Robinson to Monroe Yoder, Feb. 4, 1985. Lindsey Robinson to Executive Committee, Feb. 21, 1985, EMBMC-A.

[142] Stephen Garcia, Personal Profile, July 1985, EMBMC-A.

[143] Stephen Garcia to Lindsey Robinson, June 30, 1985. Personal Profile, July 1985, EMBMC-A.

[144] Lindsey Robinson to Executive Committee, Oct. 28, 1986.

[145] Lindsey A. Robinson to Executive Committee, Dec. 21, 1987, EMBMC-A.

[146] Don Brubaker to Ruthie Zimmerman, Sept. 8, 1988. Believers Mennonite Fellowship Support Group Meeting Minutes, May 27, 1989, EMBMC-A

[147] Believers Mennonite Fellowship Support Group Meeting Minutes, May 27, 1989, EMBMC-A. *Camp Deerpark Newsletter*, Summer 1990.

[148] *Camp Deerpark Newsletter*, Fall 1990.

[149] David W. Shenk to Pastor Mateo and Monroe Yoder, Mar. 12, 1985.

[150] Allen Brubaker to Eugene Witmer, Jan. 10, 1989, EMBMC-A.

[151] Freeman Miller, Notes on "Ethiopian Group," Jan. 28, 1989, EMBMC-A. There is a notation "Open New file NYC-Ethiopian Church Planting."

[152] Minutes Ethiopian Support Group Meeting, Apr. 24, 1989, EMBMC-A.

[153] Minutes Ethiopian Support Group, June 29, 1989, EMBMC-A.

[154] Minutes, Support Group Meeting, Ethiopian Evangelical Church, Sept. 8, 1989, EMBMC-A.

[155] Minutes, Support Group Meeting, Ethiopian Evangelical Church, Dec. 21, 1989, Mar. 9, 1990, June 7, 1990, EMBMC-A.

[156] Freeman J. Miller to Executive Committee, Mar. 7, 1990, EMBMC-A.

[157] Ethiopian Evangelical Church of New York City Support Group Meeting, June 7, 1990, EMBMC-A. *Mennonite Weekly Review*, July 7, 1991.

EPILOGUE

The New York City churches did a remarkable job in difficult circumstances of bringing the good news of Jesus Christ to hundreds of city dwellers. In planting urban churches, as in starting mission work overseas, the supporting mission boards looked to the growth of indigenous churches, capable of supporting themselves and of sending out missionaries to start new churches. The planners on the different mission boards and the workers in the field shared this vision when they began work in New York City. It proved more difficult to implement.

An outside observer might note difficulties present from the beginning and probably inherent in the initial vision for urban mission. All three mission boards retained a great deal of the decision-making process and generally took the mission workers into their confidence, but much more rarely communicated with "native" members of the churches. The East Harlem Protestant Parish had a similar pattern. They left little initiative to the members of the churches. So long as the city missions relied on young men and women who came to New York City from established congregations in Pennsylvania or Ohio, they unintentionally limited opportunities for local leadership to emerge.

The city churches in almost every case located in very poor neighborhoods. Even when strong local leadership did emerge, the congregation could rarely expect to be self-supporting and that was no more likely in the distant future. The New York City congregations remained dependent clients of the mission boards over a long period of time. Major decisions thus had to be made by the boards.

In their first years, the city churches followed a pattern established earlier in missions in towns and small cities in Pennsylvania, inviting children to mission Sunday schools and vacation Bible schools and holding outdoor evangelistic services to reach adults. They had some success in this approach in Manhattan and the Bronx, too, and influenced many people for good who never became members of any congregation.

When urban opportunities for alternative service to the military draft brought large numbers of young men from Pennsylvania, Ohio, and Kansas to the New York City Mennonite and Brethren in Christ mission churches, they expanded their ministry to include working with teenagers in athletic teams and clubs. Their intensive youth work did change lives and helped many youngsters along the road to becoming responsible adult Christians who would nurture their children in faithful discipleship.

An emphasis on bringing individuals to Jesus Christ, rather than on building church institutions, characterized all the early New York City mission outposts and they reached their goals without notably increasing their membership rolls. The self-supporting mission workers and pastors did heroic work in building church programs and visiting members and prospective members while carrying full-time employment in another field, but even their good work had its limits because of time pressure. Fidelity to cultural patterns of faithful Christian life as understood in Mennonite and Brethren in Christ homes undoubtedly raised barriers against church membership for many converts.

But the urban congregations remained small long after they abandoned initial patterns of directing program to neighborhood children and requiring members to conform to the dress code of Conference Discipline. New York City Council of Churches included sixteen urban congregations with a total of 593 members in 1995. The largest congregation, Immanuel Community Church in the Bayside section of Queens, counted just over a hundred members. Three churches had more than fifty members, Burnside Mennonite Fellowship, Ethiopian Evangelical Church, and Iglesia Unida de Avivamiento. The dozen others were all very small.

Numbers are scarcely the way to judge whether a congregation is faithful to its Lord or helping its neighbor. The stories from so many New York City churches have given evidence of half a century in discipleship and outreach and the blessings many of these small store-front churches have been to the city. But the reader is left with an unanswered question about the small congregations typical of Mennonite and Brethren in Christ churches in American cities. The New York City churches are no smaller than the churches in Philadelphia, Washington, D.C., or Los Angeles.

Emphasis on solving neighborhood problems, which characterized the East Harlem Protestant Parish in the 1950s and all of the churches by the 1960s, offered a valuable ministry for the churches and for those who relied on their pastors to lead them through a labyrinth of welfare regulations or battle at City Hall for decent housing. In neighborhoods fragmented by slum clearance projects and demoralized by drugs and crime, it did not lead to increased attendance or rapidly growing membership rolls for any of the churches. What it signaled was a commitment to the people of the city and a concern for their spiritual and material needs, when much of American society turned its back on the poor.

Did Mennonites face insurmountable odds in urban missions? From the early nineteenth century, Protestant churches of every denomination had moved uptown or out to the suburbs following a major part of their membership. Even the oldest and best established congregations suffered from the urban pattern of changing neighborhoods. A church building surrounded by blocks of one-family houses occupied by reasonably affluent Protestant families with children would in a few years become a neighborhood characterized by tenement houses where only the elderly or childless young couples or recent immigrants of a different faith or language lived.

Poorer neighborhoods, such as the sections in Manhattan and the Bronx where Mennonites and Brethren in Christ located their missions, had an even higher turnover in the second half of the twentieth century. The desolation of the South Bronx by arson was only an extreme example of a general trend. Even if a neighborhood remained an ethnic enclave for one group of immigrants over a long time, it steadily lost members of that ethnic group who could afford to move to better housing elsewhere. Mennonite and Brethren in Christ congregations established for outreach to a particular neighborhood invariably became commuter churches, with members returning for worship services and few neighborhood people in attendance.

Building a stable congregation, much less one that could be self-supporting and self-propagating, would be extremely difficult in these circumstances. Mission strategy eventually moved away from the neighborhood concept and turned to groups with a strong identity. It can be no accident that, with one exception, the larger Mennonite congregations in New York City serve ethnic minority populations without other strong institutions in the city. These congregations are genuinely indigenous in their leadership and organization.

The most recent pattern to emerge is mission to immigrant groups, not from the North American churches, but from their churches at home. The Ethiopian churches are an outreach from the Meserete Kristos Church in Ethiopia and the Amor Viviente churches of Honduras have begun churches in the New York City area among their countrymen living in the city.

Mission has moved full circle. The New York City Mennonite and Brethren in Christ churches are no longer mission outposts of well-established congregations in the Pennsylvania countryside, staffed by young men and women animated by the love of God but strangers to city ways. Today they are genuinely city churches, reaching out in love to their neighbors and to other strangers finding their way in the city. Their leaders are men and women born in New York City or long accustomed to the urban scene. Although numerically insignificant in the total urban population, they serve their communities out of all proportion to their membership. They minister from the city to the city.

INDEX

E

F

G

H

I

J

K

L

M

N

O

P

Q

R

S

T

U

V

W

Y

Z

About Pandora Press

Pandora Press is a small, independently owned press dedicated to making available modestly priced books that deal with Anabaptist, Mennonite, and Believers Church topics, both historical and theological. We welcome comments from our readers.

Visit our full-service online Bookstore:
www.pandorapress.com

Gerke van Hiele with Marion Bruggen, Ina ter Kuile and Frans Misset, *Encountering the Eternal One: A Guide for Mennonite Churches* (Kitchener: Pandora Press, 2006) Softcover, 120 pages. ISBN 1-894710-75-4

Richard MacMaster, *Mennonite and Brethren in Christ Churches of New York City* (Kitchener: Pandora Press, 2006) Softcover, 366 pages. ISBN 1-894710-70-3

Peter Riedemann, *Love is like Fire: The Confession of an Anabaptist Prisoner* (Kitchener: Pandora Press, 2006) Softcover, 84 pages. ISBN 1-894710-72-X

Andreas Ehrenpreis and Claus Felbinger, *Brotherly Community: The Highest Command of Love* (Kitchener: Pandora Press, 2006) Softcover, 146 pages. ISBN 1-894710-74-6

Jakob Hutter, *Brotherly Faithfulness: Epistles from a Time of Persecution* (Kitchener: Pandora Press, 2006) Softcover, 250 pages. ISBN 1-894710-73-8

Robert John Russell, *Cosmology, Evolution, and Resurrection Hope* (Kitchener: Pandora Press, 2006) Softcover, 118 pages. ISBN 1-894710-67-3

Nathan E. Yoder and Carol A. Scheppard, eds., *Exiles in the Empire: Believers Church Perspectives on Politics* (Kitchener: Pandora Press, 2006) Softcover, 266 pages. Scriptural and topical indexes. ISBN 1-894710-68-1

Helmut Isaak, *Menno Simons and the New Jerusalem* (Kitchener: Pandora Press, 2006) Softcover, 158 pages. Bibliography. ISBN 1-894710-69-X

Leah Dawn Bueckert and Daniel Schipani, eds. *Spiritual Caregiving in the Hospital. Windows to Chaplaincy Ministry* (Kitchener: Pandora Press, 2006) Softcover, 230 pages. ISBN 1-894710-65-7

Ralph Lebold, *Strange and Wonderful Paths. The Memoirs of Ralph Lebold.* (Kitchener: Pandora Press, 2006). Softcover, 236 pages. Bibliography, index. ISBN 1-894710-66-5

Karl Koop, ed. *Confessions of Faith in the Anabaptist Tradition, 1527-1660* ((Kitchener: Pandora Press, 2006). Softcover, 366 pages. Scripture index. ISBN 1-894710-62-2

Alle Hoekema and Hanspeter Jecker, eds. *Testing Faith and Tradition. A Global Mennonite History: Europe* (Kitchener: Pandora Press, 2006; co-published with Good Books) Softcover, 324 pages. Indexes. ISBN 1-56148-550-0

John A. Lapp and C. Arnold Snyder, gen.eds., *Anabaptist Songs in African Hearts. A Global Mennonite History: Africa* (Kitchener: Pandora Press, 2006; co-published with Good Books) Softcover, 292 pages. Indexes. ISBN 1-56148-549-7

Harry Loewen, *Between Worlds. Reflections of a Soviet-born Canadian Mennonite* (Kitchener: Pandora Press, 2006). Softcover, 358 pages. Bibliography. ISBN 1-894710-63-0

H. H. Drake Williams III, ed., *Caspar Schwenckfeld. Eight Writings on Christian Beliefs* (Kitchener: Pandora Press, 2006). Softcover, 200 pages. Index. ISBN 1-894710-64-9

Maureen Epp and Carol Ann Weaver, eds., *Sound in the Land: Essays on Mennonites and Music* (Kitchener: Pandora Press, 2006). Softcover, 220 pages. Bibliography. ISBN 1-894710-59-2

Geoffrey Dipple, *"Just as in the Time of the Apostles": Uses of History in the Radical Reformation* (Kitchener: Pandora Press, 2005). Softcover, 324 pages. Bibliography and index. ISBN 1-894710-58-4.

Harry Huebner, *Echoes of the Word: Theological Ethics as Rhetorical Practice* Anabaptist and Mennonite Studies Series (Kitchener: Pandora Press, 2005). Softcover, 274 pages. Bibliography and index. ISSN 1494-4081 ISBN 1-894710-56-8

John F. Haught, *Purpose, Evolution and the Mystery of Life,* Proceedings of the Fourth Annual Goshen Conference on Religion and Science, ed. Carl S. Helrich (Kitchener" Pandora Press, 2005). Softcover, 130 pages. Index. ISBN 1-894710-55-X

Gerald W. Schlabach, gen. ed., *Called Together to be Peacemakers: Report of the International Dialogue between the Catholic Church and Mennonite World Conference 1998-2003* (Kitchener: Pandora Press, 2005). Softcover, 77 pages. ISSN 1711-9480 ISBN 1-894710-57-6

Rodney James Sawatsky, *History and Ideology: American Mennonite Identity Definition through History* (Kitchener: Pandora Press, 2005). Softcover, 216 pages. Bibliography and index. ISBN 1-894710-53-3 ISSN 1494-4081

Harvey Neufeldt, Ruth Derksen Siemens and Robert Martens, eds., *First Nations and First Settlers in the Fraser Valley (1890-1960)* (Kitchener: Pandora Press, 2005). Softcover, 287 pages.Bibliography and index. ISBN 1-894710-54-1

David Waltner-Toews, *The Complete Tante Tina: Mennonite Blues and Recipes* (Kitchener: Pandora Press, 2004) Softcover, 129 pages. ISBN 1-894710-52-5

John Howard Yoder, *Anabaptism and Reformation in Switzerland: An Historical and Theological Analysis of the Dialogues Between Anabaptists and Reformers* (Kitchener: Pandora Press, 2004) Softcover, 509 pages. Bibliography and indexes. ISBN 1-894710-44-4 ISSN 1494-4081

Antje Jackelén, *The Dialogue Between Religion and Science: Challenges and Future Directions* (Kitchener: Pandora Press, 2004) Softcover, 143 pages. Index. ISBN 1-894710-45-2

Ivan J. Kauffman, ed., *Just Policing: Mennonite Catholic Theological Colloquium 2001-2002* (Kitchener: Pandora Press, 2004). Softcover, 127 pages. ISBN 1-894710-48-7.

Gerald W. Schlabach, ed., *On Baptism: Mennonite-Catholic Theological Colloquium 2001-2002* (Kitchener: Pandora Press, 2004). Softcover, 147 pages., ISBN 1-894710-47-9 ISSN 1711-9480.

Harvey L. Dyck, John R. Staples and John B. Toews, comp., trans. and ed. *Nestor Makhno and the Eichenfeld Massacre:* (Kitchener: Pandora Press, 2004). Softcover, 115pages. ISBN 1-894710-46-0.

Jeffrey Wayne Taylor, *The Formation of the Primitive Baptist Movement* (Kitchener: Pandora Press, 2004). Softcover, 225 pages. Bibliography and index. ISBN 1-894710-42-8 ISSN 1480-7432.

James C. Juhnke and Carol M. Hunter, *The Missing Peace: The Search for Nonviolent Alternatives in United States History,* 2nd ed. (Kitchener: Pandora Press, 2004) Softcover, 339 pp. Index.
ISBN 1-894710-46-3

Louise Hawkley and James C. Juhnke, eds., *Nonviolent America: History through the Eyes of Peace* (North Newton: Bethel College, 2004, co-published with Pandora Press) Softcover, 269 pages. Index.
ISBN 1-889239-02-X

Karl Koop, *Anabaptist-Mennonite Confessions of Faith: the Development of a Tradition* (Kitchener: Pandora Press, 2004) Softcover, 178 pages. Index. ISBN 1-894710-32-0

Lucille Marr, *The Transforming Power of a Century: Mennonite Central Committee and its Evolution in Ontario* (Kitchener: Pandora Press, 2003). Softcover, 390 pages. Bibliography and index,
ISBN 1-894710-41-x.

Erica Janzen, *Six Sugar Beets, Five Bitter Years* (Kitchener: Pandora Press, 2003). Softcover, 186 pages. ISBN 1-894710-37-1.

T. D. Regehr, *Faith Life and Witness in the Northwest, 1903–2003: Centennial History of the Northwest Mennonite Conference* (Kitchener: Pandora Press, 2003). Softcover, 524 pages. Index,
ISBN 1-894710-39-8.

George F. R. Ellis, *A Universe of Ethics Morality and Hope: Proceedings from the Second Annual Goshen Conference on Religion and Science* (Kitchener: Pandora Press, 2003) Softcover, 148 pages.
ISBN 1-894710-36-3

Donald Martin, *Old Order Mennonites of Ontario: Gelassenheit, Discipleship, Brotherhood* (Kitchener: Pandora Press, 2003). Softcover, 381 pages. Index. ISBN 1-894710-33-9

Mary A. Schiedel, *Pioneers in Ministry: Women Pastors in Ontario Mennonite Churches, 1973-2003* (Kitchener: Pandora Press, 2003) Softcover, 204 pages. ISBN 1-894710-35-5

Harry Loewen, ed., *Shepherds, Servants and Prophets* (Kitchener: Pandora Press, 2003) Softcover, 446 pages. ISBN 1-894710-35-5

Robert A. Riall, trans., Galen A. Peters, ed., *The Earliest Hymns of the* Ausbund: *Some Beautiful Christian Songs Composed and Sung in the Prison at Passau, Published 1564* (Kitchener: Pandora Press, 2003) Softcover, 468 pages. Bibliography and index. ISBN 1-894710-34-7.

John A. Harder, *From Kleefeld With Love* (Kitchener: Pandora Press, 2003) Softcover, 198 pages. ISBN 1-894710-28-2

John F. Peters, *The Plain People: A Glimpse at Life Among the Old Order Mennonites of Ontario* (Kitchener: Pandora Press, 2003) Softcover, 54 pages. ISBN 1-894710-26-6

Robert S. Kreider, *My Early Years: An Autobiography* (Kitchener: Pandora Press, 2002) Softcover, 600 pages. Index ISBN 1-894710-23-1

Helen Martens, *Hutterite Songs* (Kitchener: Pandora Press, 2002) Softcover, xxii, 328 pages. ISBN 1-894710-24-X

C. Arnold Snyder and Galen A. Peters, eds., *Reading the Anabaptist Bible: Reflections for Every Day of the Year* (Kitchener: Pandora Press, 2002) Softcover, 415 pages. ISBN 1-894710-25-8

C. Arnold Snyder, ed., *Commoners and Community: Essays in Honour of Werner O. Packull* (Kitchener: Pandora Press, 2002) Softcover, 324 pages. ISBN 1-894710-27-4

James O. Lehman, *Mennonite Tent Revivals: Howard Hammer and Myron Augsburger, 1952-1962* (Kitchener: Pandora Press, 2002) Softcover, xxiv, 318 pages. ISBN 1-894710-22-3

Lawrence Klippenstein and Jacob Dick, *Mennonite Alternative Service in Russia* (Kitchener: Pandora Press, 2002) Softcover, viii, 163 pages. ISBN 1-894710-21-5

Nancey Murphy, *Religion and Science* (Kitchener: Pandora Press, 2002) Softcover, 126 pages. ISBN 1-894710-20-7

Biblical Concordance of the Swiss Brethren, 1540. Trans. Gilbert Fast and Galen Peters; bib. intro. Joe Springer; ed. C. Arnold Snyder (Kitchener: Pandora Press, 2001) Softcover, lv, 227pages. ISBN 1-894710-16-9

Orland Gingerich, *The Amish of Canada* (Kitchener: Pandora Press, 2001) Softcover, 244 pages. Index. ISBN 1-894710-19-3

M. Darrol Bryant, *Religion in a New Key* (Kitchener: Pandora Press, 2001) Softcover, 136 pages. Bib. refs. ISBN 1-894710- 18-5

Trans. Walter Klaassen, Frank Friesen, Werner O. Packull, ed. C. Arnold Snyder, *Sources of South German/Austrian Anabaptism* (Kitchener: Pandora Press, 2001; co-published with Herald Press.) Softcover, 430 pages. Indexes. ISBN 1-894710-15-0

Pedro A. Sandín Fremaint y Pablo A. Jimémez, *Palabras Duras: Homilías* (Kitchener: Pandora Press, 2001). Softcover, 121 pages. ISBN 1-894710-17-7

Ruth Elizabeth Mooney, *Manual Para Crear Materiales de Educación Cristiana* (Kitchener: Pandora Press, 2001). Softcover, 206 pages. ISBN 1-894710-12-6

Esther and Malcolm Wenger, poetry by Ann Wenger, *Healing the Wounds* (Kitchener: Pandora Press, 2001). Softcover, 210 pages. ISBN 1-894710-09-6.

Otto H. Selles and Geraldine Selles-Ysselstein, *New Songs* (Kitchener: Pandora Press, 2001). Poetry and relief prints, 90 pages. ISBN 1-894719-14-2

Pedro A. Sandín Fremaint, *Cuentos y Encuentros: Hacia una Educación Transformadora* (Kitchener: Pandora Press, 2001). Softcover 163 pages. ISBN 1-894710-08-8.

A. James Reimer, *Mennonites and Classical Theology: Dogmatic Foundations for Christian Ethics* (Kitchener: Pandora Press, 2001) Softcover, 650 pages. ISBN 0-9685543-7-7

Walter Klaassen, *Anabaptism: Neither Catholic nor Protestant,* 3rd ed (Kitchener: Pandora Press, 2001) Softcover, 122 pages. ISBN 1-894710-01-0

Dale Schrag & James Juhnke, eds., *Anabaptist Visions for the new Millennium: A search for identity* (Kitchener: Pandora Press, 2000) Softcover, 242 pages. ISBN 1-894710-00-2

Harry Loewen, ed., *Road to Freedom: Mennonites Escape the Land of Suffering* (Kitchener: Pandora Press, 2000) Hardcover, large format, 302pages. ISBN 0-9685543-5-0

Alan Kreider and Stuart Murray, eds., *Coming Home: Stories of Anabaptists in Britain and Ireland* (Kitchener: Pandora Press, 2000) Softcover, 220pages. ISBN 0-9685543-6-9

Edna Schroeder Thiessen and Angela Showalter, *A Life Displaced: A Mennonite Woman's Flight from War-Torn Poland* (Kitchener: Pandora Press, 2000) Softcover, xii, 218 pages. ISBN 0-9685543-2-6

Stuart Murray, *Biblical Interpretation in the Anabaptist Tradition,* Studies in the Believers Tradition (Kitchener: Pandora Press, 2000) Softcover, 310pages. ISBN 0-9685543-3-4 ISSN 1480-7432.

Loren L. Johns, ed. *Apocalypticism and Millennialism* (Kitchener: Pandora Press, 2000) Softcover, 419 pages. Indexes. ISBN 0-9683462-9-4 ISSN 1480-7432

Later Writings by Pilgram Marpeck and his Circle. Volume 1. Trans. Walter Klaassen, Werner Packull, and John Rempel (Kitchener: Pandora Press, 1999) Softcover, 157 pages. ISBN 0-9683462-6-X

John Driver, *Radical Faith. An Alternative History of the Christian Church,* ed. Carrie Snyder. Kitchener: Pandora Press, 1999) Softcover, 334 pages. ISBN 0-9683462-8-6

C. Arnold Snyder, *From Anabaptist Seed.* (Kitchener: Pandora Press, 1999) Softcover, 53 pages. ISBN 0-9685543-0-X

Also available in Spanish translation: *De Semilla Anabautista,* from Pandora Press only.

John D. Thiesen, *Mennonite and Nazi? Attitudes Among Mennonite Colonists in Latin America, 1933-1945* (Kitchener: Pandora Press, 1999) Softcover, 330 pages. Bibliography, index. ISBN 0-9683462-5-1

Lifting the Veil, ed. Leonard Friesen; trans. Walter Klaassen (Kitchener: Pandora Press, 1998). Softcover, 128 pages. ISBN 0-9683462-1-9

Leonard Gross, *The Golden Years of the Hutterites,* rev. ed. (Kitchener: Pandora Press, 1998). Softcover, 280 pages. Index. ISBN 0-9683462-3-5

William H. Brackney, ed., *The Believers Church: A Voluntary Church,* (Kitchener: Pandora Press, 1998). Softcover, viii, 237 pages. Index. ISBN 0-9683462-0-0 ISSN 1480-7432.

An Annotated Hutterite Bibliography, compiled by Maria H. Krisztinkovich, ed. by Peter C. Erb (Kitchener: Pandora Press, 1998). (Ca. 2,700 entries) 312 pages. Softcover, electronic, or both. ISBN (paper) 0-9698762-8-9/(disk) 0-9698762-9-7

Jacobus ten Doornkaat Koolman, *Dirk Philips. Friend and Colleague of Menno Simons,* trans. W. E. Keeney, ed. C. A. Snyder (Kitchener: Pandora Press, 1998). Softcover, xviii, 236 pages. Index. ISBN: 0-9698762-3-8

Sarah Dyck, ed./tr., *The Silence Echoes: Memoirs of Trauma & Tears* (Kitchener: Pandora Press, 1997). Softcover, xii, 236 pages. ISBN: 0-9698762-7-0

Wes Harrison, *Andreas Ehrenpreis and Hutterite Faith and Practice* (Kitchener: Pandora Press, 1997). Softcover, xxiv, 274 pages. Index. ISBN 0-9698762-6-2

C. Arnold Snyder, *Anabaptist History and Theology: Revised Student Edition* (Kitchener: Pandora Press, 1997). Softcover, xiv, 466 pages. Index, bibliography. ISBN 0-9698762-5-4

Nancey Murphy, *Reconciling Theology and Science: A Radical Reformation Perspective* (Kitchener, Ont.: Pandora Press, 1997). Softcover, x, 103 pages. Index. ISBN 0-9698762-4-6

The Limits of Perfection: A Conversation with J. Lawrence Burkholder 2nd ed., with a new epilogue by J. Lawrence Burkholder, Rodney Sawatsky and Scott Holland, eds. (Kitchener: Pandora Press, 1996). Softcover, x, 154 pages. ISBN 0-9698762-2-X

C. Arnold Snyder, *Anabaptist History and Theology: An Introduction* (Kitchener: Pandora Press, 1995). Softcover, x, 434 pages. Index,bibliography. ISBN 0-9698762-0-3

Pandora Press

33 Kent Avenue Kitchener, ON N2G 3R2

Tel.: (519) 578-2381 / Fax: (519) 578-1826

E-mail: info@pandorapress.com

Web site: www.pandorapress.com